SOCIAL MOVEMENT
ORGANIZATIONS

SOCIAL PROBLEMS AND SOCIAL ISSUES

An Aldine de Gruyter Series of Texts and Monographs

SERIES EDITOR

Joel Best

Southern Illinois University at Carbondale

SOCIAL MOVEMENT ORGANIZATIONS

Guide to Research on Insurgent Realities

JOHN LOFLAND

ALDINE DE GRUYTER

New York

About the Author

John Lofland is Professor Emeritus and Professor, Department of Sociology, University of California, Davis. A recipient of the 1995 George Herbert Mead Award presented by the Society for the Study of Symbolic Interaction, he has served as Chair of the American Sociological Association's Section on Collective Behavior and Social Movements and as President of the Pacific Sociological Association and of the Society for the Study of Symbolic Interaction.

Author or editor of eleven prior books, whose titles may be found on p. vi, Dr. Lofland is also the founding editor of the *Journal of Contemporary Ethnography.*

Copyright © 1996 Walter de Gruyter, Inc., New York

Aldine de Gruyter
A division of Walter de Gruyter, Inc.
200 Saw Mill River Road
Hawthorne, New York 10532

This publication is printed on acid free paper

Library of Congress Cataloging-in-Publication Data
Lofland, John.
    Social movement organizations : guide to research on insurgent
realities / John Lofland.
      p. cm. — (Social problems and social issues)
    Includes bibliographical references and index.
    ISBN 0-202-30552-X (cloth : alk. paper). — ISBN 0-202-30553-8
(paper : alk. paper)
      1. Social movements—Research. 2. Social movements. I. Title.
II. Series.
   HN29.L63 1996
    303.48′4—dc20   96-4561
                                          CIP

Manufactured in the United States of America

10   9   8   7   6   5   4   3   2   1

To Herbert Blumer

who truly understood that social life is constructed
and with whom it was my great privilege to have studied

Other Books by John Lofland

Doomsday Cult
A Study of Conversion, Proselytization and Maintenance of Faith

Deviance and Identity

Analyzing Social Settings
A Guide to Qualitative Observation and Analysis
(coauthor)

Doing Social Life
The Qualitative Study of Human Interaction in Natural Settings

Interaction in Everyday Life
Social Strategies
(editor)

State Executions
Historical and Sociological Perspectives
(coauthor)

Symbolic Sit-Ins
Protest Occupations at the California State Capital
(coauthor)

Protest
Studies of Collective Behavior and Social Movements

Peace Action in the Eighties
Social Science Perspectives
(coeditor)

Peace Movement Organizations and Activists
An Analytic Bibliography
(coeditor)

Polite Protesters
The American Peace Movement of the 1980s

Contents

       I. Three Specifications   345
      II. SMO Effects: Working Inventory   347
     III. Causes and Effects   353
          Note   354

                    PART III. PERSPECTIVES
                    Dissections and Contexts

12   Dissecting Research Reports   355

       I. Format and Procedures   357
      II. Dissection Questions   359
          Note   363

13   Contextual Themes   365

       I. An Omnibus Intellectual Tool Kit   365
      II. An Implicit Guide to Moral Philosophy   366
     III. A Leitmotif of Analytic Ethnography   367
      IV. Discipline and Empowerment in the SMO Focus   368
       V. Variations in Propositional Richness   370
      VI. Variables Not Schools: Answer-Improving
          Not Theory-Bashing   372
     VII. Cumulation and Its Problems   373
    VIII. Inquiry Is Always Unfinished   375
          Notes   376

     References   379

     Index   405

List of Figures

Preface and Acknowledgments

The "reality" espoused in the mainstream of a society is but one reality: a privileged reality that excludes or represses many others. Rejecting their exclusion or repression, the insurgent realities of *social movement organizations* challenge mainstream reality and seek to establish new and better ways of life.

In this guide, I explain (1) how social scientists go about studying social movement organizations—their research *procedures*—and (2) what investigators have learned about these insurgent realities in the form of generalizations or *propositions* that answer key questions.

As a handbook or manual on social movement organizations (or SMOs, in researcher jargon), I hope this volume is of interest to people with the following (among other) concerns.

First, in featuring discussions of research procedures, people seeking to analyze social movements more generally and SMOs in particular will hopefully be helped by my reports on sources, methods, and other aspects of inquiry. Even though people doing research are an important audience, I must nonetheless distinguish between this book as a *guide to research* and books that are narrowly and only *guides to how to do research*. This latter type of volume provides much more detailed step-by-step instructions than I offer here. In contrast, in this volume I describe sources and types of data and one type of research process, but my central focus is on the *products* of research rather than on its detailed process. This is, instead, a *guide to* research rather than only a manual on "how to do" research. (Researchers seeking more detailed how-to-do-it instructions can consult the specialized manuals of instruction I recommend in Chapter 2.)

Second, people enrolled in college courses on social movements, social change, political sociology, and related subjects will find the ideas I recount of interest as they relate to these and other broad topics. In particular, in focusing on organizations and people acting in them, one can come to see that social movements and social change do not merely "happen." Instead, they are *constructed* by people in struggle. Whatever one's seemingly settled world, it is only the temporary congealment of historical strife.

Third, although this guide is substantively about SMOs, it is also about one special type of research procedure, the kind employing a "case study" and "grounded theory" approach to the development of social knowledge. While this volume is not a substitute for manuals of instructions on such research, I do explain how the approach is applied to SMOs. Instructors of courses on research methods who want to introduce case-study-grounded theory in a more topically focused way might therefore find this a useful vehicle.

Fourth and more broadly, my stress on inquiry as constituted by asking and answering eight generic questions provides an intellectual tool kit that anyone can use to good effect in analyzing virtually any topic. As such, this question-answer tool kit can be helpful in a variety of instructional contexts, especially in the teaching the logic of theory and theory construction.

Fifth, although framed as the analysis of research process and propositions, what I do here also importantly reacts to what I think is the excessive narrowness of movement studies in recent years. I am therefore trying to break out of current straitjacketing foci and to envision larger horizons. Because of this, older hands in the study of movements might find my expansionist forays of interest. (The vistas I espy, though, are in good measure a resurrection of the range of topics that have been of interest to movement scholars historically, but that have been in virtual eclipse of late.)

Sixth, this guide is "analytic" rather than "activist" in character, but I hope that, even so, social movement activists and other movement participants can profit from it. In my effort to expand the research agenda of movement studies, I also discuss many questions that are of specific concern to activists. While this guide is not a nuts-and-bolts treatment in the tradition of movement how-to-do-it manuals (a genre described in Chapter 9), much of what I report is quite pertinent to how-to-do-it concerns. Specifically, the many aspects of SMOs I treat can be read as a checklist of problem areas in the functioning and strategizing of any SMO. Seriously going through that checklist and assessing an SMO's position on each of them can serve to clarify its location in social space. I describe several possible positions and postures on many of these aspects and this knowledge of other possibilities can then serve to clarify a specific SMO's particular problems and options.

Seventh and most fundamentally, this is a book about morality that should be of interest to people seeking to sharpen their ethical awareness. As challenges to whatever is a current mainstream reality, SMOs question the morality of that reality. While I do not lay out the pros and cons of one or another moral claim, in reporting the generic claims and actions of SMOs, I of necessity canvas many dimensions of answers to the root question, How should life be lived? A reader attuned to philosophical/existential issues can, indeed, use this book as a guide to many of the most profound decisions facing a person who is trying thoughtfully to develop a reasoned, moral life.

*   *   *

As a guide to research—and therefore a compendium of it—my widest debt in writing this volume is to all the researchers who have, in fact, created this book's content. I therefore acknowledge the help of every person named in the list of references. In one way or another, every one of them has helped.

This book was initially conceived as a very brief primer that John D. McCarthy and I were going to write together. That plan was not realized, but throughout the writing of this different book, John has been a critically important confidant, sounding board, and source of support—most especially in repeatedly expressing his belief in the importance of an effort of this kind.

The following colleagues read various portions and drafts of the materials and I am grateful for their efforts and suggestions, many of which have led to significant revisions: Mitch Allen, Rob Benford, Joel Best, Hank Johnston, Lyn H. Lofland, John McCarthy, Sam Marullo, James Richardson, David Snow, Mayer Zald, and several anonymous reviewers for publishers (with special thanks to Claude Tweeles and Christine Worden).

I have used portions of the book in courses and seminars at UC, Davis, and indeed many of the parts on doing research were prompted by my efforts to help students do sociological studies of SMOs. I am therefore indebted to many UC, Davis, graduate and undergraduate students for subjecting themselves to the challenge of "doing sociology" and for allowing me to follow along with them in their struggles. I want in particular to acknowledge the help of Michael Ezell, Victoria Johnson, Tammy Lewis, Ronald Ruggerio, and Sean Wilson. Also at UC, Davis, I thank Fred Block who, as sociology chair, supported arrangements that have greatly facilitated my scholarly work.

Book production is an excruciatingly detailed and tedious process that requires a good deal of patience, goodwill, and sense of humor if all concerned are to survive it intact. Happily, the folks at Aldine de Gruyter bring these leavening virtues to this process and have made the experience pleasant rather than daunting. I am extremely grateful to them and in particular to Richard Koffler and Arlene Perazzini.

My most important debt is to Lyn H. Lofland, who has lived every step of this project with me. This is the twelfth book on which I now have such a debt, and the accumulation of them is vastly more than I can ever repay. Happily, she is a forgiving soul and has agreed to cancel at least part of it. So, I say once again, with love, thanks Lyn.

1

Introduction:

What Social Movement Organizations (SMOs) Are and Why People Study Them

This book is a guide to research on *insurgent realities*: a handbook of research on collective challenges to mainstream conceptions of how society ought to be organized and how people ought to live. Such challenges to reigning conceptions of what is true, moral, and practical come in many forms, and I here focus on the more enduring and collective variety social scientists call social movements, or more specifically, *social movement organizations*. For brevity, researchers label them SMOs.[1]

Especially well-known and dramatic examples of SMOs and their larger social movements in American history include:

- the Anti-Saloon League of the prohibitionist movement,
- the Industrial Workers of the World of the labor movement,
- the Knights of the Ku Klux Klan of the white supremacy movement,
- the Communist party of the socialist movement,
- the John Birch Society of the conservative movement,
- the Student Nonviolent Coordinating Committee of the civil rights movement,
- the Berkeley Free Speech Movement of the student movement,
- the National Organization for Women of the women's liberation movement.[2]

The guide to social science research on SMOs I offer is divided into three parts:

   I.   **procedures** for studying them,
  II.   **propositions** or generalizations about them, and
 III.   **perspectives**—wider considerations relating to them.

I. In the three chapters of Part I, on **procedures,** I report how researchers:

select SMOs for study,
collect data on them,
ask questions about them, and
answer the questions they have asked.

II. With these procedures as context, in the seven chapters of Part II, I review answers to central *questions* about SMOs and present major generalizations or **propositions** found in the extensive literature on them:

1. What are the beliefs of SMOs?
2. How are these associations structured?
3. How do they form?
4. Why do people join them?
5. What strategies do they use to achieve their goals?
6. What are social reactions to them?
7. What social effects do they have?

These seven questions raise many other questions that I also review, together with the various answers researchers have proposed.

III. In Part III, I focus on several broader **perspectives** on social movement studies.

In order most meaningfully to discuss these three matters, I must first appropriately ask and answer two logically (and psychologically) prior questions:

I.   What, more precisely, *is* an SMO?
II. Why in the world do people bother to research them?

In this chapter, I strive to provide satisfactory answers to these two questions. Premised on hopefully adequate answers to them, we can then move to understanding research *procedures* pertaining to SMOs, generalizations or *propositions* about them, and additional *perspectives* on them.

I. WHAT ARE SMOS?

Expanding on the truncated definition immediately above, SMOs are associations of persons making idealistic and moralistic claims about how human personal or group life ought be organized that, *at the time of their claims-making*, are marginal to or excluded from mainstream society—the then dominant constructions of what is realistic, reasonable, and moral.

The core feature is a *claim about reality* that is, *at the time of its assertion*, defined as improper, implausible, immoral, false, threatening, corrupting, seditious, treasonous, blasphemous, degenerate, despicable—or in some other manner not respectable or otherwise meriting serious consideration. Instead, the asserters and the realties they assert are, in mainstream views, best ignored, repressed, treated therapeutically as a sickness, or in some other manner kept excluded, marginal, or encysted.

As such, the study of SMOs is a special case of the study of *contention among deeply conflicting realities*. SMOs provide one key venue in which to probe why and how people come to have radically different ideas about how best to organize personal functioning and human group life and what happens as a consequence of these radically different ideas.

Even though my report on SMO study is sociological and scholarly neutral, the *materials studied* reverberate with philosophical, existential, and religious issues and implications. This is because the substantive materials researchers treat are addressed to the deepest of differences in human understandings about what human life *is* and how it *should be* lived.

While sociological inquirers (mostly) do not directly take sides in these reality-conflicts, they cannot but be moved by the agonies, fears, hostilities, and joys that are conspicuous concomitants of SMO-mainstream struggles. In turn, you, as a person learning about inquiry into SMOs, should not be surprised when you find yourself also moved by the deep reality-conflicts you will witness.

Deeply differing reality spurned by the mainstream is the core feature of the SMO, but that feature is (1) not unique to the SMO and (2) does not tell us enough to set the SMO off from other forms of deep reality-conflicts. We need therefore to situate the SMO in the larger context of the *range* of ways in which citizens sometimes implicitly or explicitly assert realities counter to mainstream conceptions of it. In different but roughly equivalent words, SMOs are only one way in which citizens on occasion defy authority or protest official conceptions and programs of truth and justice.

A. Mainstream and Excluded Realities

SMOs and the broader category of citizen reality in conflict with the mainstream have meaning only in relation to the existence of a *societal mainstream*. We therefore need to begin with an understanding of its features—its reality-creating and defining import.

The most prevalent form of human society possesses or displays a *mainstream:* a set of institutions and their authoritative decision-makers that can and do maintain public order, dominate economic activity, and provide plausible rationales for exercising power and authority in such matters. The core activity constituting this societal mainstream is the routine making of decisions of consequence within and for major institutions. Most prominently in the larger and more recent human societies, such decisions emanate from the upper layers of governments, corporations, the mass media, religious denominations, and scientific and educational institutions. Or, in the broader and colorful language for which Erving Goffman is noted, mainstream or institutional authorities include "priests, psychiatrists, school teachers, police, generals, government leaders, parents, males, whites, national media operators, and all the other well-placed persons who are in a position to give official imprint to versions of reality" (1983, 17).

As Goffman suggests in this passage, the process of making institutional decisions with large and binding consequences is a *reality-constructing*, defining, or in his image, an officially imprinting activity. In and through institutional decision-making and problem solving, some ideas and courses of action are (unavoidably) defined as more *true* than others, more *moral* than others, more *rational* than others, more *practical* than others, more *feasible* than others (Berger and Luckmann 1967).

Irrespective of their aims or desires, the accumulative consequence of the decisions and problem solving of institutional authorities is the social construction of mainstream societal reality as an "objective reality." Looking back on and summing up stretches of mainstream actions, perceivers see them as "This *is* reality." In reality constructionist terminology, the composite actions of authorities are gestalted as *objects* that have their own external "facticity," that are thus "objective." This objectified mainstream reality is then *the* reality—the cognitively correct, morally proper, and obvious "only real" reality. In the terms used by Goffman just above, the mainstream gives "official imprint to versions of reality."

This process of reality-creating and -reproducing would all roll along quite nicely were it not for the fact that the flip side of mainstream reality-making or -constructing is *reality-excluding*. Mainstream reality is only officially imprinted reality and not at all the only reality. Virtually every decision authorities make and problem they solve is *also* an explicit, implicit, or simply de facto exclusion if not repudiation of at least one other alternative course of action and conception of what is real, moral, and feasible. Sometimes the rejection is *explicit*, in the sense that the proponents of alternative decisions and solutions have—literally or metaphorically in recent empowerment jargon—"a seat at the table" and are directly told no. More often, the rejection is *implicit*, in that the reality asserters are not at the table—literally or metaphorically—and their alternative realities, thought by them to be "serious," are not seriously considered by authorities whether or not they are even known about.

In this way, at the same time that mainstream authorities are creating reality winners, they are also creating reality losers. In creating and reproducing mainstream reality, they also explicitly or inadvertently create rejected, marginal, submerged, or excluded realities.

This winner-loser dynamic of mainstream problem-solving and reality-making has several *causes* and *consequences* that I will elaborate in later chapters, but some main features of both need to be previewed here in explaining the "what" of SMOs.

B. Causes of Reality-Exclusion

With respect to why some realities are excluded, these are among the many factors in operation.

First, there is the question of why, in the first place, do people disagree on such reality matters as:

- What is important in life?
- What is problematic about society?
- Why are the above two topics problematic and what ought to be done about them?

Why, this is to say, is there a diversity of realities in the first place? *One* part of the answer resides in the fact of the fundamental ambiguity of reality itself in terms of knowing with any great certainty *the* right cognitive or moral depiction and course of action in any problematic situation. In the face of ambiguity, people of good will quite easily disagree, for no one can be all that certain about what is cognitively or normatively "correct."

Second, add to ambiguity the fact that humans are really quite marvelously inventive and diverse in their reactions to virtually any situation. In (metaphorically) the same way that random processes of genetic combinations are continually producing mutations of every sort, humans continually respond to situations with diverse constructions of what they are "looking at" and what to do about whatever "it" is. Humans are virtual reality-diversity machines.

Third, one key reason for this immense outpouring of diverse cognitive constructions and proposed courses of action is the fact that any existing cognitive constructions of problematic situations and in-place solutions almost never work perfectly—or even very well. Every in-place social arrangement—in the mainstream or not—can plausibly (and even correctly) be claimed by active perceivers (factor two, immediately above) to exhibit at least one conspicuous form of inefficiency, gross inequity, or sheer irrationality.

Fourth, authorities in the mainstream tend *not* to construct the character of the problems they face and the possible solutions to them in an even-handed and open fashion, taking equal account of *all* the social interests involved and *all* the pertinent information. *Instead*, they (like everyone else) tend to only a *selected* range of constructions, interests, and information. And in doing this, they are, of course, only using the mainstream construction of reality. Among the several reasons for this selectivity are simple ignorance, the need to simplify in the face of information overload, and self-deceiving self-interest in preserving or maximizing one's advantages (cf. Tuchman 1984). (Phrasing this last differently, people exhibit strong tendencies to exploit one another, especially people perceived to be different from themselves.)

Fifth, there are, objectively, different and opposing values and cognitive dispositions among which humans must select in constructing their lives. Because humans tend to select differently from among these choices, diversity of value preferences and cognitive dispositions is a fact of human life. Such opposing value choices include primacy of short-term versus long-term considerations in acting (e.g., immediate versus delayed "gratification"); risk-taking versus risk-aversion; self-centered versus group-centered existential orientation; optimistic versus pessimistic bent; belief in equality and justice versus opportunity and freedom; belief in equality of outcomes versus equality of opportunity (cf. Fine 1993).

There are many more things to be said about the causes of rejected, marginal, submerged, or excluded realities, but the above points suffice to get us started and to suggest that such realities are the inherent flip side of mainstream realities. Borrowing the phrasing without endorsing the thesis of the song "Love and Marriage" the refrain of mainstream and excluded reality is, "You can't have one without the other."

C. Consequences of Reality-Exclusion

We have, then, an image of society dominated by a mainstream reality overlying myriad alternative, competing, rejected, or merely excluded realities. This is the broad domain within which the SMOs appear as one special and key form of marginal or excluded reality.

As but *one* form of marginal or excluded reality, it is useful for us to appreciate some of the *other* and major forms of it that we find in this

Figure 1.1. Social organization of social realities: variables and forms.

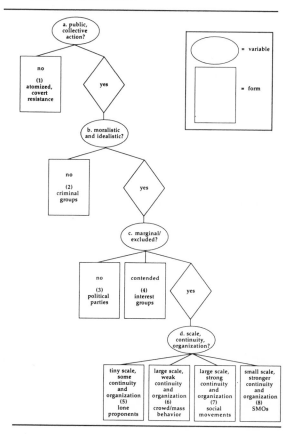

domain. Let us approach an appreciation of these other forms by examining four major ways in which realities in general vary in terms of social organization and location. By social organization and location, I refer to such matters as the number of people involved, their social power, the degree of their organization, and the persistence of their actions.

The four social organizational variables I am about to describe are depicted in summary overview in Figure 1.1, where they are represented by ovals lettered (a) through (d). As *variables*, they each assume different values. The conjunction of different values on the four variables specifies varying *social organizational forms of social realities*. Eight of these forms are also shown in Figure 1.1, where they are depicted as rectangles numbered (1) through (8). Following Figure 1.1 while reading the text that follows hopefully helps to clarify the discussion.

1. Public, Collective Actions? The most basic level of social organizational variation concerns the degree to which the marginal or excluded reality is put forth publicly and persistently in an organized fashion (oval a in Figure 1.1). For example, in any number of societies over considerable periods of time—especially societies of colonial domination—members of a large underclass widely if not universally hate or at least strongly resent and subtly resist a class of rulers they view as illegitimate. But virtually none of this resentment and resistance is publicly and collectively recognized and acted on (Scott 1985, 1990). Instead, on the surface—at the level of official, mainstream reality—everything is just fine. Official, mainstream reality is total reality and the only relevant reality.

The *first* major form (or consequence) of excluded reality is, then, *atomized covert resentment and resistance*, a pattern that James C. Scott (1985, 1990) has analyzed as *Weapons of the Weak*. Perhaps in most societies most of the time, excluded realities have taken this covert, scattered form. (This possibility is shown as rectangle 1 in Figure 1.1.)

Placing this diffuse and privatized even if widespread excluded reality to one side, let us examine variations among excluded realities that *do* achieve public recognition and action.

2. Moralistic and Idealistic? Ways of constructing reality that defy mainstream frames differ in the degree to which the alternative reality is moralistic and idealistic (oval b in Figure 1.1). A great many excluded realities are simply pragmatic and even cynical and centered on only advancing the personal or small group of the person or persons involved in it. Criminal or "thug" groupings tend in this direction. In contrast, the alternative to mainstream reality offered can claim to be morally superior and even to be a model of how all people ought to believe and act. And, this moralism can be infused with idealism, the quest to make things as they should be when viewed in higher ethical perspective. At minimum, mainstream reality—especially the behavior of authorities—is asserted to be immoral or irrational and in need of change or rejection.

A *second* major form of excluded reality is then the criminal or bandit gang. Presaging variations described just below, criminal groupings tend also to be relatively small but enduring collectivities. It is of note, in addition, that there is sometimes a contest or debate over whether a group should be thought of as a mere criminal gang or an SMO. For example, in a book titled *Bandits*, Eric Hobsbawm (1969; see also 1965) argues that outlaw bands in some places at some times are at last crypto- or proto-SMOs. (Robin Hood and his "merry band" provide the archetypal case.) (This social organizational form is shown as rectangle 2 in Figure 1.1.)

In some cases, the line between criminal groups and SMOs may reside as much in idealistic proclamations and aims as in sheer conduct. Indeed, the similarities between some criminal groups and SMOs often lead to labeling the latter as merely criminal (and one elite strategy of discrediting social movements is to treat them as merely criminals).

3. *Marginal/Excluded?* A third variation is the *degree* to which the reality is marginal/excluded (oval c in Figure 1). Realities not achieving the imprint of official reality differ in the degree to which they are *contenders* for official reality.

1. Some social realities are simply contentious and part and parcel of the mainstream rather than marginal or excluded. Such is the relation between the Republican and Democratic parties in the United States, as well as among other groupings, and provides a *third* form of reality, one that is mainstream contentious rather than marginal or excluded. This is shown in rectangle 3 of Figure 1.1.

2. One notch out from this, the contending reality may rarely if ever achieve the imprint of mainstream reality, but it is continuously in the reality-arena as a perennial but often or mostly unsuccessful contender for mainstream reality. A large number of U.S. *interest groups* occupy this status and are a *fourth* form of reality-contender. The network of such interest groups founded or inspired by Ralph Nader provides perennial examples (Walker 1991; Hofrenning 1995). (This is shown as rectangle 4 in Figure 1.1.)

3. Some formations hover at the margins of respectability and seriousness vis-à-vis the mainstream and may be "in" or "out," depending on the time period at which one is looking ("I could have been a contender"). And, of key interest here, many realities are beyond the pale in the sense that the realities they assert are simply not to be taken seriously—or perhaps even known about—in mainstream reality. Acknowledging that the distinctions among *contentious, marginal,* and *excluded* cannot be drawn with exactness, there are nonetheless realities that are, at a given point in time, marginal to or excluded from the mainstream despite their public status (variable 1) and their moralistic and idealist professions (variable 2).

Of course, for many marginal or excluded realities, the prime aim is to be taken seriously in and by mainstream reality, and the drama and romance of social movements resides in the fact that many of them *have* been successful in moving from exclusion to contention to mainstream

Figure 1.2.   Examples of realities in and out of the past and present
American mainstream.

Past In, Present In	Past Out, Present Out	Past In, Present Out	Past Out, Present In
democracy capitalism free speech freedom individualism consumerism	communism atheism anarchism socialism class struggle/ Marxism	racism sexism ableism smoking	public gay/lesbian life-styles abortion feminism/gender equality ethnic studies women's studies affirmative action labor unions

domination (and back again to marginal contention or exclusion, in some cases). In the phraseology of Eyerman and Jamison (1991), such movements have created mainstream "cognitive space." Thus, in United States history, parts or all of such a sequence can be traced for intoxicant prohibition, labor, feminist, gay and lesbian, ethnic, and physical disability movements.

Relations among what is *now* or was in the *past* in or out of the mainstream are complicated and fluid, of course. In Figure 1.2, I strive to depict some of this complexity and fluidity by showing major conjunctions between being in or out of the mainstream at the present (broadly conceived) and in the past (likewise broadly conceived). As can be seen, some realities endure as part of the mainstream, some remain enduringly outside, but yet many others leave or enter the mainstream.

4. Scale, Continuity, Organization? Publicly recognized collective actions based on a moralistically and idealistically framed marginal/excluded reality differ in their scale (or size), continuity, and degree of organization. By scale or size I mean the number of participants in the excluded reality, ranging from the single, idiosyncratic vision of a lonely proponent, through a small group, to a significant, mass sector of a society. By continuity and organization I refer to the degree to which action is ill organized, ephemeral, or short-lived versus more organized, enduring, and long-lived (cf. Best and Luckenbill 1994).

The three subvariations I package into this one variable allow a great many possibilities, of which a few are most important in the present context.

Continuing our list of forms from above, a *fifth* main social organizational form has continuity and is organized but is only the smallest of scale (rectangle 5 in Figure 1.1): This is the *lone proponent*, who perhaps has a loose band of supporters and sympathizers. Religious prophets of the Old Testament are the classic instances, although we would also want to include such marginal reality constructors as Rachel Carson and her reality construction titled *Silent Spring* (1962) and Betty Friedan and her *Feminine Mystique* (1963).[3]

Lone proponents are weak on scale but strong on continuity and (personal) organization, while *crowd/mass insurgencies* are, by definition, very large in scale but weak on continuity and organization. Examples of such insurgencies—or surges—include riots in African-American ghettoes in the 1960s and other waves of collective protests seen so prominently in the history of the United States and Europe (e.g., Stearns 1974; Lofland 1993a, Part II; Tarrow 1994). This *sixth* form of excluded but now aggressively asserted reality is weak on continuity and organization, but *not* entirely lacking either of these (McPhail 1991, 1996). As well documented, insurgencies or surges exhibit degrees of continuity and organization at some very important and basic levels (McPhail 1991, 1996; Tilly 1978; Tarrow 1994), but these are not yet the levels of more-or-less recognized leaders, spokespeople, thought-out strategies, and programs of action.

Historically, in the early and middle twentieth century, research on crowd/mass insurgencies was labeled the study of *collective behavior*. The single most influential text compiling and summarizing this research has been the several editions of Turner and Killian's *Collective Behavior* (1987, 3rd ed.).[4] As I will discuss later, toward the last quarter of the century, a widespread belief that "collective behavior" was a defective perspective that implied irrational actors and was politically anti-insurgent and conservative led to a preference for the term *collective action*. And, indeed, the words *behavior* and *action* do differ more generally in the degree to which they imply that actors are consciously choosing ("acting") versus merely behaving without conscious deliberation.[5]

To the degree that collective citizen surges of moralistically and idealistically framed excluded realities achieve significant scale, continuity and organization, they are a *seventh* form: *the social movement* (or SM) (rectangle 7 in Figure 1.1). The continuity and organization that are the marks of a social movement are signaled by the presence of several and perhaps hundreds or thousands of *named associations* that view themselves as part of "the movement" and that are carrying on *campaigns* in the name of the movement (Marwell and Oliver 1984; Oliver 1989).

These named associations are *social movement organizations*, or SMOs. They are the major building blocks of social movements, although SMOs as organizations are not always so fortunate (or unfortunate) to exist in the context of a surging social movement. Many are "loners" or "sports," who therefore do not partake in the benefits and liabilities of a surging movement context. However, because of their collective, continuing, and organized character focused on a moralistic and idealistic excluded reality, they are SMOs nonetheless. Continuing and finishing our list, the SMO is the *eighth* form of contending/excluded reality (rectangle 8 in Figure 1.1).

Elaborating the distinction between the SMO and the social movement (SMs), SMOs commonly but not always have an office, phone, publication, list of members, and other accoutrements of explicit association. Because of such features, one can literally telephone and physically visit SMOs, such as the peace movement organization called Grandmothers for Peace. In contrast, as a broad bracketing of hundreds or thousands of such movement organizations and other persons and activities, SMs cannot be located in any single place or simply dialed: you cannot, in a simple sense, telephone or visit the peace movement in America. Instead, if you want to speak by phone or visit with such a conglomeration, you have to perform visiting activities with hundreds or thousands of organizations (and individuals and activities).

Unfortunately, the terms *social movement* and *social movement organization* are often used inconsistently and sometimes interchangeably in the literature. In particular, people very often refer to a specific SMO as a "social movement" (e.g., Goldberg 1991). If one accepts the usage I give above, this is technically incorrect and, indeed, such indiscriminate use of the term *social movement* can become quite confusing.

* * *

We now see, then, the way in which the SMO is a member of a family of forms of social organization of social realities. These social realities range from large and powerful ones that form societal mainstreams (rectangle 3 in Figure 1.1) to small and scattered ones with only the most covert of existences (rectangle 1 in Figure 1.1). In between, there is a range of other possibilities, some of which are also shown in Figure 1.1. Our focus in this guide is on the special type that is the social movement organization—the SMO (rectangle 8 in Figure 1.1).

D. Similar and Different Definitional Starting Points

The focus on "insurgent realities" from which this guide begins is similar to (or virtually the same as) the starting point of many other social scientists, but also different from yet others. Because these differences lead in different directions and to different foci, it is wise to be aware of variations in starting points.

The better to understand these differences, let me first report some other ways researchers start with the same insurgent reality conception (or one that is similar to it) even though they do not use the exact same words. The classic among these is Herbert Blumer's definitional depiction of social movements as

> collective enterprises seeking to establish a new order of life. They . . . derive their motive power on one hand from dissatisfaction with the current form of life and, on the other hand, from wishes and hopes for a new scheme or system of living. (Blumer [1939] 1969a, 99)

In this definition, "new order of life" translates as insurgent reality and "current form of life" translates as the societal mainstream. "Seeking to establish" is to be insurgent.

In this same vein, Gamson and Wolfsfeld define a social movement as "a sustained and self-conscious challenge to authorities or cultural codes by a field of actors—organizations and advocacy networks—some of which employ extra-institutional means of influence" (1993, 115). Here, also, the idea of "challenge to authorities or cultural codes" means the mounting of conceptions of reality that are different from those then prevailing (cf. Traugott 1978).

There are at least two other ways to start thinking about social movements that are different than the insurgent reality vantage point just depicted. The first of these is to conceive of a movement as a collective effort "to promote or resist a change in the society . . . of which it is a part" (Turner and Killian 1987, 223). This starting point presents the problems of being too broad in one way and too narrow in another. It is too broad because societal mainstreams are full of collective efforts to promote or resist social change. As explained above, many such efforts to promote or resist change are commonly labeled political parties, lobbyists, and interest groups (rectangles 3 and 4 in Figure 1.1). There are integral parts of the mainstream and they are definitely not social movements. To include such enterprises in the study of movements is to lose sight of what is distinctive about them and therefore to dilute their study.

In addition and in another sense, this definition is too narrow in focusing on only *social* change, that is, "societal manipulation." A great many movement enterprises focus instead on *personal* transformation and reject social change (societal manipulation) as superficial or futile. However, despite these two demurs, the "promote or resist social change" and "insurgent realities" definitions do overlap a good deal and lead to similar although not identical research programs.

The second alternative starting point is to think of social movements as "collective action," a term Charles Tilly defines as "all occasions on which sets of people commit pooled resources . . . to common ends" (1981a, 17). Operationally, collective action is commonly taken to mean "contentious gathering," which "is an occasion on which a number of people gather in a publicly accessible place and visibly make claims which would, if realized, bear on the interests of some other person(s)" (Tilly 1981b, 49).

While collective actions or contentious gatherings are certainly valid and useful ways to begin and structure inquiry, they have the problem of focusing the researcher's attention on publicly observable behavioral events rather than on the insurgent realities of those events. Even more seriously limiting, many insurgent realities do not take the form of publicly observable events. A researcher attending to collective action only so construed will therefore not "see" a great deal of empirical material that is in fact relevant and discoverable using an insurgent-reality conception.

Put another way, collective action/contentious gathering analyses are too atomistically and microscopically focused. They are at least one conceptual level below insurgent reality as a more holistic, mesoscopic unit. So pitched, what movements are about in the first place—challenging constructions of reality—tends to elude collective action researchers. Conceptually, these realities fly over their heads.

Rather than being right or wrong, these various starting points simply lead to different research foci and therefore to different kinds of knowledge. Each starting point has both its strengths and weaknesses as a function of what one desires to know.[6] In this guide, we are led by the idea of insurgent realities, but other researchers quite properly strike out in other directions and come to focus on matters not encompassed by this guide.

E. A Form of Conflict

The ideas of excluded realities that are in conflict with mainstream reality that frame the foregoing discussion imply a particular arrangement of groupings and their power in society. Let me now move beyond implication to explicit statement.

The populations of a great many societies are broadly divisible into a small portion of humans who have more wealth, power, and prestige than most people—the authorities or the elites—and the mass of ordinary citizens who have relatively less or even little of these three valued objects. Further, vast disparities of wealth, power, and prestige also trace elite-citizen disparities in the respective degrees and strength of

Figure 1.3. Equal-established versus unequal-
unestablished parties in conflict.

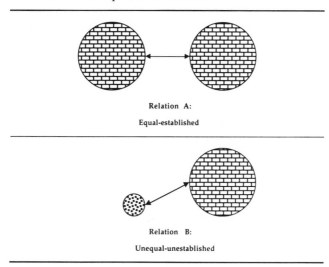

Relation A:

Equal-established

Relation B:

Unequal-unestablished

their *organization.* "Mainstream" and "marginal/excluded" realities are about these *disparities in wealth, power, prestige, and organization.*

Therefore, when we speak of citizens collectively challenging mainstream reality, we are talking about less wealthy, powerful, prestigeful, established, and organized entities in contests with wealthier, more powerful, more prestigeful, established, and organized entities. In order to foster a clear consciousness of this form of relationship, I have devised the image shown in Figure 1.3. The two parties shown in Relation B are of unequal size to signal differences in power, wealth, and prestige, and the circles symbolizing them are filled in a random versus ordered way in order to symbolize relative differences in degrees of organization.

The variations in and types of social organization shown in Figure 1.1 prompt the realization that there are many other possible features and relationships, as in, most obviously, the parties being of equal wealth, power, prestige, and organization—Relation A in Figure 1.3. So situated as one among a range of constellations of parties in conflict, we then appreciate that the study of social movements and SMOs is the study of a *special form of conflict* in which the parties are highly unequal in several respects.

This inequality is embodied in the very notion that a society *has* a mainstream against which there can therefore be social movements. The proper implication is, in fact, that a society without a mainstream is a society without social movements. Instead, the "society" is a literally chaotic and anarchic arena of more-or-less powerful contending groups striving to seize and form a mainstream. Less than a decade ago, such a possibility seemed a merely amusing academic exercise in silly possibilities that occurred only on very rare and short-lived occasions, occasions identified as "revolutionary situations" or turmoil (Goldstone 1986). But with the collapse of the Soviet Union and with other changes, societies without mainstreams have become more common and even chronic. For them, social movement analysis such as explained in this guide is likely less pertinent. What is required, instead, is a more generic perspective on conflict per se among relatively equal parties in strife as visualized in Relation A of Figure 1.3 [and as pursued by, for example, Kriesberg (1982) and Pruitt, Rubin, and Kim (1994)].

II. WHY DO PEOPLE STUDY SMOS?

If the above is, broadly speaking, *what* the study of SMOs is about, *why* do people invest time in researching or otherwise understanding them? Presented in no special order, the following are prominent among the reasons that I have heard students of movements express in conversations or that I have seen in print.

Because these reasons apply to the study of both SMOs and social movements, I use the broader term below in describing the various reasons.

A. Promoting Social Change

Most in evidence are moralistic, idealistic, and social-change advocacy reasons among people who do not like the realities promoted in and by the mainstream and who want some or all of these realities changed. This is research and study in the service of social change. By trying to understand what movements have done right and wrong in the past, one hopes to become a more effective movement participant, activist, or simply advocate or advisor (e.g., Adamson and Borgos 1984). It is no accident, for example, that the ranks of social movement scholars mushroomed over the 1970s and 1980s. This burgeoning was caused by and consisted importantly of movement people of the 1960s turning their activist aspirations to scholarly endeavors following the decline of the 1960s movements. The same impulse has continued to animate many new and younger scholars of the 1990s and I venture to guess that social change guidance remains the single largest class of reason for studying social movements.

B. Opposing Social Change

Counterpoised to this first reason, some people study social movements because they consider them one or another kind of threat to mainstream reality. In order most effectively to cope with an enemy, one must understand that enemy. In the same way that people research cancer or AIDS or dictatorship in order to figure out how to prevent or contain them, some people study social movements for the same reason.

C. Opposing a Particular SMO or Movement

Of course, some people favor some kinds of movements and the changes they propose while opposing yet others. Thus, some partisans of movements of the Left organize studies of SMOs of the Right for the purpose of exposing and damaging them. Sometimes these efforts take fairly elaborate organizational form, as in the Southern Poverty Law Center's systematic tracking of racist groups, or the many other groups that track SMOs of the religious Right. (These are described and discussed in Chapter 10, Section II.E).

D. Pragmatic Coping

More dispassionately than for any of these first three reasons, some people desire simply to cope in a pragmatic public fashion with the facts of social existence. Social movements and SMOs are quite conspicuous facts of social existence, and dealing with them effectively therefore requires knowledge of them. Because they are mushrooming in some parts of the world and are central forces in the remaking of some societies, few can escape their influences on social policies and public life— the social changes they have forged and are forging. Therefore, it is in one's sheer pragmatic self-interest to understand them as forces in the public realm. Whether one likes it or not, they are shaping the world in which one lives, the pragmatist claims.

E. Civic Duty

More moralistically rather than simply pragmatically, those inclined to be "good citizens" argue that it is the right and duty (and also privilege) of a citizen to understand and to make decisions about public policies. Some SMOs—past, present, and future—manage to become key players in making public policy. Understanding them for the purpose of supporting or opposing the policies they promote or oppose is therefore an integral part of being a good citizen.

F. Personally Relating

At the more intimate and personal level, some students of movements point out that they are likely to know someone who is or has been in an SMO—or personally to have been or will become an SMO participant. Therefore, knowing about movements can be of help in making decisions in one's private life. Through knowing about the experiences of other people in movements, one can better understand one's own personal experiences with and feelings about them.

G. Humanistic Comprehending

Students of a humanistic bent reason that all human endeavors merit our sympathetic and searching comprehension. SMOs command our attention as one key variety of the myriad of human enterprises. Like the proverbial mountains that are climbed because they are there, one climbs the SMO mountains—and their encompassing social movements—because they are there and because, as humans strivings, they are very much a part of us. Through studying them—as through studying other human activities—we achieve a better understanding of our selves as humans and—hopefully—enable ourselves to build more humane societies.

H. Moral Guidance

SMOs and SMs are integrally about morality, about answers to the question, How should life be lived? As laboratories of asserted and sometimes enacted answers to this question, SMOs can be and are studied from the point of view of what can be learned from them about right and wrong moral action and successful and unsuccessful efforts to structure life in terms of various moralities.

I. High Adventuring

As challengers of mainstream reality, SMOs often create moments or even periods of exciting drama, intense fear, immense joy, or virulent hate. SMOs are among the vehicles, that is, for creating peak or otherwise enormously engaging experiences. We ought therefore not be surprised that at least some people seek to learn about them for the same reasons that people involve themselves in other forms of significantly engaging episodes—the enchantment of adventure in challenging, consequential encounters.

J. Scientific Generalizing

For reasons similar to the humanistic comprehension reasons reported in Section G, just above, but narrower and more technical than that, some perhaps benighted souls study movements as a vehicle in the quest to discern underlying uniformities or tendencies in human social life and organization as a valid quest in and of itself. Their goal is to discern the grammar, so to speak, of human group life, to formulate generalizations that simply, accurately, and elegantly depict the order in human strivings that can be found beneath the bewildering welter of a surface reality in flux. Like astronomers who seek to know what order can be found in the universe, these seekers search for celestiallike order in the human cosmos.

Any given student of SMOs is likely, of course, to study them for more than one of these reasons—or to have yet other reasons for her or his interests.

* * *

On the optimistic assumption that one or more of the above motives expresses or engages you—the reader—let us proceed to a consideration of research **procedures**.

NOTES

1. Now used ubiquitously among movement researchers, the articulated concept of the "social movement organization" and the acronym SMO were introduced by Mayer Zald and Roberta Ash in a 1966 article titled, appropriately enough, "Social Movement Organizations."

2. These examples and the order of listing are from Robert Goldberg, *Grassroots Resistance* (1991), who provides engaging, chapter-length historical descriptions of each.

3. The current United States abounds in lone proponents and, interestingly enough, numerous journalistic investigators who publish catalogs of capsule summaries of their insurgent realities. Russ Kick's *Outposts: A Catalog of Rare and Disturbing Alternative Information* (1995) is among the more informative of these, but see also Kossy (1994) and Schultz (1989). The *Alternative Press Review: Your Guide Beyond the Mainstream* and *Factsheet 5: The Definitive Guide to the Zine Revolution* are among several periodicals that have set themselves the same task.

4. On collective behavior, see in addition Killian (1980), Curtis and Aguirre (1993), Goode (1992), Marx and McAdam (1994). On yet broader conceptions of the "unit" of collective behavior, see Gusfield (1981), Lang and Lang (1961), Lyman (1995), Morris and Mueller (1992), Rucht (1991).

5. The shift from collective "behavior" to "action" terminology and other shifts are discussed in Chapter 8, Section II, and in Chapter 13, Section VI.

6. An additional, alternative starting point conceives the social movement as a highly specialized and time-place-restricted topic and phenomenon—as merely "a distinctive nineteenth- and twentieth-century form of action" (Tilly 1983, 466). This view therefore decries the generic conceptions employed by mainstream social researchers: "My fellow sociologists have, alas, caused a great deal of confusion by combining in [the social movement] category a distinctive nineteenth- and twentieth-century form of action, which they know well, with a miscellany of other religious and political action of which they have little knowledge" (p. 466). This narrow and restricted conception of social movements is nonetheless *substantively* compatible with the broader definitions reviewed. Thus, this narrow definition allows that: "The social movement consists of a series of challenges to established authorities, especially national authorities, in the name of an unrepresented constituency" (p. 466). The definition I provide in the text sharpens and broadens this narrow conception.

I

Procedures:
Four Case Study Steps

I summarize the four steps in SMO case studies in these stark gerunds: *selecting, collecting, asking,* and *answering.* The purpose of this four-word capsule is to provide a clear image of the larger picture that the reader can employ when dealing with the details of each of the four steps.

In referring back to this four-word picture while enmeshed in detail, one is hopefully less likely to get lost. So, no matter what the immediate matter at hand, always bear in mind that the overall process is about researchers:

1. *selecting* whatever case or cases they are studying,
2. thinking broadly about diverse forms of data *collecting* on the case or cases,
3. *asking* social science questions about the data, and
4. *answering* those questions with sociological propositions.

The tasks of selecting and collecting are explained in Chapter 2 and those of asking and answering questions are discussed in Chapters 3 and 4, respectively.

2

Steps One and Two:
Selecting Cases and Collecting Data

The methodological strategy I describe in the three chapters of this part is *one* among several valid and useful ways in which researchers study SMOs (or social movements, or virtually anything else for that matter). While this strategy has no settled, agreed-upon name and set of features, it is widely referred to among sociologists as the *case study approach* or method. Sometimes this label is expanded to the "qualitative case study" method. Or, it may be called "the qualitative approach" or "grounded theory method" (Lofland and Lofland 1995; Strauss and Corbin 1990).

I. THE CASE STUDY APPROACH

Be the label question as it may, the important features of the case study approach as applied to SMOs (or to other subject matters) include the following:

1. Only **one** or a **few** cases are selected for study. This is different from studies in which *larger numbers* of units are scrutinized. Thus, Gamson's classic quantitative study of SMOs involved fifty-three cases (Gamson 1975; 1990).

2. **Extensive** and **diverse** forms of data are collected on the case (or small number of cases). This is in contrast to studies in which *limited* amounts of *one kind* of data per case are collected on a large numbers of cases. Continuing with the Gamson example, Gamson's data were drawn almost exclusively from historical reports and did not involve such other sources of data as direct observation and interviewing, surveys of SMO members, or extensive reading of each SMO's literature.

3. The data collected are importantly (but far from exclusively) **quali-tative**, meaning that various forms of prose text rather than numbers or datasets are the prime form of data employed. However, the words *importantly* and *prime* are critical in this sentence because, as we shall see, an orientation to qualitative data does not at all exclude use of quantitative data should that be feasible, available, and/or pertinent. And, referring to the Gamson study once more, his data were quantitative meaning that numerical rankings were performed on thirty-nine vari-ables for each of the fifty-three SMOs. Presented in an appendix of his study, Gamson's data are literally pages of numbers in rows of the fifty-three cases and columns of the thirty-nine variables (Gamson 1990, 319–21). As such raw data make evi-dent, quantifying or *numerizing* is the central operation of quan-titative studies.

4. The variety of the case study approach I picture in Part I begins with:

   • a *sociological orientation* to the case or cases to be studied rather than with
   • one or more *preformed hypotheses* to be tested.

   The aim of researchers is to immerse themselves in the case data and, informed by the logic of sociological analysis, **induct** sociological propositions that are highlighted in the case or cases. Otherwise often termed the "grounded theory" ap-proach, this is a process of the **immersion-induction of socio-logical propositions.** Analysis builds on researchers efforts to become intimately familiar with the case under study—on their efforts to grasp the realities of the SMO at close range. This is in contrast with studies in which all the variables of presumed interest and their possible relationships are specified before the study begins and the purpose of the study is to determine which of the relations actually obtains in the data that are col-lected. The Gamson study mentioned as illustrating other con-trasts also illustrates this one between hypothesis *testing* and hypothesis *development* or discovery.

In electing to explain and therefore de facto to promote the case study approach, I do not at all intend to suggest that other research designs are worse (or better, for that matter) per se as vehicles in the analysis of SMOs (or social movements). Instead, every variety of design has its strengths as well as its weaknesses and each can make contributions to our understanding. As we go along, I will indeed be point up the weak-nesses as well as the strengths of the case study approach.

In the same way that there is no exact, settled name for (or exact set of features of) the case study approach, there is no settled set of steps or stages for doing such studies. In such a context, one proceeds pragmatically. In this spirit, I find it helpful to think of SMO case studies as consisting of four **steps** (or phases or procedures):

1. **selecting** a case to research,
2. **collecting** data on it,
3. **asking** questions about the case, and
4. **answering** the questions posed.

I describe step (1) immediately below and step (2) in Sections II and III, respectively. Steps (3) and (4) are discussed in Chapters 3 and 4, respectively.

II. STEP (1), SELECTING: PERTINENCE, PRACTICALITY, PASSION

Sometimes selecting a case for study is not especially problematic for researchers because they are already involved in an SMO of interest. Often, however, selection is more problematic and the decision must be thought through attuned to the degree to which the prospective investigator can give positive answers to three major questions: Is it pertinent? Is it practical? Is it my passion?

A. Is It Pertinent?

The world is replete with myriad kinds of organizations, only some of which are SMOs. And, as discussed in Chapter 1, while many organizations are clearly SMOs, many others are in an ambiguous zone between mainstream reality inclusion and exclusion. Indeed, the line between SMOs and interest groups, in particular, is quite vague, despite the crispness of visualization of the distinction I present in Figure 1.1. In the minds of some investigators, in fact, this "line" is vague to the point of invisibility. But, although there is no clear boundary, there is clearly also a difference between garden variety interest groups and SMOs. Therefore, the first question SMO researchers attempt to answer about any organization they are thinking of studying is: *Is this really an SMO?* In making this decision they may consult various sources of definitions of SMOs, as in Chapter 1. Sometimes they will also solicit the views of other students of SMOs.

B. Is It Practical?

Having decided the SMO is pertinent, researchers then face the question of practicality. Within available time and resources, can they assemble enough information on the SMO to make a credible analysis? Will they able to put together a minimally adequate amount and quality of information or "data"? The exact character of a "minimally adequate amount and quality" depends, certainly, on the aspects and questions they come finally to address (Step three, discussed in Chapter 3) and the propositions they form (described in Chapter 4). Even so, there is a range of *basic activities*, at least some of which researchers feel they should complete.

In this very early stage of *preliminary reconnaissance*, researchers seek to assess the likelihood of collecting minimally adequate data within whatever context of time and resource constraints. One way this is done is to review the range of ordinary sources of data vis-à-vis the candidate SMO. Let me list these ordinary sources of data and then discuss how much of each researchers may feel they need in order to proceed with studying that SMO. (I frame this list in terms of the constraints of small-scale projects, especially those undertaken by students, and I also recognize that all of these kinds of data are not available on or from every SMO.)

1. A common very first step is to review the *scholarly literature* on the SMO. Often there is no such literature, but researchers do not assume this to be the case. By "scholarly" I mean books with the earmarks of scholarship and articles appearing in academic journals.[1] The general catalog or computer database of the holdings of a good research library is the ordinary first place to look for books; *Sociological Abstracts* and similar databases (described below, Sections II.A and II.C) are windows on scholarly articles.

2. Many SMOs give rise to a *popular literature*, which is articles of a journalistic or even sensationalistic cast that appear in mass circulation magazines and newspapers. These can provide some relatively accurate basic facts, but, more important, they are excellent sources of popular or stereotyped images. Researchers find it useful to be acquainted with many of these, if available. Preliminary reconnaissance reveals the extent of such materials.

3. The typical SMO produces its *own documents*, often in profusion. One key task of the researcher is to acquire (or at least to read) many of these. Ideally, they are available or not too hard to get.

4. Many SMOs produce a *serial publication*, a magazine or newsletter that it issues at regular intervals and has done so for some years. For the purpose of forming a holistic grasp of the SMO,

researchers find it helpful to locate a complete set of these and to read all of them—or a manageable systematic sample of them—from the start to the end (or to the present). In the stage of preliminary recognizance, though, they seek first and only to assess existence and availability.

5. Some SMOs prompt an explicitly *critical body of literature* that is not the same as the scholarly or popular literature. Instead, it overtly attacks the SMO, seeking to show the errors of its beliefs, the derelictions of its leaders, the perfidy of its members, and the like. Obviously, researchers need not believe such countermovement allegations in order to find these materials useful in understanding the SMO. The task of preliminary recognizance is to assess the degree to which there is such a literature.

6. It is possible directly to *interview representatives* of some SMOs. Researchers regard this is an appropriate or even indispensable activity if it does not put them at too much personal risk or involve inordinate expense. Hopefully, preliminary reconnaissance shows that interviewing is possible.

7. In addition, it is sometimes possible to *observe the activities* of an SMO. If the risks and costs are manageable, researchers seek to do as much of this as possible within time and other resource constraints.

Having made a preliminary reconnaissance of these seven major sources of data, researchers then ask themselves: Taking all these together, will we be able to collect enough data within the time and resources we have available? This is a difficult question to answer and researchers are guided by several "it depends" guidelines.

First, it depends on exactly how much is available in any one of these categories. If, for example, any single category offers an abundance of materials, this material might well be sufficient to the task. Researchers might select, for example, an SMO about which (and by which) nothing has been published. That is, sources 1 through 5 just above provide zero data. But, counterbalancing that, these same researchers might have rich access to sources 6 and 7. In that event, they might still judge the study to be practical (especially if they have already been trained in fieldwork and are prepared to do observation, to do appropriate interviews, and to write up good field notes).

Second, it depends on the aspects, questions, and propositions that concern the researchers and that are evident in the data, matters that I will be take up in discussing steps (3) and (4) in the next two chapters.

Third, it depends in some part on the amount of enterprising energy the researchers are prepared to put into the task of collecting data in order to overcome problems of accessibility (such as, for example, traveling to distant archives or SMO events, chapters, and members). For well-known SMOs though, researchers *begin* by exploring the practically and feasibility of getting at least *some* data from all seven of these sources.

Despite these "it depends," a rough rule of thumb is nonetheless employed: researchers reasonably expect that fairly abundant materials can be collected from at least *two* of these seven sources. Indeed, if preliminary exploration indicates to researchers that they cannot collect rather rich data from at least two, they are likely to decide not to study that particular SMO (or at least not to study it at that time).

Another way to think of practicality is in terms of a *projected basic data package* that researchers are seeking to assemble. By this I mean that researchers think ahead to the methods section they will include in their written report and they ask themselves what they will be able to say about their data in that section. So projected, they ask themselves: Will the write-up of the methods and data in the report describe adequate data? In the particular, scaled-down contexts of research in college courses, the emphasis is often on reporting the *efforts* the researchers have made to acquire data from all seven of these sources (or from yet others that I review in Section III of this chapter).

C. Is It My Passion?

Despite the fact that it can also be enormously pleasurable and even sheer fun, studying an SMO is hard work. Therefore, in periods of frustration and difficulty, researchers need some strong and personal motivational base on which to draw and that serves to carry them through the hard times. As I will discuss in Chapter 4, the process of emergent induction asks the researcher-as-analyst to exercise a great deal of enterprising diligence that involves degrees of anxiety and fear. Beyond the devices for coping with difficulties that researchers use and that I outline in that discussion, they also find it extremely important to study an SMO that they personally care about. This caring may take the form of *liking* the SMO a great deal; being concerned about the *matters addressed* by the SMO although they don't feel much about the SMO itself; or *not liking* the SMO for various strongly felt reasons. That is, the content and positive or negative emotional direction of this caring can be quite varied, as long as something about the SMO actually *matters* to the researchers. A given SMO might be quite *pertinent* and preeminently *practical*, but nonetheless a matter to which the researchers are personally indifferent. If so, researchers think hard on the question of whether pertinence and practicality can overcome their lack of passion.

The ideal SMO for study is, of course, one that the researchers can assess to be strongly **pertinent**, imminently **practical**, and central to their **passions**. Alas, the real world of making decisions rarely presents itself to researchers in such easily decidable terms. Instead, the answers to one or another of these three questions may be strongly positive while the third is negative, among numerous other combinations. The real world is often one of balancing and trade-offs. But, when researchers ask and answer these three questions seriously, they have at least advantaged themselves by the fact of consciously assessing the above three dimensions of what they are getting into.

III. STEP (2), COLLECTING: SOURCES OF DATA AND TYPES OF METHODS

Put as the question Where and how do researchers get data? I want to point to eight main or primary approaches movements researchers use effectively in their studies and that we can therefore take as models. As can be seen, these are much the same as the categories of data to scan in the preliminary reconnaissance stage, slightly modified here in terms of more in-depth data collection.

Although I will discuss each separately, it needs also to be understood that (as mentioned above) any given study tends to use more than one of these sources of data and form of method. The eight categories of data and method are arranged in a rough order of distance from or proximity to an SMO under study. I begin with the greatest distance and move slowly closer.

A. Secondary Analysis of Published Accounts

Social movements and SMOs are topics on which people write a great many book length treatments. It is common for better-known movements to generate many dozens of reports of several sorts, mostly popular or journalistic in character, but also many scholarly articles and books.

The amazingly large accumulated body of such works taken in the aggregate over all social movements is a rich resource for what is called "secondary analysis," or "research synthesis." Putting aside the conceptual frameworks of the primary authors, acute secondary analysts can and do glean information on aspects and questions about SMOs that are usable in doing new analyses of these existing data.

The classification systems of libraries are mostly *not* useful in retrieving sociologically analytic information on SMOs—information of the sort I will describe in Chapters 3 and 4. But library classification systems *are* very useful in retrieving information in terms of the *ordinary or everyday names* of SMOs because these are the kinds of categories libraries tend to use. Therefore, researchers need only become familiar with the common names given an SMO (and the names of its more famous leaders) in order to retrieve their descriptive treasures.

We are in the early stages of a revolution in the storage and retrieval of information in libraries, a revolution capsulated in the distinction between *print* and *electronic* modes of storage and retrieval. With amazing rapidity, the latter have begun to supplant the former, although the former remain, in most libraries, of major significance. Let me briefly describe major sources of information in each category that SMO researchers find to be especially helpful.

Among indexes still available primarily in print form, these are among those that are especially likely to provide leads to publications on particular SMOs, albeit SMOs only in the areas signaled by the index titles:

Alternative Press Index
America: History and Life
Bibliography of Asian Studies
Chicano Periodicals Index
Combined Retrospective Index of Journal in History, 1838–1974
Historical Abstracts
Index to Black Periodicals
Political Science Abstracts
Social Sciences Citation Index
Social Sciences Index
Sociological Abstracts
Women Studies Abstracts
Writings on American History

I need to stress that this is a small sampling from a much, much larger number of indexes that can be found in libraries. (And many of these indexes are organized in terms of geographical areas, which may or may not be a helpful category of classification relating to a given SMO.)

In addition, there are smaller-scale bibliographies, encyclopedias, and handbooks on a vast range of topics and areas that include treatments of and bibliographies on particular SMOs, such as these I happen to have at hand:

L. Wilcox (ed.), *Guide to the American Right*, 19th edition (1994b) ("directory of over 1,400 organizations, publishers, book dealers, newsletter and journals identified with the American 'right-wing'")

L. Wilcox (ed.), *Guide to the American Left,* 16th edition (1994a) (same kind of coverage as for the right)

J. G. Melton, *Encyclopedic Handbook of Cults in America,* revised and updated edition (1992)

J. George and L. Wilcox, *Nazis, Communists, Klansmen, and Others on the Fringe* (1992)

D. Gillespie, *Politics at the Periphery: Third Parties in Two-Party America* (1993)

B. Chernow and G. Vallasi (eds.), *The Columbia Encyclopedia,* 5th edition (1993)[2]

Notice that the last item in this list is a general encyclopedia rather than a specialized guide. I include it because nonspecialized compendiums can sometimes be, depending on the SMO, quite useful and fruitful as least *initial* sources of information.

E. P. Sheely (1986), *The Guide to Reference Books,* is, as the title tells, a compendium of reference books that merits review at the point of getting started. [See, further, Baker (1994, 442–50) on "Using a Library for Social Research" and Tuchman (1994), on major compendia of sources favored by historians.]

The spreading practice of electronic databasing sources of information vastly increases the speed and simplicity of searches. Simply as a practical matter, researchers prefer to use libraries that have such computerized resources. Because the specifics of holdings, access, and use of these electronic databases differ among libraries, researchers need to begin by reading the instructional material on the databases in the libraries they are using and *also* to consult with the *reference staff* in those libraries.

I want to underscore this mention of *reference staff* in libraries. Novice users of libraries often do not appreciate that the people found behind reference desks in libraries (especially in large libraries) are technically trained in the nature and breadth of library information sources. They are there precisely to be of help to inquirers like SMO researchers. Such inquirers are definitely *not* "bothering" or interrupting when they ask these librarians to help them find sources of information on a specific SMO (or other topic). Assisting researchers in finding their way around in the hundreds if not thousands of reference sources is *exactly* what they are there to do! The newness and therefore still novel character of electronic sources indeed make reference staff ever more important as sources of help and is all the more reason to seek their assistance (cf. Stewart and Kamins 1993).

Libraries differ in the particular databases they maintain or that they have access to along the "information superhighway." The following are among the more prominent and available in libraries *and* that are more likely to have SMO pertinent sources (the all capitals acronyms are the University of California user-call-up names):

MAGS	Magazines and Journal—1,500 magazines and journals
NEWS	Newspaper articles—five major U.S. newspapers
CC	Current contents—6,500 scholarly journals
CCT	Current contents—tables of contents of 6,500 scholarly journals
PSYC	PsycINFO—1,300 psychology journals and publications
UNCOVER	Magazine and journal articles—CARL Systems
LC	Library of Congress

The Gale Research Company of Detroit strives to inventory databases in its *Gale Directory of Databases* (Nolan 1994).

B. Historical Archives

As, by definition, challengers of mainstream realities, and therefore forgers of social change, SMOs—and SMs—are history. This is *not* history in the pejorative and anemic sense of "that's history," but history in the positive and robust senses of *making history* [as in Flacks's (1988a) book of that very title]. Many people in social movements are very much aware that they are making history and they frame their actions with this consciousness. One element of this consciousness of themselves as history-makers is that their actions produce *documents* and these are often consciously *saved*. A sense of posterity encourages a sense of *the record* and the need to make and *preserve* one.

Indeed, one of the key activities of elements of movement establishments (described in Chapter 11) is to institute and maintain *archives* of SMOs in particular and "movement surges" more generally. Beyond them, larger libraries often have archiving programs that feature social movements, including SMOs.

In the compass of this brief treatment of the process of SMO research, I cannot do more than call attention to the existence of a large number of these archives and to mention a few of the more famous ones that have been and are of use to SMO researchers. At the operating level, SMO researchers are likely to check into the existence of archives (also called "collections") on a movement/SMO in which they might have an interest—and especially to check into what archives might exist in their local areas. Larger libraries have a department labeled "special collections" (or a similar term) with a professional staff that is very well acquainted with that library's holdings and—equally important—is likely to be knowledgeable about *all* special collections held in the vicinity or region. [That is, archivists form their own world and are happy to tell (well-demeaned) researchers "who is who" and "what is where."] Knowledge of this latter sort calls attention to the fact that a great many archives are privately held and maintained—sometimes by a single individual—rather than deposited in public or quasi-public institutions like libraries.

Another way researchers identify the existence of archives on a particular SMO is to read the acknowledgments sections of published books on it. Often, these previous scholars/students have used even quite obscure privately held archives and they are careful to name these depositories and to thank the people who gave them permission to study the contents. (Access to many special collections is not automatic—unlike the shelf holdings of libraries—but requires permission, which in turn requires evidence of serious scholarly purpose. In ordinary cases, this permission is not difficult to obtain.)

Akin to reading the acknowledgments sections of pertinent books is the careful viewing of the credit sections of film and video programs that include coverage of a movement in which the researcher is interested. The pictures or motion pictures in these visual programs have often been obtained from archives on whatever the movement or movements treated.

Some privately held collections have not reached the level of being formally organized as archives in the sense of being a formal organization with cataloged and preserved materials whose existence is of public record. Instead, a veteran of an SMO/social movement has simply saved a great deal of material that she or he has accumulated. The collection is more in the nature of personal memorabilia rather than professionally archived material. The sentiments that have prompted these veterans to keep all those materials are also the sentiments that make them open to providing access to serious and responsible researchers. They are proud of their involvement and hope that others will take an interest in the movement; hence they are receptive to requests to examine their collections. In studying an SMO, therefore, researchers are alert to reports of the existence of such personal collections.

I have spoken of archives organized around movements or particular

SMOs, but many are not so centered. Instead, they are the papers and other materials of a well-known movement figure or leader. Therefore, researchers are often flexible in how they conceptualize what is an "archive" and how and where to find one.

Some few archives stand out as the "mother of all archives" on the particular SMOs or SMs in which they specialize. I have not surveyed all movements in terms of having or not having such a "mother of all archives," but a few that are especially well known and used by movement researchers must be reported. Assiduous researchers of other SMOs also set out to determine if there is such an archive on the movement of their special interests.

> *Movements of the Sixties:* The Bancroft Library, University of California, Berkeley
>
> *Peace movement throughout American history:* The Swarthmore College Peace Collection, Swarthmore College, Swarthmore, Pennsylvania. This collection publishes a book describing its holdings (Swarthmore College 1981). In addition, peace movement collections are so abundant that Green (1986) has compiled a small book listing them.
>
> *Labor movement:* Archives of Labor and Urban Affairs, Wayne State University, Detroit
>
> *Civil rights movement:* The Martin Luther King, Jr., Center for Nonviolent Social Change, Atlanta
>
> *Radical left SMOs:* The Labadie Collection, University of Michigan Library, Ann Arbor.
>
> *Gay and lesbian movements:* One Institute, University of Southern California Library, Los Angeles.

Archives as a general class of institution are, of course, the special interest of historians and another approach *social science* researchers use in locating pertinent ones is through historian compilations of archives, such as:

> *National Inventory of Documentary Sources in the United States* (NIDS) (Agee, Bertelsen, Holland, and Wivel, 1985)
>
> *Directory of Archives and Manuscripts Repositories in the United States* (National Historical Publications and Records Commission, 1988)
>
> *Directory of Special Libraries and Information Centers,* 13th edition (Darnay and DeMaggio 1990)

Archives per se as public or quasi-public institutions shade off into "a welter of private and quasi-public organizations [that store records], such as credit bureaus, compilers of city directories, insurance companies, schools, professional associations, fraternal societies, and alumni associations," that may, for some questions, have useful information (Hill 1993, 74; Villarejo 1980).

Of special note for the study of SMOs, some government agencies collect and archive information on persons. For the U.S. government, these are held by the U.S. National Archives and Records Administration (Davis 1988). From a movement study perspective, the mother lode of such records is, of course, the Federal Bureau of Investigation, at least some of whose records can be obtained through Freedom of Information Act requests. As Michael Hill (1993) recommends and a number of movement researchers have used, a good way to learn about the process is begin by requesting one's own files. [The process, which is not complicated, is outlined in Bitrago and Immersman (1981) and Adler (1990), among other places.]

Researchers who have the time and who are dealing with recent American SMOs that hold tax-exempt status with the federal Internal Revenue Service can learn something about the SMO's finances by filing a form 4506-A, which is a "Request for Public Inspection or Copy of Exempt Organization Tax Form." The return or returns can be examined at no charge in an IRS office or copies can be purchased for reasonable fees.

As a specialized craft, there are a number of points of procedure and of etiquette that researchers master in advance of using archives. Unlike research techniques such as survey questionnaires and direct observation though, these are not described in the numerous and widely available texts and manuals. Fortunately, that situation has begun to change and Michael Hill's brief and pointed *Archival Strategies and Techniques* (1993) is *the* indispensable primer. In particular, it is important for researchers to know *how to interact with archivists* and to treat archived materials with what archivists define as proper respect, topics on which Hill is especially informative.

C. Movement Study and Tracking Associations

Social movements as a generic category of human action and in some specific forms have spawned organized circles of (1) try-to-be-dispassionate scholars and (2) information-collecting oppositional organizations. Properly approached, these can be fruitful sources of data for SMO researchers. Because officers, editors, and pertinent addresses change so frequently and lists of these tracking organizations are therefore rapidly out of date, I do not report such specifics below. Fortunately, they or their parent organizations are listed, with details, in the *Encyclo-*

pedia of Associations (Schwartz and Turner 1995), which is revised and published each year and can be found in many libraries. Alternatively, current specifics on these organizations are common knowledge among specialists in the areas each addresses. Therefore, for a specific SMO of interest, researchers simply check around in their local milieu for who there might be such a specialist and go and see her or him.

On the more dispassionate side and addressed to social movements as a generic topic, there are several organized groupings with larger professional associations. These include:

- American Sociological Association Section on Collective Behavior and Social Movements.
- International Sociological Association Research Committee Numbers 44, 47, and 48, titled, respectively, Labor Movements, Social Movements and Social Classes, and Collective Behavior and Social Movements.

There are also a number of associations dedicated to scholarly study of some more delimited types of social movement, or even a particular social movement. These include:

- The Peace History Society, which focuses on all peace efforts but perforce does a great deal of peace movement history. (It cosponsors the journal *Peace and Change*, through which the association can be contacted.)
- The Historians of American Communism have a self-explanatory name and publish a newsletter.
- The Society for the Study of Historic Communal Societies, which publishes the journal *Communal Societies*.
- Society for the Sociological Study of Mormonism.
- Terrorist Profile Weekly, an on-line Ezine available through gopher at gopher.well.com/Publications/online-zines and Email at cdibona@mason.gnu.edu.
- Society for Utopian Studies.

SMO researchers are likely to be acquainted with yet additional specialized scholarly societies, and novice researchers locate these associations through direct contact with researchers who publish on the particular SMOs.

On the *less* dispassionate and more oppositional side, there are a number of associations that focus on "tracking" the activities of a movement or movement they *dislike*. These organizations commonly publish a variety of kinds of literature (books, pamphlets, "fact sheets," etc.).

Used cautiously, researchers find these important sources of information. Here are some well-established ones:

- Political Research Associates, Cambridge, MA, which describes itself as "providing information to progressive grassroots organizations about the American right wing." It publishes the newsletter *The Public Eye*.
- Klanwatch Project of the Southern Poverty Law Center, Montgomery, Alabama, which focuses on white supremacist groups and their activities.
- Spiritual Counterfeits Project, Berkeley, California, whose newsletter masthead reports that it provides a "biblical perspective on new religions and spiritual trends."
- Foundation for Public Affairs is described by *PR Watch* (which tracks corporate public relations activities) as having "a major mission of tracking activists," in which "it monitors more than 75 specialized activist publications and gathers information on 'more than 1,300 activist organizations, research institutions, and other groups.'" (PR Watch 1993, 3). Some of this material appears in the *Foundation's Public Interest Profiles*, described by *PR Watch* as "an impressive directory of who's who in the world of [Washington,] DC-based activism."

More specialized and private are organizations such as the Institute for Strategic Studies on Terrorism of Hereford, Texas, whose letterhead says it is "A Private, Professional Research, Consulting, Training Organization To Law Enforcement, Government, and Corporations." In addition to training courses on dealing with "terrorist organizations," in one recent year the Institute offered a "regular flow of data" to subscribers for "$2730.00 per annum."[3] In consulting arrangements, detailed information on specific groups is offered. It appears, though, that a researcher needs to be especially affluent in order to engage the services of tracking associations of this kind.

Analytically speaking, these "less dispassionate" associations are "counterSMOs" and I will consider them further in such terms in Chapter 10, Section II.E.

Hovering between and swooping back and forth between the above two patterns of movement study and tracking associations are some Internet "discussion groups" focused on a type of movement or movement reality. Among the more prominent is a discussion group with some five hundred members called The Sixties List, which is a free-flowing forum of commentaries on varied U.S. movements (including SMOs) of the 1960s. (To subscribe send the text SUBSCRIBE SIXTIES-L [your name] to SIXTIES-LISTPROC@JEFFERSONVILLAGE.VIRGINIA.EDU.)

D. Quantitative Datasets and Databases

The two sources I have just described are likely to lead to "qualitative" or narrative prose types of information on—and depiction of—SMOs. This is not the only kind of treatment that researchers often find possible and necessary. Instead, for many questions researchers need quantitative data on correlations and temporal changes. Happily and because of the computer revolution, researchers are finding data of this kind increasingly available in existing databases and datasets.

1. Secondary Analysis of Existing Datasets. For some fifty years now, scholars have been developing quantitative datasets on movements and some SMOs. The number of such existing datasets must now number in the hundreds if not the thousands. Virtually all of these datasets have long since ceased to be of much interest to their developers and lie unused among the private possessions of scholars or have been archived by one of the dataset archiving organizations. The norms of science require that these datasets be made available to serious researchers who request their use. Therefore, if the published description of a dataset appears to have pertinent information that researchers could derive by using it, they contact the author, or the organization archiving the dataset, and request a copy of it. Procedures for identifying and locating such datasets are similar to those for historical archives: they are referenced (or simply used) in publications researchers read on the particular SMO being studied.

The Inter-university Consortium for Political and Social Research (ICPSR) (1994) archives survey datasets in general and SMO researchers find some of them useful in answering some kinds of questions, particularly questions about the responses of bystander publics of movement and quasi-movement events. In the mid-nineties ICSPR had archived some three thousand surveys, representing an estimated six million variables (1994, xv–xvi). Close to four hundred colleges and universities are annual dues-paying members of this consortium, and faculty, staff, and students at those institutions can access its services at no extra charge except in "very unusual circumstances" (ICPSR 1994, viii).

Even though it is not an example of the "qualitative case study" research strategy that is the centerpiece of this guide, I would be remiss not to highlight the classic dataset of SMOs assembled by William Gamson and published in his *Strategy of Social Protest* (1975). As indicated previously, this is a study of thirty-nine variables coded on a sample of fifty-three American SMOs active in some period between 1800 and 1945. Aside from the singularity of having located and coded data on them, Gamson presents the raw data of his study in an appendix to his book, a feature that has encouraged several reanalyses of them and a good deal of debate over the findings. More useful yet, the original book together with the major critiques was republished in 1990. (Gamson's study and responses to it are reported in Chapter 9, Section IV.A.)

2. Informational Databases. As mentioned above concerning library searches, an expanding array of publications and their contents are being entered into large-scale electronic databases. The quantification of the contents of these databases is itself a technique of some note in recent movement studies. Most commonly and well known, items on specific SMOs or movements appearing in the *New York Times Index* are counted over time, or the index is used as a guide to retrieving the stories themselves and coding their contents (e.g., McAdam 1982).

The *New York Times Index* has been used most often because researchers have treated the reports therein as "objective" in the sense of assuming that this newspaper covered events with enough comprehensiveness and accuracy to make year-by-year comparisons empirically descriptive of the real world rather than merely indicators of varying levels of newspaper energy and interest. As a newspaper that styles itself the source "of record" for the United States, this use of its coverage may be justified.

However, such informational databases can be and are also treated as *constructions*, as quantitative tracings of the level of interest and concern regarding a particular SMO That is, social response to an SMO is not merely a function of its own activities, but of the intensity of interest in or concern about it that people display—in this case the people who control the contents of publications indexed in informational databases. [Gale Research publishes an intermittently updated two volume compendium of such databases (Nolan 1994).]

E. SMO Publications

In asserting realities that challenge mainstream constructions, SMOs are highly intellectual affairs. They must develop rationales, defend against detractors, spell out preferred courses of action, and so on through the range of matters entailed in argumentation on the true, the moral, and the reasonable. All this means that written items are quintessential artifacts of SMOs. As such, these items of writing command the researcher's attention—and they are a great boon as a source of data.

Often an SMO will have an official or at least dominant single publication that can be taken as expressing its point of view. These are published at more or less regular intervals and the set of them that has accumulated over some years provides a rich resource for the quantitative as well as the qualitative analysis of a wide variety of SMO units of analysis and questions about those units. (The same is true of even more ephemeral publications, such as the handbills or posters that were produced over several years.)

This category of movement publications of course overlaps with that of historical archives in that researchers can get such publications from archives and perform the above operations on them. I single out movement publications as a separate type because of the practical fact that they are often available quite apart from archives. An ordinary library might subscribe to them, for example. [Indeed, because of a librarian there named John Liberty, the library of the California State University, Sacramento, specializes in subscribing to the main publication of a great many SMOs (Liberty 1981).] Often, the national or local office of an SMO will have a complete set of its main publication that researchers can use. So also, individual pack-rat-inclined members can sometimes be discovered to have squirreled away such a publication (along with much else). Therefore, researchers must—and do—ask.

Although a great many important SMO publications do not get chronicled in conventional compilations of publications,[4] a surprising number do and directories of publications per se can therefore be an important source for identifying pertinent such serials. The marvelous and incredible mother of all compilations of publications in the United States is the four volume:

> *Gale Directory of Publications and Broadcast Media*, 128th edition (Troshynski-Thomas and Burek 1996)

In addition, there is a genre of directory that combines SMO listings with their publications, independent movement publications, and miscellaneous other types of information. There are, broadly speaking, pro-movement "movement directories" that highlight particular SMOs and their publications. Here is a sampling:

> *The Activist's Almanac: The Concerned Citizen's Guide to Leading Advocacy Organizations in America* (Walls 1993)
> *Volunteer USA: Comprehensive Guide to Worthy Causes That Need You* (Carroll and Miller 1991)
> *Organized Obsessions: 1,001 Offbeat Associations, Fan Clubs, and Microsocieties You Can Join* (Burek and Connors 1992)

> *Macrocosm USA: An Environmental, Political, and Social Solutions Hand-book with Directories* (Brockway 1992)
>
> *What Can I Do to Make a Difference?: A Positive Action Sourcebook* (Zimmerman 1992)
>
> *The World of Zines: A Guide to the Independent Magazine Revolution* (Gunderloy and Janice 1992)
>
> *The Millennium Whole Earth Catalog: Access to Tools and Ideas for the Twenty-first Century* (Rheingold 1994)
>
> *Spectrum: Guide to the Independent Press*, 23rd edition (Wilcox 1994c)

F. Computer Communication

Computer communication is a new and peculiar form of human contact that is faster and more immediate than the kinds of communications described above, but still slower and less immediate than the two forms I will treat below.

Being both recent and unprecedented, the meaning and import of computer communication is difficult to assess. But one thing is certain: An enormous throng of humans has taken it up with religiouslike enthusiasm and dedication. Such devotion is no less the case for entrepreneurs of insurgent realities than for mainstream realists. Indeed, because of the openness and freedom of computer communication, *insurgent* realities may find "cyberspace" especially attractive because of these very characteristics.

Conceived as a source of information involving a particular method, computer communication presents two main organizational forms of SMO-pertinent materials over the Internet: the online system and the newsgroup.

1. Such large commercial online systems as America Online and CompuServe are quintessentially the mainstream, but several other and smaller systems are oriented to myriad insurgent—including SMO—realities. These include Women's Wire, The WELL, the Institute for Global Communication (IGC) networks (PeaceNet, EcoNet, ConflictNet and LaborNet), and Left on Line (LBBS) (Reingold 1994, 263–65).

2. Employing a computer program called Usenet, the Internet features many thousands of "newsgroups," which are "online conferences consisting of hundreds of individual messages or postings, which are continuously broadcast over the internet 24 hours a day" (Gagnon 1995, 7). Because the Internet is open and has no centralized means of making a census of its participants, no one knows how many newsgroups there are. Assiduous, self-appointed census-takers estimate, though, that by the mid-1990s there were close to ten thousand. And entrepreneurs such as Eric Gagnon (1995) have enumerated and even reviewed some

two thousand of them! [See also King (1994), a directory of electronic journals and other more scholarly communications.]

Of pertinence here, some of these newsgroups are SMOs or at least SMO-like. Quite a number of them are identified and described in the array of newsgroup guidebooks that have come on the market. (See, for example, Gagnon 1995, Chapter 4, section on "Political Discussion and Debate Groups," Ch. 5, section on "Religion and Philosophy," and Ch. 13, section on "Off the Wall," which includes "Skinheads and Hate Groups.")

G. Survey Questionnaires

The last two forms of data/method that SMO researchers use bring us into degrees of actual and serious contact with an SMO—contact that it is *possible* to avoid with all the previous research approaches. Indeed, the possibility of avoiding face-to-face contact afforded by the above methods and data sources sometimes makes readers suspicious of a study that relies exclusively or even in a major way on them *and* in which there was no direct contact with an SMO. Such suspicion is founded on the more general proposition about social science knowledge holding that there is no substitute for the validity generated by personal immersion and, as a consequence, deep and intimate familiarity (cf. Blumer 1969b, Ch. 1; Lofland and Lofland 1995, Ch. 1).

The less intimate of the two forms of contact I want now to describe involves asking SMO people to fill out questionnaires on themselves and/or on their organizations. This method and source of data is also termed "survey research" and is one of the most practiced and codified forms of social inquiry. It is also a method in which it is possible to make a great many errors and researchers therefore do not embark on it without a reasonable amount of prior formal training in it. The wording of questions, their order in the questionnaire, the physical appearance of the questionnaire, and the approach taken in asking people to respond to it all massively affect the results one will get. Done by amateurs who make mistakes on such matters, the survey results tell us more about the researcher's errors than about the people questioned.

Nonetheless, this is not to say that researchers do not or should not do survey research on movement people or organizations. It is, however, to say that researchers take great care to know what they are doing. Measures they take to make certain they are acting correctly include, first, consulting with people who have done survey research and taking their advice, and, second, consulting with people who are familiar with the SMO they desire to survey. The best advice comes, of course, from people who combine both experiences.

Researchers who are unfamiliar with survey research (and this includes a large number of senior scholars of movements) quite properly begin this form of data collection by reading introductory texts that treat the topic, such as Babbie (1995, 1990) or Baker (1994, Ch. 7).

H. Interviewing and Observation

The most straightforward way researchers get to know an SMO is simply to approach members and to ask them about it. For most movements (but *not* all), it is my impression that this is actually quite easy and pleasant, at least in early contacts. It is commonly easy because SMOs are, as I have said, in the business of trying to convince people of the wisdom or folly of a given social or personal reality. As people in the persuasion business, participants are ordinarily quite happy to talk to a new person about such wisdom or folly. Therefore, researchers who are sympathetically attentive and not abrasively argumentative normally find early contacts and interviews quite cordial and even fun. (I include in the term "early contacts" such matters as having interviews with leaders and other public and quasi-public SMO people and attending the SMO public meetings.)

In the above, I of course assume that SMO researchers say that they are exactly that: *researchers* (or students)—persons who are open-minded at least in the sense of willing (in a civil, cordial, and fair manner) to hear members out. In such contacts they also signal that they are serious by having done some preliminary reading, having prepared questions, and taking notes during conversations. That is, SMO people are like everyone else in wanting to be taken seriously and treated with respect. Previous reading, prepared questions, and note-taking communicate attitudes of seriousness and respect.

The direct observation and interviewing I have just described may suffice for studies that employ other of the kinds of data and methods I have described above and that are preliminary in the fashion of undergraduate student term papers. Some studies, however, involve much more prolonged and in-depth observation and interviewing. At this next level, matters become very complex and socially delicate. Indeed, problems at this level are so delicate that they have given rise to an elaborate body of strategy and technique that is equivalent to the body of technique I have mentioned above regarding survey research. In the same way that it is very easy to make a mess of things in survey research if the researchers do not know what they are doing, in direct observation and interviewing, researchers can also easily make a mess of things—especially a *social* mess of things—if they do not know what they are doing.

Because of the importance of knowing how to go about such field-work, let me sketch some of the more important features of this situation and its problems.

- By definition, a great many SMOs live in a highly politicized and conflict-ridden environment, where active opposition has likely crystallized, even to the point of *covert infiltrators* of its ranks. SMO people are therefore and correctly wary of anyone who wants to "study" them and is otherwise curious and questioning of them in the ways that social analysts need to be (cf. Shupe and Bromley 1980).
- If the researchers are allowed to become known or "open" observers, there are likely to be very strong pressures to join, efforts to co-opt them, and/or tendencies to "put them on" (i.e., to lie to them), for, as nonbelievers, they may be seen as not deserving to know what is "really happening." Dealing with these kinds of problems is no easy task and special training is required.
- On the other hand, if the researcher becomes a covert or unknown observer, a range of very serious moral questions about doing this are raised. Even if such questions can be resolved, in some SMOs, covert observers are defined as potential converts and subjected to strong pressures to join, pressures that can make the researchers' lives very uncomfortable. In yet other movements, discovery that the researchers are secret observers can have very serious—even lethal—consequences.
- And, there are a series of important questions raised about the consequences of the researchers' observations. *What* do the researchers decide to report? *Who sees* the reports and *does what* with them? What are to be the researcher's positions on harming or helping an SMO by means of what they report?

A very sophisticated order of finesse and sensitivity is required in circumstance such as these. Indeed, the possible complications are such that a great many SMOs are *not* observed because of these (and other) problems. Therefore, before moving to the level of prolonged observation and interviewing of an SMO, researchers contemplating such action at least do what they also do about using other methods of direct contact (such as the survey): (1) They consult with people who have performed observation and interviewing and they learn appropriate and inappropriate practice from them. (2) They consult with people who are familiar with the SMO. Best of all, they seek the advice of people with both these kinds of experiences with the SMO or one similar to it. And, if they are unfamiliar with observation and interviewing in the first place, they begin by reading manuals on these techniques. The one I immodestly recommend is by Lyn Lofland and myself (Lofland and Lofland 1995). In addition, Earl Babbie's chapter on observation in his textbook on social research (1995, Ch. 11) is quite helpful as a brief introduction.

* * *

In this chapter I have described the first two of four major steps in (or phases of) the qualitative case study of SMOs: **selecting** an SMO and **collecting** data on it. Selecting and collecting are obviously important, but they are only the first half of the story. The other and equally important half involves **asking** questions about the data and **answering** those questions, matters to which we now proceed.

NOTES

1. The earmarks of scholarship include the following: (1) there are serious rather than "cute" titles and section captions, (2) the opening pages pose a general question or topic rather than offering narrowly descriptive text, (3) there is a bibliography or list of references, (4) sources of information are documented, (5) there is a conclusion or other assessment at the end of the report regarding what has been found or achieved in it.

2. More specialized compendiums include:

M. J. Buhle, P. Buhle, and D. Georgakas, eds., *Encyclopedia of the American Left* (1990).

R. S. Fogarty, ed., *Dictionary of American Communal and Utopian History* (1980).

C. F. Howlett, *The American Peace Movement: References and Resources* (1991).

H. Klehr, *Far Left of Center: The American Left Today* (1988).

3. Letter from Arthur E. Gerringer to John Lofland, May 31, 1994.

4. Remember, we speak of *insurgent* realities, and one of the meanings of insurgency is that the mainstream commonly *ignores* it (which is one fundamental form of exclusion). For discussion, see Chapter 10, on "reactions."

3

Step Three:
Asking Questions

In the third step of SMO case studies, researchers ask questions about the case or cases under study. My explanation of how researchers carry out this task is divided into three parts.

I. I begin with summaries of seven main questions that researchers have frequently asked about SMOs. My report of these will be brief in this chapter because each of them occupies the central position in their respective Part II chapters (5–11), where I state each in more detail (and I *answer* the questions!).

II. With these seven main questions before us, I will then show how these are (1) different kinds of *generic questions* about (2) different of *aspects* of SMOs. This will lay the basis for understanding that there are eight generic questions *and* many different aspects of SMOs that researchers address.

III. Finally, the list of eight generic questions and the list of many aspects will be conjoined in a matrix. The rich array of possibilities this matrix displays will show how the inquiries of particular researchers are of necessity quite focused within a much, much larger context.

I. SEVEN MAIN QUESTIONS ABOUT SMOS

For reasons I put to the side for the moment, only a relative few from among a great many possible questions have been asked (and answered) about SMOs with great frequency. Among these, there are seven that seem clearly to preoccupy SMO researchers and these are therefore the ones I feature in the seven chapters of Part II. Because they are elaborated on in those chapters, I here give only a brief summary of each.

To help in visualizing these questions, the object of our focus, the SMO, is symbolized as an upright rectangle in the center of Figure 3.1 and the seven main questions asked about it are arrayed in their logical relation to this symbolizing rectangle. I will explain the placement of each of the seven questions as we proceed.

A. Question 1: What Are SMO Beliefs?

Researchers use a great many different terms to refer to the cognitive— reality construction—aspects of SMOs, including beliefs, ideology, worldview, and "frame"—this last defined as "schemata of interpretation . . . that enable individuals . . . to locate, perceive, identify, and label . . . occurrences within their life space and the world at large" (Snow, Rochford, Worden, and Benford 1986, 464).

I here state the question as What are SMO beliefs? but other ways to phrase it include What matters are take to be true in and by the SMO? What are the reality-claims? How does the SMO frame issues?

A first level at which this question is answered is a summary of the SMO's proffered reality stated in its own terms. While such a summary-in-its-own-terms can be important, sociological researchers do not rest at this level. Instead, they go on to a second level, at which they ask, Of what more abstract category of beliefs or frames is the one at hand an instance? Or, What are the generic and generalizable features of the beliefs? What *kind* of reality-claims are these?

As the engine or energizing force of SMOs, I represent beliefs in Figure 3.1 as the long, oblong rectangle to the left *within* the larger rectangle symbolizing the entire SMO.

The main question, What are SMO Beliefs? leads to yet other questions, such as From where do SMOs draw their beliefs? (otherwise stated as, What are the causes of particular kinds of SMO beliefs?). After looking at the main question about beliefs in Chapter 5, I will also explore this and yet other questions about beliefs.

Moreover, the realities offered up by SMOs differ in their complexity and elaboration at various cognitive, emotional, and physical levels. As they become more complex and elaborate, these realities are usefully conceived as *cultures*. This additional aspect will also be explored in Chapter 5.

B. Question 2: How Are SMOs Organized?

The members and leaders of SMOs exhibit an overall pattern of relationship to one another. This pattern of relationship commonly involves

Figure 3.1.   Seven main questions about SMOs.

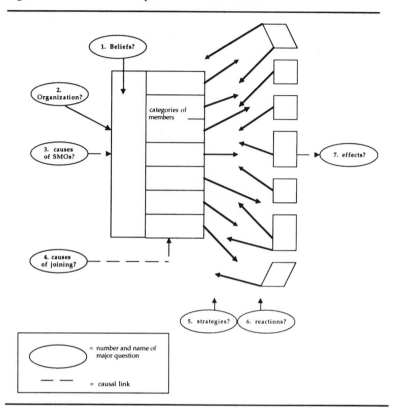

disparities in how power and other resources are distributed. What, conceived generically, are these patterns of organizational structure, particularly patterns of governance: Democratic? Autocratic? Bureaucratic? Anarchic?

In Figure 3.1, this focus on SMOs as holistic structures is symbolized by the central rectangle, which, as can be seen, also contains beliefs (just described) and members (described just below).

Once the researcher identifies a pattern of organization, there are additional questions to ask, such as Why this pattern and not some other? How and why do we see these patterns of organization change over time?

Although it might be elevated to a separate main question, I will fold the question, How are SMO financed? into the question of organization and also discuss it in Chapter 6.

C. Question 3: What Are Causes of SMOs?

The question of the "causes" of SMOs (and of social movements) is without doubt the dominant if not preeminent preoccupation of social movement scholars. Attention devoted to answering this question is so overwhelming in the literature that it might even be regarded as an obsession or fixation. Commonly, indeed, this causal question is the *only* question asked in a study and in the minds of some researchers it is virtually synonymous with the entire study of SMOs (and social movements). Therefore, I give much attention to it in Chapter 7, including the tricky matter of how best to state the question itself, other phrasings for which include, How do SMOs get organized? What factors facilitate or inhibit SMO crystallization? and When do SMOs form?

In Figure 3.1, this question is shown (1) external and to the (2) left of the box symbolizing the SMO. This representation expresses the conventional conception that causes of things precede them in time and are external to them. Time itself is commonly represented as proceeding linearly from left to right across a visual field, and I adopt that convention here.

D. Question 4: Why Do People Join SMOs?

Also often asked is the question of causes of SMO participation. The distinction here is between the causes of an organization (question 3) and the causes of joining an organization (question 4). It is one thing to bring an organization into existence, but quite another "simply" to join a preexisting organization. Another phrasing of this question is, How, if at all, are people who join SMOs different from people who do not?

In Figure 3.1, members are symbolized as composed of several categories within the right-hand box depicting an SMO. Like the depiction of causes of SMOs, causes of joining are depicted as external and prior in time and thus shown physically external and to the left in Figure 3.1. (In Chapter 8, however, we will see that causal analysis is messier than this initial, orienting depiction and can involve SMO-internal and ongoing variables).

E. Question 5: What Are SMO Strategies?

All SMOs engage in goal-seeking or attainment activities or strategies. What are these? How might the strategies of a particular SMO be best characterized abstractly and analytically? Related to this question, what factors enter into the selection of one rather than another line of action, or the change of a strategy?

Because they are viewed as products or productions—as what SMOs do—strategies are shown as external and to the right of the box symbolizing the SMO. The various arrows symbolizing diverse strategies are shown as going in various directions and over different distances in order to suggest that strategies exhibit such qualities.

F. Question 6: What Are Reactions to SMOs?

SMOs exist in complex environments of diverse social entities with which they passively interact, aggressively target in the pursuit of goals, or otherwise strategize about What do these other entities make of given SMOs? How do groupings such as ruling elites, the media of mass communication, and similar SMOs manage their relations to SMOs, and in turn how do SMOs react to those reactions?

In Figure 3.1, the series of small boxes to the right represent varied *reactors* and the arrows pointing back to SMO strategy arrows symbolize their *reactions*.

G. Question 7: What Are Effects of SMOs?

Reactions to SMOs are in one sense effects or consequences of SMOs, but such near-time, ongoing, and close-in effects need to be distinguished from longer-term and wider consequences of various sorts that stem from SMOs. These latter are the focus of the seventh main question and I address them in Chapter 11.

Continuing to follow the conventions of (1) representing time from left to right in a visual field and (2) causes and consequences as external to the topic of focus, in Figure 3.1 I place the question of the larger and longer-term effects to the far right, external to all that has gone before.

II. SEPARATING ASPECTS AND GENERIC QUESTIONS

The seven main questions just described and that will be answered in Chapters 5–11, respectively, are, in fact, a small subset of a much larger set of questions formed by the conjunction of SMO (1) **aspects** and (2) generic **questions** about those aspects. Indeed, I have telegraphed this fact in references I have made just above to "additional questions" and matters such as "culture" and "financing."

Let me explain this larger context by now separating out aspects and generic questions as two separate topics that have merely been conjoined in one special way in the above list of seven main questions.

A. Aspects

The term "aspect" refers to any substantive part, dimension, or unit of a reality "out there" that a researcher singles out and attends to separately.

1. Five Main Aspects.   Looking at the seven main questions as they are stated above, we see that while there are seven questions, there are only five separate aspects we are asking questions about. Specifically:

1.   Question 1: *beliefs.*
2.   Questions 2, 3, and 7: the SMO is taken as a holistic entity, an *organization*, and different questions asked about it.
3.   Question 4: *members.*
4.   Question 5: *strategies.*
5.   Question 6: *reactions.*

(Anticipating the discussion just slightly, these five are shown in the left-hand column of Figure 3.3 as "main aspects.")

2. Four Additional Aspects.   However, there are, in fact, a great many additional aspects that are integral to the study of SMOs, some of which I have already smuggled into the above brief elaborations of the seven main questions. Let me list those that I will in fact discuss as subsidiary foci in the chapters of Part II:

1.   *Culture*—the broader set of values, expressive symbolism, and cultural artifacts that impart distinctive identities to SMOs (Chapter 5).
2.   *Financing*—forms and sources of funding (Chapter 6).
3.   *Leaders*—activists and others who speak for and organize events in SMOs (Chapter 8).
4.   *Recruitment*—ways in which new people are brought into SMOs (Chapter 8).

(Again to anticipate, these are also listed in the left-hand column of Figure 3.3.)

3. Selected Reactors.   Several other aspects are divisions within the broad aspect of "reactions," the aspect on which the sixth main question focuses:

1.   *Ruling elites*—policymaking and associated strata targeted by an SMO in an effort to achieve or resist social change.

2. *Dissident elites*—elite strata who doubt the wisdom of the actions of the ruling elites and who support an SMO, including elite funders, people with significant discretionary wealth who fund SMOs.
3. *Media*—the means of mass communication, including television, newspapers magazines, books, videotapes.
4. *Similar SMOs*—SMOs whose beliefs or other aspects create the presumption of similarity and relationship with a given SMO.
5. *Counter-SMOs*—SMOs mobilized expressly to counter a particular SMO.
6. *Bystander publics*—the mass of the spectator public whose positive or negative opinions are often objects of contest between SMOs and other interaction partners.
7. *Beneficiary constituents*—people not participating in the SMO but in whose name it speaks and who it is claimed benefit from the SMO's actions.
8. *Conscience constituents*—people not thought directly to benefit from the SMO but who are sympathetic with it and who, taken collectively, form a field of allies for the SMO.

(Again, most of the reactors also appear in Figure 3.3.)

I must stress that among researchers there is no definitive formulation of "the" proper aspects for research. Although researchers agree that the SMO must be treated as a unit, beyond that views vary widely. The five I have selected for emphasis in the seven main questions can doubtless be disputed; and the two lists of additional aspects and reactors can be surely be extended, shortened, and otherwise revised.

Indeed, one of the key features and functions of the case study approach I am explaining is that it *facilitates* and even *encourages* researchers to be alert to the possibility and necessity of identifying *new aspects* that provide a better understanding of SMOs. (I will discuss how this in done in Sections III and IV of the next chapter.)

B. Generic Questions

Looking once more at the seven main questions, let us this time ask, What *kind* of question is being asked in each? Ignoring differences in aspects, what are the *generic* questions being posed? So scrutinized, we find that there are only three generic questions posed among the seven main questions Specifically:

Generic question	Seven main questions
What are the aspect's types (variations)?	1. What are SMO Beliefs? 2. How are SMOs organized? 5. What are SMO strategies? 6. What are reactions to SMOs?
What are the aspect's causes?	3. What are causes of SMOs? 4. Why do people join SMOs?
What are the aspect's consequences?	7. What are effects of SMOs?

In the same way that the seven questions contain only a few of possible aspects (five of them), they also only contain a few (three) of a larger number of generic questions that can also be pertinent to ask in the course of researching SMOs. Indeed (and as with aspects), some of these other generic questions are already smuggled into the above capsule description of questions.

Paralleling the larger set of aspects, what is the larger set of generic questions that researchers ask? As commonly reckoned, there are eight questions that we humans often ask about most anything we encounter, including SMOs and their aspects. In order to make these as clear as possible, I have devised the schematic representation of them shown in Figure 3.2, which attempts to depict their differences and relations by

Figure 3.2. Eight generic questions.

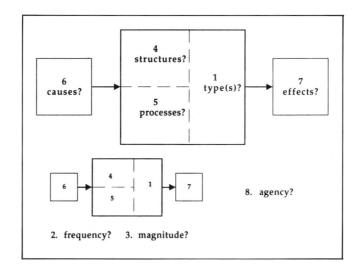

means of their arrangement in space. In Figure 3.2, the central box is intended to symbolize whatever the particular aspect, be it the SMO as a holistic entity, its beliefs, members, or strategies.

As a memory device, the eight questions can be conceived as **four pairs** of two questions each based on how the members of each pair are associated with one another. This pairing works best for the third and fourth pairs, but is also serviceable for the first two.

- Questions 1 and 8, *Type(s) and Agency*, ask, respectively, what the aspect *is* and how people strategize in and toward it.
- Questions 2 and 3, *Frequencies and Magnitudes*, ask how often we observe the aspect and its strength or size.
- Questions 4 and 5, *Structures and Processes*, ask how, in detail, the aspect is organized (structured) and how it operates over time (processes).
- Questions 6 and 7, *Causes and Effects*, ask what factors bring a aspect into existence (causes) and what effects it has (consequences).

The boxes representing the eight questions in Figure 3.2 are arranged in space so as to indicate their relation to the unit under study:

- Looking first at the box representing a topic, questions 1, 4, and 5 are shown inside it in order to suggest that the basic kind of thing an aspect "is" inheres in it (question 1), that its detailed structure is also to be found there (question 4), along with processes in terms of which it operates (question 5).
- A small duplicate of the larger set of boxes is given below the larger set in order to represent that the question of frequency involves counting cases (question 2) and the magnitude is a matter of estimating relative size or strength (question 3).
- Questions 6 and 7, causes and effects (consequences), are show to the left and right of the larger central box, symbolizing the aspect, respectively, in order physically to represent causes as coming *before* the aspect in time and in order physically to represent consequences as coming *after* the aspect in time. (The phrase "causes and consequences" is a common coupling in social science language—as is "structure and process," described just above.)
- Question 8 is show outside both the large and small set of boxes in order to represent it as an entirely different kind of question, that of active human agency.

I want now briefly to elaborate the meaning of each of these eight generic questions. Looking back at Figure 3.2 as we go along will, hopefully, be helpful in grasping each question and its relation to other questions.

1. What Are the Aspect's Types (Variations)?   A first question researchers may ask about any aspect is, What are its basic or defining features? In simplest terms, this is a definition of an abstract or generic idea. For example, what do we mean by the concept of SMO beliefs? We can begin with common sense and general definitions, but we need also to become more specific and precise. What *kinds* of reality-claims do we observe? Do the participants, for example, want a revolution? Do they want to change themselves rather than society? Or, do they want to change just a part of a society? In this manner, we can begin to think of *types* of realities or beliefs, as in "revolutionary," "personal transformation," or "reformist." We might think of these as "master types" within an aspect. But even these are still quite general. Often, researchers want to push the definitions to finer distinctions, specifying subtypes within such master types. For example, revolutionary beliefs can be Marxist-Leninist, fascist, religious, and the like.[1]

The same process of typing and subtyping applies to any aspect, as in types of leaders or financing. In sociological jargon, this is the procedure of "multiple typing."

In a different but logically equivalent language, many researchers think of a type or types as a *variable* of concern rather than in type terms. Continuing with the above examples, rather than asking about types of beliefs, the researcher may ask what is the *degree* to which an SMO's beliefs are, for example, totalistic or vilify opponents (two variables discussed in Section III of Chapter 5). The case or cases at hand are then placed on the continuum formed by that variable.

2. What Are the Aspect's Frequencies?   It is often useful and important for researchers to count how often something occurs, as with questions of how often SMOs of various forms are observed. Some SMOs and various aspects are, in fact, much more common—statistically—than others, and knowing such differences helps to answer yet other of the eight generic questions.

The question of frequency is often otherwise termed "descriptive statistics" and involves such common summarizing measures as a total number, means, modes, medians, percentages, and other measures of central tendency as well as measures of dispersion. There are some quite elaborate procedures for counting and analyzing many kinds of social phenomena, procedures codified under such rubrics as "descriptive and inferential statistics," "sampling," "survey research," and "systematic observation techniques." Short of such advanced complexity, however, there are a great many quite important while still simple counts that researchers make.

3. What Are the Aspect's Magnitudes? The question of frequency refers to occasions of something occurring, whereas the question of magnitude refers to the strength, intensity, or size of occurrences. As with the determination of frequencies, determining magnitudes is a quantitative question that in more sophisticated forms involves very complicated *measurement* procedures. And as with frequency, measurement operations can be complex, but many of its basic forms are quite simple and sometimes important to perform.

Questions of magnitude—or more abstractly *variation* and its *measurement*—are very often joined with questions of causes and consequences. Because of these close associations, I postpone further discussion of magnitudes until the discussions of cause and consequences.

4. What Are the Aspect's Structures? It is often useful to move beyond a simple depiction of an aspect (a "master type") or a set of types and toward a detailed rendition of the elements of which the type is composed when viewed as a static or "frozen" entity. Metaphorically, this is the difference between providing a very *rough sketch* of the overall features of, for example, a house, and working out the *detailed drawings* of how the house is actually assembled (i.e., the plans for its construction).

One particularly common and fruitful procedure for doing such structural analysis is called *ideal typing*. In this procedure, the researcher views the features of an SMO (or an aspect of one) from the angle of what would a pure case, a logical extreme, or a hypothetically ideal form look like? In formulating such an ideal type, the analyst then inspects the empirical case or cases at hand in terms of how close to or far from the ideal type it seems to be. An example of such ideal type analysis is provided in Chapter 6, where Rothschild and Whitt's ideal type contrast between bureaucratic and democratic-collectivist organization is displayed graphically (in Figure 6.1).

5. What Are the Aspect's Processes? The word *process* is commonly defined in dictionaries as "the action of . . . going along through each of a succession of acts, events or developmental states." As regards SMOs, researchers are often interested in depicting how aspects of them exhibit changes over time that divide into periods, phases, or stages.

Processes themselves may be thought of being of one or another of three general forms or types:

1. Some processes are *cycles*, meaning that one can observe a set of stages recurring again and again. After the last phase, the process "resets," so to speak, and begins again. Such cycles signal a degree of stability in functioning.
2. Other processes do not exhibit the stability of cycles. Instead, they display a pattern of a continuously spreading and accelerating increase or decrease. These are termed *spirals*. Spirals of increase are said to be in *escalation*; those of decrease in *de-escalation*.
3. Processes that are not cycles or spirals are simply *sequences*, "a time-ordered series of steps or phases" (Lofland and Lofland 1984, 108).

In some analyses the line between process and causal questions and answers is blurred, in that one can ask a causal question in a process manner, as in:

> What are the stages in terms of which an SMO changes?
> What are the stages of experience through which a person goes in becoming involved in an SMO?

While researchers are concerned to depict a process, the answers they develop can also move over to the question of the causes, to which we now come.

6. What Are the Aspect's Causes?   The question that preoccupies humans is, of course, that of "causes." It is a question that is phrased in many ways, as in:

> On what factors does some variation depend?
> What facilitates or inhibits its occurrence?
> Under what conditions is it present and under what conditions is it absent?
> What circumstances make it more likely to occur or less likely to occur? (Adapted from Lofland and Lofland 1984, 100.)

Looking at the schematic of the eight generic questions in Figure 3.2, we see that in asking the causal question researchers are no longer looking at the aspect per se—unlike the type, structure, process, magnitude, and frequency questions, which require direct inspection of it. Instead, they direct their attention to matters that are *prior in time* to the object they want to explain in the sense of specifying its causes.

Temporality priority is, indeed, a *first* and prime requirement of making a valid causal inference that researchers face. Nothing can be a cause of something—an independent variable—unless it can be shown to occur before the matter researchers want to explain—the dependent variable.

The *second* requirement for valid causal inference is that the two variables—the unit (or variable) to be explained and its possible cause—must vary together, that is, they must be *correlated*.

But, in the famous slogan, correlation does not prove causation. There is therefore a *third* requirement of valid causal inference with which researchers must wrestle. The possible influence of third variables must be ruled out, for the first two can be changing together not because of a causal relation between them, but because of a causal relation to a third variable. This is called the requirement of ruling out *spurious correlation*.

In sociological studies (as well as in all human inquiry) it is exceedingly difficult to meet all three of these requirements of valid causal inference. Caution and humility about casual conjectures are therefore required in research.

7. What Are the Aspect's Effects?   The question of consequences once again directs the researcher's attention away from the aspect per se. This time, though, instead of looking back in time, the researcher looks forward—as depicted schematically in Figure 3.2. In the causal question (immediately above), the unit was the dependent variable, for which the researcher was seeking independent variables that cause it. Now, in contrast, the unit becomes the independent variable for which the researcher seeks to specify a range of variables that are dependent on it.

It is important to appreciate that the same three requirements of valid causal inference applying to causal assertions also apply to consequences/effects assertions: (1) time order, (2) correlation, (3) control for third variables or spuriousness. And, therefore, the same requirements of caution and tentativeness also apply.

As with the question of causes, the question of consequences can be worded in many ways—ways that stimulate the researcher to think more broadly about the question:

What are the *consequences* of the aspect we are inspecting?
What *functions* are served by the aspect that would not be served if it did not have this form?
What *role* does this aspect play in the maintenance or change of this movement or some aspect of it?
What are its *products*? (Adapted from Lofland and Lofland 1984, 113–14.)

As mentioned above, the most conspicuous question of consequences researchers tend to ask about SMOs (and social movements as well) is, How effective are their strategies in achieving their goals? But there is much more than this to look at, as we shall see in Chapter 11.

8. What Is Human Agency?   We need, finally, to add a different kind of generic question to the seven just reviewed. Instead of focusing on the types, causes, and consequences (and the like) of an aspect, researchers also want to know how people go about doing things—the *strategies* they employ in dealing with the situations they confront. Instead of only viewing people and their associations as the *products* of social forces, researchers view them, in addition, as active *constructors* of their action in efforts creatively to address situations as they define them. This difference has otherwise been termed a distinction between *structure* ("products") and *agency* (constructors) (Blumer 1969b).

In posing this question, researchers bracket all the previous seven questions as themselves forming a single set of matters toward which people construct their actions. This switch is shown graphically in Figure 3.2 as the large rectangle that contains all the seven previous questions outside of which people adopt a strategic stance (8. agency? in Figure 3.2).

III. COMBINING ASPECTS AND GENERIC
QUESTIONS: A RESOURCE MATRIX

I began this chapter with a list of the seven main questions that researchers have frequently asked (and answered) about SMOs. We can now see specifically what it means for me to report that this list of seven is but a small and selected subset within a much, much *larger set of both aspects and generic questions*. In order to show this contrast with the greatest clarity, in Figure 3.3 I have cross-classified the list of aspects given in Section II.A and the list of eight generic questions just explained in Section II.B.

As can be seen in Figure 3.3, the entire matrix specifies more than a hundred distinct questions—the exact number depending on how you devise a list of aspects. In contrast to this, the heavier outlined cells of Figure 3.3·indicate only the seven main questions explained in the first section of this chapter.

I single out seven main questions, but I do not want to give the impression that these are the only questions that researchers have found of much interest. This is quite definitely false. Instead, there are rich, albeit smaller bodies of materials dealing with a great many of these other aspects and questions, and I will review some of these materials as ancillary topics in the chapters of Part II.

SMO researchers might find it useful to regard the matrix shown in Figure 3.3 as a rapid-access resource guide in thinking about any SMO they are studying. In bringing a wide array of possibilities together in this stark and summary form, careful reflection on specific aspect and question conjunctions might be of assistance in focusing an ongoing case study.

Figure 3.3. Aspect-question matrix.

Aspects ⬇	Questions ➡							
	1. Type(s)?	2. Frequen-cies?	3. Magni-tudes?	4. Structures?	5. Processes?	6. Causes?	7. Effects?	8. Agency?
I. Main Aspects ⬇								
1. Beliefs	1 (Chapter 5)	2	3	4	5	6	7	8
2. Organization	9 (Chapter 6)	10	11	12	13	14 (Chapter 7)	15 (Chapter 11)	16
3. Members	17	18	19	20	21	22 (Chapter 8)	23	24
4. Strategies	25 (Chapter 9)	26	27	28	29	30	31	32
5. Reactions	33 (Chapter 10)	34	35	36	37	38	39	40
II. Additional Aspects ⬇								
1. Culture	41	42	43	44	45	46	47	48
2. Financing	49	50	51	52	53	54	55	56
3. Leaders	57	58	59	60	61	62	63	64
4. Recruitment	65	66	67	68	69	70	71	72
III. Selected Reactors ⬇								
1. Ruling Elites	73	74	75	76	77	78	79	80
2. Dissident Elites	81	82	83	84	85	86	87	88
3. Media	89	90	91	92	93	94	95	96
4. Similar SMOs	97	98	99	100	101	102	103	104
5. Counter SMOs	105	106	107	108	109	110	111	112

Note: The seven cells with thicker borders and containing chapter numbers indicate the seven main questions treated in the respective seven chapters of Part II.

* * *

In the logic of the matter, *questions* cry out for *answers*, the latter being the fourth task or phase in the case study process. Let us turn to that phase.

NOTE

1. Many thanks to Hank Johnston for his suggested phrasings, which I have adopted in this paragraph.

4

Step Four:
Answering Questions

Researchers gather the fruits of their plantings and cultivations in the previous three steps in the fourth step of *answering* questions. This step or task consists of six lines of activity as follows.

I. Moving forth from types of generic questions, researchers develop answers that can also be called *generic propositions*.

II. Beyond the more technical matters of formulating sociological propositions, there is the broader matter of the *mind-set* that researchers bring to their studies of SMOs. I explore these mind-set or general approach matters in Section II, focusing in particular on developing "sociological consciousness."

III. Attuned to answering questions with an appropriately broad mind-set, in the case study approach researchers *immerse* themselves in their data and emergently *induct* sociological propositions from the interactions of their knowledge of SMO questions and answers, their mind-set, their sensibilities, and their data.

IV. This process of immersion-induction utilizes and is facilitated by a number of routine *physical procedures*, including such mundane actions as filing (or "coding," to use the fancier term). I describe these in Section IV and I stress the fact that such procedures in case studies of SMOs are very much like those used in any and all forms of scholarly endeavor.

V. Even with the help of routine physical procedures, the process of immersion-induction can be fearsome, frustrating, and *anxiety producing* for researchers. These are perfectly normal reactions, and researchers undertake a number of actions to deal with them, which I describe in Section V.

VI. A key proximate both goal and result of the researcher's endeavor is a *written report*. In order for a written report to be readable and useful, researchers follow a number of conventions in assembling it. I explain these conventions, formulated as a checklist of desirable features, in Section VI.

I. GENERIC PROPOSITIONS AS ANSWERS TO QUESTIONS

The most basic goal of the social-scientific study of SMOs is to formulate accurate generalizations about them in answer to questions the researcher has asked. This aim, it should be understood, suffuses the social-scientific study of human social organization in general. It has therefore been linguistically rendered in a wide variety of ways in the course of analysts struggling to achieve it.

The phrasing I employ in this guide is the search for *generic propositions*, but this is only one among many, many possibilities and ongoing usages. Let me list some of these *other* phrasings that researchers use to express the same point and that communicate the spirit of this quest for generalizations (quoted, adapted, and extended from Lofland and Lofland 1995, 156):

forming a *hypothesis*   identifying a *story line*
developing a *thesis*   telling a *story*
elaborating a *concept,*   constructing general *principles*

formulating an *assertion*   providing a *general interpretation*

putting forth an *idea*   *framing* the data
constructing a theory   making a *point*
propounding a unifying   reporting an *analysis*
    theme
addressing a *problem*   offering a *generalization*

A. Eight Basic Types of Propositional Answers

Following from the eight questions enumerated in Chapter 3, there are eight basic forms of propositions that are answers to the eight questions.

1. *The Type Proposition:* A type of (or variation in) an aspect of something simply exists. Example: There are reformist versus revolutionary (types/variations in) SMO beliefs (an aspect of an SMO).
2. *The Frequency Proposition:* Some types of an aspect of something occur more (or less) frequently than others. Example: Reformist beliefs are more common than revolutionary beliefs.
3. *The Magnitude Proposition:* Some types of an aspect of something are larger, more intense, or stronger than others. Example: Reformist beliefs are held less intensely than revolutionary beliefs.
4. *The Structure Proposition:* A type of an aspect of something exhibits certain detailed features of composition, construction, configuration, or makeup. Example: Revolutionary beliefs of a certain kind have several further and correlative features beyond the core (type) feature of being revolutionary.
5. *The Process Proposition:* A type of an aspect of something operates in terms of certain temporal phases, cycles, or sequences. Example: Beliefs move through the temporal phases of indifference, mainstream, reform, and revolution.
6. *The Cause Proposition:* A type of aspect of something comes about because of certain causal factors. Example: Revolutionary beliefs are caused by repressive societies.
7. *The Effect Proposition:* A type of an aspect of something has certain consequences. Example: Revolutionary beliefs lead to violent actions.
8. *The Agency Proposition:* In a particular situation, people strategize in certain ways. Example: Movement strategies continually change in response to ways in which authorities strategize to neutralize previous movement strategies.

B. Case versus Generic Propositional Answers

Propositional answers differ in whether they are stated as:

1. applying only to a *case* or cases at hand in the data the researcher is studying, or as
2. applying to a more *general class* of which the case or cases under study are simply instances.

The first is a *case proposition* and the second is a *generic proposition*.

Here are examples of this distinction in answering each of the eight generic questions.

1. Type Propositions.   Answers to the question of types are relatively simple distinctions among kinds of units, summary descriptions of or labels for units, or definitions. Here is a case and generalized type proposition example in which the SMO taken as a whole is the "aspect":

- *Case:*   In the 1980s the SMO Sane/Freeze was organized in terms of a national office and several dozen state affiliates over which the national office had little control.
- ▶ *Generic:*   SMOs such as Sane/Freeze exhibit a *loosely federated* structure, a central feature of which is little or no national control of local units but various degrees of cooperation and coordination, nonetheless.

(In order to highlight generic propositions, I label the more succinct of them with the graphic device of the bold-face arrow, i.e., ▶. Some generic propositions are, however, too complicated to formulate as pithy declarative sentences. Those are not so labeled, as with, for example, the enormously complex propositional answers to the questions, What are causes of SMOs? and Why do people join SMOs?)

2. Frequency Propositions.   Even with case studies, some matters are so clearly more or less frequent than others that frequency estimations are easily made. Thus, frequency propositions of this character may be offered:

- *Case:*   In the American peace movement of the 1980s, violence as a strategy was extremely rare and almost undetectable (Lofland 1993a).
- ▶ *Generic:*   Generically, highly restrained and civil action is an instance of *polite protest* (Lofland 1993a).

Here is a second example:

- *Case:*   Chapters of Mothers Against Drunk Driving (MADD) formed at a rapid rate over the early 1980s (McCarthy and Wolfson 1992).
- ▶ *Generic:*   MADD exhibited a pattern of *exponential growth.*

3. Magnitude Propositions.   Many aspects of SMOs are matters of magnitude or degree, that is, are variables in terms of which an SMO can have more or less (e.g., financing) or that can be can be stronger or weaker (e.g., recruitment programs). Focusing on culture, for example, some SMOs seem to have much more of it than others, leading to these propositions:

- *Case:* The Unification Church (the so-called "Moonies") has elaborated one of the most complex cultures of contemporary SMOs (Lofland 1985, Ch. 9; see also Section V of Chapter 5 in this guide).
- ◗ *Generic:* The generic dimensions in terms of which cultures vary in degree are sharing, distinctiveness, scope, elaboration, quantity, and expressiveness. (Lofland 1995b; see also Chapter 5 in this guide)

4. Structure Propositions. As indicated in Sections II.B.1 and II.B.4 of Chapter 3, structural questions and answers are more elaborate and detailed depictions of type questions and answers. The more systematic of these are called "ideal types," an example of which is given in Figure 6.1, Rothschild and Whitt's (1986) contrast between "bureaucratic" and "collectivist-democratic" forms of organization. Despite the complexity of the structural contrast they draw, the central proposition involved is relatively straightforward:

- *Case:* Six "countercultural" organizations studied in a southern California city rejected ordinary ideas of hierarchically organizing their associations.
- ◗ *Generic:* Bureaucratic and collectivist-democratic forms are two contrasting patterns of formal organization.

5. Process Propositions. Analyses of processes commonly attempt to depict changes through which the SMO as a whole or some other aspect has moved. In his case study of an SMO called the Townsend movement (after the name of its leader), Messinger formulated the following case proposition:

- *Case:* After its major goal of providing financial security for the elderly was achieved in the Social Security Act, thereby preempting its program, the Townsend movement underwent a process of shifting its foci to sheer sociability and individualistic health care palliatives (Messinger 1955).

Raised to the next level of abstraction and generalization, Messinger's case-specific generalization can be stated:

- ◗ *Generic:* An SMO whose structural change goals are achieved or preempted will tend to shift to member direct benefit strategies.

6. Cause Propositions. Mindful of the requirements and hazards of valid causal inference reported in Chapter 3 regarding causal questions (Section II.B.6.) causal propositions are most often tentative hypotheses that the case study researcher puts forth with due qualification and recognition of the limitations of causal arguments. But, so qualified and tentative, case study researchers also do not hesitate to engage in causal thinking—the formulation of causal propositions.

In SMO case studies, one potent stimulus to causal thinking is comparison of *major changes or contrasts* in the SMO's history (combined with searching for concomitant variations that may explain the contrast). Using the language of "variables," a change over an SMO's history is a variation in a "dependent variable" that the researcher can relate to other changing variables, which are "independent variables."

For example, in comparing markedly different levels of success over several decades in efforts to form successful unions among farm workers, Jenkins related that variation in the dependent variable to the independent variable of *also* changing levels of support from several elite strata in the larger society. Finding a correlation, his proposition is:

- *Case:* A major cause of successful union organizing among California migrant agricultural farm workers in the 1970s was new and broad support among elite sectors of the society (Jenkins 1983).

Raised one level of abstraction and generalization, the proposition is:

- *Generic:* As the degree of support by elite sectors for a disadvantaged group increases, the chances of successful organizing among that group increase.

While many causal answers/propositions are usefully as simple as one dependent variable related to one independent variable, as given immediately above, *multiple* independent variables are more commonly formulated as related to a single dependent variable. For example, a very large number of independent variables are involved in the formation of new SMOs, as we shall see in Chapter 7.

7. Effects Propositions. Recasting the causal question, an SMO as a whole, or other aspect, is focused on in terms of what follows from it. The dependent variable now becomes the independent variable. Here is an example regarding the consequences of participation in an SMO drawn from Doug McAdam's (1988a) survey of people who participated in the civil rights movement Freedom Summer voter registration project of 1964:

- *Case:* Later in their adult lives, participants in the Freedom Summer project differ from people who were accepted into the project but did not follow through and actually participate in several marital, occupational, and political participation ways.

◆ *Generic:*   People who engage in dramatic and high-risk movement activism in early adulthood tend to engage in more activism throughout their lives (and to have several distinctive demographic features, such as having fewer children) than do others who are otherwise like them, but who have not had that early experience (McAdam 1988a).

8. Agency Propositions.   Looking over the shoulders, so to speak, of particular SMO actors, what kinds of strategies do we see them devising in order to deal with situations as they define them?

- *Case:*   The Rev. Sun Myung Moon's leadership of his Unification Church is characterized by a decades-long succession of crisis campaigns in which members are deployed and dispersed in an emergency fashion on new and difficult projects that must be pursued with great haste.
- ◆ *Generic:*   SMOs with grandiose, world-saving goals that are held up by leaders as realizable in the imminent future have special problems sustaining the hope and moral of members. Leaders of such SMOs are therefore under pressure to adopt a strategy of frequent and repeated crisis precipitation and broad new campaigns that serve to energize members in new, hopeful pursuits (Lofland [1966] 1977).

C. The Quest and the Purpose

For the social science researcher, *case* propositions are an indispensable first step in analyzing SMOs, but the higher quest is for *generic* propositions. One key purpose of this quest is, of course, to learn from experience by abstracting from it. To formulate a generic or generalized proposition or concept out of a case or cases is to strengthen our ability to recognize such patterns when we encounter them in yet other instances. For example, to study a very unusual leader of an SMO without a concept of, say, "charisma," is to thwart our capacity to see that kind of leadership when we come upon it again. To formulate generic (or generalized) concepts of leadership is, in contrast, to strengthen our ability to "see" leadership in new cases by being able to compare and contrast it with our existing concepts.

The aim is to use facts to rise above facts, so to speak, and to take better control of facts with propositions, concepts, and all those other ways to speak of answers to questions that I list above. Our quest is to move from seeing merely the trees that are the facts, to seeing the forest that is composed of those facts-trees. The alternative—in different imagery—is to be adrift and awash in oceans of facts, drowning in information that we cannot use because we have not organized it into meaningful patterns (cf. Prus 1994).

D. Three Contrasts with Generic Propositions

Formulating generic propositions is a distinctive kind of intellectual endeavor that can be contrasted with other kinds of endeavors in a variety of ways. That is, the idea of generic propositions reflects other distinctions drawn among types of intellectual work. Let me sharpen the above depiction of generic propositions by reporting three of these other ways in which this kind of effort can be conceived as differing from other forms of writing or reporting. These are the contrasts between

(1) subject and idea writing,
(2) historically particular writing and sociological writing, and
(3) review/summary and analysis/report writing.

In each of these three, it is the second label that most resembles "generic propositions" (i.e., idea writing, sociological writing, and analysis/ report writing.)[1]

1. Subject versus Idea Writing.   In the broader domain of writing per se, a distinction is drawn between *subject* writing, which describes a topic or area, and *idea* writing, which propounds a thesis or makes an assertion.

> Some people use the word *idea* to mean something like "topic" or "subject," phrases that indicate an *area* of potential interest, such as "economics" or "a cure for cancer." . . . These phrases might be said to be "broad" or "narrow" subjects, but they are not yet ideas because they do not say anything about economics, or a cancer cure. . . . The noun *economics* is not an idea. . . . "Economics is bull" *is* an idea. . . . The difference between noun phrases that are not ideas and statements that are ideas lies in the predication: Ideas are sentences; they complete a thought by connecting a verb to the noun phrase. Saying something about a subject requires making some kind of connection between it and something else. (Gage 1987, 48–49)

In parallel, generic propositions about SMOs represent idea writing rather than subject writing. Propositions are assertions about SMOs. Notice that each of the abstract formulations of propositions stated in Section I.A, Eight Basic Forms of Propositional Answers, contains a *verb* that serves to transform the subject into an idea, that is, a topic into an answer/proposition. Specifically, these verbs are, in order, *exists, occur, are, exhibits, operates, comes, has, strategize.* So cast, a report on an SMO is more than a compilation of "facts" the researcher has gathered on the SMO. Rather, it is a set of assertions about the SMO and/or that the SMO exemplifies.

2. Historically Particular versus Sociological Writing. A second way to speak of the difference between "case" and "generic" propositions is as the difference between historically particular and sociological writing. By "historically particular" I mean focusing primarily on the ideas we find used by participants to tell their own story and their descriptive reporting of their own and other people's activities. In order to show this contrast clearly, I have assembled examples of such writing in the middle column of Figure 4.1. While these examples are diverse, their common focus is that of a specific location in historical time.

The social-scientific—sociological—quest is, in contrast, for abstract propositions and concepts of which the historical particulars are instances, a quest that is also termed, as previously said, the search for generic propositions or concepts. Examples of these are shown in the right-hand column of Figure 4.1 and they are juxtaposed to the historically particular (or "topical") versions of the same example given in the middle column.

Max Heirich's two published analyses of movement activity on the campus of the University of California in 1964–1965 (shown in the bottom row of Figure 4.1) provide an especially apt illustration of this contrast. Knowing that different audiences are attuned to different kinds of accounts, Heirich's publisher arranged for him to put out two books on exactly the same events! One is titled *The Beginning: Berkeley, 1964* (1970). Its 317 pages are divided into sixteen chapters that only report the sheer history of the events involved. The second—the sociological—book contains the same historical account, but is also much longer (502 pages divided into twenty-one chapters) and provides an extremely detailed sociological analysis of the historical events. Appropriately, it bears a title signaling the presence of that analysis, which is: *The Spiral of Conflict: Demonstrations at Berkeley, 1964–1965* (1971).

3. Review/Summary versus Analysis/Report Writing. Some students from garden variety educational backgrounds tend to approach social science writing as if it were the same as the task of composing an ordinary term paper. The two are, however, in fact very different. Ordinary term papers and social science analyses are alike in that both are constructed of sentences, paragraphs, and sections set successively on sheets of paper, but the similarity of the two pretty much ends right there.

Figure 4.1.   Historically particular versus sociological writing.

| | **Two Types of Answers ➡** | |
Questions ⬇	**Historically Particular**	**Sociological**
What are the SMO's beliefs?	description of a specific philosophy, point of view, or ideology, e.g., Mormonism, Communism	type of point of view, e.g., totalism, sectarianism, millenarianism
How is the SMO organized?	description of a specific named organization	type or form of organization, e.g., vanguard party, democratic-collectivist
What is the SMO's leadership?	descriptions of particular persons	types of leaders, e.g., charismatic
What are the SMO's strategies?	descriptions of events and activities	type of strategy, e.g., direct benefit, public education, strike, boycott
Book-length Example: Max Heirich's study of movement activity at UC, Berkeley in 1964-1965, published as two books, one of each type.	*The Beginning: Berkeley, 1964* (1970), sixteen chapters running 317 pages.	*The Spiral of Conflict: Demonstrations at Berkeley, 1964* (1971), twenty-one chapters running 502 pages.

Ordinary term papers—including many student efforts to write them on SMOs—are smorgasbords or cook's tours of miscellaneous facts about their topic. Indeed, ordinary term papers seem often to be modeled on encyclopedia or other reference book articles, sources from which much of the information in these papers has often been taken. Applying the two sets of distinctions made immediately above, the ordinary term paper tends to be subject rather than idea framed and historically particular rather than sociologically framed.

Let me try to capture the difference between an ordinary term paper and a social science analysis in these two, two-word couplets:

> 1. *review/summary*
> versus
> 2. *analysis/report*

The first couplet centers on surveying information available on a topic and presenting a summary of it. Above I use the terms "subject writing" and "historically particular writing" to refer to this kind of work.

The second couplet denotes a central focus on one or more concepts—analysis—on which one is making a report. In the language used above, the analysis/report is a propositional answer to a question about an aspect of an SMO.

The first is what a student is commonly doing in an ordinary term paper, the ordinary term paper being itself an application of the model of the encyclopedia or reference book article or review. The second is what a researcher is doing in SMO inquiry—and in social science research more generally. Thus, in discussing the organization of social science papers, Lee Cuba speaks of it as the task of constructing "general principles from a set of observations" in which one "always sees the world in terms of the question: What is this an example of?" (1988, 35). Such papers therefore begin with and treat some "broader, unifying theme," "general interpretation," or "larger question" (p. 36).

There is a procedural similarity between the ordinary term paper and *some* SMO analysis that seems to induce the ordinary term paper mind-set. Data on some SMOs can be collected in libraries, the very same place one assembles information for an ordinary term paper. Sometimes, it is important even to read a great many encyclopedia and encyclopedia-type articles on the SMO under study. The very physical similarity—or even identity—of the acts of data collection can trigger the ordinary term paper mind-set.

Fortunately, this is a problem and miscue that can be overcome. First, knowing that such an inappropriate mind-set can beset researchers, they can learn to resist it by being aware of the need to resist it. Second, researchers can make every effort to use a *variety* of sources of information not found in the reference works of libraries.

The moral is this: Researchers put aside notions of ordinary term papers when they undertake SMO analysis, an act of putting aside that needs to be maintained up through the activity of writing the paper.[2]

E. How Many Propositions in a Given Study?

Exactly how many propositions do researchers put forth and develop in their reports? The equivocating but accurate initial answer is that they differ. But, having said that, I think it is also accurate to say that paper-length reports by professional researchers commonly dwell on only one or a few answers/propositions, with others simply mentioned or treated briefly. In book-length reports, each chapter likewise tends to focus only on one proposition. These are, though, the works of professional researchers who have gone to the time and trouble to glean enough data on a few propositions to make a grounded story with regard to some delimited set of questions. Such work often requires at least many months and sometimes years.

But what about research contexts in which time and data are more limited and work is performed under a deadline? I have in mind college courses in which the novice researcher may study an SMO over some ten to fifteen weeks and be required to make a report on that effort. In that context, it can be extremely difficult to single out one or a few propositions and successfully assemble and analyze pertinent data by the deadline. Such fine-grained concentration and development can sometimes be achieved and this is an extraordinarily laudable achievement, but often limitations of access to data render in-depth focus enormously difficult or impossible.

For such contexts of research, it may be better to think in terms of a scaled-down and broadened out form of analysis and reporting, a form that can be termed the *propositional profile report*. Rather than striving to pare down the propositional foci to only one or a few aspects or items that focus the data, the researcher thinks in terms of *compiling a list* of answers/propositions suggested by diverse portions of the data. The result is a variety of "minianalyses" that can themselves be sorted and ordered into a propositional profile of the SMO. Stated in the procedural terms I use below in discussing memoing (Section IV.B), the second-level *sorting memos* on a variety of propositions are loosely organized with appropriate *integrating memos*.

The exact number of such minianalyses that are appropriate is, of course, a question and the answer will vary in terms of course length, standards of effort and achievement prevailing at given institutions, the place of the report in the course or seminar, and the like. For myself and for contexts where the report is a major focus, on the order of a dozen propositions in the profile seems appropriate.

F. Overview of Answers to Questions about Main Aspects of SMOs

Part II of this volume is a guide to—a tour of—a wide array of generic, propositional answers to questions that researchers have posed about SMOs. This tour is organized in terms of the generic *questions* and *aspects* I have described in the preceding chapter and above in this chapter.

In drawing together the main propositions of hundreds of studies conducted over several decades, the tour I give in Chapters 5–11 threatens to become too complicated. Mindful of this problem, I have tried to use a number of simplifying and clarifying devices. The diagram of seven main questions about SMOs given in Figure 3.1 and my presentation of material in outline format are two among other simplifying devices.

Having explained the ideas of "questions" and "aspects" as combined with *answers* I want now to provide yet another simplifying device. This is an overview of the actual *answers* to questions that researchers have offered about five main aspects of SMOs. Overviews (i.e., summaries) of the most elaborate of these answers appear in the cells of the aspects-questions matrix in Figure 4.2.

Two features of Figure 4.2 bear explanation and comment. First, Figure 4.2 contains answers to questions about only the five aspects I am calling *"main* aspects," namely, beliefs, organization, members, strategies, and reactions. As indicated in Chapter 3 and as displayed in Figure 3.3, in Part II I in fact treat four *"additional* aspects," which are culture, financing, leaders, and recruitment. Specifically, culture is treated as ancillary to beliefs in Chapter 5, financing as ancillary to organization in Chapter 6, and leaders and recruitment as ancillary to members in Chapter 8. Moreover, the category of "reactions" contains several categories of "reactors" that are not presented in Figure 4.2. For the sake of clarity, I have left all these "additional aspects" and "selected reactors" out of Figure 4.2. Nonetheless, these other aspects follow the same logic of analysis and equivalent matrices of answers regarding them can be constructed by anyone interested in doing so.

Second, it can be seen that there are quite a few empty answer-cells in Figure 4.2. This is because I do not report answers to those questions about given aspects—or that my report is too brief to merit rostering in Figure 4.2. My lack of (or scanty) reporting is due to one or more of these factors: (1) lack of research on that aspect-question; (2) my failure to discover research that exists; (3) my decision not to treat the matter at this time.

Figure 4.2, then, is an additional source to consult while reading or otherwise reviewing the several chapters making up this volume's Part II. It follows on to the more specific level of *answers* from the broader orientation provided to questions and aspects by Figures 3.1 and 3.3.

II. MIND-SET IN ANSWERING QUESTIONS

I use the term "mind-set" to call attention to researchers' overall approaches to analysis—to the attitudes or postures they bring to making sense of the raw materials with which they are working. I divide mind-set concerns into the two matters of (1) the posture researchers strike toward the claims they encounter and (2) self-management in the process of analysis (as well as in data collection).

Figure 4.2. Overview of answers to questions about main aspects of SMOs.

Main Aspects ➡		
Generic Questions ⬇	**1. Beliefs** (Chapter 5)	**2. Organization** (Chapters 6, 7, 11)

1. Types/ Variations?	*Ch. 5, III, Differences:*
	A. Two Parameter Variations: Amount & Locus of Change
	B. Existential Variations
	  1. Adversary Versus Exemplary
	  2. Degree Totalistic
	  3. Type of Cognitive Mode
	  4. Type of Time Construction
	  5. Degree Nihilistic
	  6. Combinations of Existential Variations
	C. Mundane Variations
	  1. Substantive and Institutional Content
	  2. Aggregate versus Adversary Frames
	  3. Vilification
		Ch. 6, II, Differences:
		A. Individual-Organizational Members
		B. Fragility and Temporariness of Organization
		C. Formalization and Centralization
		D. Member Absorption
		E. Volunteer Spare-time Absorption
		F. Form Diversity and Complexity
		G. Scale
		H. Democratic-Oligarchic

2. Frequencies?		*Ch. 6, V. A: Frequencies*
3. Magnitudes?		*Ch. 6, V. B. Magnitudes*
4. Structures?		*Ch. 6, III: Structures:* A. Collectivist-Democratic Structure B. Professional Social Movement Organizations (PSMOs) C. Marketed Social Movement Organizations *Ch. 6, IV: Other Variations*
5. Processes?		*Ch. 6, V. E: Processes*

6. Causes?	*Ch. 5, IV, A.: Causes of SMO Beliefs*
	Ch 5, IV.B: Causes of Selected Variations in SMO Beliefs
		Ch. 7. IV, V: Causes of SMOs:
		  1. Social Inequality and Change
		  2. Political Opportunity
		  3. State Penetration of Citizen Life
		  4. Prosperity
		  5. Geographical Concentration
		  6. Prior Organization and Collective Identity
		  7. Cross-cutting Solidarities
		  8. Perceptions and Cultures of Injustice
		  9. Regime Crises and Contested Political Arenas
		 10. Recent Decline of Amount of Repression
		 11. Focal Points/Focusing Crises
		 12. Citizen Surge Synergy
		 13. Leadership Availability
		 14. Communication Networks and Similar Resources
		 15. Network Integration among Potential Formers
		 16. Situational Availability among Potential Formers
		 17. Frame Alignment and Alignment Skill
		 18. Belief in the Necessity and Effectiveness
		
		Ch. 7.VII: Sustaining Causes

7. Effects?	*Ch. 5, IV: Effects of Selected Variations in SMO beliefs*	*Ch. 11: II: Effects of SMOs per se:* A. Changes in Governments, Laws, Policies, Policy Systems. B. Winning Acceptance C. New or Enlarged Movement Establishment D. New Items of Mainstream Culture E. Shifts in Norms, Cultural Images, and Symbols F. Change in the Interaction Order G. The Shape of Strata Structures H. Cultural Clarification and Reaffirmation I. Entertainment and Spectacle J. Violence and Tyranny K. Scholarly Trade L. Models for Later SMOs *Ch. 6, V.D: Effects of Selected Variations:* 1. Cadre Versus Mass-membership 2. Formalization and Centralization
8. Agency?		

Note: Cells with thicker borders are the respective seven main questions and answers of Chapters 5 through 11.

Figure 4.2. Continued

3. Members (Chapter 8)	4. Strategies (Chapter 9)	5. Reactions (Chapter 10)
Ch. 8. I. Four Complications in the Study of Joining A. What Is Joined? B. What Is Joining? C. What Are Experiences of Joining? D. What is Membership? 　1. The Body of Members 　　a. Formal Schemes of Roles 　　b. Analyst Articulated Patterns 　　c. ... Hierarchy and Membership ... 　2. The Leaders 　　a. Organizers 　　b. Speakers 　　c. Writers 　　d. Generalists and Specialists	*Ch. 9. II. Differences:* A. Larger-Scope or Scale Substantive Differences 　1. Main Objectives 　2. Overt Versus Covert 　3. Frontal Assault versus Attrition 　4. Degree of Contentiousness 　5. Tactical Mechanisms 　6. Target, Force ... Combinations 　7. Strategic Organizational Postures B. Smaller-Scope or Scale Substantive Differences 　1. Framing Issues 　2. Local Amelioration 　3. Nonviolent Action 　4. Staid, Conventional Actions C. Dramaturgic Differences 　1. Dramaturgic Dimensions 　2. Dramaturgic Ingratiation 　3. Personal Bearing 　4. Speech Practices	*Ch. 10.I. The Concept of Reactions* *Ch. 10.II: Primary Reactors and Types of Reactions:* A. Ruling Elites 　1. Basic Forms 　2. Government Efforts to Damage or 　　Facilitate 　3. Counterframes B. Dissident Elites C. Media 　1. Trends and Variations 　2. Causes of Varying Reactions D. Similar SMOs E. Counter SMOs (CSMOs) 　1. CSMO Formation 　2. Astroturf CSMOs and Counter-CSMOs *Ch. 10. III. Other Reactors* *Ch. 10.IV. Potpourri of Other Reactions*
		Ch. 10.V. A Third Point of View: Interaction A. Schematics of Interaction Fields B. Interaction Processes
Ch. 8. II.III: Why People Join: 　1. Biological 　2. Deep Motivation 　3. Self-concept 　4. Belief and Socialization 　5. Active Seeking 　6. Benefit Calculation/Rational Choice 　7. Experimentation 　8. Macrostructure 　9. Organizational Membership 　10. Prior Activism 　11. Prior Contact/Network 　12. Suddenly Imposed Grievances 　13. Situational Stress 　14. Biographical Availability 　15. Coercive Persuasion 　16. Affective Bonds *Ch. 8. IV: Membership Maintenance*	*Ch. 9.III: Factors Affecting Selection:* A. Images For Thinking About SMO Strategizing 　1. Strategic Dilemmas 　2. Tactical Interaction B. General Schemes of Causes 　1. Causes of Repertoires of Collective 　　Action 　2. Limiting Factors in Selecting Strategies 　3. Factors Affecting Strategic Options C. Specific Strategies and Cases 　1. Causes of a Type of Strategy 　2. Case Study of Causes	
Ch. 8. V: Membership Consequences A. Psychological Consequences B. Life Course Consequences	*Ch. 9.IV. Effects and Success:* A. Combat Willingness and Readiness B. Radical Flank Effects C. Confrontation and Crisis D. Great Turns and Crises of History	
Ch. 8, VII.A. Recruitment Strategies	*Ch. 9.V: Other Questions and Answers*	

A. Posture toward Claims

How do serious case study researchers routinely regard assertions about the facts and morality of the persons and organizations they are studying? The presumptions they make about facts and morality in their role as open-minded inquirers concern (1) their conceptions of "good" and "bad" guys, (2) their exercise of critical intelligence, (3) their willingness to live with an inherent tension between them and the SMO they are studying, and (4) their leap into "sociological consciousness."[3]

1. Good and Bad Guys in SMO Studies. The species *Homo sapiens* exhibits a quite remarkable—and perhaps dismal—propensity to divide itself into juxtaposed categories in which all virtues adhere to one or a few categories of the species ("our kind") and all vices adhere to some other category of "them" ("their kind"). We may think of this as the "good guy–bad guy" propensity or even syndrome of human functioning. One can easily understand the attractiveness of this form of thinking: It simplifies the task of dealing with people one encounters. You need only to "code" any new person (or topic) as a "good guy" or "bad guy" and proceed then in terms of the simple script attaching to each. In contrast, it is much more difficult to assess each new human one sees in terms of her or his own combination of specific characteristics.

Alas, students of social movements sometimes tend to be very much like most everyone else in their propensities to divide the world into good guys and bad guys. One prominent form of this is to believe that all social movements are good guys and that all holders of power targeted by movements are bad guys. Another prominent form is to presume that social movements of the political left are good guys, while those of the political right are bad guys. Or, that political movements are the good guys and religious and other personal change movements are the bad guys. Indeed, I venture to generalize that one unstated but strong tendency among contemporary movement researchers is to think that political movements of the left are the quintessential good guys.

But the higher ethical values of researchers as humans admonish them not to assess individuals or their groups as either totally good or bad. Instead, all humans exhibit both good and bad characteristics. In such appeals for appreciation of complexity, mixture, and nuance, no person (or at least hardly any person) is accurately or properly categorized as either a "good guy" or "bad guy."

A great many SMO researchers strive to practice this more complicated view and to avoid the propensity to divide the world into good and bad guys. I do so myself, but I must confess that I also recognize my inclination to do otherwise. I therefore do not claim to have transcended the good guy–bad guy syndrome, only that along with many other researchers I try to be reflexively self-critical in how I portray various "actors" in movement dramas.

Even so, some readers are likely to think that researchers who strive for a more complicated view, including me, are too critical of movements. We ought, it can be said, to be more protective of them as social enterprises. My answer to this concern is the same as that given by movement organizers Madeline Adamson and Seth Borgos in explaining their book *This Mighty Dream*:

> [A] tradition which has been whitewashed to erase the harsh texture of struggle is of little aid to understanding the conflicts and setbacks of the present. Even its inspirational value is ultimately suspect. . . . To acknowledge . . . internal conflicts, prejudices, false starts, and strategic errors . . . is not to diminish [the] heroic stature [of previous movements] but to clarify it. (Adamson and Borgos 1984, 16–17)

In seeking to grasp moral complexity, then, researchers do not take the easy path of selectively marshaling their data to produce cardboard cutouts of heroes, villains and fools.

2. Critical Intelligence. Avoiding the easy out of good guy–bad guy stereotypes is an application of a broader mind-set with which researchers approach their data and its analysis, the mind-set of *critical intelligence*. This is the quite amazing and hard-won modern posture of liberal science, the institutionalization of the view that no assertion is beyond constant questioning, checking, and unending skepticism (Rauch 1993). Instead of accepting versions of reality proffered by others, critical intelligence takes all claimed realities as themselves objects to be analyzed. In using critical intelligence, nothing is "of course" or taken for granted. Most especially, even the researcher's own most passionate commitments are properly the subjects of searching inspection and critique. *All* claims, that is, require inspection in terms of factual adequacy, comfortable self-serving myths, hidden vested interests, and other forms of mystification or mere intellectual laziness. Even critical intelligence itself is subjected to critical intelligence: Just what sort of self-canceling operation is this? In the spirit of unfettered skepticism, critical intelligence is brought to bear on the critical intelligence that is applied to critical intelligence.

As an approach in collecting and analyzing data, critical intelligence calls on researchers always to question the veracity of claims they encounter and that they are themselves are making. For example, SMO spokespersons claim one hundred thousand members. How do they know that? What do they mean by "member"? Could they be wrong, or have reasons to inflate the number or to mislead outsiders? Indeed, researchers are likely not to have an independent way to check a great many things that an SMO claims and this situation of uncertainty therefore requires that researchers treat all claims with caution.

And researchers treat their own claims with the same skepticism as they do SMO claims. For example, given researchers may think that variables A and B are linked in a given way. What is the evidence for that? Could they be wrong? Could the evidence on which they base the assertion be faulty? Have they made a logical error of inference? Therefore, in reporting, researchers treat *all* claims as exactly that: claims.

3. Activist-Analyst Tensions.   Critical intelligence (or, more broadly, liberal science) is a distinctive mind-set that is often at odds with the mind-sets of many SMO activists. While researchers, as analysts, must doubt and check *all* claims, movement activists want to—and perhaps must—*believe* their own claims. This creates an unavoidable tension between the researcher/analyst and the activist. It is a tension that arises in the process of data collection and becomes all the more evident to one in the process of analysis—if the researchers are exercising critical intelligence.

Indeed, if, in doing analysis, researchers do not experience tension between their critical inspection of the data and what SMO people are wont routinely to claim, they ask themselves if they are merely "whitewashing" the SMO rather than analyzing it. It is *possible*, of course, that they are studying an SMO in which there is a great deal of critical intelligence and therefore their exercise of it does not create tension. But it is also possible—and more likely—that such researchers are too accepting of the SMO's version of reality.

4. Sociological Consciousness.   The three topics of "good and bad guys," "critical intelligence," and "activist-analyst tensions" are ways of preparing for a yet broader way to explain and express the researcher's posture toward claims. This broader formulation is often termed *sociological consciousness* (although not all sociologists have this consciousness and it has been given other names, such as "humanistic consciousness").

Following Peter Berger's formulation as presented in his classic and brilliant *Invitation to Sociology* (1963), by sociological consciousness I mean the state of awareness in which a person steps outside the "taken-for-granted routines of society" and becomes conscious of society as a construction. In this act, human social life or "society" is bracketed and beheld rather than assumed and unthinkingly lived. Berger thus uses the term "ecstasy" from the root *ekstasis*—meaning "standing or stepping outside"—as a way to describe sociological consciousness, a consciousness that "transforms one's awareness of society . . . such . . . that *giveness* becomes *possibility*" (p. 136).

Sociological consciousness can be shocking and many people there-fore avoid it or shrink from it when it happens to them. But, for the intellectually and otherwise bold this ecstasy generates the *excitement of discovery* by transforming the familiar into the unfamiliar. Such discovery is "'culture shock' minus geographical displacement." By means of it, "the sociologist travels at home—with shocking results" (p. 23).

The centerpiece of this exciting consciousness of society as a brack-eted and beheld unfamiliar object is the proposition that "*things are not what they seem*," a declaration Berger terms "the first wisdom of soci-ology" (p. 23, emphasis added). This means a person with sociological consciousness

- is interested in looking some distance beyond the commonly ac-cepted or officially defined goals of humans actions . . .
- [has] a certain awareness that human events have different levels of meaning, some of which are hidden from the consciousness of everyday life . . .
- may [have] a measure of suspicion about the way in which human events are officially interpreted by the authorities, be they politi-cal, juridical or religious in character. (p. 29)

Other phrases denoting this consciousness include "seeing through" and "looking behind," as in the process of looking behind or "'seeing through' the facades of social structures" (pp. 30–31).

Berger suggests that there are at least four key dimensions or motifs of sociological consciousness:

First, "by the logic of [this consciousness, the sociologist] is driven time and again to debunk" any social setting under study and this *de-bunking motif* is "inherent in sociological consciousness" (p. 38). One common and famous form of debunking is to document the ironic con-sequences of actions; that is, the unrecognized and unintended conse-quences of action that confront and contradict the actors' intentions. Another prominent form of debunking documents how high-minded rationales for social arrangements are "verbal smoke screens" for hidden and self-interested motivations, as in insurance salesmen who present themselves as "fatherly advisors to young families" (p. 41).

Second, in being "detached from the taken-for-granted postures of . . . society," a person with sociological consciousness becomes aware of "worlds other than that of middle-class respectability," which leads to "fascination with the *unrespectable view of society*" (pp. 47, 46, 43, empha-sis added). This is seen in the pronounced degree to which sociologists focus on, among other *demimonde* matters, the "'other America' of dirty language and disenchanted attitudes, that state of mind that refuses to be impressed, moved, or befuddled by the official ideologies" (p. 44). Sociological consciousness exhibits a "irreverent curiosity and clear-sightedness" that "manages to free itself from the goggles of respectability" (p. 45).

Third, sociological consciousness is *relativizing* in that it is (as an instance of "modernity") "mobile, participates vicariously in the lives of others differently located from oneself, [and] easily imagines itself changing occupation or residence" (p. 48). As a consequence, sociological consciousness views identities and ideas as "relative to specific social locations" (p. 52).

Last, sociological consciousness exhibits *cosmopolitanism* in the historical sense of the urban cosmopolitan who "roams through the whole wide world" but "is at home wherever there are other [people] who think." Like urban cosmopolitanism, sociological consciousness provides a "broad, open, emancipated vista on human life." At its best, this consciousness has "a taste for other lands, [is] inwardly open to the measureless richness of human possibilities, [and is] eager for new horizons and new worlds of human meaning" (p. 53). This is in contrast to "narrow parochialism in . . . interest [which] is always a danger signal for the sociological venture" (p. 53).

For some, sociological consciousness is justified by the sheer joy of it, the excitement of delving into the ways in which society is simultaneously much like a prison, puppet theater, and comic drama (the three main sociological perspectives Berger treats as "man in society," "society in man," and "society as drama"). As laudable as joy and excitement certainly are, the experience of them in sociological consciousness points, though, to broader moral and ethical meanings of this consciousness.

For Berger and for me as the author of this research guide, these meanings center on being aware that we are (1) molded and controlled by society, (2) taken in by our own social performances, *and* (3) have the capacity and creativity to construct our actions (society as prison, puppet theater, and comic drama). It is precisely this kind of awareness that is one critical condition of personal and societal freedom. With this awareness, we can see that we often move as puppets in a theater, but we can also "grasp a decisive difference between the puppet theater and our own drama. Unlike the puppets, we have the possibility of stopping in our movements, looking up and perceiving the machinery by which we have been moved. In this act lies the first step toward freedom" (p. 176).

And with this awareness, we are able to see the machinery by which all social shows are moved and by which people come to believe they "must" do what they do and that they "really are" what "society" (or other grouping) says they are or that they define themselves as being. In this way, "society provides . . . a gigantic mechanism by which [people] can hide from [themselves their] own freedom" (p. 145).

In explicating the machinery of society and exposing the possibilities of choice against claims of nature and necessity, sociological consciousness is a profound humanism that counsels us not to be "taken in by [any] act being performed" (p. 156). It is a humanism that "does not easily wave banners, that is suspicious of too much enthusiasm and too much certainty. It is an uneasy, hesitant thing, aware of its own precariousness, circumspect in its moral assertions" (p. 162).

In the special context of the case study of SMOs, the humanism of sociological consciousness means that one is "compassionate and skeptical at the same time" and seeks to "understand without bias" (p. 171). In this way, sociological analysis so understood

> can attain to the dignity of political relevance . . . , not because it has a particular political ideology of its own to offer, but just because it has not. Especially to those who have become disillusioned with the more fervent political eschatologies of our era, sociology can be of assistance in pointing to possibilities of political engagement that do not demand the sacrifice of one's soul and of one's sense of humor. (p. 171)

B. Self-Management

Separate from the above issues of the researcher's posture regarding claims, several aspects of how the researcher relates to her- or himself during analysis (and in data collection as well) bear reporting.

1. The Negative Side of Freedom.   In doing their own research on an SMO, researchers have a great deal of freedom relative to other kinds of, especially, college activities (such as regular quizzes, weekly exercises, or papers and exams on specific reading).

One referent of the term "freedom" is wide personal discretion in determining what one will or will not do in various situations. Such wide personal discretion is often lauded as the kind of circumstance required in order for people best to exercise their creativity and innovative enterprise. Freedom is an essential condition of excellence.

While this is true, freedom is also a two-edged sword. At the same time that freedom provides one key ingredient for achieving true excellence, it also creates the circumstance in which someone can be an abysmal flop. The freedom necessary truly to excel is also the freedom that allows a person seriously to fail.

Therefore, freedom needs to be treated cautiously. Some people come to be in situations of freedom who are not prepared to manage it—and they dither away their opportunity for creativity and excellence.

Such a two-edgedness is present in case study SMO research—in the emergent and inductive discovery of generic propositions about SMOs. This process provides researchers an opportunity to do outstanding work *and also* the opportunity to find that they do lousy work—or lack the training or disposition to organize their own work. In college course research contexts, an instructor can organizationally mask this dismaying possibility by giving such novice researchers written and verbal feedback and grades that are more positive than they have earned. But instructors cannot protect such researchers from what they personally discover about themselves—about their own self-discipline, responsibility, energy, insight, creativity, and the like. In emergently inducting propositions about SMOs, researchers may be ecstatically delighted with what they find about themselves on these and other scores—or they may be severely disappointed. Such are always the dual possibilities of freedom.

But forewarning about unpleasant possibilities can also create the awareness of a possibility that researchers can strive to avoid. This is the reason I have called attention to the negative side of freedom that attends the collection and analysis of data. In knowing these dangers in advance, researchers are better equipped to avoid them.

2. Creative Possibilities.   In the next section I will point out several positive and negative concomitants of the process of doing the "immersion-induction" of generic propositions about SMOs. Among possible negative concomitants, I will mention anxiety and fear. Among the positive concomitants, there can be exultation, playful fun, and a sense of adventure. To these sometime concomitants we need to add the fact that researchers can and sometimes do also have the profound experience of being creative. I mean by this that it is entirely possible to discover or formulate an important generic proposition about SMOs that the researcher experiences as a thrilling revelation, a moment of the blinders falling from her or his eyes and beholding a shining new order in the data and—hopefully—in social reality. This creative insight may or may not be original—the first time anyone has ever formulated it—but this does not detract from the reality and authenticity of the creative experience.

It takes further and careful checking to determine whether the discovery is original as well as creative, but the researcher's accomplishment is not diminished by having had predecessors.[4] On the other hand, further checking may determine that the researcher has done something new and important that deserves a wider audience. In that case, he or she can add an achievement of consequence to the experience of creativity.

3. Intensive, Enterprising Diligence. One oft-quoted maxim about creativity (or genius) is that it "is one percent inspiration, ninety-nine percent perspiration" (Thomas Edison, quoted in King 1995, 71). People often experience creative insight as something that happens *to* them. But, so goes conventional wisdom, creative moments seems to happen more often to people who are otherwise working very hard on whatever their project. The moral is that researchers can be creative, but the best way to ensure this is to exercise a great deal of enterprising diligence.

Short of creativity per se, there is still the very impressive and more common level of executing excellent or elegant work that is impressively thorough, clear, and carefully organized. Impressive qualities such as these do not depend on blinding flashes of creativity, or even an especially sharp intelligence. Rather, they are functions of the sustained application of methodical effort and careful, well-organized, and sustained activity. And these qualities of elegance and thoroughness are products of venturing enterprise in searching out data that are available but not actually acquired by less diligent researchers and by carrying analysis beyond the point where the less diligent stop.

Most dramatically and even frequently, enterprising diligence stands in contrast to passive dependence on someone else to tell one what to do next and to check on and approve every small step one has taken. Such timidity and hesitancy is sometimes an almost passive-aggressive lethargy, a stonelike immobility in a situation that instead calls on the person to organize his or her own action and to go out and find and to develop materials. Unsurprisingly, people with such a passive approach to data collection and analysis fail to accomplish very much at all.

Between creativity and passivity then, there is a dependable research path to excellence: *intense, enterprising diligence.*

III. IMMERSION-INDUCTION IN ANSWERING QUESTIONS

The matters I describe in the first four chapters of this guide form a universe of pertinent concerns, a subject matter that is carved out from the immense universe of all possible subject matters. In capsule form, these "carved out" and therefore specifying matters focus on:

1. *Aspects* of SMOs (Chapter 3, Section II.A).
2. *Questions* about such aspects of SMOs (Chapter 3, Section II.B).

3. *Generic propositions* rather than "case" or other answers to ques-
    tions about SMOs (Section I, this chapter).
4. *Case studies* as vehicles for developing answers/propositions
    (Chapter 2, Section I).

The task of getting *from* aspects and questions *to* answers/propositions
raises the question, Exactly how does the researcher get from one to the
other?

The beginning and basic answer is: researchers *immerse* themselves in
the materials of the SMO case or cases they are studying and let the data
they encounter interact with their intuitions and sensibilities as these are
informed by their knowledge of aspects and questions. Often termed
"grounded theory" in the jargon of social science, researchers begin
with an open-ended and open-minded desire to know an SMO and they
are guided by the data and themselves as agents of induction in the task
of emergently formulating one or more generic propositions (Strauss
and Corbin 1990; Lofland and Lofland 1995).

This immersion-induction or "grounded theory" perspective means
that researchers approach the existing literature on SMOs and social
movements as *sources of flexible and variable consultation* that stimulate
their quest rather than as materials to be mastered in some strictly mem-
orized fashion and applied in a mechanical manner. In the instance of
this guide, for example, researchers read here and there in order to
follow leads rather than reading from start to finish in a linear progression (although they can also of course read it in a linear fashion).

Let me further explain this "consultation" as opposed to "linear reading" view of the literature by immersion-induction researchers by means
of an analogy with field manuals published on birds, plants, and other
creatures of particular regions. Paramount examples of such field guides
include, of course, those by Roger Tory Peterson on butterflies, animal
tracks, and you name it (e.g., Peterson 1990). Books of this field manual
sort are not assembled for the primary purpose of reading from start to
finish. Instead, they are to be carried—*literally* carried—into the field
(and are often designed to fit jacket pockets) so that they can be *consulted*
when questions arise as to what one is observing and how to interpret it.

However, this analogy between the literature on SMOs (including this
guide) and biological field manuals is one of spirit rather than of exact
correspondence. This is because, unlike biology, the field of social movements and its SMOs has not yet developed a widely recognized set of
species and subspecies, processes, and so forth. Instead, students of
SMOs are still at the stage of identifying characteristics of species rather
than species themselves. Here called "aspects," these characteristics are
what published materials on SMOs (and the Part II chapters of this

guide) help researchers identify. A biological field manual exactly parallel to the existing literature (and this guide) would—on birds, for example—provide chapters on such characteristics (aspects) as wings, beaks, colors, diet, and migration patterns. Most biological field manuals are obviously not organized in such terms.

The existing literature's organization in terms of characteristics (aspects) rather than species is nonetheless extremely helpful. By having already identified an array of salient matters (aspects) to which to attend and how those aspects can vary, researchers can construct their own profiles of species from the unique combination of features they discern. Or, put in the language I have used above, to develop generic propositional *answers* to *questions* about *aspects* of SMOs. In such a fashion, sociological researchers are field investigators like earlier field biologists, who performed an immense task of species identification.

IV. PHYSICAL PROCEDURES IN ANSWERING QUESTIONS

The process of immersion-induction is open-ended, but this does not mean that it lacks all structure and has no form at all. Instead, there are series of routine physical procedures that researchers commonly use and that are much the same as the procedures used in scholarship of all kinds. These are described in detail in many standard manuals and it is therefore not necessary to go into great detail here (see, e.g., Lofland and Lofland 1995; Jacobus 1989, esp. Ch. 10; Strauss and Corbin 1990; Cuba 1988; Barzun and Graff 1977). It is nonetheless important to describe these procedures in detail sufficient to indicate what they are and how they are employed in immersion-induction. These procedures are (1) coding, (2) memoing, and (3) charting.

A. Coding.

The word *coding* is the fancy name some researchers give the act of looking at a datum and asking and answering questions of these sorts:

- What is this an example of?
- What is this about?
- What does this tell us about this SMO? (Cuba 1988, 35; Lofland and Lofland 1995, 186).

Or, in the language of this guide: What *question* about what aspect of this SMO does this datum *answer*?

The word or few words (a caption or phrase) that these questions evoke is a "code," or what can otherwise be called a classification, categorization or simply file label heading. In being more abstract than the case, it is a rudimentary generic proposition, or at least the beginning of one.

This sorting and classifying of the incoming flow of data is the primal stream or level of analysis for the researcher. Its historic and brute physical form was (and is) to sort data-notes and other data-items into literal physical piles on some flat surface. The physical piles of items were (or are) the basic code categories—the topics of attention, the types of aspects of the SMO under development. Within such physical piles, there might be subsorts or subcodes of some complexity.

Moving up from such piles, researchers—historically—placed the piles in separate file folders and worked within folders in the elaboration of codes (that is, analysis or answers to questions about aspects). With the advent of the personal computer (PC), data are—with increasing frequency—entered into a database that is coded, but the logic of categorizing items of information is the same as that of placing a datum in one pile rather than another on some flat surface:

> [Regardless of the physical method, coding begins] the process of *categorizing* and *sorting* data. Codes then serve as shorthand devices to *label, separate, compile,* and *organize* data. . . . Codes [also] serve to summarize, synthesize, and sort many observations made of the data. By providing the pivotal link between the data collection and its conceptual rendering, coding becomes the fundamental *means* of developing the analysis. (Charmaz 1983, 111, 112, emphasis in the original)

Researchers who want to explore how this process can be performed on a personal computer will find it helpful to consult Weitzman and Miles's (1995) review of some two dozen programs designed to perform qualitative data analysis.

B. Memoing

Codes are labels for—or categories of—data, while *memos* are explanations of the codes, prose that "tells what the code is about" (Charmaz 1983, 120). As such, memos differ greatly in length, ranging from a sentence or paragraph to several pages. In "telling what the code is about,"

> [m]emos are primarily conceptual in intent. They don't just report data; they tie together different pieces of data into a recognizable cluster, often to show that those data are instances of a general concept. Memos can also go well beyond codes and their relationships to any aspect of the study—

personal methodological, and substantive. They are one of the most useful and powerful sense-making tools at hand. (Miles and Huberman 1994, 72)

Some researchers distinguish among three types of memos in terms of their breadth and stage in the research. The first type—sometimes called the *elemental* (or "small piece") *memo*--has been described immediately above: It is the basic level of written prose on the codes and their data. These are the prose building blocks of the analysis. As the metaphorical bricks from which the building of larger analysis rises, even in quite small projects assiduous researchers are likely to write several dozen elemental memos.

The accumulation of many elemental memos creates a need for a next level of analysis, analyses that address questions of how the elemental memos themselves fit together. Written work addressed to this emergent level of analysis constitutes a second type of memo, one termed the *sorting memo*. "By going through accumulated [elemental] memos and sorting them, researchers gain insight into . . . core variables, key phases in a process, . . . major issues," or whatever the emerging content (Charmaz 1983, 122). "The discoveries one makes in this sorting are then themselves written up. As *analysis written on analysis*, these sorting memos achieve a higher level of abstraction and generalization than do elemental memos" (Lofland and Lofland 1995, 205).

Third and last, the corpus of elemental memos that are overlaid with sorting memos creates yet a next level of needed analysis: explanations of connections and relationships among the sorting memos! These are termed *integrating memos* and they seek to show how relations among various parts of the entire analytic effort.

The concrete procedural tasks of immersion-induction (that is, of analysis) are, then, coding and memoing. The *content* of coding and memoing is, of course, versions of *questions* about *aspects* of SMOs that result in *generic propositional answers*.

C. Charting

In both coding and memoing, researchers often find it helpful to think visually about their nalyses, that is, to develop succinct graphic representations of the concepts/propositions that are the codes and memos. Such "charting" has sometimes also been spoken of as *display*, which is, as defined by Miles and Huberman, "a visual format that presents information systematically" (1994, 91).

Following Lofland and Lofland (1995, ch. 9), let me point to four main forms of the visual displays often used by researchers: typologizing, matrix-making, concept-charting, and flowcharting.

1. Typologizing. Typologizing or cross-classifying refers, in the simplest instance, to the visual display of the intersection of two variables. In the most rudimentary version of this simplest form, each variable assumes only two values, creating a four-cell table. An example of this is given in Section III.H of Chapter 5, where the dichotomized variable of degree of change desired (partial versus total) is cross-classified with locus of change (individual versus society), creating the four cells—that is, types of SMO beliefs—of reform, revolution, redemption, and transformation. (Other examples include Figures 8.1 and 9.1.)

In writing about the sociological imagination, C. Wright Mills has stressed that ongoing cross-classifications in research work are "very often genuine tools of production. They clarify the 'dimensions' of the types [you are working on], which they also help you to imagine and build" (1959, 213). Indeed, Mills declares:

> I do not believe I have written more than a dozen pages first-draft without some little cross-classification [i.e., typology]—although, of course, I do not always or even usually display such diagrams. Most of them flop, in which case you have still learned something. When they work, they help you to think more clearly and to write more explicitly. They enable you to discover the range and the full relationships of the very terms in which you are thinking and of the facts with which you are working.
>
> For a working sociologist, cross-classification is what diagramming a sentence is for a diligent grammarian. In many ways, cross-classification is the very grammar of the sociological imagination. (p. 213)

2. Matrix-Making. As defined by Miles and Huberman a matrix is "the 'crossing' of two lists . . . set up as rows and columns" (1994, 93). They differ from typologies in the complexity of the "lists" involved and in using only two lists (while typologies may use many variables). We need not look far for an example of a matrix. As ought to be evident, this guide is built squarely on one: Figure 3.3, the Aspect-Question Matrix. (Other examples include Figures 1.2, 4.2, and 7.1.)

3. Concept-Charting. In some cases, a set of concepts may be clarified by arranging symbolic representations of them (say squares or circles with concept names in them) on a sheet of paper or physically arranging and rearranging such representations on a flat surface. In this way, physical placements and the distances among the parts displays relationships. Various types of lines (solid, broken, etc.) and directional arrowheads between and among the concepts can be used to represent varying types of relations. Again, we do not need to look far for examples of concept-charting. Two of them also appear in Chapter 3: Figure 3.1, Diagram of Seven Main Questions about SMOs, and Figure 3.2, Eight Generic Questions.

4. *Flowcharting.* Concept- and flowcharts are alike in visualizing relations among concepts, but differ in that the former depict their static structural relations while the latter arranges the concepts in terms of *time* or in terms of a temporal *sequence* in a *process.* I report several studies of such processes in Part II, but for one or another of several reasons I have not reprinted the flowcharts that may have accompanied those analyses. Two studies described in Part II that feature flowcharts that can be seen in the original publications are Heirich (1971) on spirals of conflict (described in Chapter 10, Section V), and Freeman (1979; 1983b) on factors affecting strategic options (described in Chapter 9, Section II.A.7).

Coding, memoing, and charting, then, are basic physical procedures researchers employ in the immersion-induction of analysis. If desired, more detailed discussion of these procedures appears in the several works cited at the start of this section.

V. FRUSTRATION, ANXIETY, EXHILARATION IN ANSWERING QUESTIONS

Aspects, questions, generic propositional answers to questions, immersion-induction, and other of the matters I have described orient researchers, but even taken collectively they still leave them in a rather undefined and ambiguous situation.[5] The emergent and inductive character of the quest for generic propositions involves a high degree of openness and therefore calls on researchers to *construct* sociological order. Moreover, there is almost always one or another problem in collecting data in any research undertaking.

These features of openness, ambiguity, and data snags tend to cause anxiety, fear, and feelings of frustration in researchers. Success in forging sociological order in what at first appear to be only chaotic materials can even seem impossible to many, especially novice researchers.

Fortunately, there are several widely practiced and successful methods for coping with feelings of anxiety and difficulty that researchers can and do employ in the face of open-ended tasks. Let me point up four of these.

The *first* and most important mode of management is for researchers consciously and un-self-consciously *to recognize and to accept* the mundane fact that emergent and inductive analysis resulting in generic propositions is not a mechanical and easy task. Feelings of anxiety and difficulty in the face of such open-ended tasks are common and normal. This situation *of course* causes anxiety and concern. When researchers recognize and accept this fact they normalize the anxiety and associated concerns and emotions. They therefore relax—for they are like most everyone else.

Steeled by this recognition, a *second* mode of management is *persistently to work* at the task of collecting data with an eye to an emergent and inductive analysis of generic propositional form. The sheer accumulation of information is in itself anxiety reducing because it ensures that researchers will, at minimum, be able to say *something*, even if that something is not as analytic as they might like and is not known to them at the moment.

Moreover, the physical procedures of coding, memoing, and charting that I have just described provide researchers with some very specific operations to engage in as a way to cope with their fear and anxiety. Coding, especially, brings order and order brings calm—the sense that the flux of stuff can be made sense of.

Based on these two modes of coping, researchers then (and *third*) *have faith* that they will inductively emerge with a statement of one or more generic propositions—that is, propositional answers to one or more questions regarding one or more aspects of the SMO they are studying. This faith is bolstered by the common *fourth* practice of participating in a group of people who are doing the same or similar kind of research. In trendy terminology, researchers form "support groups" of like-minded fellow inquirers among whom there is the solidarity of all being in the same boat on rough seas. Commonly, these groups involve as few as two or three persons, but they do the job.

One aspect of maintaining faith pertains to researchers *believing that they will be successful* in their quest and that they will achieve a significant personal and emotional reward in the form of the *joy and exhilaration of discovery*. Very much like the satisfaction felt in solving any other puzzle, finding one or more generic propositions in the chaos of "mere data" can be an enormously powerful and positive emotional experience—and even a "high." Reduced to a slogan, researchers "go for the high!"

VI. DESIRABLE FEATURES OF REPORTS:
A CHECKLIST

There are a number of conventions and standards that guide researchers in organizing and composing their research reports. Equally as important, these conventions and standards guide serious *readers* of research reports in making evaluations of the quality of research efforts. Therefore, researchers who desire positive responses from serious readers learn these conventions and standards and employ them in composing their research reports.

I report these conventions and standards below in the form of a *checklist of questions* that researchers ask about their reports at several points in the process of composing them. Most obviously, these questions are asked about drafts of the final report close to the conclusion of the research. But these questions are also posed in prior stages and they help researchers assess what they have completed and what remains to be done.[6]

My report of these questions attempts accurately to represent the wider world of professional scholarship, but it is also drawn somewhat more broadly in order to take account of projects completed as part of college and university courses (and framed as the preliminary propositional profile papers I refer to in Section I.E above).

1. Basic Features

1.1. Does the *title* of the report have a generic propositional or kindred conceptual referent (e.g., "the marketed social movement"), or, if it is a propositional profile, is that fact signaled in the title?

1.2. Is there an *abstract* and/or a table of contents?

1.3. Does the *first paragraph* of the report (or at least the first paragraphs) state a sociological proposition, thesis, or the like that will be used in approaching the data? Or, if the paper is a propositional profile, is this reported right at the start?

1.4. Is there an introductory section that provides an *overview* of what will be covered in the paper. Requoting Babbie's quotation of an "old forensic dictum," one reasonable practice is to "[t]ell them what you're going to tell them; tell them; and tell them what you have told them" (1995, A11).

1.5. Is there an early section that reviews social science writing that is pertinent to the proposition or propositions being treated? (The standard phrase for this section is "review of the literature.") (In fieldwork or kindred reports completed under time constraints this section might be brief or omitted.)

1.6. Is there an early section that reports the *sources* of the data and the *methods* used? Does this section also indicate possible faults with the data or sources of bias and how these have been dealt with? (In some forms of research this section is called "study design and execution.")

1.7. Is there a *main*, data-reporting, and analyzing *body* of the report that is divided (and subdivided, if required) with informative headings? (This portion of a report is sometimes called the "analysis and interpretation.") In propositional profile papers, the main body of the paper would consist of these propositions (and the data and analysis associated with each of them).

1.8. Is there a *summary and conclusion section* that summarizes what has been reported, draws conclusions about it, and suggests what further research is appropriate?

1.9. Is there a list of *references* or other appropriate bibliographic apparatus?

1.10. Are appropriate *stylistic conventions* employed? Stylistic conventions in research reporting mean, among other things, standard margins, numbered pages, clear and consist placement of headings, and properly formatted references. Some of these stylistic conventions are now the default settings of many word-processing programs, but many are not. Stylistic conventions are detailed in manuals of style such as Turabian (1996), Jacobus (1989), and Cuba (1988).

1.11. Is the writing grammatical and are the words spelled correctly?

2. Methodological Caution

In addition to cautions that may be expressed in the methods section (question 1.6), are the data and analysis treated throughout with a concern for error and bias? Is the researcher appropriately critical of the data and analysis and her or his own claims about them?

3. Research Effort and Success

3.1. Is there evidence that reasonable efforts to locate data adequate to the topics treated have been expended?

3.2. Is there evidence that those efforts were reasonably successful?

4. Data Quality, Quantity, Pertinence

4.1. Taking account of differing course and other contexts, are data of adequate quality and quantity presented in the report?

4.2. Even if quantitatively and qualitatively adequate as a general matter, are the data pertinent to the conceptual focus or foci of the report?

5. Clarity, Logical Order, Generic Propositional Framing

5.1. Even though the report might have the eleven elements indicated in 1.1 through 1.11, is the report clearly organized even so?

5.2. Does the report clearly put forth one or more generic propositions that are answers to questions?

6. Analytic Thoroughness

6.1. Is the main body of the report (question 1.7 above) organized in terms of a detailed scheme of categories of analysis or in terms of a profile of propositions?

6.2. If there is a detailed scheme, is it intertwined with whatever data are used, as opposed to presenting the scheme in one place and the data in another?

6.3. Are the concepts used and the captions employed serious phrasings (or do they run to the literary and to the stylistically "cute")?

7. Balance[7]

7.1. Does the report have too much or too little material quoted from published or other sources?

7.2. Does the paper have a balance between description and analysis?

7.3. Are the sections of the paper balanced?

8. Truth and Plausibility

8.1. To what degree are the data true and accurate?

8.2. Are the data presented consistent with the analysis?

8.3. Are the data and analysis presented consistent with other data and analyses?

9. Originality or Newness

Taking account of the context (e.g., college courses versus professional research), does the report make an advance over what is already known and discussed in whatever the context?

* * *

In the three chapters comprising Part I of this guide, I have reported the four major steps or phrases in the case study of social movement organizations—the case study of SMOs. Reduced to a single word each, these are the steps (or procedures) of *selecting, collecting, asking,* and *answering.* Together, they form a *case study* methodological approach to the study of SMOs.

The purpose of research procedures is, of course, to find out things about whatever is studied. Such "finding out" is at least in part guided by questions and answers that other researchers have already explored. These are the matters to which we now turn in Part II.

NOTES

1.   Many other and much wider contrasts can be drawn among rhetorical or "discourse" styles. I focus on these three narrower contrasts as most salient to the task at hand. Among wider and more sweeping comparative analyses consider, though, Brown's (1966) exposition of "five primary types" of prose styles: deliberative (persuasion), expository (e.g., a treatise), tumbling, prophetic (e.g., Biblical), and indenture (e.g., legal documents). Close to this same sweep, Lannon (1986, 165) distinguishes among the "three major goals" and associated forms of writing: the expressive ("centers on you"), explanatory ("centers on your view . . . of some outside subject"), and persuasive ("centers on your audience") (emphases omitted). Writing about writing social science has of course been a major preoccupation in recent times. A bibliography and brief discussion are provided in Lofland and Lofland (1995, 217).

2.   A yet additional contrast may seem too obvious to mention but, in my experience, it is not—alas. It is the contrast between empirical and normative questions and answers/proportions about SMOs. Empirical questions and answers strive to represent the way reality simply *is,* irrespective of one's moral preferences or values about it. In contrast, normative statements assert the way some matter *ought* to be. Thus, an empirical (or "is") assertion might say: "This SMO uses violence as a strategy." A normative (or "ought") statement on the same topic, in contrast, reads: "This SMO ought to use violence as a strategy." In this guide, I am concerned with empirical (or "is") rather than normative (or "ought") statements. As Berelson and Steiner quote Samuel Butler: "Let us settle the facts first and fight about the moral tendencies afterwards" (1964, 2).

3.   Some of the themes in this section are repeated and revised from Lofland and Lofland (1995, Ch. 8, Section II).

4.   Indeed, independent formulation of similar or identical creative ideas is not uncommon and is an almost regular feature of the process of expanding human knowledge.

5.   The themes developed in this section are adapted from Lofland and Lofland (1995, Ch. 9, Section II).

6. In developing this checklist, I have drawn on Babbie (1995, Appendix B) and on Lofland and Lofland (1984, Ch. 10). The list given here is an abbreviated version of an expanded treatment in Lofland and (Lofland 1995, Ch. 10, Section II).

7. The concept of "balance" and its three forms are from Cuba (1988, 71–72).

II

Propositions:
Answers to Questions about Aspects

In this Part II, I attempt accurately to represent a fair portion of the generic social scientific propositions that researchers have developed on SMOs. I do so in terms of the seven main questions overviewed at the start of Chapter 3 and schematized in Figure 3.1. In summary recapitulation, these are as follows:

1. Simply thinking about people acting together with some continuity to do anything, we recognize that they must, as a very first matter, devise and put forth some kind of definition of their situation or **beliefs** about what is true, moral, and possible. Knowing and otherwise understanding these beliefs is therefore our initial task—and it is the main task of the next chapter.

2. The beliefs of concern in analyzing SMOs involve acting together in some fashion, which is a question of how people are going to be arrayed in some form of **organization**. How are SMOs organized? This is the main question addressed in Chapter 6.

3. Knowing something about various forms of their organization, what are the conditions under which SMOs come into existence? Or, to use the title of Chapter 7, What are **causes** of SMOs?

4. If there is to be SMO action, there must be participants—"members" as well as leaders. From where do these come and under what conditions? In the terminology of Chapter 8's title. Why do people **join** SMOs?

5. SMOs are about people acting together to realize realities at that time excluded from the mainstream. How do they go about doing this? In the calculative terminology used in the title of Chapter 9, What are SMO **strategies**?

6. As promoters of excluded or at least highly contentious realities, mainstream and other groupings in society are not likely to be merely neutral about or indifferent to specific SMOs. What, indeed, are the **reactions** of various groupings?

7. Finally and as framed by the title of Chapter 11, What are **effects** of SMOs? What difference, if any, do they make?

This list, then, forms a simple sequence of:

1. beliefs?
2. organization?
3. causes?
4. joining?
5. strategies?
6. reactions?
7. effects?

As we move in closer, the picture becomes more complicated than this, of course. But these seven questions do provide a larger frame of reference into which to fit our more detailed delvings.

5

What Are SMO Beliefs?

The term *beliefs* is commonly defined as "matters taken to be true." In the context of movement studies it is shorthand for "challenging/insurgent constructions of reality." Conceived as more or less systematic bodies of assertions, beliefs answer basic questions of being: Who are we? What are our problems and why do we have them? What should be done about our problems and who is to do it? Other words sometimes also used to refer to beliefs include *ideologies, worldviews, doctrines, creeds, outlooks, views, frames,* and *perspectives.*

This chapter is divided into five sections. The first four address aspects of SMO beliefs, as follows:

I. We need to begin with the recognition that SMO beliefs are a matter of their social location rather than of their substance, content, or form. *Any* belief can be an SMO *or* mainstream belief.

II. Even so, SMO beliefs do have some features in common, some *similarities* that answer the question, What are SMO Beliefs?

III. Equally or more important, SMO beliefs *differ* in a great many important ways that also answer the question, What are SMO Beliefs? I will inventory several of the most basic of these.

IV. Sections II and III answer generic question (1), What are the aspect's types? In Section IV we attend to some answers to generic questions (6) and (7) as applied to beliefs. These are, What are *causes* of SMO beliefs? and What are *consequences* of SMO beliefs?

In Section V I place beliefs in the larger or encompassing context of *culture,* a different but closely related aspect of SMOs. There, I pose generic question (3) as applied to culture: What is the *magnitude* of SMO culture? After explaining differing cultural magnitudes, I review se-

101

lected propositions about the *causes* and *consequences* of variations in magnitude.

I. SMO BELIEFS ARE CONTEXTUAL RATHER THAN INHERENT

Researchers proceed on the assumption that no beliefs are inherently either SMO or mainstream because of their substance, empirical truth, logic, or any other feature. Instead, they assume that *any* belief, no matter how bizarre from the researchers' personal or other point of view, is or could become a dominant, mainstream reality *or* a marginalized, excluded, or even repressed reality in a society.

Only the briefest contemplation of beliefs currently excluded from the American mainstream that have been mainstream realism and reality in other times and/or societies makes this point: National Socialism in Germany of the 1930s, Marxist-Leninism in the Soviet Union of the 1920s and later, the divine right of kings in several European countries in many periods.

Reciprocally, in these three example contexts and others, reality as constructed by the current American mainstream was or is marginalized, excluded, or even suppressed and repressed. Thus, such American reality constructions as "democracy," "capitalism," "personal freedom," and "human rights" are regarded as false, subversive, antisocial, degenerate, or just plain sick in the three examples of mainstream contexts given just above (as well as in many other contexts). When we speak of the sheer substance of SMO beliefs, therefore, we are speaking of the *social location* of beliefs rather than of their essential or substantive character.

Howard Becker's (1963) distinction between *conventional* and *unconventional sentimentality* can be used to elaborate this point. *Conventional sentimentality* is the prejudging sentiment that (1) a belief must be true, better, and rational because it is mainstream and that (2) a belief must be false, worse, and irrational if it is marginal or excluded.

Unconventional sentimentality is the reverse form of prejudicing presumption: (1) a belief is truer, better, or more rational because it is marginal or excluded, and (2) a belief is false, worse, and irrational because it is part of the mainstream.

Sweeping and frequent changes in the social standing of many beliefs—from marginal to mainstream and the reverse—suggests little or no relation between the truth, moral merit, and rationality of a belief and its mainstream-marginal location. Mainstream or marginal beliefs are de facto neither true, moral, or rational, nor false, immoral, or irrational. Instead, beliefs need to be assessed on their own merits and demerits rather than subjected to the prejudices of *conventional* or *unconventional sentimentality*. And, most pertinent here, as dispassionate inquirers, researchers strive to suspend all sentimentalities—conventional and unconventional alike—as they do their research.

II. WHAT SMO BELIEFS ARE: SIMILARITIES

From the point of view of researchers examining the beliefs of a specific SMO, the answer to the question, What are SMO beliefs? calls for two levels of consideration: the *case* itself—the concrete beliefs in their own terms—and the more generalized—*generic*—characterization of the beliefs that the case data suggest.[1]

Although researchers study and master an SMO's beliefs in their own terms and in a simple narrative fashion (the *case* level), such a straightforward recounting is not in itself and yet of social scientific interest. Instead and based on their narrative mastery of the beliefs, researchers organize their treatments of them in terms of more generic or generalized features that the beliefs may exhibit.

Researchers seek generalized features of SMO beliefs in two directions: *similarities* and *differences* (or variations)

In the similarity direction, the first item on the agenda is of course an answer to the most basic form of the question, What are the aspect's types? That most basic form is a *definition* of SMO belief, which we have already encountered several times: moralistically and idealistically rendered reality constructions that challenge mainstream conceptions of the real, the moral, and the possible.

Beyond a definition, thinking about generalized similarities has involved conceiving the logical components of any belief system advocating change. One of the more durable and useful of these formulations has been John Wilson's list of three structural parts of movement belief systems:

1. **Diagnosis:** a statement of what is wrong or the current problems.
2. **Prognosis:** a statement of what must be done, the solutions to the problems.
3. **Rationale:** a statement of who must do the job, that is, a rationale for the movement (edited and quoted from Wilson 1973, 95, Ch. 3).

Elaborating on these distinctions in terms of beliefs as "frames" (that is, "schematic of interpretation"[2]), David Snow and Robert Benford have treated these categories as

> three core framing tasks: (1) a diagnosis of some event or aspect of social life as problematic and in need of alteration; (2) a proposed solution to the diagnosed problem that specifies what needs to be done; and (3) a call to arms or rationale for engaging in ameliorative or corrective action. (Snow and Benford 1988, 199)

In further work likewise in part building on Wilson, these analysts work up the concepts of beliefs and frames into the idea of the *collective action frame*, which they define as "an interpretative schemata that simplifies and condenses the 'world out there' by selectively punctuating and encoding objects, situations, events, experiences, and sequences of action's within one's present or past environment" (p. 137). Pertinent to similarities in SMO beliefs, these analysts suggest that all collective action frames share certain characteristics.[3] These are

[1: Punctuation] [C]ollective action frames . . . punctuate or single out some existing social condition . . . and define it as unjust, intolerable, and deserving of corrective action. . . .

[2: Attribution] [They make] diagnostic and prognostic attributions. . . . In . . . the former, movement activists attribute blame for some problematic condition by identifying culpable agents. . . . And in . . . prognostic attribution, [there are suggestions for] both a general line of action for ameliorating the problem and the assignment of responsibility for carrying out that action. . . .

[3: Articulation] [C]ollective action frames enable activists to articulate and align a vast array of events and experiences so that they hang together in a relatively unified and meaningful fashion. (pp. 137–38).[4]

III. WHAT SMO BELIEFS ARE: DIFFERENCES

Beyond such generic or logical similarities, researchers have been more concerned with generalized differences or *variations* in SMO beliefs. The following are among the main types of these that researchers have identified. The reader will notice that a number of these variations overlap with one another in several ways and to different degrees. This is because I am making a report of researches on variations rather than constructing a mutually exclusive and exhaustive classification of how beliefs are different and vary.

I have singled out these I describe and not others for special exhibit for one or more of these reasons: (1) the *breadth* of variation they identify, with emphasis on wide variations, (2) their *legitimacy* in the research tradition, and (3) their sheer *substantive importance* in comprehending SMOs. Alas, there are yet other very intriguing variations that constraints on space foreclose reporting.[5]

The *order* in which I report these variations is a question of some importance and I will explain why some are discussed before or after others as we go along.

A. Two-Parameter Variations: Amount and Locus of Change

Perhaps most frequently, researchers have distinguished among SMO beliefs in terms of the *amount* and *locus* of the changes envisioned.[6] In "insurgent reality" terminology, just *how much* new reality *about what* is proposed?

1. **Amount.** Most fundamentally, how much change is envisioned in the beliefs? Does the *total* social order or person require reconstitution or are only *partial* changes needed?

2. **Locus.** Separate from amount, at what level is the change thought necessary? Is the *person* focused on as the prime unit needing change or is it social *structure*? Another term for structure is "supraindividual," which refers to, as used by Aberle, "the economic order . . . the political order, a total society or culture, the world or indeed the cosmos" ([1962] 1982, 316).

The intersection of these two dichotomized dimensions specifies four main variations in (or types of) SMO beliefs. Here are the four types with David Aberle's names for them in italics type, along with some other names that diverse researchers have used generically to characterize each pattern.

1. *Partial change of structure:* reform, norm-oriented (Smelser 1962), *reformative* (Aberle 1966) beliefs. Examples of SMOs with such beliefs include the National Women's Suffrage Association and the National Association for the Advancement of Colored People (cf. Wilson 1973, 24).

2. *Total change of structure:* revolutionary, value-oriented (Smelser 1962), *transformative* (Aberle 1982), millenarian beliefs. I discuss characteristics of these beliefs in Section III.B.6 below.

3. *Partial change of persons:* *alterative* (Aberle 1982), ego (Lofland 1985) beliefs. "Various birth control movements are examples insofar as they do not involve efforts to change . . . legislation (in which case they are reformative)" (Aberle 1982, 317). To the degree that it promotes narrow, individual packages of self-manipulation techniques, the SMO Transcendental Meditation has exhibited alterative beliefs (Johnston 1980; Ch. 6, Section III.C in this guide; Back [1972] 1987).

4. *Total change of persons:* *redemptive* (Aberle 1982), expressive (Blumer [1939] 1969a) beliefs. Examples of SMOs espousing redemptive beliefs include the Salvation Army, Soka Gakkai, Moral Re-Armament, specific Pentecostal congregations (Wilson 1973, 25), and certain psychoanalytic associations (Aberle 1982, 320).

I begin with this classic typology of two dichotomized variations that display four basic kinds of SMO beliefs because it so clearly sets forth the really quite *magnificent sweep* of ways in which insurgent humans generate social realities.

The proper domain of movement studies in general and SMO analyses in particular is this magnificent sweep in all its varieties and complexities and not simply one subset within it. I mention this because of the tendency of researchers in recent times to focus much more commonly on SMOs and movements whose beliefs exhibit pattern number (1), immediately above (partial changes of structure) rather than the other three patterns. While attention to pattern (1) is obviously in order, excessive preoccupation with it clearly also distorts one's picture of SMOs.

B. Existential Variations

In the spirit of encouraging more sensitivity to broader differences in SMO beliefs, I want to feature variations that catch at the more profound range of possibilities for human collective definition and action and that confront the human condition in more radical epistemological fashions than have prevailed in most societal mainstreams most of the time. I label such variations "existential" and assemble five of them in this section. After reporting these, I will turn to variations that are more "mundane," although certainly no less important because of that.

1. Adversary versus Exemplary. It is one thing to advocate that reality ought to be different, but it is quite another collectively to live that advocated reality. In the fashionable phrases "talking the talk" is not the same as "walking the walk." Researchers have otherwise written of this as the difference between:

- beliefs that *advocate* personal and/or social changes but do little or nothing to affect such changes *in the lives of SMO members,* and
- beliefs asserting that "the future is now" and seeking to *exemplify* as well as advocate changes in the lives of SMO members.

Paul Starr uses this distinction to classify organizations, but his characterization applies as well to systems of SMO beliefs:

> An adversary [SMO], such as a political party, a union, or a reform group, is primarily concerned with altering the prevailing social order. Oriented toward conflict, it may not exhibit in its own organization all the values that its supporters hope eventually to realize. Whereas the members of an exemplary organization typically regard its activities as intrinsically valuable, the participants in an adversary organization regard its activities primarily as a means toward an end. For exemplary organization, the goals mainly involve changes in internal structure, while for adversary organization, the goals involve changes outside. The exemplary [SMO] invests its energies in building up a model of what its organizers would like the world to be; the adversary organization expends its resources against the larger world of power. (1979, 247)

Conceived more generically, Albert Hirschman (1970) has dubbed this distinction "exit" (exemplary) versus "voice" (adversary). Exit as a generic is "any form of unilateral departure from an economic or political entity," while voice is "any attempt to exert influence [on society] by directing complaining to it" (Starr 1979, 249). Among SMOs, exit beliefs spell out an "organized exit from a dominant institutional system, whereas adversary [beliefs] are a form of organized voice" (p. 249).

2. Degree Totalistic. SMO beliefs vary in the degree to which their component assertions are:

1. *explicitly formulated,*
2. internally integrated with one another or *systematized,*
3. *comprehensive* in the scope of realities to which they refer,
4. applied with a sense of *urgency* and imperativeness that is accompanied by aroused affect and promulgated authoritatively,
5. *intensely concentrated* on and systematically integrated around certain central propositions or evaluations (adapted from Shils 1968, 68, 66).

In composite, these variations form a *variable* that, for want of better terms and drawing on Shil's analysis of ideology, I label degree *totalistic,* or degree *ideologized.*

As a variable, researchers begin with the assumption that *all* patterns of human beliefs as a general class vary along the above five dimensions.

Perhaps most commonly among humans, patterns of belief are *not* very explicit, systematic, comprehensive, accompanied by a sense of urgency, or focused on a few central ideas. Terming these lower ranges on the totalism variable simply **outlooks**, Shills characterizes them as vague, diffuse, subject to less pressure to be observed in action, and less accompanied by high emotional arousal or sense of urgency.

In ethnomethodological terms, "outlooks" exhibit the "common sense attitude" or the "attitude of everyday life" in which events are not thought to have "unequivocally stable meanings." Negotiating daily life and life more generally therefore requires supple and shifting "practical judgment" that draws on multiple, ever-changing, and perhaps contradictory frames of reference (Bittner 1963, 930).

The essence of totalistic thinking—of ideologizing—is, in contrast, to reject mere "outlooks" and the "heterogeneous interpretation of meaning" in the common-sense outlook and to move toward, in the phrase of Bittner, *"a unified and internally consistent interpretation of the meaning of the world"* (1963, 932, emphasis in the original).

Such systems of *total belief* and demand for consistency "shaped by an overarching principle" (Wilson 1973, 94) are difficult for people not extensively exposed to them to grasp, and a clear example of one is therefore in order. The example I offer is what its proponents call Unification Thought, which is the ideology of the Unification Church (UC) or Movement founded and headed by Sun Myung Moon. In one introduction to UC beliefs as a "comprehensive philosophical system," a UC intellectual quotes Moon as describing Unification Thought as

> a new view of life, a new view of the world, a new view of the universe and a new view of the providence of history that has never before existed. It is also a principle of integration that can encompass the whole into one unity. . . . God's truth is sent to earth as a revelation given through certain providential persons. God's truth is the absolute truth, which is an almighty key capable of solving any problem, no matter how difficult it may be. I have encountered the living God through a lifetime of prayer and meditation, and have been given this absolute truth. Its remarkable contents clarify all the secrets hidden behind the entire universe, behind human life and behind human history (Moon quoted in Tenabe 1992, 18).

A number of assertions and words in this passage are noteworthy as indicators of a very high degree of totalism:

- *All* of life, the world and the universe—not simply one or a few institutional realms—are encompassed by it.
- The truth that believers know is not partial, imperfect, and situational but *absolute*, as well as *total*.

- *All* problems are solved by it; it is comprehensive.
- *All* secrets and unknowns are now known.
- Moon and "certain providential persons" reveal this total system of explaining problems and solutions to humans.

In the context of Moon's characterization of Unification Thought, this UC intellectual then summarizes it as:

> a philosophical theory dealing with questions of being, logic, cognition, value, art, history, and practice; a theory assuming theological nature in that it deals with the attributes of God, creation, providence, etc.; a theory of standards for settling actual problems; a reform theory which is aimed at restoration of the original world; a complementary theory which recognizes the truth in existing philosophies and theologies; a theory for cultural revolution which provides the basis for the culture of the Kingdom of Heaven; and the true liberation theory which aims to liberate all humankind from Satan and thus to liberate God. (Tenabe 1992, 18)

Commenting on his summary, the UC intellectual declares: "This is a formidable list! Clearly, Unification Thought sets itself a great task" (p. 18).

3. Type of Cognitive Mode. Historically, SMO researchers and other writers tended to assume that all SMO beliefs were highly totalistic systems of assertions (e.g., Wilson 1973, Ch. 3). While it is true that some—perhaps many—SMO belief systems tend to be totalistic, it is also true that many are not, even among SMOs whose beliefs (and actions) are also exemplary (in the sense this term is discussed above). This variation has been documented with special clarity by John Hall in his comparative ethnographic analyses of some two dozen exemplary-oriented communes. In this study, Hall conceives highly totalistic communes as adopting a:

[1] **produced** enactment of their beliefs in that the members sought to realize in their group reality a systematic and comprehensive philosophical scheme from which their commune was derived or deducted. "Daily conduct involves an attempt to live out a coherent, unified and comprehensive system of belief" (1978, 12–13).

Among the groups Hall studied, however, this "produced"—that is, totalistic—belief enactment was but one of *three* that he observed. He refers to the second as simply a:

[2] **natural** enactment, in which people "may subject events to scrutiny, analysis and reinterpretation, but no socially unifying philosophy, system of belief or set of ethics provides collectively
legitimized rules for interpretation of experience" (p. 12). In
"natural enactments" group members are "simply holding out a
vague ideal of communalism, or living together principally as
friends, family, or for convenience" (1988, 690).

Above, I have used the terms and phrases "outlook," "common-sense
outlook" and "attitude of everyday life" to call attention to what Hall
here labels the "natural" cognitive mode of reality construction.

These two degrees of totalistic belief—the produced and the natural—
set the stage for Hall pointing to a third possibility in "cognitive modes
of social enactment," that of

[3] **transcendental** enactment in which "taken-for-granted preconceptions of how the world 'is' and normative statements of how it
'should be' are bracketed or set aside. In such a mystical mod-
ification of attention, consciousness is immersed in immediately
given phenomenal experience prior to meaningful interpretation, belief or ethical assessment" (1978, 13). "As a central group
activity, . . . group participants try to attain a mystical, symbolically transcendent form of consciousness and act in terms of
that 'vision'" (1988, 690).

In the same way that a totalistic/produced belief system is difficult to
grasp and therefore requires an example such as the Unification Church,
the transcendental belief system/mode of cognitive enactment might
seem alien and therefore needs exemplification. Paralleling the fame and
infamy of the totalistic/produced beliefs of the Unification Church
among the new religions of the 1970s were the *transcendental beliefs* of the
saffron-robed and street-corner-chanting devotees called Hare Krishna
or, formally, the International Society for Krishna Consciousness. As
represented by John Hall, chanting the Hare Krishna mantra is the key
activity because

chanting provides transcendence of the everyday lifeworld and entry into
a special world of eternally available timeless consciousness. The devotee
achieved an attention to life which would seem to lie somewhere between
full awakeness and dreaming. . . . The constant repetition of a single
mantra routinizes the stream of consciousness. All moments merge indis-
tinguishably into the same moment. . . . After sufficient chanting, the
mantra becomes thematic in consciousness whether it is actively chanted
or not. It *is* the stream of consciousness. . . . Devotees say the sound
vibrations of repetitious chanting provide access to the "third eye" of

consciousness, "seeing" that is innate and prior to any sensory input. (1978, 76–77)

Hall concretizes these characteristics with a quote from an interview in which he asks a devotee: "What's the attraction of chanting?" The devotee answers:

> Well, once you have the pattern, it allows you to tune into places and sources that are beyond time because they transcend the concept of time. Once you've found the key and been to those places, your mind naturally goes to those places because that's where it is most natural and comfortable. (pp. 76–77)

4. Type of Time Construction. Cross-cutting variations we have examined is variance in how *time* is centrally conceptualized or *constructed* in an SMO. How is time immediately experienced in the "perception, memory and anticipation" of the streams of consciousness of the members (Hall 1978, 11)? Drawing on and modifying Karl Mannheim's ([1929] 1936) treatment of the "utopian mentality" Hall suggests that there are "three distinct modes of cognizing and socially constructing time":

[1] In **diachronic time,** the given moment is experienced as one of a linear succession of moments, and immediately given meaning directs attention to remembered past events and an anticipated future as coordinates which contextualize action. (Hall 1978, 11, emphasis added). [For example, in diachronic time, the communal groups Hall studied] calculate members' labor contributions in terms of objective temporal measurements and either pay them wages or credit them with having fulfilled their labor obligations on the basis of accumulated credits. (Hall 1988, 690)

[2] **Synchronic time** . . . involves the experience of *durée*, or accent on the subjectively experienced immediately given moment in and of itself, without a referencing frame of remembrance or anticipation, and without a linear succession of objectified units of time to order the flow of time. (Hall 1978, 11)

[3] **Apocalyptic time** involves cognition of the last days of a prevailing order—the end of historical time (i.e. societal diachronic time)—giving way to a new, typically timeless world. Though this orientation . . . contain[s] both diachronic and synchronic elements, it is the juxtaposition of these elements in a focus on the end of one epoch and the beginning of another that makes it distinctive. (Hall 1978, 12, emphasis added) [In apocalyptic time, an SMO has] a well developed theory of the end of histo-

ry, in which members consider . . . themselves as existing or paving the way for existence beyond 'this' world, in an exclusive heaven-on-earth of the chosen or saved. (Hall 1988, 690)

Variations in time constructions sometime correlate with but are not the same as the previous variations I have reviewed. The fact of *some* correlation does, though, allow me to use the SMO cases described above also to illustrate differences in time constructions. Thus:

- Diachronic time tends to be the time construction of "outlooks," "the attitude of everyday life," or "natural" modes of cognition.
- Synchronic time tends to be the time construction of the transcendental cognitive mode of constructing reality, as in the Hare Krishna.
- Apocalyptic time tends to be the time construction of highly totalistic or "produced" SMOs, as exemplified by the Unification Church.

The phrase "tends to be" is crucial in each of these examples. This is because *some* groups exhibit *other* combinations of these variables, as in, for example, having both a "produced" (totalistic) construction of reality and an apocalyptic construction of time. Indeed, a good part of Hall's analyses of communes traces out such "discrepant" combinations of variations in beliefs. [In that tracing, the produced/apocalyptic combination is, for example, the "other-worldly sect," which is one of five main ideal types (Hall 1978, 1988).]

5. Degree Nihilistic.   In one sense, SMO beliefs stride out on the existential plains of the universe in daring to say that mainstream reality is not the only "real" reality or that it is not "really real." Most often, this striding on those existential plains is not likely striding at all but timid tiptoeing, mild and cautious adversarial probing (it is, that is, "mundane"). Nonetheless, some SMO explorers do exuberantly bound into new universes of meaning. They leap into the vertigo of alternative realities, and they voyage on the expansive space oceans of the cosmic void, pressing for cognitive possibilities beyond the limits of known constructions of reality.

In so questing for new worlds of meaning, in the sheer reasoning calculus of the matter such seekers come upon the logical possibility that life has no meaning. All reality is constructed; therefore, all constructions are arbitrary; and, indeed, they are all oppressive and harmful. Therefore, "existence is senseless and useless" and "social conditions warrant destruction," the quoted phrases being dictionary definitions of the idea of *nihilism*—the enchanting and horrifying realization of the void available to every assiduous movement voyager.

Like many other matters, nihilism is a variable, a construction of reality that can be more or less present, and it is associated with some more than other of the variations in SMO beliefs that I have reviewed above. Two such associations are of special note, those with the *transcendental* cognition of reality (Section B.3) and those with the *synchronic* construction of time (Section B.4). With regard to the former, if human society and life are meaningless as reckoned by the numerically more common "natural" and "produced" cognitive constructions, transcendental immersion in mystical or cosmic vision opens the door to nihilism—to the vertigo of meaninglessness—although not yet fully going through that door. And regarding the latter, diachronic and apocalyptic constructions of time can be eschewed in favor of synchronic time, a stress on "the subjectively experienced immediately given moment" (Hall 1978, 11). Synchronic time, too, opens the door to nihilism in its rejection of any "referencing frame of remembrance or anticipation" (p. 11).

Transcendental cognition joined with synchronic time creates an extremely *individuated mind-set* that in *some* constructions within it results in the "rejection of *all belief systems*" in the sense of rejecting "any system of norms or rules (external to the individual) for guiding human behavior" (Carter 1990, 259, emphasis in the original). Lewis Carter argues that such a construction developed in the Rajneesh movement, an SMO that flourished in the 1980s and was most noted for its conflicts with the local people of eastern Oregon over its "colonies"—especially the city of Rajneeshpuram—and other ventures.

Like some other SMOs, Rajneesh taught the necessity to "throw off" the fettering and corrupting reality constructions of society and to become a "new person" in search of "peace" and "bliss," a process featuring varied exercises that promoted transcendental cognition and synchronic time construction. But unlike other SMOs in which such "throwing off" of the corrupting is replaced with a new system of social ethics and conduct, Rajneesh provided "no *new* belief system" (Carter 1990, 261, emphasis in the original).

The upshot was an SMO without a moral order, without an ethical scheme that guided social relations and organization. Since moral orders were regarded as arbitrary and without any rightful claim on the individual, organization and decision-making both within the SMO and in relations with outsiders were marked by arbitrariness, coerciveness, authoritarianism, and amoral manipulation—these being the only ways left to make decisions and to organize enterprises. In particular, transcendental cognition and synchronic time rendered *consistency* in decision-making and in personal character irrelevant. What one "says today in the moment is true but its opposite may be true in the next moment" and, as Carter observes, "this stance precludes analysis, criticism, and negotiation." Indeed, Rajneesh denied that "reality is knowable through negotiation (with agreed-upon rules), but rather point[ed] to a Diony-sian wisdom, a subjective 'knowing' " (p. 268). Regarding personal char-acter, the very concept of character itself had "been dropped along with the prior socialization" that created it. Therefore, a Rajneesh felt no need to speak or act consistent with her or his prior speech or action and, Carter relates, "rejection of consistency and chronicity (time sequence) means that it [was] difficult to converse with [members] concerning motives and intentions" (p. 269).

The form and degree of nihilist beliefs embraced by the Rajneesh was expressed in violating a wide range of local, state, and national laws (as well as in violating many customs of civil and respectful interaction). Authorities at all these levels of government mobilized law enforcement measures that, by the late 1980s, ran the SMO into virtual extinction (or at least out of eastern Oregon) (Carter 1990).

Nihilistic tendencies may be especially associated with mind-sets that feature transcendental cognition and synchronic time, but such tenden-cies are not confined to them. In particular, some forms of strong *apoca-lyptic* SMO beliefs may be prone to nihilistic directions under conditions such as extreme external duress. At least, a turn of this sort is often suggested with regard to the famous mass suicide/homicide events that punctuated Jim Jones's Jonestown (Hall 1987) and David Koresh's Branch Davidians. In those episodes, the possibility of much more homicide than suicide does not gainsay the sense of nihilism that seem clearly also to have been present at least among key leaders.

6. Combinations of Existential Variations. Using the above or other variations as points of reference, researchers seek to formulate particular combinations of them as (1) derived generic patterns or as (2) profiles of specific cases.

(1) With regard to derived generic patterns, Aberle, for example, elab-orates pattern (2) in the amount and locus of change typology—total change of structure (Section III.A)—as having several "constant charac-teristics." The *transformative* social changes envisioned are:

> 1. *imminent and cataclysmic*—to begin soon and to be completed speedily. . . .
> 2. *teleological* . . . in the sense that the transformation is viewed as des-tined, willed by God, or the outcome of entelechous forces. . . . The trans-formation [is] part of God's total plan . . . , or, in the case of . . . secular movements, . . . the product of such forces as evolution, the dialectic process, the long course of history, the destiny of the race, and so on. . . .

> 3. *led by charismatic figures*—those who regard themselves and are regarded by their followers as in touch with superior forces or has having superior knowledge of the forces of destiny. . . .
> 4. *[furthered by] increased social or spatial segregation* of [SMO] members from the larger society [in] an effort to withdraw energy from the larger society . . . so as to will, or to work for the transformation. (adapted from Aberle 1982, 318–19)

Some versions of this complex of transformative beliefs have otherwise been termed *apocalyptic*, as described above, or *millenarian*.

(2) While perhaps most commonly embodied in supernatural or religious ideologies in which supernatural forces of good and evil do cosmic battle, there are also secular varieties of the above pattern, of which James Rhodes has argued that the National Socialism of Adolph Hitler is a very notable instance.[7] Rhodes pictures this generic apocalyptic or "millennial consciousness" as composed of six themes or beliefs:

1. Believers view life as a catastrophe or *disaster* and see themselves as its victims.
2. A sudden *revelation* has explained their sufferings and promises release or salvation from hardships.
3. This revelation unmasks the previously concealed existence of a *demonic conspiracy* that causes their suffering and that surrounds them with secret agents that lead society into cooperating with its own downfall by "succumbing to clever temptations" laid in its path (Rhodes 1980, 29).
4. The believers have "been chosen to fight and defeat the wicked forces, thereby saving themselves and the world from satanic afflictions" (p. 29). The believers are *the elect* who have a "sacred mission to battle the conspiracy" (Brink 1982, 483).
5. The forces of evil and their minions are "preparing to administer coups de grace to the good" and the eschatological *battles of Armageddon are at hand*. The believers must therefore "rise up and eliminate evil from the earth by smashing [it] in short, titanic wars" (Rhodes 1980, 30).
6. The believers will be victorious in this eschatological war and establish a new order of being or *"paradise on earth"* (Brink 1982, 484).

As can be seen in looking back over the existential variations described above, this particular millenarian belief system is an amalgam of several of those variations, namely, of high *totalism*, a *produced* cognitive mode, and an *apocalyptic* construction of time (cf. Walzer 1974).

C. Mundane Variations

Having now traveled to some of the further—more existential—reaches of variations in SMO beliefs, let us come back to milder and more mundane ways in which SMO beliefs have been identified as varying.

1. Substantive and Institutional Content. Historically, researchers focused on providing generalized characterizations of beliefs in terms of the larger, *substantive* "camp" or category into which instances fit. Thus, in his 1951 treatise, *Social Movements*, Rudolf Heberle classifies and discusses in some detail "the ideas in social movements" using the categories of:

- liberalism
- communism
- socialism
- anarchism
- conservatism
- fascism

Heberle's analysis includes major variations on each of these, most notably the Marxist and Leninist variations on socialism and communism (Heberle 1951, Part 1).[8]

In this same vein but broadened out from the political realm, beliefs can be characterized in terms of the *institutional realm* to which they may primarily refer. Such institutional realm classification assumes, though, that the beliefs are framed so that they apply only or primarily to a specific realm. This is often true, but it is also true that many belief systems (such as those mentioned above, e.g., liberalism, fascism) are sweeping in character and make assertions about most or *all* institutional realms. Indeed, many beliefs framed for a specific institutional realm will tend to be (or under pressure to be) *expansive* and thus range into other realms.

With this proviso in mind, the following is a working formulation of institutional realms together with an example of a specific SMO belief—in the context of the current U.S. mainstream—found in each.

> **economic:** the government should run the economy
> **political:** abolish governments
> **religious:** God will end the world soon
> **social class:** tax the rich out of existence
> **ethnicity:** race is the most fundamental human difference and some races are superior to others
> **gender:** prohibit abortion, keep women at home
> **age:** children should all have the same rights as adults

family/intimate relations: gay/lesbian marriages should have the same legal and social standing as other marriages

education: abolish the public schools

crime and justice: legalize all drugs, abolish prisons

health and health care: give mainstream standing to holistic health approaches

media: abolish television

military: abolish the armed forces

natural environment: *Homo Sapiens* is a violent, out of control species that is destroying itself and human extinction is a good thing

built environment: abolish the automobile, stop suburbanization

Classification of SMO beliefs in substantive or institutional ways serves to locate them in social space, so to speak, but for recent social researchers, this is only a first and not yet very analytic step. Indeed, in recent decades sheer substance or institutional realm per se has been of little interest to researchers, oddly enough. (They have focused, instead, on other of the variations I report—or have ignored beliefs altogether and focused on organization.)

2. Aggregate versus Adversary Frames. Using the terminology of "frames" rather than of beliefs (but about beliefs nonetheless), William Gamson distinguishes two ways in which an SMO insurgent reality can conceptualize the nature of problems faced and who is responsible for them—the *target* of remedial action:

[1. **Aggregate:**] Some groups attempt to mobilize their constituents with an all-inclusive "we." We are the world, humankind, or, in the case of domestic issues, all good citizens. Such an aggregate turns the "we" into a pool of individuals rather than a potential collective actor. The call to action is personal—for example, to make peace, hunger or the environment one's own responsibility. . . . Framing the target as an abstraction—hunger, pollution, war, poverty, disease—makes invisible both the "we" and the "they" involved. If pollution is the problem and we are all polluters, then "we" are "they" and neither agent or target is a collective actor. . . .

[2. **Adversary:**] In adversarial frames, in contrast, "we" and "they" are differentiated rather than conflated. [These frames thus] have the advantage of [facilitating a sense of injustice]. Only an injustice frame . . . taps the righteous anger that puts fire in the belly and iron in the soul. It is what cognitive psychologists call a "hot cognition"—one laden with emotion. . . . An injustice frame calls attention to a group of motivated human actors who carry some of the onus for bringing about harm and suffering. By defining a "they" who are responsible and can change things, adversarial frames supply the target for indignation and action in a way that aggregate frames cannot. Vague and abstract definitions of the target diffuse indignation and make it seem foolish. An adversarial frame [in contrast, supplies] both a "we," who can act as an agent of change, and a "they" who are responsible for injustice and can be called to account. (Gamson 1995, 13)[9]

Gamson frames his discussion of this variation as a "dilemma," as a "damned if you do and damned if you don't" circumstance. For, while there are definite advantages to targeting "motivated human actors," there are also some "serious disadvantages"—or at least some fairly common emergent problems and consequences for SMOs (Gamson 1995, 13).

3. Vilification. One of these problems or consequences, Gamson suggests, is that "many collective actions involve doing something disruptive, embarrassing, or harmful to the target. To enable such actions, one must remove this adversary, at minimum, from the universe of obligation that extends to one's supporters and neutral third parties. 'They' have forfeited their right to dignity and respect—and sometimes even to life integrity rights—through their perpetration or complicity in injustice. . . . Hence, it is quite possible for adversarial frames to create new victims in the name of overcoming past injustices" (Gamson 1995, 14).

While this seems clearly an inherent *tendency* in adversarial beliefs, it is also a *variable* and SMO belief systems differ in the degree to which they portray their opponents or antagonists and nonmembers as *villains*, as persons who are in their beings evil and who must as treated accordingly. As formulated by Turner and Killian (1972, 240ff.; 1987, 217ff.), this variation is composed of a number of dimensions in terms of which degrees of vilification can be gauged:

[1] What is the degree to which people outside the SMO are sharply divided into friends versus foes? To what degree are outsiders neither of these, but, rather, viewed as neutral, perplexed, or simply ignorant? Folk SMO slogans associated with more extremely polarized categorizations of outsiders include "if you are not part of the solution, you are part of the problem" and "he who is not for me is against me."

[2] What is the degree to which "the enemy is viewed as wholly devoid of redeeming qualities"? (Turner and Killian 1972, 240). In more extreme vilification and as formulated by Turner and Killian, "characterizations of the enemy exhibit fairly standard features. . . .

First, the enemy's motivation is simple and not [a] mixture of sometimes reinforcing and sometimes contradictory impulses. . . .

Second, the enemy's attitudes are not measurable as degrees on a continuum but are polarized. . . .

Third, the enemy's normal practice is deception with respect to real intentions, attitudes, and motives. Hence it is acceptable and even required to discount the enemy's reasonable actions and to take occasional reprehensible actions as indications of the real person. To provoke the enemy into finally abandoning any reasonable and genteel facade is simply to expose a deeper reality" (Turner and Killian 1972 240; 1987, 218).

In intensely vilifying belief systems, "the enemy is inherently perfidious, insolent, sordid, cruel, degenerate, lacking in compassion, and enjoys aggression for its own sake. Everything [the enemy] does tends to be interpreted in the most unfavorable light. If one's comrades retreat in the face of formidable opposition, they are making strategic withdrawal; if the enemy does the same thing, he [or she] is a coward. If one's comrades fight on under such circumstances, they are credited with great courage; should the enemy do the same thing, he [or she] is dismissed as a fanatic" (Shibutani 1970, 226).

[3] In such a context, what is the degree to which there is "preoccupation with loyalty . . . and virtue" among SMO members and leaders? (Turner and Killian 1987, 218). The internal reverberations of strong vilification of opponents can be "anxious preoccupation" with the loyalty of one's associates. In more intense versions, "anyone who questions or criticizes the goals, the ideology, and even the capability of the in-group [is likely to] be charged with disloyalty" (Turner and Killian 1987, 218).

Historically, lesser degrees of vilification have been associated with substantive belief systems of *nonviolence*, which stress the diversity and mix of motivations of people outside an SMO, the essential goodness and redeemability of all humans, and condemnation of *actions* rather than of *persons* (Holmes 1990; Sharp 1973). Indeed, Gamson refers to this "Gandhian tradition of *satyagraha* and *ahimsa*" as "the most serious and sustained effort to deal with [the dilemma of] how to tap the mobilizing power of righteous indignation without directing it in ways that create a 'they' who is outside the universe of obligation of life integrity rights" (1995, 14).

(Treating vilification as a way in which SMO belief systems vary is, of course, entirely different from the treating the empirical question of the actual degree to which the opponents of an SMO do, in fact, exhibit villainous features.)

*   *   *

These, then, are some of the more existential and more mundane ways in which social researchers have identified variations in SMO beliefs. Such variations are useful to researchers in getting an initial conceptual purchase on any new SMO they encounter. With the new instance at hand, researchers ask, How does it show up on each of these (or yet other) variations? The resulting profile of the beliefs composed of where the SMO falls along the above dimensions of variation helps researchers locate the case in social space, so to speak, and thus be better able to relate it to other cases that it may be like or *unlike*.

It can also be the case that the beliefs of the SMO at hand seem not to be adequately captured by any already reported variation. In that event, researchers set about trying to articulate what it is about the beliefs of the SMO under scrutiny that requires identification of a *new* variation in order properly to capture it. It is such perplexity, indeed, that has given rise to the inventory of variations I have presented above (and to others rostered in note 5 of this chapter).

IV. QUESTIONS AND ANSWERS ABOUT
VARIATIONS IN SMO BELIEFS

Beyond accurate characterization—answers to the question, What is the aspect's type?, specifically, What are SMO beliefs?—there are the *other seven generic questions* that researchers ask. Now that the "dependent variable" is before them, they can go on to ask questions of frequency, magnitude, structures, processes, causes, consequences, and strategies (the generic questions explained in Section II.B. of Chapter 3).

Answering all these questions with regard to every variation in SMO belief is obviously a large undertaking and one that is beyond the scope of this guide. In the present context, I will review materials relating to only three questions: causes of SMO beliefs in general; causes of one specific variation in them; and one effect of a specific variation in them.

A. Causes of SMO Beliefs

The first of these questions is: What are causes of SMO beliefs as a general class? This question is often combined or merged with the question of "what are causes of SMOs?" (the central question of Chapter 7). For some purposes this collapsing or merging is fine in that an answer to one question is also an answer to the other.

But collapsing or merging the two questions can also result in disattending the sources of the specially ideational content of SMOs. In order to achieve this more specific understanding, we must keep the two questions separate. So focused, the causal question can be rendered, What are the sources of given SMO beliefs? From where do they come? Why are the SMO beliefs *these* beliefs and not some others that are logically possible or plausible contenders in the context?

In the second edition of their classic text on *Collective Behavior* Ralph Turner and Lewis Killian have offered an enduring and comprehensive answer to this question. Their answer proposes five classes of variables as each in part identifying sources of SMO beliefs.

[1] Far from being wholly novel creations, [SMOs] draw heavily upon themes in the *traditional culture*. . . . Every culture is a storehouse so replete with diverse ideas that to increase the emphasis on some at the expense of others . . . can supply the justification and direction or restructuring society.

[2] [SMOs] rely especially on the world view of the class or other social segment of that constitutes the [SMO's] prime constituency. [In addition to social class as a *subculture world*] regional and ethnic traditions have played a great . . . part in supplying [SMO beliefs]. [For example,] the constitutive ideas for the abolition . . . and the woman suffrage movement in the United States were congenial with the regional culture of the industrial Northeast but antithetical to the Southern plantation view. . . .

[3] In some respects the [SMO's beliefs] may be in contrast to the established values, according to the theory of the dialectical process [in which SMOs] formulate their [beliefs] as contrast conceptions to established ideas. [In this *dialectical contrast*] dissatisfaction with the present generates an image of its opposite when life would be as idyllic as it is now tragic. [For example,] the theme of the upside-down class system recurs from the early Christian declaration that "Many that are first shall be last; and the last first." . . .

[4] It is well established that [SMOs] come in clusters that share elements of ideology and pursue closely related and mutually sup-

portive goals, leading us to speak of *general movements* as a major source of [SMO beliefs. A] general movement is . . . a social trend and a mass preoccupation with certain values, which is both reflected in and facilitated by specific [SMOs]. [General movements redirect attention from narrower SMO conditions and] to broader changes in the culture and in the social structure. Thus, the ideas incorporated into the woman suffrage movement did not have their origin uniquely in the situation of women but in the wider transformation of society that generated a broad value of humanitarianism.

[5] [SMOs] respond to the *focal problems of an era,* so that the issues of one generation's movements are not those of the next generation's movements. [The focal problems of an era are the broader background that condition general movements and are social changes] that create problems of an unusually fundamental and pervasive sort for a population segment. [Historically, the focal problems of eras have often involved] readjustments among social classes [but other kinds of changes can create different focal problems, as in economic depressions, a "pig in the python" demographic structure, massive immigration, extensive internal migration, and first- to third-world capital flight.] (Adapted from Turner and Killian 1972, 278–84, emphases added)

B. Causes of Selected Variations in SMO Beliefs

The five variations I label "existential variations" in Section III.B of this chapter range along a master variation of being "less" to "more" radical in revising mundane, disjointed, situational human coping. In different ways, each of them rejects more muddling-through, tentative, situationally devised ways of conceiving and acting toward successions of situations. Thus:

- Exemplary beliefs, when acted on, tend to be more radical in the above sense than adversary ones.
- "Totalistic" belief systems are, indeed, systematic rejections of mere muddling-through "outlooks" (that is, "the common-sense attitude" or the "attitude of everyday life").
- Transcendental and produced cognitive modes are more epistemologically daring than "natural" ones.
- Apocalyptic and synchronic time constructions involve more systemic cognitive effort than diachronic time constructions.

- Nihilistic constructions of the amoral character of all social orders are more ontologically breathtaking than belief in moral
  obligation.
- Transformative and redemptive beliefs (including their apocalyptic
  and millenarian versions) are more sweepingly comprehensive
  than reformative and alterative ones.

The *generic* causal question researchers pose about one or more of
these variations in degrees of radicalness is, What is the aspect's causes?
In this case, the "aspect" is the variable "degree of radicalness" in the
varied senses just enumerated.

One more specific formation of the generic question of causes is,
therefore, What are the causes of more radical beliefs, of such more
radical realities constructions that challenge a mainstream reality? And
each of the several versions of radicalness can be substituted in this
question, as in, for example, What are the causes of highly totalistic
versus less totalistic beliefs?

A good deal of effort has gone into answering these questions, much
of which overlaps with the central question of Chapter 7, When do
SMOs form?—and with the yet broader question, What are the causes of
social movements, or of social movements of particular types? Because
of this overlap, we will encounter elements of answers to these questions in Chapter 7 and I therefore will not report those parts here.
Instead, let me provide a summary of propositions researchers have
developed that are particularly attuned to the degree of radicalness of
belief.

These accounts divide into (1) those that point to more macroscopic
matters of large historical and structural changes in society as distinguished from (2) those focusing on more meso- and microscopic factors
at the level of individuals and face-to-face interaction.

1. Macrocauses. Reviewing the research of Frederick Engels, Karl
Mannheim ([1929] 1936), and Norman Cohn (1961) on these matters,
John Hall provides this statement of conducive causal macrohistorical or
structural conditions of more radical beliefs (or what he terms
"countercultures"):

A sociohistorical model that synthesizes their views suggests that
[1] rapid social and economic change creates a situation in which
[2] certain people, marginal to the established order,
[3] perceive glaring inadequacies in previous "recipes" and legitima-
tions concerned participation in the social order.

[4] Under these conditions, people who seek survival or a new meaningful relation to the world form groups under the aegis of one
or another utopian vision [i.e., radical belief]. Whether these
visions be secular or religious, they may be said to be prophetic
in so far as they promise this-worldly or other-worldly salvation
based on new missions. (Adapted from Hall 1978, 7)

The variables of "rapid social change," "marginality," perceived "glaring inadequacies" central to this answer—and yet other variables—are
taken up in more detail in Chapter 7, on the causes of SMOs.

2. Mesomicrocauses.   Moving in closer to the kind of macrohistorical
circumstance Hall summarizes immediately above as conducive to invention of SMO beliefs, Rodney Stark and William Bainbridge have
proposed the three mesomicroscopic variables[10] of (1) psychopathology,
(2) entrepreneurship, and (3) subculture development as variously often
involved in "how and why individuals invent or discover" in particular,
"new religious ideas" (1985, 172):

[1] The psychopathology variable highlights the fact that insurgent
realties are *sometimes* "the result of individual psychopathology
that finds successful social expression." In one variation on this
possibility, the inventors "achieve their novel visions during
psychotic episodes. . . . After the episode, the individual will be
most likely to succeed in forming a cult [a new SMO] around his
vision if the society contains many other person suffering from
problems similar to those originally faced by the cult founder, to
whose solution, therefore, they are likely to respond. . . .
Therefore, such cults most often succeed during times of
societal crisis, when large numbers of persons suffer from similar unresolved problems" (p. 174; cf. Hall, summarized just
above).
[2] The entrepreneur variable focuses on the fact that some new SMO
systems of beliefs are successfully marketed and profitable
product packages that their inventors and salespersons modify
over time in order to maximize market acceptance and penetration. Some are the "cultural equivalent of recombinant DNA
genetic engineering. Essentially the innovator takes the cultural
configuration of an existing cult, removes some components,
and replaces them with other components taken from other
sources" (Stark and Bainbridge 1987, 183; Bainbridge 1984).
[3] The psychopathology and entrepreneur variables "stress the role
of the individual innovator," but the subcultural development
variable "emphasizes group interaction processes. It suggests

and it points out that even radical development can be achieved through many small steps. [In this pattern,] a few intimately interacting individuals [over time] become relatively encapsulated [and] once separated to some degree from external social control, the evolving cult develops and consolidates a novel culture, energized by the need to facilitate the exchange of rewards and compensators, and inspired by essentially accidental factors" (Stark and Bainbridge 1987, 183).

Stark and Bainbridge stress that these are three *compatible* variables: "Any pair, or even all three [can] combine validly to explain the process of innovation that [has] produced a given" new SMO, especially one featuring religious beliefs (p. 173).

C. Effects of Selected Variations in SMO Beliefs

Continuing to focus on "degree of radicalness" as one underlying meaning of each of the seven variables, let us now conceive it as an *independent variable*, as something that might be among the *causes* of other things. (In contrast, just above it is treated as a *dependent* variable, as an *effect* for which we seek to specify causes.)

One way to state the consequences question is, What effects do varying degree of radicalness have on other matters? The tricky part of this question is, of course, what do you mean by "other matters"? *What* other matters? The answer is that there are an enormous number of possible and legitimate "other matters." Many of them were enumerated as "aspects" in Chapter 3 (Section II.A) and they are listed in the left-hand column of Figure 3.3, the aspect-question matrix. Among the fourteen aspects listed in Figure 3.3, let me report one proposition each for the "aspect" of the SMO itself taken as a whole (second on the list, labeled "organization") and "members" (third on the list).

1. One major question about the SMO as a unit concerns its structure—which is generic question (4), What is the aspect's structure? As we shall see in the next chapter, SMO structures vary in many ways and one major dimension of their variation is the degree to which they are democratic versus oligarchic, autocratic, or authoritarian. How might the variable of degree of radicalness be related to the degree to which an SMO is democratic versus autocratic? Or, cast in consequences or effects terms:

What effects do nonradical versus radical beliefs have on SMOs being democratic versus autocratic in organization?

The tentatively held propositional answer to this consequences question is:

♦ The more radical the beliefs (in one or more of the several senses described above), the more likely that the SMO will be autocratically organized.

The qualifying phrases "tentatively held" and "more likely" are critical in thinking about the truth or falsity of this proposition or the circumstances in which it may be true or false. This is because (1) our data are imperfect, (2) the concepts themselves are subject to shifting and contentious operationalization in specific cases, and (3) we know of cases where the proposition, as stated, does not accurately describe the reality (e.g., Rothschild and Whitt 1986). Especially because of this third reason—negative cases exist—virtually all propositional answers describe only *trends* and *tendencies* for which there are acknowledged exceptions. (A great many such exceptions, though, cast doubt on the proposition itself. But negative cases that are simply exceptions to the general trend call forth efforts to specify the special conditions under which there are exceptions.)

Assuming that this belief-organization proposition is reasonably accurate, there is then, of course, the need to figure out *why* such a relation might obtain. What are the causes of certain forms of radical beliefs being associated with autocratic organization? When is the proposition more true and less true? The short answer is: If you know what the truth is, what is there to be democratic about? Just DO IT! This is obviously a flip short answer (with a core of truth), and I will report more elaborate answers in the next chapter.

2. What effects might certain kinds of radical beliefs have on participants? Pertinent aspects of participants include their *self-conceptions*—their constructions of "who" they are, why they are alive, and what they are doing. Among other ways, self-conceptions vary in terms of the *degree of certainty and sense of mission and purpose* about the meaning and goals of everyday action and life itself that the beliefs provide. These senses of certainty and mission are themselves productive of a high sense of *satisfaction with being alive*.

Linking radicalness of beliefs to this self-conception variable, the proposition is:

♦ The more radical the beliefs, the stronger the participant's sense of cognitive certainly, sense of mission, and associated satisfaction with being alive.

The theory propounded in this proposition is that at least certain forms of radical beliefs provide all-embracing cognitive cocoons that in their sweeping comprehensiveness and finality of understanding make their believers quite happy and happier than believers in less radical beliefs (within limits and other factors being equal, of course).

One interesting source of data on this proposition comes from the experiences of *ex-believers* in radical systems. Based on interviews with ex-believers in several such systems, Norman Skonovd reports that many experience a "definite longing for" these aspects of their former self-conception even while at the same time expressing hatred for the now rejected beliefs (Skonovd 1981, 176). Some "admit that they would love to return, but have come to value the freedom and integrity which comes from an autonomous existence" (p. 176).

This report by an ex-believer in the radical beliefs of the Unification Church describes this longing and is further helpful for the explicit contrast she draws between the "outlook" or "muddling through" construction of life and a cognitively radicalized construction:

> Being a person trying to struggle with the complexities of reality—the ambiguities, the unknowns, the knowledge that you're acting without guarantees that your actions are leading toward a more perfected world—I have a profound respect for people who are struggling within that totalistic, simplistic, very alluring world in which you have a sense of total rightness— . . . where you know that what you are doing is right. . . .
>
> I mean, to me, it's much more difficult to live in the world than it is to live in the [Unification] church. It would be so much easier to go back to the church. I've thought that many times. But it would be dishonest toward what I now really perceive. (Skonovd 1981, 176, emphasis omitted)

Such sweeping cognitive and moral certainty is heady stuff, so heady that some of its ex-imbibers have even likened it, Skonovd reports, to "a drug addict's craving for the euphoric high of opiates." Another former member of the Unification Church interviewed by Skonovd was quite explicit:

> I just have to restrain myself because it would be very easy for me to fall into another group or religion. . . . It's like being a drug addict. Even now, even though I know how wrong it is, there'll be moments when I just long to be with people like that again. . . .
>
> You know it's bad for you, but you long for it—you, know, the certainty, the truth. *Can you imagine just to know the truth? To know exactly why you're here. To know the purpose of everything?* . . .
>
> I can see I have that need but I want to fulfill it in a different way. (Skonovd 1981, 176–77, emphasis in the original and some emphasis omitted)

In a different framing of the above proposition, *some* SMO belief systems might be thought of as providing *adventures*, as creating involvements marked by the features Georg Simmel adduces in his generic delineation of "the adventure":

- an experience that is in marked contrast with everyday life,
- that is conceived as having a sharp beginning and end,
- that involves the possibility of great loss or great gain,
- which is thought of as highly significant, and
- is intense in its emotional engagement in that it "gathers all passions into itself" (Simmel 1959, 248).

V. THE BROADER CONTEXT OF BELIEFS: CULTURE

Beliefs are central to understanding SMOs and therefore in need of the explicit treatment I have accorded them. But they are also but one component of the SMO's broader and larger ideational and cognitively meaningful content. This "broader and larger ideational content" is often referred to as the *culture* of the SMO, the complex of positively cathected valued ends or purposes of life, norms, physical objects, memories or stories, occasions, social roles, member styles of interaction ("persona"), and other accoutrements of ideas and action that form the SMO's "lifeway." In the same manner that we speak of societies, ethnic groups, and other formations as embodying culture, SMOs manifest one or another degree of culture.[11]

A. Culture As Collective Identity

The topic of culture is also often spoken of as (or in relation to) the topic of *collective identity*, a concept defined as "the shared definition of a group that derives from members' common interests, experiences, and solidarity" (Taylor and Whittier 1992, 105). Or, "[t]he collective identity of [an SMO] is a shorthand designation announcing a status—a set of attitudes, commitments, and rules for behavior—that those who assume the identity can be expected to subscribe to [and] an individual announcement of affiliation, of connection with others" (Friedman and McAdam 1992, 157; see also Nagel 1994).

Stressing the need to separate the individual and cultural levels in researching collective identity, Gamson observes that

> the locus of collective identity is cultural; it is manifested through the language and symbols by which it is publicly expressed. We know a collec-

tive identity through the cultural icons and artifacts displayed by those who embrace it. It is manifested in style of dress, language, and demeanor. Collective identity need not be treated as some mysterious intangible but can be as empirically observable as a T-short or a haircut. To measure it one would ask people about the meaning of labels and other cultural symbols, not about their own personal identity. (1992b, 60)

B. What Is the Magnitude of SMO Culture?

Among the eight generic questions researchers ask about culture, I want here to focus on number (3) on that list, What is the aspect's magnitude?[12] In case study perspective, the research specification of this question is, What is the magnitude of an SMO's culture?

By "magnitude" of SMO culture I mean the *amount or degree* of it that we find in an SMO. So viewed, culture is a *variable*, a something that some SMOs have more of than do others.

1. Dimensions of Extent. Conceived formally (as distinct from specific content), and thinking in terms of *enumeration* or counting units of culture, these are more specific dimensions of cultural extent within which units can be counted:

1. SMOs vary with respect to the degree that their participants agree on or *share* the same complex of cultural items, be these items that are distinctive to the SMO or not. This is the question of cultural diversity versus consensus within an SMO.
2. Holding aside (or "constant") cultural agreement or sharing, SMOs vary in terms of the number or proportion of their cultural items that are *distinctive* to it. At one extreme, the SMO elaborates a wide range of distinctive cultural items; at the other, participants are almost culturally indistinguishable from other members of society.
3. Like beliefs, cultures can be quite narrow or situation-specific in *scope* or quite wide, specifying, for example, appropriate beliefs and actions for every conceivable circumstance and topic.
4. Within a particular category of cultural item, there is variation in degrees of *elaboration* or complexity.
5. Some forms of culture—particularly items of material culture— vary in terms of their sheer numbers or the *quantity* in which they are produced, a matter related to complexity but not the same as it.
6. Specific items of culture and the array of cultural matters differ in the degree to which members emotionally and positively experience them as expressing or embodying their values and life

circumstances, as providing occasions of transcending the mundane in *expressive symbolism* (Jaeger and Selznick 1964).

These six dimensions (and others we might use) allow researchers to chart degrees of movement culture, to assess the extent to which (and ways in which) an SMO is "doing culture." SMOs tending to higher quantitative values on these dimensions are—in a noninvidious and technical sense—"more cultured," "culturally rich," or "culturally developed." SMOs that are "lower" in these respects are "less cultured," "culturally poor," or "culturally undeveloped."

2. Social Locations of Culture.   Informed by these dimensions of extent, there is then the question of where exactly to look in assessing the degree of the presence of each. Among other possible locations, let me draw attention to six very basic ones:

1. Expressions of general *values* that the SMO seeks to realize.
2. Physical *symbolic objects* and associated iconic personages that are held in high public esteem in an SMO.
3. Everyday *stories* told and retold with strong positive or negative emotional expression among participants in an SMO.
4. Characteristics of the SMO's *occasions* (gatherings) that are regarded as positive features of it.
5. Social *roles* that specialize in the creation and dissemination of ideas, artifacts, and performances endowed with positive value.
6. Ways in which these specialized and other roles are expressed in the *persona* exhibited by participants.

3. Social Locations and Extent.   In the interest of brevity, let me report how extent of culture can be assessed in only three of the above six locations, numbers (2), (4), and (5).[13]

a. Symbolic objects.   In cultural perspective, the symbolic objects of an SMO are all those material items that participants view as physically expressing their enterprise, including remembrances of its successes, traumatic challenges, and hopes for its future. Such objects are of several kinds, three of which are: (i) key artifacts, (ii) symbolic places and (iii) iconic persons.[14]

i. Key artifacts.   Perhaps the most physically cultural way to look at an SMO is simply to inventory the transportable and literal objects that are "part" of it. Such inventories vary across SMOs in terms of their number, their size and weight, market value, distinctiveness, and the like. Presumptively, the higher an SMO's rank on these dimensions (comparatively speaking), the more materialistic it is, as well as the more cultured.

Artifacts divide into those endowed with symbolic value or expressive symbolism by participants and those regarded as mere neutral instruments. In being symbolic or "expressive," participants emotionally experience the artifact (or whatever) as portraying their deepest felt commitments, aspirations, hopes, and noblest sentiments. By definition, highly expressive cultural matters prompt emotional experiences that are described with words such as poignant, spiritual, touching, invigorating, and enlivening. Artifacts or other matters *lacking* in expressive symbolism are labeled with such terms as vacuous, dull, empty, and dead.[15]

A key matter is therefore to scrutinize the artifacts observed on the bodies of participants, brought to their gatherings, and found at places of SMO habitation is in terms of which if any are fondly regarded (i.e., have symbolic significance). Prime prosaic candidates for such regard include posters from past campaigns, particular copies of certain books and other publications, unusual souvenirs from past striking events, and pictures of movement people.

ii. Symbolic places.   SMOs vary in the degree to which given spaces or places come to be defined as recalling and expressing "the movement." For a few SMOs, a *single*, particular place gets defined as *the* revered place—the either literal or metaphorical Mecca of the movement. Applying the five dimensions of extent, to what degree are culturally endowed SMO places:

- known to SMO members (shared in the sheer sense of knowledge)?
- the same as or different from revered places in the culture at large (distinctiveness)?
- addressed to a diverse or narrow range of matters of concern in human life (scope)?
- simple or complex (or expensive or inexpensive) in their construction and furnishing (elaboration)?
- abundant versus few in number (quantity)?
- evocative of intense emotional experiences and scenes of public and dramatic emotional display (as in gyrations of joy or torrents of tears) (expressiveness)?

iii. Iconic persons.   The phenomenon of the charismatic leader is the most fully developed case of persons as highly expressive symbolic objects for SMOs. Instances of such symbolic persons in diverse SMOs have included Jesus, Karl Marx, V. I. Lenin, Adolph Hitler, Mao Tse-Tung, and Sun Myung Moon. Among SMOs as a general class though, charismatic personages are rather rare. Instead, selected figures come to be venerated and endowed with symbolic expressiveness without their also being thought to possess extraordinary capacities that transcend normal human limitations (cf. Wilson 1973, Ch. 6). (Charisma is discussed in Section I.D.2 of Chapter 8.)

One important way to begin to gauge the cultural contours of an SMO is to conduct a census of SMO persons who are mentioned publicly with some frequency and referred to as sources of authoritative or other important enunciations. This list can then be scrutinized in terms of the five dimensions of cultural extent regarding the degree to which these people:

- are known to and revered by participants in the SMO (sharing);
- overlap with revered figures in the larger society (distinctiveness);
- represent diverse institutional realms (scope);
- are subjects of a great deal of or very little symbolic representations (as in hanging their pictures or placing their statues in conspicuous places, distributing writings by and about them) (elaboration);
- are large or small in number when viewed in comparative SMO perspective (quantity);
- stimulate expressive emotional experiences in movement members (expressiveness).

b. Occasions.   The occasions on which SMO participants assemble face-to-face provide many opportunities for richer or poorer cultural enactment. Even gatherings that are instructional or task oriented in character—as opposed to celebrations per se—can vary in the distinctiveness and extent of cultural display. On a virtually global scale, the quintessential form of SMO occasion has become the march/rally. Irrespective of society, culture, or movement, march/rallies exhibit a remarkably similar form that features marchers carrying banners and placards and a parade of speakers from organizations in coalition that are punctuated by "folksy" musical entertainment. One cultural challenge to SMOs in particular and movements more generally is, indeed, to avoid the deadly sameness and repetitiveness of this kind of key event. In recent times, cultural innovation with respect to the march/rally has, in fact, been seen with increasing frequency and these innovations are reasonably viewed as responding to a need for increased degrees of cultural expressiveness (see, e.g., Epstein 1991).

The music sung (or not sung) at movement occasions is always, of course, of particular cultural interest. Similar to the prevalence of the standard march/rally, the song "We Shall Overcome" has become the virtually global and all-purpose movement anthem, sung even in conservative movements despite its leftist origin.

c. Roles. While culture pertains to everyone, "everyone" does not have an equal relation to it or an equal role in its creation, elaboration, preservation, chronicling, performance, or dissemination. Instead, some people are likely to "do" culture much more than others. And SMOs differ in the *degree* to which, in the *variety* with which, and in *numbers* in which people are engaged in such specialized cultural roles. Specialized culture roles themselves divide into those that *create* (and/or elaborate) culture and those that are particularly occupied with *disseminating* it.

i. Creators.   One key category of culture is the ensemble of concepts, assertions, precepts, presumed facts, and other cognitions labeled "knowledge." This body of "knowledge" is mostly created by people who work at that task with continuity and diligence. These are therefore "knowledge workers," otherwise called "intellectuals," "artists," and "scholars." So, too, the products of knowledge workers divide roughly into items that are more "scientific" or "analytic," versus "artistic" or "humanistic." The former are said to produce "thought," "analysis," or "science" while the latter provide "art" or "literature."

Institutions of higher education and journalism, along with the wealth of foundations and individuals, have created an infrastructure on which has risen a social class of intellectuals. Portions of this social class function as the continuing culture creators (and elaborators) of many SMOs. In inspecting an SMO, one basic task is to determine whether or not it even has strata of analytic and/or humanistic intellectuals and to profile each in terms of the six dimensions of cultural extent. In particular, there are these kinds of questions:

- How many people can we say function as analytic or humanistic intellectuals in this SMO?
- Among the analytic intellectuals, how many journals and other publications claim to be doing serious scholarship and seek to engage mainstream intellectuals working on the same topics?
- How productive are the analytic and humanistic intellectuals along such lines as the number of books, journal articles, novels, poems, plays, musical compositions, literary criticisms, and the like that they create in given units of time?
- Using conventional categories of scholarship, what sort of intellectuals do these tend to be (e.g., historians, physicists, economists, theologians, or whatever)?
- What is the general size of the corpus of SMO intellectual materials that these intellectuals have produced over one or more decades?

ii. Disseminators.   While creators of an SMO's culture obviously also disseminate it to a degree, culture is probably most effectively spread when people set about doing it in social roles geared to that objective. There are at least three major sorts of these specialized disseminator roles, not all of which appear with much force in all SMOs (or social movements).

(a.) The creators may produce materials that can be assigned monetary value and offered to a market by *culture retailers*. Given such a supply, we can then ask:

   i.   How many retailers of the SMO's culture are there?
   ii.   What is the scale of their operation?
   iii.   What is the range of their offerings?

(b.) SMO dancers, actors, comedians, musicians, and kindred *artistic performers* in troupe or solo form differ in the degree to which they can make a living from the SMO or must depend on broader audiences. In the recent United States, for example, only a very few SMOs have sustained artistic performers—and these only for brief periods. That is, most of the time, most SMOs tend to be so small that a "movement" performer must "reach out" beyond an SMO in order to make a living.

(c.) *Formal educators* are people who make a living teaching in educational institutions from kindergarten through the most advanced graduate training. The way they earn their livelihood encourages them to be more than normally sensitive to ideas and ideals, to conceptions of the way the world is, what is wrong with it, and how it might and should be changed. We ought therefore not be surprised to discover that the ranks of formal educators are disproportionately populated with activists, participants, fellow travelers, and sympathizers for virtually every SMO— left, right, or whatever. SMOs differ, though, in the degree of their respective strengths among formal educators, including the extent to which educators overtly promote movement ideas and culture in educational activities. For some few SMOs, their ideas and culture have achieved formal curricular recognition and a measure of legitimacy, most especially in post-secondary educational organizations. This is particularly the case for the women's movement, several ethnic movements, the peace movement, and movements of the left.

*   *   *

The above, then, outlines a research path for answering the question of the *magnitude* (the extent) of an SMO's culture.

C. Other Questions and Answers about Culture

While such profiles of cultural extent are interesting in themselves[16] and in comparative SMO perspective, this variation becomes much more interesting when we conjoin it with questions (6) and (7) on the list cf eight generic questions, the questions, that is, of the *causes* of given degrees of cultural extent or development and of the *consequences* of given degrees of extent or development.

Regarding the question of causes, cultural extent is, otherwise stated, a "dependent variable" that changes as a function of other, "independent variables." Why are some SMO cultures much more developed than others? What variations in social contexts and other variables lead some SMOs to have cultures—collective identities—that are differentially developed along a variety of dimensions? For example, certain kinds of *beliefs* may be linked with degrees of culture developments, as in this proposition:

▶ The more totalistic (i.e., sweeping and grandiose) the beliefs of an SMO, the more sweeping and grandiose the culture that SMO leaders and other cultural architects will attempt to generate.

What about the context provided by *other* cultures in which an SMO develops determines what cultural elements will or will not be adopted in a given SMO? Cast in different terms, existing cultures are resources that are differentially accessed by given movements (Nagel 1994). How does this happen and with what consequences for degrees of SMO culture?

Regarding consequences, variation in cultural magnitude or extent is also treated as an "independent variable" by researchers, as among the variables that affect a wide variety of "dependent variables" of central interest in SMO studies. Widely and tentatively accepted propositional answers to this consequences question include:

▶ The greater the degree of cultural development, the higher are participant morale and, therefore, commitment and tenacity in the face of adversity, and retention of movement participants (e.g., Taylor 1989; Kanter 1972, 1973).

▶ The greater the degree of cultural development, the greater are the likelihood of success in SMO campaigns and overall degree of SMO success (e. g. Oberschall 1973, 144).

The qualifying phrase "tentatively accepted" is important in approaching these two propositions because in several not well-specified circumstances these relationships do not obtain. One research task is, indeed, to specify when the above generalizations do and do not hold in specific cases.

*   *   *

We have now examined some questions and answers that researchers bring to the *cognitive content* or beliefs of SMOs. I have treated this topic first among the seven main questions organizing Part II because it ranks, I think, as likely the most fundamental thing we need to comprehend about any SMO—or as at least among the small number of most fundamental things we must initially understand.

But beliefs are hardly all we need to know about. Beliefs imply things about how people can and will *organize* themselves in SMOs, including the possibility that they will not form SMOs at all. These are matters to which we move in Chapters 6 and 7.

NOTES

1. This distinction is explained in Section I.B of the previous chapter.

2. Goffman (1974, 21), as quoted in Snow and Benford (1988, 214, note 3).

3. Snow and Benford shift between seeing these similarities as characteristics and as performing certain functions, that is, between generic questions (1) and (6).

4. Wilson's scheme is also employed in Snow et al. (1986). In addition, Turner and Killian (1987, 278–82) present a series of candidate similarities (called functions) of belief systems, or what they call "value orientations." See also Heberle on a movement's "constitutive ideas" that "usually concern three main problems: (1) . . . final goals . . . (2) . . . ways . . . the goal is to be attained, and (3) . . . justification of the movement" (1951, 24).

5. Among them:

Lakey's (1994) deep structural reading of many SMO beliefs systems as constructed around the "game" roles identified in transactional analysis as victim, persecutor, and rescuer;

Lofland and Richardson's trinity of political, religious, and ego beliefs (Lofland 1985, Ch. 7);

the traditional degree-of-radicalness spectrum, as in, for example, the environmental movement center-to-left sequence of Audubon Society—Sierra Club—Greenpeace—Sea Shepherd—Earth First!;

the vision of hierarchical relations that will obtain in the new order, as in the spectrum of (i) obliteration in assimilation to the mainstream, (ii) categorical convergence (as in gender androgyny), (iii) egalitarian pluralism, (iv) inversion of whatever the categories of hierarchy at issue ("the last shall be first and the first last"), (v) geographical separation or secession, (vi) expulsion, and (vii) genocide.

6. The variations are classic but the terminology here is Aberle's (1982).

7. In the views of other analysts, secular millenarian SMOs have included Leninist Marxism, The Symbionese Liberation Army (Hall 1978), the Charles Manson Family, and numerous Marx-inspired "political sects" (O'Toole 1977).

8. Reviving this practice, Garner's (1996) depiction of movements is organized in terms of eight "ideologies": (1) conservatism, (2) liberalism, (3) "socialism, the new left, and populism," (4) "movements of religious orientation," (5) nationalism, (6) "fascists, nazis, neo-nazis," (7) "feminism, women's movements, movements of sexual orientation," (8) environmental.

9. The distinction between aggregate and adversary frames has also been treated as the difference between "consensus" and "conflict" movements by, among others, Lofland (1993a, Ch. 2) and McCarthy and Wolfson (1992). On the relation between these two sets of paired concepts, see Gamson (1992a, 260).

10. Stark and Bainbridge refer to and treat their three variables as full-blown "models." Consonant with my effort to "deschool" movement study thinking, I have changed the terminology to "variables" (see Section VI of Chapter 13).

11. My treatment of culture in this chapter is abbreviated and revised from Lofland (1995b).

12. This is cell 43 in Figure 3.3, the aspect-question matrix.

13. Discussions of the other three appear in my fuller treatment, Lofland (1995b), which is a chapter in Johnston and Klanderman's *Social Movements and Culture* (1995).

14. Additional categories of symbolic objects are treated in Lofland (1995b).

15. The theoretical framework and rationale for treating "expressiveness" as a variable dimension of culture has been elaborated by Jaeger and Selznick (1964). In the perspective they develop, the "symbolic value" or "expressive symbolism" of culture, arises

> in order to continue and sustain meaningful experience. The wearing of black respects and prolongs the experience of mourning, of confronted death. Festivities rich in symbolism can help consummate an experience that would otherwise be brief and incomplete. In the presence of the symbol, people respond in ways that nurture rather than attenuate the experience. Moreover, having had "an experience," [humans] create a symbol of it in order that the experience may be re-evoked and relived.

*   *   *

> [Expressive] symbols help to provide focus, direction, and shape to what otherwise might disintegrate into chaotic feeling or the absence of feeling. . . . By serving as vehicles of response, symbols can help transform a "mere" feeling, a vague somatic tension, into genuine emotion. Thus symbols do more than sustain emotion. They contribute to the emergence of emotion as a uniquely human attribute. (1964, 662–63).

16. Case studies profiles of different degrees of cultural extent include Lofland (1985, Ch. 9) on the amazingly elaborated culture of the Unification Church and Taylor (1989) on the National Women's Party in the "doldrums."

6

How Are SMOs Organized?

SMOs are a species of more or less formalized human associating, albeit a specialized one because their beliefs challenge mainstream conceptions of reality. SMOs are organizations nonetheless and after first asking about beliefs that make them "movements" (as in Chapter 5), researchers have a prime interest in them *as* organizations. SMOs as holistic organizational entities are thus now the central focus of analysis.

My report on them so viewed is organized into six parts:

I. The same eight generic questions obtain, the first of which is, What is the aspect's type? Specified for SMOs, this question can read, How are SMOs organized? Or using different words, What prominent similarities and differences do researchers observe them exhibiting? In Section I of this chapter, I describe SMO organizational *similarities*, which is a fancy way of saying I will repeat the definition of them given in Chapter 1 and elaborate its elements.

II. With the object of our attention before us, I will then review various organizational ways in which researchers have thought SMOs *vary* significantly.

III. Applying the distinction drawn between "type" and "structure" questions on the list of eight generic questions [numbers (1) and (4)], I will report on analyses that move beyond depiction of a simple "type" as a point on a variable and that render detailed *structural* analyses.

IV. The inventories of variations and structures I give in Sections II and III are, for want of space, only a small selection from a much larger number of also quite important both variables and structures. In acknowledgment of this fact, in Section IV I itemize a number of others.

V. All these variations and structures raise a number of additional questions that I will explore in Section V.

VI.   Finally, I will discuss *financing*, an "aspect" that is closely re-
      lated to organization but is not exactly the same thing.

I. HOW SMOS ARE ORGANIZED: SIMILARITIES

Recall that in Chapter 1 I portrayed marginal or excluded realities as a
generic domain involving four major variables. Variations in these variables allow us to specify eight forms of social realities, most of which are
marginal to or excluded from the mainstream. As summarized in Figure
1.1 of that chapter, one of these eight forms, the *SMO*, displays the
following values on the four variables depicting the larger domain:

1.   The social reality is public and collective.
2.   It is moralistic and idealistic.
3.   It is marginal to or excluded from the societal mainstream.
4.   It is comparatively small in scale but displays continuity and
     organization.

So specified, SMOs are set off from seven other forms, specifically, atomized, covert resistance, criminal groups, political parties, interest
groups, lone proponents, crowd or mass insurgencies, and social movements (Section I.C of Chapter 1).

For purposes of precision, I want now to elaborate on the fourth of
these four variables: scale-continuity-organization. Exactly how large,
continuous, and organized should an entity with the first three features
be in order to merit the appellation SMO? Going by the various entities
researchers have actually studied, the general answer appears to be not
very with regard to size, continuity, and organization. My operational
rule of thumb is that the threshold SMO consists of at least two people
who act together in terms of a shared movement reality on at least two
occasions. That is, two people cooperating twice is the rock bottom in
SMO scale, organization, and continuity. Obviously, the larger the number of cooperators and the number of occasions of their cooperation, the
greater (by definition) the SMO scale, organization, and continuity.

The concepts in this formulation are obviously still not clear in the
sense of strictly operationalized. Thus, what is an "occasion" and what
is "once" versus "twice" or more? Using Gamson's classic Holiday Inn
sessions of goading citizens into challenging unjust authority as empirical points of departure, for example, we might say that Gamson created
one occasion of cooperation that sometimes threatened to become an
SMO when the rebels began to lay plans to meet the next day and in

another location (Gamson, Fireman, and Rytina 1982). Had any rebels so met (Gamson and associates report they managed to stop all of them), at that next meeting they would have been a rudimentary SMO. Generalizing from the Gamson episodes, "two occasions" might be operationally defined as at least two instances of face-to-face assembling that are separated by at least several hours (cf. Best and Luckenbill 1994; Klandermans 1989).

These primal facts of *successive occasions of acting together* create a number of emergent and unavoidable similarities of SMOs, features that are similarities in the sense of matters that any SMO must deal with—problems that must be solved—if there are to be continuing occasions of acting together. Among these similarities or ongoing problems that must be solved are (1) an allocation of tasks in a division of labor, (2) ways of deciding what the tasks will be, (3) ways of deciding who will do what tasks, (4) the raising of resources that finance and otherwise make the tasks possible, (5) maintaining the interest and morale of people performing tasks. Put another way, successive-occasions-of-acting-together is an exceedingly fragile and problematic human project and accomplishment. It is an enterprise that is fraught with all manner of difficulties such as those just enumerated, as well as many others. As organizations, such matters make up the common plight of SMOs—their similarities.

II. HOW SMOS ARE ORGANIZED: DIFFERENCES/VARIATIONS

As in practically every other area of life, SMOs vary in how they organize themselves to deal with their common plight qua organizations. Or, put more broadly, SMOs form an analytic category, but they vary in a great many ways within that category. In the same way I reviewed a number of major variations in beliefs in the previous chapter, I want now to report some major forms of organizational variation.

I begin with differences/variations that are simpler, fundamental, or rudimentary and move to those that are more complex, derived, and sophisticated.

A. Individual-Organizational Members

In a significant but unknown portion of SMOs, the unit of membership is *another organization* rather than the individual person. Thus, the famous Montgomery Improvement Association (MIA)—often consid-

ered the founding SMO of the U.S. civil rights movement of the 1960s—
began as the cooperative effort of a number of African-American
churches in Montgomery, Alabama. The key founding "members" were
representatives of churches—their ministers—who, by their participation, were committing their church congregations to a boycott of the
Montgomery bus system. Like many other *coalitions*, the MIA was an
organization of organizations as the major unit rather than of individual
per se (Branch 1988; Freeman 1983a).

Such coalitional organizations are fragile constructions and tend to
disband after the event or campaign for which they were devised. If they
do survive the termination of the founding, initial task (e.g., a rally) or
campaign (e.g., a boycott), they tend to do so by shifting to individuals
as the unit of membership, a process sometimes involving uneasy coex-
istence with continuing organizational memberships (Kleidman 1993).

B. Fragility and Temporariness of Organization

Even though correlated with "organizations of organizations," *fragility*
and *temporariness* are variables in their own right irrespective of the
organization-individual unit of membership. Even so, more fragile and
temporary SMO organization is often seen in specific, strategic coalitional campaigns directed to achieving proximate objectives, such as in the
MIA example just given.

As efforts that hover between simple strategic activities and solid
SMO existence, leadership and organization are highly problematic. I
have thus characterized fifteen such fragile sit-in SMOs that Michael
Finke and I studied and that used sit-in protest actions at the California
capitol building as:

> tentative, groping, emergently negotiated, and somewhat internally disor-
> ganized, and decentralized in terms of the factions composing the protest
> effort. (Lofland 1985, 311)

Most often, leadership came from a "circle of situationally shifting" persons rather than from *a* leader. And in this circle, "leaders seemed ex-
ceptionally polite to one another—almost gingerly polite" (p. 311).

In an enumeration of the universe of all SMOs that have ever existed,
it may well be that most tend to the more fragile and temporary states of
these two variables.

C. Formalization and Centralization

Formalization as a variable refers to the degree to which an SMO has an
explicit (e.g., written) scheme of organization—a division of labor—that

it strives to enact in its routine activities. *Centralization* refers to the degree to which an SMO's activities are devised and directed by a well-identified SMO-wide leadership as opposed to activities originating and pursued by multiple, relatively independent SMO subgroupings. In theory, these two variables can vary independently, but in practice they tend to be rather strongly correlated. An SMO high on one is likely to be high on the other and vice versa.

Before focusing specifically on SMO variations in these variables, it is important to identify and place to the side a widespread confusion among researchers. This is the tendency to *confuse informal and decentralized SMOs with social movements* (SMs).

SMs are, by definition, composed of multiple SMOs that are independent entities even though they share enough beliefs with those other SMOs to justify conceiving all of them as a single social movement. SMs are, in this sense, *decentralized* (and its SMOs often vary widely in the degree of their formalization and centralization). Some researchers mistakenly construe SMs, in being decentralized, as simply decentralized SMOs. It is not uncommon, in particular, to misread the well-known formulation of Luther Gerlach and Virginia Hine (1970) regarding the organization of SMs as a depiction of a less formalized and centralized SMO. But Gerlach and Hine are clearly speaking of SMs and not SMOs in their formulation. Thus, these are the three features they suggest as characteristic of SMs:

1. *Segmentary:* A movement is composed of diverse groups, or cells, which grow and die, divide and fuse, proliferate and contract.
2. *Polycephalous:* [A movement] does not have a central command or decision-making structure; rather it has many leaders or rivals for leadership, not only within the movement as a whole, but within each movement cell.
3. *Reticulate:* These diverse groups [are] not . . . simply an amorphous collection; rather they are organized into a network of reticulate structure through cross-cutting links, "traveling evangelists" or spokesmen, overlapping participation, joint activities, and sharing of common objectives and opposition. (Gerlach 1983, 135)

Seen through the lens of low degrees of formalization and centralization, it is understandable that some researchers would misread Gerlach and Hine as taking about less formalized and decentralized SMOs. But inspection of their report on the two movements from which they derive this characterization—black power and pentecostalism—shows that this is not their meaning (Gerlach and Hine 1970).

Variation in degrees of formalization and centralization in SMOs has been of great interest to researchers because, among other reasons, it is of key or even central interest in a great many social movements where members see themselves as in revolt against hierarchical and centralized forms of society per se. Beyond aiming to abolish these features in the larger society (an *adversary* belief), many SMOs have sought to "walk the walk" and to implement *exemplary* forms of less formalized and decentralized SMO organization (see Chapter 5, Section III.B.1). Segments of the U.S. women's liberation movement of the 1970s have been among movements so concerned and these segments have exhibited a "great emphasis . . . on what are called leaderless, structureless groups as the main, if not sole organizational form of the movement. The source of this idea was a natural reaction against the overstructured society in which most of us found ourselves" [Freeman (1982, 1), Baker (1982), Ferree and Yancey (1995). On such beliefs and practices in other movements see Breines (1980), Barkan (1979), Downey (1986), Smith (1990), and Schiffman (1991).]

Researchers have especially focused on the *consequences* of varying degrees of formalization and centralization in SMOs and I will discuss propositions regarding these in Section V.D below.

D. Member Absorption

What is the *degree* to which the modal or statistically common member of an SMO dedicates her or his life to it? SMOs can be arrayed along the dimension of very low to very high such absorption or scope of involvement. Absorption or scope refers to "the number of activities in which . . . participants are jointly involved" (Etzioni 1961, 160). For SMOs, such "number of activities" refer to

1. working,
2. maintaining an abode,
3. engaging in familial relations,
4. socializing, and
5. participating in occasions of thinking about how one is related to the world at large or ultimate reality (e.g., religious ceremonies, political rallies).

The most absorbing SMOs attempt to organize all these activities—the total round of life—in a single, territorially amalgamated scheme of living. At the other end of the continuum, the SMO organizes only some of the spare time of most members, who otherwise work, reside, and organize their familial relations apart from the SMO. Surveying common forms of SMOs in this perspective, six basic degrees of absorption are identifiable. Arrayed from highest to lowest these are as follows:

1. *Associations* sustained by spare time volunteers.
2. *Bureaus* in which most members are ordinary workers or staffers and who otherwise live apart from the SMO.
3. *Troops* in the sense of mobile units whose entire round of life is simplified and temporarily absorbed into the SMO for the purpose of emergency and temporary missions. These might be troops in the military sense of soldiers, as in guerrilla armies, or troops in the metaphorical sense of civilians formed into a dedicated cadre, such as the fleet of van-based fund-raising units once operated by the Unification Church (Bromley and Shupe 1979).
4. *Communes* composed of people who maintain a shared household, but who work outside it.
5. *Collectives*, in which a distinctive scheme of economically productive work is organized, but the participants otherwise organize their lives separately.
6. *Utopias*, in which there is a effort to bring all the basic aspects of living under a single geographically consolidated scheme of working, residing, familial relations, socializing, and understanding existence (Lofland 1985, Ch. 8).

Another way to think about the dynamic underlying this progression of levels of absorption is in terms of a contrast between what Zald and Ash term *inclusive* versus *exclusive* SMOs. Inclusive SMOs "require minimal levels of initial commitment, . . . a short indoctrination period, or none at all. On the other hand, the 'exclusive' organization is likely to hold the new recruit in a long 'novitiate' period, [and] to require the recruit to subject himself [*sic*] to organization discipline and orders" (1966, 331; Curtis and Zurcher 1974).

E. Volunteer Spare-Time Absorption

It is likely that the garden variety SMO form in industrial democracies is, at the lowest level of absorption, the spare-time *volunteer association*, which may have one or more part- or full-time staff but in which the *modal member* is an unpaid volunteer (number 1 in Section D, immediately above). For this reason, it deserves close analytic attention and one line of such attention has been to think about how associations vary among themselves. Continuing to focus on the variable of the degree of member absorption or corporateness, five such degrees have been observed:

1. Least corporate, most fragile, and transitory are *study groups*, which include the kinds of discussion meetings and "audience cults" found in the "cultic milieu" of the United States, consciousness-raising groups of the women's liberation movement of the 1970s (Freeman 1975), and therapy groups of the self-help movement.

2. More enduring but still primitive in terms of organizational accoutrements are *fellowships*, examples of which include "affinity groups" in the antinuclear and peace movements (e.g., Epstein 1985; Barkan 1979) and "block clubs" or "building organizations" in urban neighborhoods (e.g., Bailey 1974, 54–55; Lawson 1983).

3. At the point of establishing its own office, or more still, its own *building*, from which it can organize and deploy a range of activities, an SMO might be termed a *congregation*. Such a building level of volunteer focus is likely more aimed toward and is more common among religious than among political SMOs, names for which include center, headquarters, or house—in political cases—and fellowship hall, temple, or church—in religious cases.

4. Congregational volunteer associations that work up their beliefs and involvement with particular intensity and conceive reality in a strongly dualistic fashion—as deeply divided between the forces of good versus evil—are often termed *sects*. Irrespective of the specific religious or political content of this all-absorbing dualism, demands on involvement tend to the "unbounded," even while still at the level of a part-time, volunteer involvement.

5. When underground or illegal operations guided by conspiratorial schemes are added to sectarian formations, associations may take the form of secrecy and security concerned *cells* (see further Lofland 1985, Ch. 8, especially pp. 215–16).

F. Form Diversity and Complexity

Even though most SMOs are organizationally quite simple, some few *do* exhibit a great deal of complexity in the *constellation* or assortment of the basic units (such as those given above) they are able to organize. That is, within some single SMOs, we may find units of *several* of the basic types of absorption levels and several basic levels of associations enumerated above.

And the particular profile and mix of these forms may change in response to new visions of strategy and to environmental changes.

Among some SMOs, there is a pronounced penchant for proliferating diverse units that result in structures that look rather like multinational corporate empires. Very complex organizational charts are necessary in order to visualize and thereby to comprehend them. Notable reports on such SMOs include Richardson, Steward and Simmonds (1979) on an extraordinarily complex Christian "commune"; Bromley and Shupe (1980) on the dozens of diverse units created within the Unification Church; and Carter (1990) on the Rajneesh worldwide empire of the 1980s.

G. Scale

Variation in form diversity and complexity can otherwise be viewed as variation in SMO *scale*, that is, variation in the number of basic units that compose the SMO and how these units are interrelated. Here are three commonly observed levels of scale:

1. *SMO Locals.* One of the most common SMO forms in the U.S. experience at least is the local, *freestanding circle of people* pursuing a movement activity. This circle may have a name and perhaps even an office and telephone. Even so, many such "grassroots" groups are quite informal, in such ways as lacking a clear name, operating out of a leader's home, or using her or his private telephone.

2. *National SMOs with Locals.* Considerably less common in the U.S. experience have been SMOs that operate a national office with staff in or near a center of state power, an office that is itself supported by and coordinated with multiple SMO locals. In recent years, the National Organization for Women (NOW) has been among the more successful and effective in establishing and maintaining such a "two-tiered" organization.

3. *National SMOs with No Locals.* Some of the best-known U.S. SMOs are primarily if not wholly national, staff-operated offices that have few or no SMO locals. They are likely, however, to have large and sophisticated mailing lists and direct-mail operations that generate funds and that therefore provide the impression of a national membership that is organized into locals.

H. Democratic-Oligarchic

In ordinary discourse, the term *oligarchy* means "government in the hands of a few" or "government in which the power is confined to a few persons." The contrasting concept that makes oligarchy a position on a variable is, of course, *democracy*, which is sometimes defined as government (or a smaller polity or group) of, by, and for the people (the members). Earmark features of democracy versus oligarchy include having a written and enforced constitution or bylaws, universal right to vote in open and fair elections, proportionate representation of whatever diverse groupings there are within the group, free dissent, richly developed internal groupings that are vehicles of expressing diverse viewpoints, open meetings of full and sober policy deliberation, open access to all pertinent policy information, and monitored and restrained leaders.

Using such earmarks, there is a tradition of case studies in which researchers have inquired into the degree various SMOs are or are not democratic versus oligarchic. Robert Michels's *Political Parties*, published in 1911, founded his line of inquiry by assessing the degree of democracy in left, democracy-professing political parties and unions in Europe. He concluded that oligarchy was the rule rather than exception in those cases and he formulated the more sweeping proposition that organization itself—"the technical indispensability of leadership"—makes oligarchy unavoidable even in professedly and formally democratic associations. Calling this "the iron law of oligarchy," he declares, "It is organization which gives birth to the dominion of the elected over the electors. . . . Who says organization, says oligarchy" (Michels [1911] 1959, 401).

A stream of studies seeking to find exceptions to this "iron law" has mostly uncovered yet more oligarchy,[1] but also some exceptions. While oligarchy is much the dominant tendency, democracy is found under some special conditions. (These are discussed in Lipset, Martin, Trow, and Coleman 1956; Breines 1980; Rothschild-Whitt 1976; 1979; Lofland and Fahey 1995).

Of course, oligarchy is a dilemma or problem only among SMOs that profess support for democracy in the larger society and therefore, by implication if not by explicit profession, its practice in the SMO itself. The fact is, though, that a very large portion of SMOs do not even formally profess democracy for the larger society, much less for themselves. This is especially and quite unsurprisingly the case among SMOs of the more existential bent I describe in Chapter 5. For example, beliefs tending in the totalistic, apocalyptic, nihilistic direction either *know* the truth (so democracy is pointless), or think there is no moral reason to prefer one form of decision-making over another.

Updating and slightly softening Michels:

♦ Who says SMO, likely says oligarchy.

Frequencies of democracy or oligarchy aside, a *process proposition* is also attached to this variable, which asserts that SMOs tend to start with democracy and evolve into oligarchy. Because this is a process, I will report on this proposition in Section V.E on process.

III. WHAT ARE SMO STRUCTURES?

Although we can *glimpse* structures in the variations and types I report above, this is not the same as achieving a detailed understanding of how such cryptically captured types (and variables) operate. As I put it previously, this difference is like that between a crude drawing of a house and a blueprint for its construction (Chapter 3, Section II.B). Among work on such detailed specifications, I want to point up efforts focused on questions of hierarchy and decision-making and on three other examples of patterns of SMO structure.

A. Collectivist-Democratic Structure

Questions of hierarchy are often more consciously and articulately problematic in many SMOs than they are in large sections of mainstream organizational life. In particular, "ordinary" conceptions of how to organize and to delegate responsibility may be rejected under the aegis of *exemplary* beliefs (as described in Chapter 5, Section III.B). This rejection is expressed in experimentation with "alternative" forms of hierarchy and decision-making. Some of these run in the egalitarian and consensus decision-making direction and yet others move in the opposite direction of rigid forms of authoritarianism and charismatic leadership. Put more generally, a portion of SMO structuring is a search for alternatives to the kind of "pluralistic" or compromised forms of organization that pass for proper human association in a societal mainstream.

In the egalitarian and consensus democracy direction, among several analytic efforts to grasp such structures, perhaps the most systematic has been that of Joyce Rothschild and Allen Whitt, who studied several "alternative" or "countercultural" organizations in an effort to isolate their structural principles. They formulated their results as an "ideal type," their summary of which I report in Figure 6.1. As can be inferred from the complexity and detail of Figure 6.1, in their longer treatment Rothschild and Whitt strive to dissect *precisely* how this SMO pattern is organized and how it operates. As such, it—and others like it—is a virtual blueprint for others who would try their hand at it—including the recognition that the structure is exceedingly difficult both to establish and to maintain and has an extremely high rate of failure.

Figure 6.1.   Bureaucratic versus collectivist-democratic organizational
structure.

Dimensions ⬇	Bureaucratic organization	Collectivist-democratic Organization
1. Authority	1. Authority resides in individuals by virtue of incumbency in office and/or expertise; hierarchical organization of offices. Compliance is to universal fixed rules as these are implemented by office incumbents.	1. Authority resides in the collectivity as a whole; delegated, if at all, only temporarily and subject to recall. Compliance is to the consensus of the collective which is always fluid and open to negotiation.
2. Rules	2. Formalization of fixed and universal rules; calculability and appeal of decisions on the basis of correspondence to the formal, written law.	2. Minimal stipulated rules; primacy of ad hoc, individual decisions; some calculability possible on the basis of knowing the substantive ethics involved in the situation.
3. Social Control	3. Organizational behavior is subject to social control primarily through direct supervision or standardized rules and sanctions, tertiarily through the selection of homogeneous personnel, especially at top levels.	3. Social controls are primarily based on personalistic or moralistic appeals and the selection of homogeneous personnel.
4. Social Relations	4. Ideals of impersonality. Relations are to be role-based, segmental, and instrumental.	4. Ideal of community. Relations are to be wholistic, personal, of value in themselves.
5. Recruitment and Advancement	5a. Employment based on specialized training and formal certification. 5b. Employment constitutes a career; advancement based on seniority or achievement.	5a. Employment based on friends, social-political values, personality attributes, and informally assessed knowledge and skills. 5b. Concept of career advancement not meaningful; no hierarchy of positions.
6. Incentive Structure	6. Remunerative incentives are primary.	6. Normative and solidarity incentives are primary; material incentives are secondary.
7. Social Stratification	7. Isomorphic distribution of prestige, privilege, and power (i. e., differential rewards by office); hierarchy justifies inequality.	7. Egalitarian; reward differentials, if any, are strictly limited by the collectivity.
8. Differentiation	8a. Maximal division of labor; dichotomy between intellectual work and manual work and between administrative tasks and performance tasks. 8b. Maximal specialization of jobs and functions; segmental roles. Technical expertise is exclusively held: ideal of the specialist-expert.	8a. Minimal division of labor: administration is combined with performance tasks; division between intellectual and manual work is reduced 8b. Generalization of job functions; wholistic roles. Demystification of expertise: ideal of the amateur factotum.

Source: Rothschild and Whitt (1986, 61-62, Table 3.1, "Comparisons of two ideal types of organization").

B. Professional Social Movement Organizations (PSMOs)

While not developed in the structural detail we see in the Rothschild and Whitt analysis, perhaps the single best-known structural identification of a type of SMO in the last generation has been that of the **professional social movement organization** or PSMO. Delineated by McCarthy and Zald in 1973, its key features include:

[1] A leadership that devotes full time to the [SMO].
[2] A large proportion of resources originating outside the aggrieved group that the movement claims to represent.
[3] A very small or nonexistent membership base or a paper membership [, one that] implies little more than allowing one's name to be used on membership rolls . . . .
[4] Attempts to impart the image of . . . speaking for a potential constituency . . . .
[5] Attempts to influence policy toward that same constituency. (Adapted from McCarthy and Zald 1987a; see also McAdam, McCarthy, and Zald 1988, 717)

Like the structural depiction offered by Rothschild and Whitt, this formulation of the PSMO should be regarded as an *ideal type*, as a form to which many SMOs can be seen to tend rather than exactly to replicate (as its formulators have themselves said) (McAdam, McCarthy, and Zald 1988, 717).

McCarthy and Zald attach a *frequency* proposition to their depiction of the PSMO, one that asserts that they have become much more common in the middle and later twentieth century. As such a proposition, I will discuss it further in Section V.A on frequency.

C. Marketed Social Movement Organizations

Hank Johnston (1980) formulated the ideal type of the "marketed social movement organization" as a way to articulate the features of an SMO called Transcendental Meditation (TM), although TM is not the only instance of this type. In Johnston's depiction, the marketed social movement has several major features, none of which are necessarily distinctive to the type but which, in composite, make up a distinctive structure:

(1) the use of sophisticated promotional and recruiting techniques;
(2) a radical divergence in the status of the membership;
(3) participation as a product package; and,

(4) the extension of membership as the dominant goal of the movement. (Johnston 1980, 333)

Johnston's analysis of TM as a marketed social movement is organized into four main parts. I think it is helpful to review these in order to convey a concrete sense of a somewhat more informal pattern of depicting structure that provides a contrast to the more formal style exemplified by Rothchild and Whitt in Figure 6.1.

In the first main part of his report, Johnston says that he was prompted to think of TM as a marketed social movement because that SMO was not accurately depicted by McCarthy and Zald's formulation of the ideal type of the "professional movement organization" (described immediately above). In particular, the ideal type of the professional movement organization presumes that although articulate social and political grievances may not figure heavily in the causes of such SMOs, they are nonetheless present and SMO leaders refer to them in organizational activities. Such was not the case for TM. So too, the goals of professional movement organizations are specifically political or economic, rather than general and vague, as was the case with TM. For these and other reasons, then, "I . . . develop the concept of the marketed social movement" organization (Johnston 1980, 336).

The second main part of Johnston's analysis traces the three phases of TM's organizational development:

1. *The cultic period from 1959 to 1965.*
2. *The invention and rise of the marketing orientation from 1965 to about 1972.* This period was marked by the creation of distinct product packages that were directed to "four distinct target populations." Spiritual aspects of TM were deemphasized and stress was placed on TM as a pragmatic and scientific activity.
3. *The transition to a multinational organization starting in 1972.*

In the third main part of his report, Johnston turns to the question of causes or reasons why TM would develop this kind of organization and why TM was able to grow so rapidly in the second historical period. He offers four reasons: wide and heightened interest in Eastern religions at that time; widespread media coverage that TM encouraged; self-help and self-improvement themes in American culture; and "deep respect for science and technology" in American culture, a respect that TM exploited.

Having thus set the stage in these three main parts by (1) indicating what prompted him to formulate the type, (2) describing the empirical features of the organization and its history, and (3) suggesting social conditions that facilitated its rise, in the fourth and final main part,

Johnston provides a more formal profile of the abstract features of the marketed social movement. Three of these are discussed under the headings:

- objectification of membership
- the movement as a product package
- member grievances—diffuse and ersatz (Johnston 1980, 345–49)

He concludes with a summary of these four main parts, with suggestions on other SMOs that might be instances of this type, and with other suggestions for further investigation.

IV. OTHER DIFFERENCES/VARIATIONS AND STRUCTURES

Various additional delineations of SMO variations and structures are important, but for want of space I will only list their names and salient places where they are discussed:

Degree of Factionalism or Propensity to Schism: SMOs vary in terms of (1) the degree to which internal decision-making is contentious and conflictful, (2) the degree to which internal "tendencies" or "factions" have crystallized, and (3) the actual occurrence of splintering or schism (Georgakas 1990d). Zald and Ash (1966, 337) offer the *causal proposition* that "exclusive" SMOs are more prone to these conflictful possibilities than are "inclusive" ones. (As reported above in Section II.D, by "exclusive" they mean SMOs that are more absorbing and "require the recruit to subject himself [sic] to organization discipline and orders." "Inclusive" SMOs move in the opposite direction.) [See further, Stark and Bainbridge (1985, Ch. 5), on "causes of religious dissent and schism," and Morris (1984, 42–44).]

Combat Party, also called *Organizational Weapon* or *Vanguard Party*: The generic structure of the Communist Party USA (Selznick [1952] 1960). A key historical theorist and practitioner of this "party of a different type" was, of course, V. I. Lenin, as expressed in his 1902 *What Is to Be Done?* Georgakas defines a vanguard party as "a political party composed of professional revolutionaries [that acts as] the general staff of the revolution. . . . [It] is organized on a modified military model under a schema termed democratic centralism" (1990a, 813) [Gross (1974) provides a wide ranging history and analysis of this form.]

Preparty Formations: "Under Leninist doctrine a vanguard party is necessary to make a successful revolution, but that party cannot be instantly born out of the proletarian brow. Various publishing groups, militant unions, special-interest movements, ethnic federations and other social forces must become active before a vanguard party is possible" (Georgakas 1990b, 96).

Front Organization (or group): "Radical organizations often seek to influence political events by creating groups that deal with only one aspects of their general program. . . . Activists in a front are usually aware of the forces that shaped the front, but the general public is likely to perceive the organization as spontaneously formed" (Georgakas 1990c, 248; see also Goldberg 1991, 127).

Activist Art Groups: These are "characterized by the innovative use of public space to address issues of sociopolitical and cultural significance, and to encourage community or public participation as a means of effecting social change" (Felshin 1995, 9).

World-Transforming: Generic features of the Unification Church (Bromley and Shupe 1979).

Movement Halfway House: Certain freestanding SMOs and sympathetic community associations that sometimes serve as training and launching sites of SMOs (Morris 1984).

Cults and Sects: A large literature strives for structural analysis of these. Wallis (1977) assembles candidate features and synthesizes them for the case of Scientology.

Social Movement Schools and *Movement Mentor Organizations:* These "encourage, support, and facilitate collective action, but typically are not the organizational vehicles of that action" (Edwards and McCarthy 1992, 548–49).[2]

V. SELECTED OTHER QUESTIONS AND ANSWERS ABOUT GIVEN VARIATIONS

All the variations and structures I have reported in Sections II, III, and IV are, of course, answers to only generic questions (1) What is the aspect's type? (its variations) and (2) What is the aspect's structure? Obviously researchers *also* bring one or more of the other six generic questions to bear on answers to these two questions. Let me review five of these with regard to SMOs per se or selected organizational variations in them: frequencies, magnitudes, causes, effects, and processes.

A. Frequencies

The question of how frequent SMOs are poses the descriptive task of "simply" counting them in a given geographical area at a specific time. At first glance, this may seem easy to do, but it is in fact often a major undertaking that is plagued with definitional quandaries and is quite laborious.

Happily, however, in many *social movements* the puzzle of exactly how many SMOs there are (and where they are and what they are doing) is a puzzle to one or more movement *promoters*, who undertake themselves to perform censuses and to publish directories. Alert researchers of SMOs and social movements are therefore always on the lookout for these directories and the group or groups involved in their production. (Indeed, groups devoted to their construction are themselves a distinctive kind of SMO; they pursue, that is, a distinctive strategy of SM promotion.)

In the context of the recent and current U.S. scene, the larger and established social movements (a seeming contradiction I explain in Chapter 7) consist of on the order of five to fifty thousand SMOs. The labor movement, with its myriad union locals, may well be, in this SMO sense, the largest movement in the United States. However, the women's, the several ethnic movements, and the conservative movement may consist of SMOs of the same order of magnitude (depending in part on whether one considers conservative churches SMOs). Smaller but still sizable movements such as the peace movement likely consist of at least some five thousand SMOs.

The absolute number and relative frequency of SMOs in various movements vary across states, cities, and towns, with some of these having much heavier concentrations of some movements than others. For example, peace SMOs cluster heavily on the Eastern and Western seaboards, with scant relative representation in the rest of the country (Colwell 1989). Of some note, the metropolitan areas of Boston, New York, and Washington tend to have more SMOs of almost all sorts—both absolutely and relative to population size—than other areas in the United States. University and college towns also tend to have SMOs in strong disproportion to population. Indeed, areas with concentrations of universities and colleges tend to become virtual *SMO regions*, as has happened in western Massachusetts and which is related to the five postsecondary institutions clustered there.

Researchers also focus on the frequency of various organizational forms of SMOs over time, initially seeking simply to describe the rise (or fall) in the numbers of given organizational forms of SMOs. As mentioned in Section II.B, one of the key *frequency propositions* in recent decades has been McCarthy and Zald's thesis that professional social movements (PSMOS) have, since World War II, risen in number and as a proportion of all SMOs (McCarthy and Zald 1987a).

A second key frequency proposition in the recent period is that what are called "new social movement" SMOs have risen in number and as a proportion of all SMOs in the industrial democracies since perhaps the 1970s (see Section IV.A.3 of Chapter 7).

B. Magnitudes

Researchers commonly conceptualize the size or strength of an SMO along such dimensions as number of members, size of budget or of income, complexity or scale of organization, and amount of power. The first two of these are most commonly the referents of magnitude questions and are often as difficult to determine as the frequency of SMOs (just discussed).

Indeed, members and money are very much what SMOs must be about (as is virtually any organization for that matter) and, as coin of the realm, are subject to contentious claims. People who speak for given SMOs have an obvious interest in putting whatever they believe to be the best face on things as regards members and money. This can include exaggerations that *minimize* one or the other, and not simply the better-appreciated tendency to *inflate* membership and monetary support. The artfulness of varying definitions and classifications of "members" and "money" often make accurate figures difficult to come by—and all the more difficult because the researcher must her- or himself make definitional and classificational judgments that are murky and contentious (Lofland 1993a, 86–90, 135–40).

Putting counting problems to the side for the moment, taking all SMOs as a set and extrapolating from the limited data we have (e.g., Colwell 1989; McCarthy and Wolfson 1992), I venture the guess that the vast majority of SMOs in at least the industrial democracies have well less than fifty members, with many having twenty-five members or less. Only a small percentage have memberships of more than ten thousand, although some very few have been (or are), of course, very much larger. Thus, focusing on the end of major periods of mobilization, Schwartz and Paul report that the AFL-CIO had 5,000,000 members at its organizing peak in 1940; the Southern Farmers' Alliance had 850,000 members in 1890; the National Organization for Women had 250,000 in 1983; and, the Woman's Christian Temperance Union had 150,000 in 1890 (Schwartz and Paul 1992, 206).

Two reputedly enormous SMOs in U.S. history—Students for a Democratic Society and the Communist party—had only 100,000 and 80,000 members, respectively, in their peak years (1969 for the former and 1939 for the latter) (Schwartz and Paul 1992, 206). With 25,000 members in 1985, an SMO such as Mothers Against Drunk Driving, though small relative to the others just mentioned, may in fact be one of the larger recently founded U.S. SMOs.

In speaking of magnitude, it is critical to distinguish between SMOs and social movements. Since the latter may be composed of thousands upon thousands of even small SMOs, and large numbers of participants who are *not members of any SMO*, the sheer numbers of people involved in a *social movement* can be very large, indeed. At peak mobilizations or soaring, albeit briefly, millions of people might be involved.

C. Causes

Causal questions regarding SMOs qua organizations divide into two categories:

1. causes of them per se—their occurrence or nonoccurrence as a general class,
2. causes of how existing SMOs vary in some fashion, as, for example, in terms of such variables described above as scale, degree of member absorption, and organizational diversity and complexity.

The first category is the central question addressed in the next chapter (number 7) and I will therefore to postpone discussion of it. Instead, I want here to describe and illustrate answers to the second category.

Answers to the second category of causal questions of course require inspection and assessment of the relative role of a wide variety of possible factors or causes. As in the parallel discussion of the causes of variations in SMO beliefs in the previous chapter, the list of diverse aspects given in Figure 3.3 (the aspect-question matrix) is one pertinent source to consult in forming hypotheses about causes. Among the fourteen listed in Figure 3.3, let me single out *ruling elites* as of more than mean importance in understanding variations in SMO organizational forms.

As the quintessential definers of mainstream reality and the persons who act to protect their monopoly on the exercise of physical violence, ruling elites, more than others, call the tune to which SMOs dance, so to speak. For example, in "the long history of progressive social movements in the United States, widespread repressive social control efforts" have perforce shaped the organizational forms of SMOs, including the formation of secret cells and the destruction of SMOs (McCarthy, Britt and Wolfson 1991, 49). Such "direct" responses are, however, "costly, crude, and potentially dangerous for . . . [ruling elites], since they expose the power and control of the central state in channeling dissent" (p. 49).

We ought therefore to expect ruling elites also to sponsor "less direct . . . mechanisms" that channel SMOs in a wide variety of ways, *including* the shaping of their organizational forms (p. 46). In seeking to specify these "less direct . . . mechanisms" in the recent United States, McCarthy, Britt, and Wolfson have proposed that the Federal Tax Code and the Internal Revenue Service (IRS) provide one among several sets of mechanisms that create a web of constraints and incentives that mold the organizational forms of many SMOs. The specific provisions are tax code sections 501(c)(3) and 501(c)(4), which grant tax exemption to "charitable," nonprofit organizations and tax deductions for contributions to them. These are attractive organizational advantages for which the price is refraining from "any partisan campaign activities and from most other political activities if they are substantial" (p. 54).

The range of permitted "charitable" activities is nonetheless very broad and abstractly stated (e.g., "lessen neighborhood tensions . . . defend human and civil rights secured by law . . . combat community deterioration"). Construing this breadth and abstractness as consistent with SMO beliefs , 501 status is thus enticing to, sought by, and acquired by many organizations that are SMOs. But acquisition of 501 status comes at the price of IRS oversight and audit, the fear of which, McCarthy, Britt, and Wolfson propose, causes many SMOs to *organize* themselves in ways the IRS defines as acceptable and to *act* in ways that will not jeopardize that status.

Combined with the effects of many yet other entities, such as the Postal Service, this "interlocking web of regulations, and the incentives that support them [provides] a template for a consensual social movement organizational form." In this inducing template, "certain organizational elements are explicit criteria for qualification for 501 status [such as,] goals must be specific and articulated and be achievable by means other than grass-roots lobbying exclusively" (p. 66).

This is an example, then, of *one* set of variables that can have causal impacts on the form of organization of an SMO (and on yet other aspects, such as strategies).

D. Effects

Like the question of causes discussed just above, the generic question of effects as regards SMOs divides into the questions of (1) their effects

per se as a general class, and (2) the effects of particular, specific variations in them. The first question has a complex and multifaceted answer
that I reserve for separate treatment in Chapter 11, "What Are Effects of
SMOs?"

The second question has been addressed prominently as regards (1)
effects of cadre versus mass-membership organizational form and (2)
effects of degrees of formalization and centralization.

1. Cadre versus Mass Membership.   Several of the eight main variations I review in Section II (items A through H) catch at the question of
the degree to which an SMO strives to be a large, stable, enduring, and
democratic association versus a smaller, temporary, and absorbing cadre
formation. The fragility and temporariness (II.B), absorption (II.D), scale
(II.G), and democratic-oligarchic (II.H) variations on that list are particularly pertinent to thinking about this cadre-mass distinction. The cadre
organization is more fragile and temporary, highly absorbing, smaller in
scale and likely less democratic than the mass membership organization.

Francis Fox Piven and Richard Cloward have argued:

> ◗ In those rare but heady moments when a mass of unjustly treated
> people defy authorities, *mass-membership* SMOs have the effect of
> subduing protest and insurgency rather than facilitating, encour-
> aging, and enlarging it (Piven and Cloward 1977; Cloward and
> Piven 1984).

In their view, American activists working among insurgent populations have been informed by the mass-membership model in which the
"goal was to build stable membership organizations at the local level and
then unite them through a national structure. This conviction about
organization was, in turn, inextricably tied to a more fundamental conviction that real and sustained political leverage depended not on disruptive protest, but on bringing large numbers of people together in
formal organizations that would represent their interests" (Cloward and
Piven 1984, 591–92).

Piven and Cloward offer the counterproposition that "sustained political leverage" for poor people, at least, is won by *disruption* rather than
by enduring formal organization. And disruption requires a *different type*
of organization, the *cadre* organization, a form they also term the "leadership" organization or "organizations of organizers" (p. 595). The goal
of this alternative form is "organizing demonstrations and confronta-
tions, not membership organization" (p. 592).

In their massive and classic *Poor People's Movements* (1977) Piven and
Cloward review the unemployed workers', the industrial workers', the
civil rights, and the welfare rights movements in these terms. Regarding

the civil rights movement, for example, they observe that "people were not recruited as organization members; they were only being recruited for collective defiance of caste rules" (Cloward and Piven 1984, 594).

By contrast, they argue that periods of defiance among renters and welfare recipients have been unsuccessful because the SMOs mounted in those periods were mass membership rather than cadre. In particular, "the formally-structured mass-membership organization [attempted by the National Welfare Rights Organization] was unsuited for marshaling disruptive resources" (p. 596).

Piven and Cloward believe that their focus on disruption and SMO structure appropriate to it has often been misread as a celebration of anarchy and "blind militancy" (p. 598). Indeed, some critics have charged that their work is an "anti-organizational philippic" (Gamson and Schmeidler 1984, 584). They vigorously reject such accusations and say that their goal is exactly the same as some of their critics say it ought to be:

> The intellectual task [is] figuring out what types of organization are likely to facilitate insurgency or abandon their oppositional politics under different historical conditions. (Gamson and Schmeidler 1984, 583)

My own reading of this brouhaha is that Piven and Cloward have been misread. They have, indeed, addressed the intellectual task stated just above, albeit they may not have done so with the clarity and detail that may be necessary.

2. Formalization and Centralization. Related to but not the same as the cadre–mass-membership variation is the question of the effects of variations in *formalization and centralization* (Section II.C) and/or the structure of the *professional social movement organization* (Section III.B). Amalgamating these variables as a contrast between *formalized* and *informal* SMOs, Susan Staggenborg has traced consequences of this variation among eight formalized and twelve informal prochoice SMOs operating in the Chicago area from the late sixties to the early eighties. In Staggenborg's classification, *formalized* SMOs

> have established procedures or structures that enable them to perform certain tasks routinely and to continue to function with changes in leadership. . . . [They] have bureaucratic procedures for decision making, a developed division of labor with positions for various functions, explicit criteria for membership, and rules governing subunits. . . .
>
> In contrast, *informal* SMOs . . . have few established procedures, loose membership requirements, and minimum division of labor. Decisions . . . tend to be made in an ad hoc rather than routine manner. . . . The organizational structure . . . is frequently adjusted; assignments among personnel and procedures are developed to meet immediate needs. . . .

> Individual leaders . . . exert an important influence on the organization; major changes in SMO structure and activities are likely to occur with changes in leadership. Any subunits . . . tend to be autonomous and loosely connected to one another. . . . Nonprofessional, largely volunteer, leaders [dominate]. (1988, 589–90; see also Staggenborg 1986; 1989a; 1989b)

Thus delineating the variable formalized-informal, Staggenborg poses the question: what difference, if any, does this variation make? Her answer is that it makes a great deal of difference in at least three areas:

[Maintenance/Expansion/Decline:] [In contrast to informal SMOs] formalized SMOs have been stable organizations that helped to sustain the movement. . . .

[Major Strategies and Tactics:] Formalization . . . affect[s] the strategic and tactical choices of SMOs. First, formalized SMOs tend to engage in institutionalized tactics and do not initiate disruptive direct-action tactics. Second, formalized SMOs are more likely than informal SMOs to engage in activities that help to achieve organizational maintenance and expansion as well as influence on external targets. . . .

[Coalition Work:] In my sample, formalized SMOs have played the dominant roles in lasting coalitions. (Staggenborg 1988, 597–602; see also Staggenborg 1986; 1989a; 1989b; Kleidman 1994)

E. Processes

In the context of analyzing an SMO qua organization, the generic question What are the aspect's processes? is answered in one or more of the general forms of *sequences, cycles,* and *spirals* displayed by the SMO taken as a global or holistic entity.

As discussed in Section II.B.5 of Chapter 3, process answers/propositions are distinctive in isolating a **series** of *phases, periods,* or *steps* in a process sequence, cycle, or spiral. In describing *multiple,* time-ordered and interrelated phases/periods/steps, process propositions are different from cause or effect propositions in that these latter two consist of only two interrelated classes of variables. For example, Staggenborg's effects propositions reported immediately above consist of only *formalized-informal SMOs,* on the one side, and *three kinds of effects,* on the other side. In contrast, a process analysis of the same data would feature phases, periods, or steps in a sequence, cycle, or spiral that linked these variables.

Processes analyses of SMOs qua organizations have more commonly been in the form of sequences than of cycles or spirals.[3] Among sequence analyses, the early and dominant imagery offered by researchers was that of SMOs moving "from democratic decision structures—a situation of dispersed power, to centralization and oligarchy" (Zald and Ash 1966, 328). Sometimes labeled the "Weber-Michels model of routinization and oligarchization" (McAdam et al. 1988, 718) in recognition of its early describers—Max Weber (1958) and Robert Michels ([1911] 1959)—this is the democratic-oligarchic variable I describe above fitted as a process onto the history of SMOs (Section II.H).

While such a process clearly characterizes *some* SMOs, researchers have noted that it is far from universal among them. Instead, there are, in terms used by McAdam et al., "a variety of other SMO trajectories" (1988, 718):

> a variety of other transformation processes that take place, including coalitions with other organizations, organizational disappearances, factional splits, increased rather than decreased radicalism, and the like. (Zald and Ash 1966, 328)

The searching, case study scrutiny of specific cases provides one key way in which to understand such "trajectories." Thus, Richard Ofshe has sought to understand Synanon, a prominent SMO of the United States in the seventies, in terms of its four distinct stages of "evolution." He carefully states, though, that these four stages were

> not phases in a natural process of organizational evolution. There was no inherent logic of social organization at work . . . which demanded and insured the development [of the four stages]. At the same time, however, the . . . the dramatic shifts were not arbitrary or accidental either; they are the work neither of madness nor of randomness. Rather, these several transformations of the Synanon organization can best be understood as strategic responses to events . . . aimed at extending and protecting the organization and its power structure. There is a logic to this process, but it is managerial, not evolutionary. Likewise, there is also an unpredictability about these events, but it enters the process as a contingency for strategic management decisions, not as a controlling principle of development. (Ofshe 1980, 115)

Ofshe's analysis is in two parts: (1) a depiction of the four stages themselves and (2) a separate analysis of the managerial strategies and other factors involved in the three transformations involved in those stages (i.e., change (i) from stage one to two, (ii) from two to three, and (iii) from three to four].

The stages themselves are discerned from quite dramatic changes in the organization:

1. *Voluntary Association: January–September, 1958.* [Involved in Alcoholics Anonymous (AA) in the Los Angeles area, one Charles Dederich en-

courages the formation of AA groups composed primarily of narcotics rather than alcohol addicts and splits these groups off from AA.]

2. *Therapeutic Community: 1958–1968.* Synanon [develops] a reputation as a therapeutic community for the treatment of narcotic addicts. . . . In 1966, Synanon started operating game clubs, encounter groups for non-addicts who now could play the famous "Synanon Game." . . . By 1968, Synanon claimed game club membership of 3,400 individuals. . . .

3. *Social Movement and Alternative Society: 1969–1975.* Until 1968 the only residents of Synanon houses were former narcotic addicts, polydrug abusers and a few alcoholics. In March, 1968, there were 1007 such residents. . . . During the latter part of 1968 and through early 1969, two decisions were made and implemented. First, the program leading to graduation [moving from a Synanon house and getting an external job] was abolished. . . . The second decision was to redefine Synanon as a social movement and to open its doors to residents drawn from the game clubs. . . . The rhetoric of Synanon . . . became that of an experimental society. . . . Using the vocabulary of the human potential movement, Synanon was the "growing edge of humanity," and living in Synanon was like living in the twenty-first century. . . . By 1972 Synanon reached its maximum population of almost 1700 residents. . . . During this period, Synanon was often characterized as a commune . . ., but others also saw it as a business . . . for the organization began to develop successful business operations and substantial real estate holdings. In 1964 Dederich announced a plan to build a Synanon City in Northern California. . . . [H]oldings of about 3,300 acres [were acquired and] an estimated five million dollars worth of buildings were constructed or renovated. . . . The organization continued to develop . . . "hustling" operations [consisting of] soliciting goods or cash from business organizations or individual across the nation. . . .

4. *Religion: 1975–[1980s]:* In August, 1974, Synanon's Board of Directors adopted a resolution proclaiming the Synanon Religion. . . . The central tenet of the Synanon Religion is called the *reconciliatory principle* [which holds that] while dichotomies such as good and evil exist . . . "at the same time we must understand that they are ultimately resolved [and] in that sense, they do not really matter at all" [Ofshe quote from a Synanon pamphlet]. . . . Dederich was named the highest spiritual authority of the Synanon religion, the court of last resort in all disputes. He alone could promulgate the laws and decisions of the group. . . . Synanon's disputes with California authorities since 1975 . . . involved allegations of child abuse . . . , of financial improprieties concerning the use of charitable funds for the purchase of weapons, and of excessively large remuneration to corporate officers. . . . It has been alleged that Synanon residents carried out a series of violent incidents of assault and false imprisonment . . . , beginning with the beating of a neighboring rancher in 1975. . . . [L]aw enforcement organizations have investigated (and in some cases charged) Synanon residents in connection with a series of

incidents culminating with the allegation of an attempted murder by
rattlesnake of attorney Paul Morantz in October, 1978. Synanon has also
received attention for other unusual practices, such as dissolving marriages and re-pairing couples . . . and the manner in which the requirement was enforced that some male "communicants" secure vasectomies.
(Ofshe 1980, 109–14)

This is a dramatically contrasting set of phases or stages and one next
step in understanding them is to ask how and why Synanon moved
from one to another or, in Ofshe's terms, underwent "three transformations." "Taking each of the three transformations in turn" in his report,
Ofshe proceeds to

(a) outline the steps in the transformation process,
(b) identity the methods used to control the formal authority structure of
the organization, and
(c) examine the role of techniques of coercive conversion. (p. 116)

In briefest compass, Ofshe identifies

two central elements of the transformation from voluntary association to
therapeutic community. [i.e., movement from the first to the second
stage]

First, the recruitment of addicts and the split from AA created a group
dependent on Dederich. . . . [F]or the . . . addicts who lived, slept and
ate at the store [a rented location], the organization was . . . their way of
life, and they depended on it for their existence. . . .

Second, the incorporation of Synanon established a formal instrument of
control for Dederich. (p. 116)

Although different in ways Ofshe also describes, both of the other two
transformations

employed the same set of strategic moves, use of formal authority and
coercive interpersonal techniques to produce a controlled conversion to
a new model of the organization. The pattern Dederich employed was
straightforward.

[1] In each case he first modified the corporate charter of the
organization.

[2] Next, he announced an intention to make a major change in existing
arrangements.

[3] He then set about creating a miniature working model of the new
organizational form and the training of a corps of underlings who
represented the new incarnation of the organization. This created
two versions of the organization.

[4] At this point the informal social control system was brought into play.
The remaining residents were pressured, though a conversion experience, to transfer allegiance to the value system and norms of
the management-preferred model or to depart. (p. 117)

VI. HOW ARE SMOS FINANCED?

The above focus on forms of SMO organization highlights them as small *polities*, as divisions of labor in which there is decision-making for the purpose of carrying out collective activities. SMOs are, in addition, small *economies*, collective enterprises that require financial resources in order to get things done. In what forms and from where does this financing come?

The short answer is: The forms and sources tend to be *varied* and are varied in two senses. One, SMOs differ among themselves in the kind of sources of funding on which they most depend. Two, any individual SMO tends to be funded from several or many sources, rather than from just a single or small number.

Of course, these generalizations are not understandable apart from knowing what is meant by "forms and sources" of funding. What, specifically, are we talking about? What is the spectrum of possibilities within which SMOs can differ at the two levels of financing across SMOs and within given SMOs?

In a strict or narrow construal, "financing" or "funding" refers to literal money, to—in the U.S. context—"cash dollars" with which to buy and pay for goods and services. While we certainly need to give central attention to financing in this sense, to attend to it alone would seriously narrow and therefore distort our perception of SMO as *economies*. In the interest of this broader understanding, some researchers therefore include nonmonetary or "in-kind" inputs that are the *practical equivalent* of cash money. Therefore, there is a key distinction in financing between what is termed "in-kind donations" and literal money.

A. In-Kind Donations

Four kinds of in-kind donations figure heavily in SMO economies.

1. Participation. SMO members commonly pay their own expenses of participating in SMO activities—activities that sometimes involve, for example, overnight travel to distant protest locations and, therefore, transport, meal, and lodging costs. Unlike mainstream employment, paid expenses are virtually unheard of among SMOs. Therefore and in the aggregate, participant self-financing is a huge element in SMO economies.

2. Work. As largely volunteer associations (as discussed above), getting things done in SMOs importantly depends on unpaid both unskilled (e.g., answering the telephone) and skilled (e.g., organizing a major rally) labor. Even though the quality of this donated work cannot be controlled in the ways used in paid employment (e.g., selective recruitment, pay cuts, or raises), work does nonetheless get done. Even if is sometimes weak on quality, it happens and has a very significant monetary value.

3. Lifestyle. It is one thing to donate work for some hours or other period, it is another thing to give an SMO one's life. But some people do, and inherited wealth, retirement pensions, affluent and supportive spouses, and part-time subsistence jobs combined with spartan lifestyles are among arrangements that make this possible. These are self-financing activists and some SMOs profit enormously from their full-time work donated dedication (Richardson 1988).

4. Good and Services. SMO-sympathetic business people sometimes donate whatever goods or services they otherwise sell. A landlord may give free or reduced rent in an office building. A caterer may donate prepared food for a fund-raising event. More broadly, SMO-sympathetic individuals sometimes donate personal items—such as replaced personal computers or filing cabinets—to an SMO. Indeed, the newsletters of many SMOs often carry "wish lists" of items they would like someone to give them in order to encourage such donations.

We see, then, that while none of these is cash money, each can be, for practical purposes, as good as cash. Here is the point cast as a sociological proposition or hypothesis:

◗ Major portions of the activities of most SMOs in most movements most of the time are dependent on a rich infusion of in-kind donations.

B. Money

The forms and sources of actual money are much more varied than those of in-kind donations. I am going briefly to sketch thirteen of them, but this list is far from complete, although I think it does encompass major forms and sources.[4] The items on this list are ordered roughly in terms of their importance in less radical American SMOs since the Second World War. In other societies and eras, both the forms and their order of importance may be very different.

1. Grants. In the United States and other industrial democracies, there has arisen a world of project funding organizations commonly called "foundations." The vast bulk of the billions of dollars foundations grant to projects each year go to mainstream and staid endeavors such as education, research, and community improvement. But some few foundations do specialize in funding activities of SMOs and in times of movement surging even otherwise conservative foundations fund the milder of newly surging SMOs [see, e.g., Jenkins and Eckert (1986) on foundation funding of the civil rights movement of the 1960s; Lofland (1993a) and Wright, Rodriquez, and Waitzkin (1986) on foundation funding of the peace movement of the 1980s].

2. Angels. In general as well as movement usage, an "angel" is a person of some wealth who provides large lump sums that make projects or organizations possible. Some few SMOs are virtually the in-perpetuity creatures of such "major donors," but in others they may fund only shorter-term projects. Sometimes, the identities of the angels will be known only to the SMO leadership and the gifts are publicly announced as "anonymous" (sometimes such gifts appear truly to be anonymous). Because of the shadowy role of angels, it is difficult to gauge their importance in SMOs as a category. Given all the "rumors of angels" heard in various SMOs, my own guess is that they are much more important than commonly recognized.[5] One special form of angeling is the *bequest*, or *annuity* in which elderly SMO members or sympathizers are encouraged to make will or trust arrangements that benefit the SMO. (Solicitations to do this are seen with some regularity in SMO publications—as they are in the publications and mail solicitations of virtually every institution of higher education, for that matter.)[6]

3. Dues. Perhaps surprisingly, dues vary quite widely in their importance to SMO financing. Some few SMOs/movements have, historically, been able to impose and collect dues that were most or even all of SMO spending. Labor movement SMOs are the prototypical case, which because of their workplace base have more leverage over members than SMOs whose members are geographically more dispersed. Other SMOs may have dues leverage based on their epistemologically radical beliefs (as discussed in Chapter 5) that are religious. In these, dues are termed "tithing" (or a similar word) and conceived as the sacred duty of upright believers. But for more garden variety volunteer SMOs, the amount of dues and yearly *renewals* are quite problematic. Kept low in order to encourage renewal, dues in such SMOs often make up half or less of yearly spending (e.g., Lofland 1993a, 166–68).

4. Direct Mail. Direct mail solicitations to buy merchandise burgeoned in the United States from the seventies through the nineties. The success of this strategy did not pass unnoticed among many SMOs, which began to develop their own specialized mailing lists and letters soliciting donations. Although not as large scale and professionally slick as those of mainstream merchandise retailers, SMO mail solicitations provide important portions of many SMO budgets. (SMO direct mail is discussed in Oliver and Marwell 1992, 261.)

5. Phone Banks. Likewise what is called "telemarketing" among retailers and "phone banking" among SMOs burgeoned in the United States over that same period. This has proved a successful tactic for many SMOs and it is especially lucrative in periods of heightened sensitivity to given issues. For example, during the 1980s surge of citizen concern over Reagan administration bellicosity regarding nuclear weapons, SANE's "phonaton" program was raising on the order of one million dollars a year (Lofland 1993a, 162). (No tactic is without its problems, however, and telemarketing and phone banking came up against the phone answering machine in the nineties—and likely stimulated the growth of the answering machine industry.)[7]

6. Fundraising Events. One standard way to raise money for election campaigns in the U.S. political mainstream is to stage a fund-raising event, a "fund-raiser." These vary greatly in the degree of glitter of the locale, the formality of the occasion, and the cost of admission (the "donation"), ranging from thousands of dollars per person down to quite modest amounts. As with techniques just described, fund-raiser possibilities have not been lost on SMOs, which have done their own commonly more modest versions. The organizing foci of such gatherings are quite varied, including talks by movement celebrities, concerts by movement-oriented performers, motion picture showings, runs, walks, dances, tours of exotic buildings or places, and simple "cocktail" type shmoozing in someone's large home. For some SMOs, such events form a significant percentage of a year's income. (Some contingencies in organizing fundraising events are reported in Oliver and Marwell 1992, 264–65.)

7. Sales Revenue. A small percentage of SMOs are "firms," which Knoke and Prensky define as organizations "distinguished primarily by the production of goods and services for sale in a marketplace in order to make profits" (1984, 3). SMOs enacting *exemplary* beliefs (Chapter 5, Section II.B) are more likely to be firms in this meaning than are adversary SMOs and to be formed as geographically consolidated communes or "utopias" (as defined above in Section II.B). Less absorbing exemplary SMOs tend to be publishing businesses (books, magazines, newspapers), or to offer educational or health services (e.g., Rothschild and Whitt 1986). Totalistic and exemplary-based religious SMOs such as the Unification Church have a special penchant for starting and operating a wide variety of firms in which members are employed.

Occasionally, an adversary SMO will have an internal literature and paraphernalia sales component of some economic significance (as does, for example, the Fellowship of Reconciliation). A few adversary SMOs focus their economies on a combination of publications and associated bookstores that feature what they publish, as among various radical Marxist SMOs in major North American and European cities [e.g., O'Toole (1977), which describes this pattern in Canada]. At the most modest level of depending on sales, an SMO may hold a yearly or more frequent bake or yard sale. The economic force of these is signaled in the widely circulated movement slogan "It will be a great day when our day care centers have all the money they need and the navy has to hold a bake sale to buy battleships."

8. Public Place Solicitation and Selling. Sales revenue as a source of financing is traditional or "mainstream" in character in that it involves a settled place of business and the fabrication or retailing of products in traditional settings of exchange. Moving beyond this model, some SMOs literally "take to the streets" in search of money using solicitation or selling, or a combination of both techniques. In *solicitation*, strangers are approached in a public place and asked to give money to a worthy cause. In *selling*, an item of some claimed value is offered in exchange for a requested amount. Combining the techniques, an item such as a flower, pamphlet, or book is offered in exchange for a "donation." In a variation called "tabling," a cardtable or ironing board is set up, signatures on petitions may be solicited, and literature for sale displayed. In the recent American past, religious more than secular SMOs have fielded these techniques, sometimes with extremely lucrative outcomes. [Bromley and Shupe (1980) estimate that in these ways the Unification Church raised twenty-five million dollars in each year of the late 1970s.]

9. Canvassing. While not common among SMOs in general, the 1970s innovation called "the canvass" merits mention. Reported to have been invented in the early 1970s as an explicit application of door-to-door encyclopedia selling to community organizing, canvassing involves a corps of solicitors who go door to door in the early evening hours offering memberships in and contributions to a particular SMO. The canvassers are ordinarily paid a minimum stipend and a percentage of what they collect (Oliver and Marwell 1992, 261–62).

10. Gambling. One proposition about funding I might insert as an aside is that the closer to the mainstream are the animating beliefs of an SMO, the more likely it is to employ mainstream techniques in raising funds. At least, this possibility is suggested by the tendency of less radical SMOs to employ such milder forms of gambling as raffles and lotteries that are much like those seen among mainstream civic and community groups.

11. Hat Passing.   Although it seems on the decline in the twentieth century, passing a hat (or whatever container) through an emotionally aroused crowd of the faithful has been historically a standard and apparently lucrative way to raise funds. While stereotypically associated with SMOs of "religious" rather than "political" beliefs, it is by no means confined to them and the practice continues in some SMOs.

12. Expropriation.   SMOs whose beliefs tilt in one or more of the several "existential" directions I enumerated in Chapter 5 (Section III.B), and who are therefore, by definition, most condemning of the mainstream, can more easily begin to conceive mainstream financial resources as illegitimately and illegally held. Especially when the beliefs are apocalyptic or millenarian and feature secret malevolent conspiracies among holders of wealth (Chapter 5, Section III.B.6), such holders are not seen as merely undeserving of their wealth. Instead, the SMO has every *right* and a *duty* to take it from them in order to finance the forces of good that the SMO embodies. Hence, *expropriation*, meaning to "take over by preeminent right," as in the Bolshevik sentiment "we steal what has already been stolen." [8] Mainstream labels for this, of course, include theft, robbery, embezzlement, and fraud, depending on the particulars.

In framings of this kind, *banks* and kindred financial institutions and wealthy persons, rather than nonbanking organizations or ordinarily citizens, become targets of choice because they are portrayed as key forces in the conspiracy of evil (and they are of course also more likely to repay one's trouble). It is of particular note that *both* ultraright and ultraleft framings along these lines converge on much the same view of expropriation. (That is, while ultraleft and ultraright groups view each other as their worst enemies, they nonetheless come to the same conclusion about the correct *targets* of expropriation and its *morality*.)

13. Government Aid.   My mention of illegal, coercive, and violent SMO fund-raising moves us decisively beyond the largely "mild" forms and sources on the above list. Having so moved, I certainly cannot conclude without listing a yet more important type of player in "hardball" financing: the governments of many countries attempting to undo (or prop up) the governments of other countries by funding (or subverting) SMOs that oppose (or support) those enemy governments. Commonly secret and illegal, these practices have a long, complicated, and shadowy history—as in the German government engineering Lenin's return to Russia;[9] the Soviet Union subsidizing the U.S. Communist party; the Reagan administration giving aid to the Nicaraguan "contras."

Indeed, in the heyday of the cold war, the Soviet Union and the United States vied in clandestine campaigns of helping (or hindering) SMOs virtually around the world as regards governments each liked or disliked. It is conceivable and highly ironic that governments themselves may be among the most potent mainstream angels of SMOs in the twentieth century (although these have mostly been SMOs outside their own countries).

C. Other Questions and Answers about Financing

One prime task of researchers in profiling the finances of SMOs is to sort through and categorize forms and sources using categories such those I have just given. The profile so discovered then raises a number of further questions for researchers. These include the following.

1. Causes.   Whatever the funding profile, why *this* one and not some other? For example, in North America in the 1970s, public-place solicitation and selling was quite in vogue among new religions. Why was that? And it passed out of vogue in the 1980s. What caused this change? [Bromley and Shupe (1980) propose answers to this question.]

2. Consequences.   What advantages and disadvantages are imposed by a particular pattern of financing? That is, what are the strengths and weaknesses of one SMO financing profile versus another? Consider these two dilemmas (or propositions) posed by two different (but related) profiles of funding.

First, there is the *financial ripsaw dilemma*. Many peace movement SMOs of the 1980s were heavily funded by grants and angels. This had the enormous advantage or strength of quickly available large sums of money that supported very rapid membership growth and high levels of activity. The flip side of grant and angel funding, though, was that each source was *time and task delimited*. When the time of the grant was up or the task completed, the funding need not continue—and in this movement it did not. Therefore, jolting or fatal fund cessations were an enormous weakness or disadvantage. This special profile of funding, indeed, created a financial ripsaw for an entire movement (Lofland 1993a, Part Two).

Second, there can be a *source and control dilemma*. Sources of funding differ in terms of coming from the SMO's own members and its beneficiary constituency—people who stand to benefit by SMO success—or from outsiders, such as foundations and many angels, who do not stand directly to benefit from the SMO. Assuming that "he who pays the piper calls the tune," to depend heavily on outside support is to hand over much control of SMO activities to those outsiders. On the other hand, if the SMO and its beneficiary constituency are poor, not to accept outside funding can be to condemn the SMO to meager efforts focused mostly on simply surviving. Either way, a significant price can be paid, which is why it is a dilemma (McAdam et al. 1988, 725–26).

* * *

In this chapter we have seen how researchers focus on the question of how SMOs are organized. On our list of eight generic questions, the focus has been question (1), What are the aspect's types?—its values on the several variables described in Section II. In Section III, we examined several answers to the expanded form of question (1)—generic question (4), What is the aspect's structure? Called "forms and sources," the main treatment of financing (in Section V) also answered the question, What are the aspect's types?

Now having before us a more textured conception of *what* is organized when researchers speak of SMO organization, we can more knowl-edgeably go on to inspect how researchers ask *why* there is SMO organi-zation in the first place. Phrased as, What are causes of SMOs? this is the central question treated in the next chapter.

NOTES

1.   In some SMOs, though, the pattern of governance is perhaps better con-ceived as fumbling clique domination rather than something as sweepingly grandiose as oligarchy. For example, based on early and mideighties organiza-tional improvement workshops with many peace groups, Ayvazian formulated their "seven deadly sins"—a set of descriptive characteristics. In her view, many tended to exhibit "Founders' Disease [domination by the initial members] lack of long-range planning . . . burnout . . . growth with no plan . . . no clear lines of accountability . . . poor or nonexistent office systems . . . horrendous meetings" (Avyazian 1986, 3–15). On frequent vacillation, indecision, and "buffeting" re-garding courses of action, see also Marullo (1990), Wernette (1990), Benford and Zurcher (1990), and Price (1990).

2.   Numerous other researchers have proposed types of SMOs but the formu-lations are not developed in detail sufficient to think of them as structural an-alyses. Such formulations include my own effort to enumerate thirteen forms of volunteer SMO organizations in the American peace movement of the 1980s (Lofland 1993a, Ch. 4). See, further, Curtis and Zurcher (1974), Zurcher and Curtis (1973), and Klandermans, Kriesi, Tarrow (1988).

3.   On cycles of SMO process functioning, see, though Lofland ([1966] 1977, Ch. 12), which dissects cycles of hope and despair in an SMO's history. (This study is summarized in Section V.B.1 of Chapter 8 in this guide.)

4. Longer and more detailed or differently formed lists are given in Lofland (1993a, Ch. 4) and Oliver and Marwell (1992). SMO fund-raising is sometimes viewed as a species of "nonprofit organization" fundraising and numerous manuals provide guidance on ways to raise money in many of the thirteen categories I explain above (and in many other ways). See, for example, Klein (1988) and Krit (1991).

5. "A major source of funding, both to the Party coffers and for Lenin's private needs, came from private benefactors" (Volkogonov 1994, Ch. 1).

6. For further discussion of grants and angels, see Oliver and Marwell (1992, 260), who refer to them taken together as "professionalized technologies."

7. Additional aspects of SMO telemarketing are discussed in Oliver and Marwell (1992, 262–63).

8. Volkogonov (1994, 54) details how V. I. Lenin lived comfortably in Europe for many years partly on proceeds from Bolshevik robberies in Russia.

9. Volkogonov (1994, 123ff.). Volkogonov also reviews evidence pertaining to large sums of money the Kaiser's government gave to Lenin and company in support of their political work in Russia—i.e., in support of weakening Russia in the war against Germany.

7

What Are Causes of SMOs?

In the title of this chapter I phrase generic question number (5) (What are the aspect's causes?) as applied to SMOs as, What are causes of SMOs? I am not pleased with this way of stating the question and I use it only because it is slightly less problematic than the alternatives. Numbering this phrasing (1), other even more problematic phrasings include:

2. How do people successfully start SMOs?
3. When do SMOs form?
4. Why do SMOs form?
5. What are the causes of SMOs?

The problem with these five ways of casting or framing the causal question about SMOs is that each encourages the researcher to attend or disattend to some things more than to others. Specifically, numbers (2) and (3) tilt us in the direction of active human agency, encouraging us to focus on how people organize SMOs—the beliefs, techniques, and broader strategies organizers employ in creating SMOs. This is fine but it is a "tilt." What these framings tilt away from is signaled in numbers (4) and (5), which tilt the framing in the opposite direction, toward impersonal, structural, and historical circumstances that may facilitate or inhibit SMOs. While properly moving toward structure, numbers (4) and (5) tilt away from human belief and agency as causal forces.[1]

Of course, researchers rightly seek a phrasing that gives them both worlds, the worlds of agency *and* of structure. The closest to such balance that researchers come at this time is the workable but still structure-tilted phrasing, What are causes of SMOs? or perhaps When and why do SMOs form?

I. THE DEPENDENT VARIABLE REEMPHASIZED

We need to keep clearly in mind that we want to explain the *SMO* and *not* three related (and important) dependent variables.

The first of these is the *social movement* (the SM), the larger constellation of SMOs, campaigns, activists, and events within which many (but not all) SMOs are situated. As elaborated in Chapter 1, examples of such SMs include the labor, civil rights, women's, and prolife movements. Explaining the occurrence of the *surging* or burgeoning of these rapid upswellings of a broad range of protest activism is what "theories of social movements" are mostly about. Identifying the causes of movement surges is certainly pertinent to explaining the causes of SMOs—and many of the causes are the same. But, the surging social movement—the SM—is nonetheless a very different dependent variable. The SM is a diffuse, diverse, and broad range of upsweeping activism involving a great many SMOs. In contrast, the SMO is space and time focused. While it is often difficult (and contentious) to say when an SM "began," the beginnings of SMOs can commonly be traced to specific days, places, and persons. For example and as reported by Jo Freeman the National Organization for Women began on June 30, 1966 when Betty Friedan coined the name and "twenty-eight women paid five dollars each to join" (1983a, 19).

The second related but very different dependent variable is *individual participation or membership* in an SMO or SM. The causes of such "joining" have also been the subject of enormous research (perhaps more even than the causes of SMs). As collectivities of people (or organizations), SMOs are clearly different from individuals and the causal variables at play in the one are quite different in key respects than those at play in the other. (As a matter that affects SMOs, however, in the next chapter I review answers to the question, Why do people join SMOs?)

A third oft focused on dependent variable we want to keep separate from the SMO is the episode or episodes of crowd insurgency. An archetypal instance is the "Stonewall Rebellion," the name given several evenings of late June 1969 over which patrons of a New York City bar called the Stonewall Inn rioted in resistance to police harassment of them at that establishment This episode is often taken as the space- and time-specific start of the gay and lesbian rights movement, but it did not directly involve SMOs. Instead, it was an emergent crowd and protest response to chronic grievances. Such crowd (and mass) actions have their distinct causal dynamics that are importantly different from SMOs. (On such dynamics see McPhail 1991; 1996; Tarrow 1994).

II. ORGANIZING CAUSAL VARIABLES

As complex social phenomena, SMOs have complex causes that operate at several (1) levels of social organization and (2) degrees of immediate change involved leading to the formation of the SMO. That is, researchers *classify the causes* of SMOs in terms of the two variations of:

1. macro-, meso-, or micro *scale* of social organization, time, and geography, and,
2. *standing arrangements versus situational changes* in fostering or inhibiting SMO formation.

The first variable—*macro-meso-micro scale*—seeks to take account of the fact that causes operate at different geographical and temporal distances from SMO formation and at varying scales of social organization—from *micro* circumstances of immediate face-to-face encounters, through *meso-* (meaning middle) arrangements of workplaces, milieux, networks, neighborhoods, and the like, to *macro* structures and events, such as repressive governments, capitalist economies, individualistic cultures, wars, and massive migrations (McAdam et al. 1988).

The second variable—*standing arrangements versus situational changes*—seeks to recognize that from the point of view of new SMO formation, certain factors that are in fact among causal forces have not changed recently in ways that proximately stimulate (or dampen) or facilitate (or inhibit) the SMO. Instead, in proximate perspective, these factors are "standing arrangements" that nonetheless facilitate or inhibit SMO formation. (This does not mean, however, that though these variables are unchanging or have never changed, simply that even though they are stable, they have causal significance in the proximate situation of SMO formation).

In order to simplify reporting, I am going to treat these two variables for classifying causes as *dichotomies*, i.e., as assuming only two values each. It needs nonetheless to be recognized that these are continuous variables rather than dichotomies. This simplification is shown in Figure 7.1, where, in particular, "meso" is combined with "micro."

This scheme for organizing causal variables differs from the approach of movement researchers who prefer to think of causes in term of competing "schools," "perspectives," or "theories" that are pitted against one another in pseudocontests over correctness. For reasons I give in Chapter 13 of this guide and elsewhere (Lofland 1993b), I am critical of this "theory-bashing" approach and I do not use that mind-set here. I have tried instead to select important and valid elements from every and

Figure 7.1. SMO causes.

	Macro	Meso-Micro
Standing Arrange-ments	1. Social Inequality and Change 2. Political Opportunity 3. State Penetration of Citizen Life 4. Prosperity 5. Geographical Concentration 6. Prior Organization and Collective Identity 7. Cross-cutting Solidarities 8. Perceptions and Cultures of Injustice	13. Leadership Availability 14. Communication Networks and Similar Resources 15. Network Integration among Potential Formers 16. Situational Availability among Potential Formers
Situational Changes	9. Regime Crises and Contested Political Arenas 10. Recent Decline in Amount of Repression 11. Focal Points/Focusing Crises 12. Citizen Surge Synergy	17. Frame Alignment and Alignment Skill 18. Belief in the Necessity and Effectiveness of Forming

any perspective on the causes of SMs and SMOs and to assemble them into a synthesized account tailored to SMOs.

Happily, other researchers have also thought that synthesizing accounts are preferable to sterile "theory-bashing" and their efforts inform this inventory. Specifically, the comprehensive statement by Doug McAdam, John McCarthy, and Mayer Zald (1988) is especially valuable and I adopt both their broad approach and many of their detailed statements of variables, albeit with some reorganization, alternations, and additions. Because I cite them so frequently, I try to save a tree branch or two by abbreviating their names as MMZ. (Their treatment is itself, of course, a synthesizing compilation of previous variables and schemes of variables and I strive also to acknowledge and to incorporate those efforts.[2])

III. CAUSAL LOGIC

The variables I am going to explain are summarized in the four cells of Figure 7.1. Before examining them, we need to think about the logic of the way each, alone or in combination, may or may not be a causal factor or causal factors in SMO formation.

The first critical appreciation is that all of the eighteen variables shown in Figure 7.1 are exactly that: *variables*. They can be present or absent or *present to one or another degree* (i.e., in varying strength) in any given case. Because all eighteen can have different strengths from case to case, every specific case might well exhibit a somewhat different or even unique profile of the strength of each variable. But summed or otherwise composited over all eighteen, each case will have a level of *composite causal* force behind it. So composited, some cases will have very low causal force while yet others may be very high.

Cases with the *same* composite casual force that have led to SMO formation may be composed of variables that are individually quite different in the strength of specific variables. But these differences are nonetheless composite in strength sufficient to form an SMO. For example:

SMO A's macro variables may all be strong, while all its micro variables are weak, whereas
SMO B's variables are the reverse—all its macro variables are weak and its micro variables are strong.

Nonetheless, both SMOs form because there is sufficient *composite causal force* in each case, despite the fact that the strengths of the variables are different in each case.

Among more extreme possibilities of combinations of strengths of causal variables, it is possible that some or even perhaps many variables can be *zero* (i.e., they are absent), *but* enough *other* variables are of strengths sufficient to lead to SMO formation despite zero strength or absent variables (cf. Amenta and Zylan 1991; Lieberson 1992).

All of this is background to saying that researchers are reasonably but tentatively confident that these eighteen variables (or a successor formulation of them) are involved in SMO formation, but the *degree* of the exact role of any of them in given cases is *variable and uncertain*.

The list in Figure 7.1 and my text explaining it should therefore be taken as the specification of a *range of causal possibilities* that will have different causal force and salience from case to case.

Proceeding now to the variables, I first report standing arrangements and situational changes in *macro* variables affecting the formation of SMOs.

IV. MACRO–SMO CAUSAL VARIABLES

As just explained, macro variables differ among themselves in terms of being structural arrangements that are more or less static but that nonetheless facilitate or inhibit the occurrence—the formation—of an SMO. These need to be distinguished from changes in the proximate situation that promotes or retards the crystallization of an SMO.

A. Standing Arrangements

Drawing on and adapting MMZ and other compositors, as indicated, the following are among eight main macro "standing arrangements" that, in sufficient strength in combination with other variables, are productive of SMO formation.

1. Social Inequality and Change.   Inequality in its myriad forms and possibilities is *a* if not *the* central standing arrangement that sets the stage for SMOs (as well as for SMs, a twin fact that is so often true that I will make not make specific mention of it hereafter). By inequality, researchers mean unequal distribution of the valued things of life: physical wholeness; good health and health care; education; meaningful, powerful, safe, and highly paid work; power to influence economic and political affairs; wealth; pleasant natural and human-built environments; respectful and dignified treatment in everyday life.

The unequal distribution of such valued things has been, of course organized on various bases or "principles," some main forms of these being physical condition, gender, age, ethnicity, nationality, social class, and religious creed. Devising hierarchically ordered categories on one or more of these bases, *some* rather than *other* people are asserted to deserve more of what is valued, as in, at one or another time and place:

- the physically able more than the physically challenged,
- men more than women,
- adults more than children,
- whites more than blacks,

- English more than Irish,
- middle more than working class,

and on and on and on through a very, very long list.

Inequality is not, of course, in itself enough to cause an SMO (or other collective objection). Unequal distributions of valued things are historically and contemporaneously ubiquitous and constant, while SMOs form only some of the time. Because a variable (SMOs) cannot be explained with a constant (inequality), inequality alone is insufficient as a causal account. Nonetheless, it grinds away in the background of standing arrangements. But when *combined with* other variables the probability of an SMO increases.

Since every viable and enduring post-hunting-and-gathering society has been fundamentally hierarchical and therefore highly unequal in a great many ways, there is an ironic sense in which society is itself a root cause of SMOs. An updated version of Michels's "iron law," which says "who says organization says oligarchy," might well read "who says society says SMOs."[3]

Moreover, forms of *social change* continually create new forms of inequality and exacerbate others.

> Population growth, migration, the growth of cities and of industry, changes in technology, in modes of production, communication, organization and the scale of society are everywhere accompanied by changes in the everyday lives and security of ordinary people. Some groups advance while other stand still or decline. . . . It is the rising and declining groups and classes formed and transformed during periods of change that usually constitute the core of social movements and organized groups who seek to reform and revolutionize existing institutions or, on the contrary, defend the social order under attack. (Oberschall 1973, 34–35)

Oberschall also refers to such alternations in hierarchy as "changes in basic life conditions . . . likely to produce discontent and ineffectiveness in the usual ways for providing relief and handling problems" (Oberschall 1993, 17). Among myriad instances of this "demand side" variable (as Oberschall terms it), MacLean (1994), as summarized by Blee, has argued that the Ku Klux Klan of the 1920s was, in part, responding to a

> growing demand for rights by women, African American and young people [, a fact that] caused widespread anxiety among white men. To these men it appeared that the new assertiveness of women, men, youth and African Americans threatened their authority both in the home and in the political sphere. At the same time, the growing chasm between elite owners and militant workers seemed to jeopardize the economic security and social respectability of petty-producer households. The Klan, MacLean argues, mounted a powerful appeal to white middle-class men by down-

playing social class divisions and emphasizing those based on race and gender. In the Klan white men fought to recover racial privilege, to reclaim control over their wives and children, and to assert their place in the new economic order. (Blee 1995, 346)

Although the inequalities and changes at issue may be economic or political in character (as is evident in the Klan example), they can also be *cultural*, meaning "designs for social organization" that have come under attack and that SMOs are now defending (Oberschall 1993, 377). Gusfield (1963) has termed these more culture- or life-style-spurred SMOs *symbolic crusades*. As summarized by Snow and Worden, the causal dynamic is that

should the life-style of a status group that has enjoyed some measure of prestige and dominance [be] challenged by another status group, or by various changes within the ambient society, then the threatened group may well become the social base for a movement that seeks to preserve or enhance the "honor" of its lifestyle. The rhetoric of such a movement is usually moral in tone and seeks through public acts to reaffirm the propriety of its way of life. Law becomes the primary avenue for this public affirmation, either in the legislature or the courtroom. (Snow and Worden 1993, 342).

Taking "everyday life" as starting point in thinking about movements, Flacks phrases these matters of inequality and change in this way:

There would be no basis [for social movements] if society were organized so that every member had the opportunity for a safe, secure and self-governing private life—presumably if a ruling elite could guarantee such circumstances, its legitimacy would be unchallenged. [But in] advanced capitalist societies . . . gross inequalities exist with respect to the chances people have for decent everyday existence. . . . Massive structural contradictions give rise to periodic crises in the economy that disrupt material conditions for everyday well-being. Massive misallocation of power and resources generate chronic experiences of threat to security and safety— e.g., crime, pollution, deterioration of public service, tax burdens. These inherent features of the social order create a continuing basis for mass movements aimed at resisting unwanted encroachment on daily life. In addition to such structural contradictions, there is a rich diversity of cultural contractions stemming from cultural values emphasizing equality, freedom and dignity, from the endless circulation of conflicting ideas about the good life, and from the many ways in which the culture legitimates but the social order fails to implement a variety of personal needs. (Flacks 1976, 278–79)

Social movement researchers have a special appreciation of the inequality and change backdrop of social movements. This appreciation makes them prone to speculate on what will be the next great social movement surges of SMO formation. Attuned to ideas like those I re-count just above, they scan the social horizon for such things as "the mismatch between individual potential and social opportunity in an aging population" or "structural lag of human institutions behind the changes in human lives." At one point in the 1990s, speculators fixed on *age* inequalities as likely the next great engine of movement activity, as in this prediction: "After grasping the contradictions that [the book *Age and Social Lag*] lays out, I found it almost necessary to predict a twenty-first century revolutionary transformation of age-related structures as tho-rough-going as the civil rights and feminist revolutions of the twentieth" (Smelser 1995, 273, commenting on Riley, Kahn, and Foner 1995).

2. Political Opportunity. Societies differ in the extent to which they are receptive to ("vulnerable" to) SMO action (MMZ 1988, 699; Kitschelt 1986). This variation is termed the degree of *political opportunity* and in attending to it researchers seek to specify ways in which and the degrees to which there are opportunities to undertake movement action.

Conceived in the broadest terms, some commentators have suggested a curvilinear relation between political opportunities in the sense of the degree to which a society has a "fully democratic, participatory system" and the degree to which there are SMOs. The hypothesis of cur-vilinearity suggests that there are few or no new SMOs in societies in which elites prohibit all or most forms of democratic participation—societies, that is, of consistent repression. Thus, most of the histories of the Soviet Union and of the nations of Eastern Europe dominated by the Soviet Union were marked by the *absence* of surging SMOs. But in those nations (and in other nations), as opportunities for participation in-creased, so did SMOs. At the other extreme, this theory holds, a com-pletely or fully democratic society would also not have new SMOs, for problematic conditions developing among all segments of the popula-tion would receive receptive and corrective attention long before any impetus to marginal, excluded reality constructions and actions.

SMOs may therefore be especially characteristic of quasi-democratic societies—societies in which there is *some* semblance of honoring demo-cratic participation, but democracy that has not been fully realized. As put by movement strategist Bill Moyer regarding the United States: "We only need such pressure because *our* system won't respond to meet the true, obvious social needs unless we push it to" (1988, 6, emphasis in the original). [See also Eisinger (1973), on the paradox of protest and, in addition, Amenta and Zylan (1991; 1992), Jasper (1990), Jasper and Nelkin (1992).]

Conceived more narrowly, the political opportunity variable as it oper-ates in semidemocratic societies can refer to the degree to which a political processes is organized in a way that does or does not provide occasions that people can target for action. An instructive example of this variation in the availability of feasible targets is seen in the contrast between France and the United States regarding political processes attendant to siting and constructing nuclear power plants. In the United States, siting and constructing nuclear power plants have required an elaborate set of pubic hearings and other forms of opportunity for public attention. In France, in contrast, there have been few or no occasions of public hearing and review. In political opportunity terms, the United States has been much richer in political opportunities than France. And, in fact, anti–nuclear power SMOs have been much more frequent (and stronger) in the United States than in France (Kitschelt 1986).

3. State Penetration of Citizen Life.   One long-term trend in relations between states and citizens is expansion of the range of ways in which (and the degree to which) the former has control of or power over the latter. To the degree that these penetrations advance, the stage is set for citizens to target the state and its agents. Put differently, in penetrating citizen life, the state can be defined as *responsible* for citizen life. The more responsibility the state assumes, the greater is the likelihood that citizens will demand the state live up to its responsibilities.

This proposition applies in a broad way to SMOs of all varieties, but some researchers have thought it applies most strongly to SMOs in what are called the "new" social movements, meaning mostly the women's, environmental, and peace movements (which are distinguished from "old" social movements, referring principally to labor and ethnic-group movements). These new social movement are thought by some theorists to be resisting the "politicization of private life" and attempting "to regain control over decisions and areas of life increasingly subject to state control" (MMZ 1988, 701). For the state to penetrate citizen life is also to "create new status groups who are dependent" on the state for "the satisfaction of a wide range of material and status needs" (p. 702). Such dependency without full democracy (variable 2, above) sponsors conditions of frustration and resentment that set the stage for ensembles of new SMOs (Kerbo 1982; Melucci 1989; Larana, Johnston, and Gusfield 1994; Calhoun 1994).

4. Prosperity.   One commonsense or "folk" belief about the causes of SMOs is that people most economically deprived are the most prone to react to this deprivation by forming SMOs with the aim of ending their deprivation. An extension of this proposition holds that as societies become more prosperous, the incidence of SMOs declines. A quite considerable body of research literature finds little or no support for either of these propositions! Instead, within limits, the reality is the opposite.

Prosperity or lack of it operates at two levels: the individual and societal. At the individual level, severe economic deprivation weakens the will and capacity of people to sustain more than "momentary insurgency" (MMZ 1988, 702) (what I depict as "crowd/mass insurgency" in Chapter 1). Recall that one of the "earmark" characteristics of SMOs (and SMs) is that they are *enduring* as opposed to ephemeral efforts to achieve social or personal change (Chapter 1, Section I.C.4). Among the most economically deprived we *do* find various forms of transient or ephemeral protest or violent action, meaning, especially, various forms of rioting. This is not, however, SMO or SM action.

At the societal level, prosperity as a feature of social organization increases the availability of a wide range of resources that facilitate SMOs. Among these are such things as telephones, cheap document reproduction, and—increasingly—access to computer and other electronic technology (e.g., electronic bulletin boards, faxes), which have been critically helpful to more recent SMOs (McCarthy and Zald 1987a; 1987b).

The paradox then is that prosperous societies (that are also not yet fully democratic, a la variable 2, above) are hotbeds of SMOs.

5. Geographical Concentration. The variables so far described address aspects of the larger, *containing environment* to which people react. The four variables to which we now come, in contrast, focus on the *internal structure of a population* from which SMOs may arise. As variables, these four may or may not assume states that facilitate or inhibit the formation of new SMOs.

The first of these is degree of geographic—or "ecological"—concentration, referring to the degree to which the people who might participate in an SMO live in physical proximity to one another and, allied with this, are also homogeneous on other social characteristics (such as economic level, language, religion, and culture). To the degree that people are concentrated and homogeneous in these senses, new SMOs are facilitated (assuming facilitating states of other variables). The reasoning here is that proximity and social homogeneity increase the physical and psychological ease of interaction, which in turn facilitates collective action of all kinds, including new SMOs. Conversely, geographical dispersion and social heterogeneity inhibit collective action.

Such geographical concentrations that are productive of SMOs (as well as other insurgencies) have been well documented among workers in territorially isolated occupations (Kerr and Siegel 1954), ethnic/racial enclaves or ghettoes (Morris 1984), and "youth ghettoes" (Heirich 1971; Lofland 1985, Ch. 3), among other ecological amalgamations.

Ironically, in their zeal to repress and punish insurgent realities, main-

stream elites sometimes themselves create concentrated enclaves of insurgents, which become ecological training grounds for even more re-
silient SMO insurgency. One especially clear and colorful instance is the
British internment, at Frongoch, North Wales, of over 1,800 Irishmen
who participated in the Easter Rising of 1916. As reported by Sean
O'Mahony, the British let the internees organize their own affairs in the
camp and it became a "university of revolution" (the subtitle of his book
on Frongoch). "The Frongoch Internment camp provided an ideal opportunity for the [Irish Republican Army] to develop the philosophy of
revolution. The internees returned home to Ireland to organize and later
to engage the might of the British Empire in a war of independence"
(1987, 246).

   6. Prior Organization and Collective Identity. Populations that exhibit high degrees of geographical/ecological concentration and social
homogeneity can and do still differ in the degree to which their people
have also created forms of social organization among themselves—a
variable that is also sometimes referred to as differential *density* of organization. Being close together and similar (variable 5 immediately above)
is more potent when it is reinforced by occurring in a population that
already has a great many ways in which people are meeting together in
preexisting or prior organization. The reasoning here is that SMOs, by
definition, involve organization. To the degree that organization is not
already there, it must now be constructed in some crisis/opportunity
situation. But to the degree that it already exists, one need not perform
that step in forging collective action. Existing organization (meeting
places, telephones, printing machinery, settled hierarchies, relations of
knowing and trust, etc.) can simply be *turned to* the new movement
purposes.
   Researchers of varied dispositions have devised a variety of labels for
such prior organization. In historical sequence, these include:

- "pre-existing friendship nets" (Lofland [1966] 1977, 60–62),
- "solidary community" and "bloc recruitment"(Oberschall 1973, 121,125),
- co-optable and "preexisting communications networks or infra-structure" (Freeman 1975, 48),
- a category of people forming a network (abbreviated "catnet") (Tilly 1978, 63),
- movement "half-way houses" (Morris 1981),
- "indigenous organizational strength" (McAdam 1982, 43–48),
- "micro-mobilization contexts" (MMZ 1988, 709-11).

As one of the more widespread and facilitating forms of organization
among Americans, the *churches* of the several religious denominations of

that nation have been, historically, among the most important kind of prior organization out of which any number of new SMOs—of the political *left, center, and right*—have arisen.

The sloganized proposition that captures this variable is: *New organization arises out of old organization.* Like all slogans, this one is, strictly speaking, only approximately accurate, but it does capture the spirit of the truth that new SMOs are often incubated and hatched in and around ordinary and preexisting association. It is such an appreciation, indeed, that prompts totalitarian governments to try to either *prohibit* organization among its citizens or *totally to manage* all organization among citizens.

7. Cross-Cutting Solidarities. The new SMO potential of a population is increased to the degree its members *lack* "ties to other groups in society" (MMZ 1988, 704; Oberschall 1973, Ch. IV). To have many and strong ties to members of other groups is to be compromised by one's loyalties to them (and one's economic and other dependence on them) and to be susceptible to appeals to loyalty by them. Moreover, when such separation or segregation is quite pronounced, these other groups are likely to lack "the minimum ties required to threaten political or economic reprisal" (MMZ 1988, 704). Potential SMO participants can perceive this lack of power to take reprisals and be all the more emboldened because of this realization.

The reluctance that many women have displayed regarding women's movement SMOs is frequently interpreted in terms of this variable. Not only have women been dispersed (variable 4), they have been "linked to men through a wide variety of social, political, and economic ties" (p. 704). "Efforts to create groups or communities free from male influence, such as consciousness raising groups or feminist communes, attest to the seriousness of the problem as well as to the attempts of feminists to deal with it" (p. 704).

8. Perceptions and Cultures of Injustice. The variables I have reported to this point pertain to political, economic, and population arrangements. While these are all important, they neglect a critical matter: the degree to which the population in which SMOs might develop has a perception or "sense" that some social arrangement or personal condition is *unjust*. The perception of injustice is a very special cognition in that it goes beyond the belief that something is wrong but that is the way life *is*. It does this by asserting that something is wrong and *it does not have to be the way it is*. It *can* be changed and *should* be changed because there are *insufficient good reasons* to leave it that way and *more than sufficient reasons* to justify changing it. Moreover, at least in theory and under proper circumstances it *could* (or can) be changed. It happens that such perceptions of injustice are quite variable in human populations (at least until recently) and have only been achieved in certain circumstances.

Even so, many ethnic, national, and religious enclaves harbor *standing perceptions of injustice*, or as Snow and Oliver phrase it, "cultural traditions of activism." Beyond their structural meaning for SMO formation, such enclaves

> often give rise to ongoing cultures of resistance and struggle that are transmitted across generations. In these contexts, children grow up with almost continuous exposure to a structure of grievances and beliefs that justify activism. [e.g., SMO formation] (1994, 580)[4]

Moreover, subpopulations not themselves already possessing senses or cultures of injustice can become aware that such perceptions are active and actively promoted in yet other subpopulations. Given the objective ubiquitousness of social inequality and change and misfortune in general in human life, perceptions of self as unjustly treated might, in some circumstances, produce entire "nations of victims" (Sykes 1992).

* * *

The foregoing macro variables are all more or less continuing conditions that affect the likelihood of SMO crystallization. These variables increase or decrease the likelihood of an SMO occurring at the general level of establishing or not establishing an auspicious stage on which such collective action might take place. In functionalist theory, these macro variables are sometimes labeled matters of "conduciveness" (can it happen) and/or "strain" (impetus to happen) (Smelser 1962). However, these macro conditions only make an SMO more likely; they do not absolutely ensure that one will occur.

B. Situational Changes

To these continuing conditions, we need to add temporary, more proximate changes in macro variables that begin to alter people's conceptions of legitimacy, feasibility, and timeliness of SMO formation and action.

9. Regime Crises and Contested Political Arenas. The likelihood of SMOs is increased to the degree that the major dominant and hegemonic groups of a society begin to contest among themselves for the control of central institutions. Such struggles are assessed by yet other sectors of society as increasing the likelihood of their own successful action should they now begin to act. In the terms used by Turner and Killian (1987, 245–48), in witnessing the larger turmoil and troubles of elites, less powerful and organized potential SMO forgers begin to reassess the *feasibility and timeliness* of movement action.

Such regime crisis are themselves sometimes precipitated by events of these kinds:

- The ruling elite becomes involved in a losing military venture (e.g., the United States in Vietnam, Russia/Soviet Union in World War I).
- The state fiscally overextends itself or makes promises of material prosperity or other forms of social justice to segments of the population on which it cannot deliver (Goldstone 1986).
- Elites embark on a bold program of initiatives that run counter to existing understandings about the bounds of elite action (e.g., the Reagan administration's aggressive posture on nuclear weapons, which violated existing conceptions of restraint) (Meyer 1990; MMZ 1988, 700).

A next level of causal question is, Why and how do elites embark on courses of action that are so clearly (in the eyes of a host of citizen onlookers) disastrous? Answers to this question form, of course, an entire discipline in itself. One guide to it that I particularly appreciate is Barbara Tuchman's (1984) *The March of Folly from Troy to Vietnam*.

As I present them here, the two variables of the degree of political opportunity (variable 2 above) and degree of regime crisis differ in that the former refers to characteristics of a stable political arrangement while the latter refers to a new instability in the relations among all the "previously dominant groups or coalitions" (MMZ 1988, 700).[5]

10. Recent Decline in Amount of Repression. Dominant groups in a society react to SMOs and their larger movements with varying degrees of repression or receptiveness at two levels: (1) longstanding and overall stable pattern of repression-receptiveness versus (2) changes in this level made in the recent past and the ongoing present. I have discussed the first level above with regard to the broader conception of the degree of political opportunity variable (variable 2).

We need now to add the second and more proximate level, the level at which dominant groups may begin to relax their repression or controls over various segments of the population, or become simply unable any more to apply controls effectively. Thus, McAdam (1982, 87–90) has documented declining use of the most repressive means of control over African-Americans in the period just preceding the surge of civil rights SMOs in the late fifties and the early and middle sixties. More broadly, one concomitant of some regime crises is "the collapse of the state as a repressive agent," a proximate change that powerfully encourages the citizen perceptions of new opportunities (or dangers) that are so central to SMO formation (MMZ 1988, 701; variable 18 below; see also Useem 1980).

11. Focal Points/Focusing Crises. One of the variables that stimulates or sharpens a sense of injustice (and also interacts with other variables in fostering or inhibiting new SMOs) is the degree to which incidents occur that serve to *dramatize*, heighten, or *focus* otherwise unfocused or diffuse discontent. Egregious court decisions, large-scale industrial accidents, and major military defeats in ongoing wars are among more familiar types of focal points that have critically fueled the formation of new SMOs. As dramatic episodes or incidents, they furnish vehicles that summarize injustice and provide rallying points for possible collective action.

As with preexisting organization, researchers have used varied labels in speaking of this variable:

- "[P]recipitating factors," meaning "events [that] provide a concrete setting toward which collective action can be directed" (Smelser 1962, 17).
- "[F]ocal points . . . signal hope of success and the weakness of existing social control mechanisms" (Oberschall 1973, 138).
- "[A] crisis [is] usually one or more events that symbolically embody the underlying discontent [and that] galvanizes [a network] into spontaneous action in a new direction" (Freeman 1975, 49).
- Groups can "find themselves confronted with a suddenly realized [e.g., Love Canal] or suddenly imposed (court-ordered busing, a major oil spill, etc.) grievance." The accident at the Three Mile Island nuclear power plant in 1979 was one in a "growing number of instances where suddenly imposed major grievances have been important in explaining grass roots mobilization phenomena" (Walsh 1981, 2, 17; see also Haines 1992).

Events constructed as "focal points" or "crises" must, of course, be exactly that: *cognitively constructed* by definers of them as such. Events "out there" also obviously differ in the ease with which this construction-as-crisis/focal point can be accomplished. Some, especially of a "natural" disaster sort, may be much more amenable to a crisis construction than events that are more simply "social" in character (Killian 1984). Given that enterprise can be required in defining an event as a focal point or crisis, adroit movement entrepreneurs are often on the "lookout" for episodes that can be so responded to—or can even set about to *create* such episodes (cf. Alinsky [1946] 1969; 1972).

12. Citizen Surge Synergy. SMOs tend to form in spurts or "surges." This fact clues us to the special pertinence of the macro situational changes just enumerated (variables 9 through 11) and, in addition, to the possibility that previous SMO formations in a surging series encourage subsequent SMO formations. Earlier formations function as models for and encouragers of an expanding number of later formations. "If they can do it, so can we" is one folk expression of an emergent atmosphere of *synergy* in which existing SMOs stimulate new ones. In this way, SMO formations feed on themselves.

This synergistic process among SMOs is itself embedded in a *wider field* of forces and events that are also interacting with SMOs and among themselves. As Sam Marullo and I view it, this wider field can display a "ratcheting effect [that is] multiplied over several classes of events" in a "synergistic or feedback fashion" (Lofland and Marullo 1993, 240–41). In the case we dissected, that of soaring formations of peace SMOs in the 1980s, eight such classes of events were part of this synergy or interaction spiral:

> (1) ruling elite goading events, (2) local dissenting events, (3) dissident elite legitimizing events, (4) national dissenting events, (5) coalescing events [our name for SMO formations], (6) media events, (7) funding events, (8) public opining events. (p. 243; see also Downs 1972)

This is to say that SMO formers were responding to previous SMO formations *and also* to a complex, ongoing, reinforcing, and synergistic interplay of seven other classes of events (Hilgartner and Bosk 1988; Katsiafricas 1987; Mauss 1975; Snow and Benford 1992).

* * *

Continuing with the discussion of causal logic begun in Section III, researchers posit that these standing and situational macro variables *interact among themselves* and not only in effects on SMOs. For example, there is likely a strong *reinforcing* interaction between increase in state penetration and dependency (variable 3) and a semidemocratic society (variable 2). As the former increases without sufficient increase in the latter, the discrepancy between the power of the state over a person and the person's capacity to affect remedies for dissatisfactions increases. Conversely, there is likely a *dissipating* interaction between high geographical concentration (variable 5) and high degrees of cross-cutting solidarities (variable 7). Considering several or all these variables simultaneously creates a quite complex set of reinforcing and dissipating interactions. Studies of particular cases invite assessment of how these and yet others variables interplay in various ways that do and do not result in new SMOs of several types and scales, especially as regards the level of *contentiousness* we observe in the actions of SMOs (discussed in Chapter 9).

In analyzing one or more SMOs, one task is to assess the degree to which these—or other—macro causal variables would appear to be operative and at what level of strength. Such assessments of all these variables yields profile of causal variables.

V. MESO-MICRO–SMO CAUSAL VARIABLES

In order further to increase the likelihood of an SMO, we need to add particular constellations of a second level of variables—those of meso-micro contexts—in which actual SMO action may or may not occur as a function of the strength of several variables at this level and in these contexts.

The degrees of presence and strength of *macro* variables describes a world that is "out there" from the point of view of potential SMO formers. That macro world provides *possible* stimuli to action and *possible* opportunities for action.[6] Such possibilities have not yet, however, been translated into a *shared belief* that collective action *should* be taken, *can* be taken, and *will* be taken. By themselves, macro variables do not describe and account for the development of the *active capacity to act* or the *decision* to act in an SMO. How, therefore, do this capacity and such decisions come about? At least six meso-microscopic variables (13–18) are involved, variables that are greatly dependent on their *joint operation* for causal effectiveness.

Another way to think of these meso-micro variables is as ways in which the immediate face-to-face and interactional situations of potential participants vary, a level that MMZ (1988) label "micro mobilization contexts." Some forms of these immediate situations are more supportive of collective action in SMOs than others. The ways in which these immediate contexts can vary in supportive and not supportive ways are captured (at least in part) in the following six variables.

A. Standing Arrangements

As among macro variables, meso-micro variables are of two types: *standing* meso-microscopic arrangements versus *situational* meso-microscopic *changes.* (These are shown in the two right-hand cells of Figure 7.1.)

13. Leadership Availability. In a great many situations, human beings are quite reluctant to "stick their neck out," to use the colloquial phrase, and to take risks in a public and organized way, especially on socially quarrelsome matters that are the, by definition, objects of movement-type activity. People must be *encouraged* to take risks on socially or personally contentious, shameful, or other emotionally invested topics and they need to be shown how to do so by yet others who are willing to take the lead. People who so encourage and organize are, by definition, leaders, or at least organizers.[7]

Populations vary in the degree to which they contain people who are prepared to assume these tasks of leadership—of defining a situation quarrelsomely, suggesting action regarding it, and organizing concrete action in which others will participate—the rudiments of the SMO. Despite strong degrees of the twelve *macro* variables listed, populations lacking in such leaders will be populations tending not to have new SMOs (although there may be many ephemeral forms of rioting and other collective defiance).

In order for people to follow, people must *trust* these would-be SMO leaders; they must think they will act wisely and can deliver astute leadership. It is no accident, as a consequence, that leaders of SMOs tend also to have *already been leaders* in some context—to have already shown that they know how to lead and be trusted to lead. In some circumstances such trust is founded in family affiliations, as appears in part to have been the case with Martin Luther King, Jr. Both his father and grandfather were prominent in "the national Baptist movement [and] when King came on the scene, . . . 'you probably couldn't find a black Baptist preacher who wouldn't have known who he was, because they knew his family'" (Clayborne Carson quoted in the *Chronicle of Higher Education* 1992, A7).[8]

The key point here is that a population lacking in such preexisting leaders is a population less likely to crystallize new SMOs. (This is only one of a large number of ironic ways in which the unconventional—insurgent reality—behavior of SMOs is intimately tied to the most conventional aspects of standing social organization.)

14. Communication Networks and Similar Resources. Leaders need resources with which to communicate with one another and possible participants, to field projects of action, and to stimulate certain collective cognitive processes to which I will come shortly. Concretely, they (and participants more generally) need places to meet, telephones or other means of contact, document duplication equipment and supplies, and the like. The particular states of geographical concentration (variable 5), prior organization and collective identity (variable 6), and cross-cutting solidarities (variable 7) figure strongly in the degree to which such resources will be at hand.

But the mere strong presence of such resources is not enough. More than proximate, they must be *available* by consent or other arrangement with those who control them. Sometimes would-be leaders are the custodians of such resources and therefore simply use them. Aldon Morris reports:

> Nearly all the direct-action organizations that initiated . . . early [civil rights movement] sit-ins were closely associated with the [African-American] church[es]. The church supplied these organizations not only with an established communication network, but also leaders and organized masses, finances, and a safe environment in which to hold political meetings. Direct-action organizations clung to the church because their survival depended on it. (Morris 1981, 748)

In a yet more "amenable" pattern, *existing* SMOs of certain varieties may be willing and even enthusiastic about having themselves "used" as staging grounds and launching platforms for new SMOs of compatible beliefs. Morris has termed these SMOs as a class the "movement halfway house," which is:

> an established group or organization that is only partially integrated into the large society because its participants are actively involved in efforts to bring about a desired social change in society. The American Friends Service Committee, The Fellowship of Reconciliation, the War Resisters League, and the Highlander Folk School are examples of modern American halfway houses. . . .
>
> Several preexisting movement halfway houses assisted . . . emerging civil rights movement [SMOs] in a number of important ways. For example, halfway houses assisted in disseminating the tactic of nonviolent direct action, developing mass education programs and publicizing local movements. (1984, 139–40)[9]

At other times, allies need to be coaxed into granting access and use. And at yet other times, these networks and other resources must be used "on the sly," that is, "coopted" (Freeman 1973, 48).

Social networks and other such resources are *variables* and they are simply lacking in some situations—or they are available in only the most modest and insufficient degree. Jackson and associates (1960) have nicely documented such a case in an "attempted property tax revolt in California" where "there was no . . . pre-established network of communication which could quickly be employed to link the suburban residential properly owners who constituted the primary base for the movement" (p. 38, quoted in MMZ 1988, 715).

15. Network Integration among Potential Formers. The three macro variables of ecological concentration (variable 5), prior organization (variable 6), and cross-cutting solidarities (variable 7) are abstract ways of describing the degree to which—at the meso-micro (face-to-face) level—potential SMO formers have (or do not have) strong lines of established interaction and, therefore, interpersonal ties. The consistent finding is that "the more integrated the person is into the aggrieved community, the more readily he or she can be mobilized" into new SMOs and their activities (MMZ 1988, 715).

The integration variable has two referents: the degree or density of such ties in a population taken as a whole versus the degree to which any given individual is integrated. In both cases, the greater the integration, the greater the likelihood of SMO formation. Therefore, the greater the degree of integration, the more likely new and vigorous SMOs.

16. Situational Availability among Potential Formers. Potential participants vary in terms of how easy or difficult it is for them as a practical matter in their everyday lives to be involved in SMO formation and action. This variation is itself a function of how the potential participant's day is structured (the amount of discretionary time in it, for example) and the nature of the action proposed (how easy or difficult it is to fit into the potential former's day or longer period). Potential participants who are involved in a highly regimented day are, other things equal, less available and new SMOs are therefore inhibited. Conversely, potential participants with loosely structured days and with discretion over expenditures of time are more available to form and act in terms of new SMOs. It is thus no accident that populations of affluent students at elite colleges are more frequently the sites of new SMOs than are more regimented populations (McCarthy and Zald 1987a, 341–58).

B. Situational Changes

The above four meso-micro variables (13–16) are all structural or organizational in the sense that they deal with how people are related to one another, their social organization, their behavior skills, or the organization of their daily lives. The presence of all four of these variables in reasonably strong states provide social contexts in which people can carry on discussion of appropriate action. This is discussion, that is, among people who already know one another. Such settings constitute, again, what MMZ label "micro mobilization contexts."

It is in such settings that at least two fundamentally important kinds of *cognitive* processes can take place (or fail to take place). These two processes relate, first, to developing a rationale that *legitimates* the SMO's formation and action, and, second, to developing a belief that the SMO and its actions are *necessary* and will be in some sense worth the effort or be *effective*.

17. Frame Alignment and Aligning Skill. The first of these collective cognitive processes is sometimes spoken of as the problem of aligning the idea of the SMO and its new actions with existing ways in which reality is conceived (i.e., the "frames" that people use to order reality). It is here that the work of leaders assumes such supreme importance, for it is their task to fashion rationales that legitimate the SMO and its "behavioral proscriptions" and prescriptions (MMZ 1988, 713). The success with which leaders can do this is a function of a great many other variables, including the degree of divergence between the SMO and its proposed actions and existing behavioral routines, and the complexity and substance of existing, legitimate frames that can be drawn on in performing the work of alignment. In cases of only small degrees of divergence, leaders need only "bridge," "amplify," or "extend" frames (Snow et al. 1986). In circumstances of high divergence, "transformation" is required.[10]

Here is a nice example of aligning work performed by Rev. Martin Luther King, Jr., before a mass meeting of potential bus boycotters the evening of December 5, 1995, the event at which the Montgomery, Alabama, bus boycott was publicly proclaimed:

> We are not wrong in what we are doing.
> If we are wrong, the Supreme Court of this nation is wrong,
> If we are wrong, the Constitution of the United States in wrong.
> If we are wrong, God Almighty is wrong.[11]

Astute leaders do not bother to orate about matters that are not problematic. King's assertion, "We are not wrong," therefore tells us that some significant portion of those involved are worried about the moral and/or legal propriety of the impending bus boycott. King's skillful, strategic alignment tactic here (his "frame") is the assertion that definitive sources of moral authority *higher* than the city of Montgomery and the state of Alabama define the boycott as moral. Both these entities may define them as wrong (which they would in fact do), but the boycotters were right in the moral light of the Supreme Court, the Constitution, and God. (Generically, this is the "higher law" alignment strategy. This and other alignment strategies are analyzed in Snow et al. 1986.)

And, in the same way that there can be a surfeit of leaders skilled in more mundane tasks of organizing, leaders skilled in frame alignment can be in short or inadequate supply.

18. Belief in the Necessity and Effectiveness of Forming. Potential SMO formers and participants can believe that a condition is unjust (variable 10) and that the proposed SMO and its actions are proper or legitimate (variable 17), but still decline to act because they do not think *their own* action is necessary or will make any difference, or that collective action itself will not be effective. The more cynical reasons for this belief have been labeled "the free-rider problem," which is the following sentiment, stated here as a first-person declaration:

> Why should I bother to do anything? All you other folks are acting, therefore my action will not make any difference and is not needed. If the rest of you *do not* achieve the change we desire, I will not have wasted my time, energy and other resources. If you *do* achieve the change, I will get the benefits anyway and will not have incurred the risks and costs you will have paid. (adapted from the classic formal statement of Olson 1965)

There are less cynical versions of these sentiments, of course. In good faith, a person can believe that others are unlikely to join in forming the SMO and acting (so one's personal action will be ineffective), that her or his action makes no difference in successfully forming the SMO and acting, and that even if many people participate, the effort will be unsuccessful (Klandermans 1984, 585; Oliver 1983; 1984).

What variables are involved, therefore, in *overcoming* such beliefs—such cognitive barriers to action? Or what factors might prevent the development of such beliefs in the first place?

A *first* variable researchers of this matter point to is an amalgam of variables 13, 14, and 15 (in the top right-hand cell of Figure 7.1) and what ensues when these three variables are reasonably strong: participants integrated in rich networks of communication in the presence of skilled leadership engage in *collective, mutual conversion*. In face-to-face discussions, participants mutually convince one another and themselves that the SMO and its actions are necessary and will be effective. One important part of this is the possibility of gathering information that others are more likely to participate if you participate, and vice versa, a process sometimes labeled "mutual facilitation" of action. It has also been captioned with the yet fancier terms "value expectancy" and "aggregation of choice" (MMZ 1988, 714). In such micro mobilization contexts, a person is also more likely to hear plausible arguments that if many people act, the SMO will be effective—as well as other reasons for both effectiveness and necessity.

A *second* variable of note concerns the fact that people engage in action for reasons other than sheer calculations of necessity and effectiveness. As member of groups in which they want to be well thought of, people will "go along" in order to "get along." In fancier terms, these are "solidarity incentives," the rewards of status, positive regard, experiences of comradeship, fellowship, good times, and the like.

Third, a minority of possible participants—but a critical and catalytic minority—has long ago developed *ideological commitments* to dissenting action and SMO formation, if and when the time should be appropriate.

Such a prior resolve makes this minority more likely to construct a current situation as *the* time and therefore to be key players in the process of mutual facilitation just described.

Fourth, barriers to formation and action are overcome to the degree that the *macro* "focal point" or "focusing crisis" (variable 11) can be, at the *micro* level, be defined as a matter of *urgency* associated with perceptions of *new dangers*, threats and/or *opportunities* that are at hand. The situation is defined as "something unusual is happening." Life is plausibly asserted to be no longer simply "normal" or "routine." *New kinds of actions and advocacy* (for those undertaking them) are now required because some emergent circumstance of threat, danger, or opportunity demands them. Here are some quotations from participants in the black southern sit-in SMO campaigns that illustrate such perceptions and actions:

> [I]t took all our time, and we were really totally immersed in it. . . . When things were really hot we called a meeting at eight o'clock in the morning. We'd call one for twelve that day . . . and the place would be full. We had what we called our wire service. People got on the telephone . . . and they would fill the building . . . in . . . a . . . relatively short time. . . .
>
> I called back to Atlanta and . . . I said "this is the thing. You must tell Martin [Luther King, Jr.] that we must get with this, and really this can shake up the world." (participants quoted in Morris 1981, 763, 757; see further Benford 1993a)

It is thought necessary to act with haste because of new threats and harms that must be *countered* and/or new opportunities that must be *seized* before they recede. In the terms offered by Turner and Killian (1987, 245–48), there is a radical revision of the sense of "feasibility and timeliness."

The term "variable" is central in considering variables 17 and 18 and factors affecting them. The more attenuated either variable (and other variables, for that matter), the less likely that a new SMO will occur. And the empirical fact appears to be that, most frequently, at least several of the variables are rather weak and a new SMO does not emerge.

VI. CAUSES OF SMO DIFFERENCES

All of the above is directed to the question of SMO formation, of their presence or absence as a phenomenon per se irrespective of how they differ. This, though, is not the only use to which this inventory of causal variables can be put. As reported in Chapters 5 and 6, SMOs also *differ* in their beliefs, organization, sizes, or magnitudes, and in many other ways. In those two chapters I also described a few of the causal variables

researchers have used in attempting to account for these and other variations (Chapter 5, Section IV.A.1, Chapter 6, Section IV.A).

But many more than the few variables I have previously reported are
in fact involved in explaining SMO differences, *and* the above variables
are among those that researchers use in this task.

VII. SUSTAINING CAUSES

The central SMO questions above concern (1) causes of SMOs coming
into existence (Sections IV and V) and (2) causes of variations in SMOs
(Section VI).

There is yet a third way to think about the causes of SMOs: Once in
existence, what factors sustain or support continuing existence (or fail to
do so)?

Once afloat, so to speak, what factors keep SMOs viable and continuing, or, in their absence or weakness, lead to their demise? Verta Taylor
has provided important leads in answering this question in her analysis
of the "abeyance process" as it operated in the women's movement—
specifically the SMO The National Woman's Party—during its doldrums
period of the thirties through the fifties. Causal factors she describes as
supporting a stable abeyance include:

- the relative social homogeneity of the participants,
- a high degree of organizational centralization,
- the presence of a charismatic leader, and,
- the existence of a rich, supportive culture.[12]

* * *

As indicated at the start of this chapter, people joining an existing
SMO is a very different matter than starting one up in the first place and
"from scratch" (although we have seen that start-ups are not truly "from
scratch"). In the next chapter, we examine what researchers have had to
say about this very different matter of "joining."

NOTES

1.   The agency-structure distinction is explained in Chapter 3, Section II.B.8,
on generic question (8), What is Human Agency?

2.   Such previous general schemes include:

- Smelser's (1962) six "value-added" factors,
- Freeman's four factors in movement/SMO formation (1983a),

- Wood and Jackson's (1982) multichapter review,
- Ferree and Miller's (1985) "integration of . . . perspectives,"
- Turner and Killian's (1987, Ch. 13) "model for social movements,"
- Oberschall's (1993, 16–25) four "dimensions of collective action" (two on the "demand" side and two on the "supply" side).

3. Michels on oligarchy is discussed in Section II.H of Chapter 6.

4. Snow and Oliver (1995, 580). Causes of the perception/sense of injustice are elaborated in Turner and Killian (1987, 242–45). See further Johnston (1991).

5. Other formulations, though, treat a great many other matters, including variable (9), as "political opportunity," as does, for example, Tarrow (1994, 87). Indeed, the idea of political opportunity is so elastic that in some formulations it means *anything* that facilities a movement.

6. In Neil Smelser's scheme of six value-added determinants, these are termed "conduciveness" ("Do certain structural characteristics, more than others, permit or encourage" certain possibilities?) as distinct from "strain" ("ambiguities, deprivations, conflicts . . . discrepancies") (Smelser 1962, 15, 16).

7. In many situations the terms *leader* and *leadership* are too grandiose and concepts such as *organizer* seem more accurate. For simplicity's sake here though, I use the term *leader* to mean both leaders and organizers. This matter is treated in more detail in Section I.2 of Chapter 8.

8. See further Oberschall (1973, 146–78) ["the upper and middle strata . . . supply the substantial bulk of opposition leaders in all manner of social movements in proportions far above that of the percentage in the population at large" (p. 155)]; Freeman (1983a), who ranks the skilled organizer as one of four conditions necessary for a social movement ["the art of 'constructing' a social movement is something that requires considerable skill and experience" (p. 26)].

9. The four SMOs that Morris lists have also played key roles in other SMs/SMOs. On the importance of "communication networks and similar resources" the first three of these SMOs in the peace movement of the 1980s, see Lofland (1993a, 225–30) and sources cited therein. On the role of the fourth listed in a variety of movements, see Edwards and McCarthy (1992) on "social movement schools" and "movement mentor organizations."

10. These four degrees of convergence-divergence are discussed in Section VI.B.1 of Chapter 8.

11. This is my transcription from the sound track of "Awakening," the first segment of the television series *Eyes on the Prize: America's Civil Rights Years 1954–1965.*

12. Taylor (1989, 756–70). The classic forerunner study of factors affecting the longevity of SMOs of a communal variety is Kanter (1972). Using different statistical techniques, Hall (1988) revises certain of Kanter's findings. See also Hirsch (1986) and Edwards and Marullo (1995).

8

Why Do People Join SMOs?

Good answers to the question, Why do people join SMOs? presuppose agreement on the meanings of "join" and "SMO." Or we need at least to understand the range of meanings that these terms are often assigned. Moreover, there are yet *additional* terms and units of analysis that are, *as prior matters*, necessary to clarify in order sensibly to speak of causes of SMO participation.

I. Therefore, I begin this chapter with an effort to sort out and to clarify the *terminology* of "joining," "joining what," and membership or participation.

II. Despite the complicating consequences of multiple referents and meanings of "joining" and related concepts, in Sections II and III I review variables that researchers have used to account for "joining," that is, to formulate its causes. Section II focuses on *individual* variables affecting joining.

III. Section III addresses *structural* variables that can be involved.

IV. With that review before us, its complexity demands that we once again think about how any or all of the variables might enter (or not enter) into particular cases of joining.

V. Researchers view membership or participation as continuously problematic rather than as established once and for all. Another form of the joining question is therefore, How is participation *maintained* or not? This is the subject of Section V.

VI. Being (or having been) in an SMO can have various kinds of *consequences*. I review what some of these might be in Section VI.

VII. Conceptually separate from joining and factors affecting it is the question of how SMOs may or may not go about consciously to bring new people into their ranks. Such *recruitment* efforts (or lack of them) are taken up in Section VII.

I. FOUR COMPLICATIONS IN THE STUDY
OF JOINING

Causal accounts of joining are bedeviled by slippery, varied, and shifting referents regarding four aspects of it. First, what—exactly—*is* being joined? The unit "joined" is not always an SMO, and SMOs vary in ways that complicate causal accounts. Second, what *is* "joining" in the first place versus other possible forms of participation? Third, what are people's phenomenological experiences of joining? For example, is it a major event in a person's life, an unremarkable moment, or what? Fourth, even among people researchers agree are "members," participation is quite varied. It is so varied that different causal factors might account for different extents and types of participation. Revising a folk phrase, Does one size [theory] fit all?

Let us consider each of these complications.

A. What Is Joined?

The first two complications are distinguished by one being about the unit itself that is joined and the other about what we might mean by "joining," whatever the unit may be.

Regarding complications of What is the unit? research studies of movement "members" divide into those that use an SMO as the unit "joined" and those that use some other "unit" of membership/participation. Regarding the latter, these are among such "dependent variables" seen in studies and sometimes characterized as "membership":

- sympathetic attitudes toward the goals of an SM (e.g., McCarthy and Zald 1987b, 20),
- participation in an SM event, such as a march or rally (e.g., Oegama and Klandermans 1994; Klandermans and Oegema 1987; Sherkat and Blocker 1993; Opp 1988),
- contributions of money or in-kind goods to an SM event or SMO (e.g., Cohn, Barkan, and Whitaker 1993).

Each of these is better thought of as an *action* rather than as joining or membership. For purposes of understanding participation in *SMs*, such actions are obviously important but these are *membership* in only the weakest of senses. Moreover, such actions are not—in and of themselves—evidence of SMO joining or membership.[1]

Further, we need to recognize that some people who are well identified with an SM—and who are even quite famous spokespeople for it—may not be members of *any* SMO (or at least only "checkbook" or "nominal" members of one or more SMOs). Such people have "joined" a *social movement*, but this is quite different from having joined an SMO.

Where an SMO *is* the unit "joined," the research suggests that these entities vary in three key ways that complicate and constrain causal theories of joining.

1. SMOs vary in the degree of involvement they require of members, a variable described in Chapter 6 as "degree of member absorption." Turner and Killian have phrased this as a "continuum from those requiring only *segmental involvement* to those requiring *total absorption*" and they generalize that "the dynamics of recruitment, commitment and control are quite different depending upon how total or segmental are the requirements of adherency" (1987, 325, emphasis in the original).

2. Related to absorption but not the same as it, SMOs differ in the degree to which joining is defined as involving a deep discontinuity with the person's previous life and a radical reorganization of life-style and personal identity. For many SMOs, there is almost no such discontinuity and reorganization. "Joining" is "merely" a matter of *activating* some of the person's energy in SMO terms. For others though, the discontinuity is great and joining is better termed *conversion*. In cases of mere activation, indeed, causal factors in "joining" may be very similar those attendant to getting involved in prosaic avocational groups.

3. SMOs vary in the forms and degrees of *personal risk* that membership entails. By definition, all SMO membership is risky, but the nature and intensity of it are variable. Some obvious dimensions of variation include social stigma or reprehension, state prosecution and incarceration, and threats of physical assault and actual assault. One candidate proposition about the relation between risk and joining is:

◆ The greater the personal risk of joining, the stronger that certain causal variables reviewed below need to be.[2]

Substituting the degrees of absorption and discontinuity variables for risk in this proposition, the same relation likely applies.

B. What Is "Joining"?

Confining our attention to SMOs, how can we tell who is or is not a member of one? The simplest answer and one that often works is (1) ask people who claim to speak for the SMO who the members are, and/or (2) ask "suspected" members themselves whether they are members or not. This is a "phenomenological" solution to the problem, meaning that researchers take the participants' definitions of membership as definitive.

However, it is hazardous to depend on such a phenomenological approach alone. As ought to be clear, many circumstances prompt self-claimed SMO speakers and members not to be candid about membership; both are to prone to simple errors in such matters; and "members" may not agree among themselves about who is "really" a member.

Such problematics mean that researchers often also go on to formulate their own indicators of membership, indicators that take account of the phenomenology of "members" but that are not confined to them. Dimensions that often enter into formulating these indicators include the following:

- How frequently does the person participate in SMO activities?
- How much money (or in-kind donations) does the person give to the SMO?
- How well known is the person to people who are the most active SMO members and how much power and influence does she or he appear to have?
- What is the degree to which the person expresses disagreement or agreement with the beliefs of the SMO?

C. What Are Experiences of Joining?

Separate from these more "objective" matters of operationalization and measurement are questions of what joining may or may not *mean* to joiners, the manner in which joining is *experienced*.

Dimensions along which experiences of joining vary include:

1. The degree the person feels under *pressure* (and is under pressure) to join. Experiences vary *from* being completely "self-engineered" and decided on the person's own *to* being surrounded by many people who are urging the person to join (or at least to participate in the next step leading to joining).
2. The *rapidity* with which a decision to be a member is made. This ranges from a long, drawn-out, and gradual process to a sharp, space-time-bound acute episode of sudden embracing of membership.
3. The degree of emotional or affective *arousal*, ranging from the flat, calm emotions of humdrum life to ecstatic epiphany.
4. The *content* of the emotions or affect, including the possibilities of curiosity, excitement, illumination, awe, love, hate, and fear.

5. The degree that the physical action of joining coincides with inner acceptance of the SMO's beliefs. In many cases, there are discrepancies between believing and participating. Participating may precede believing and vice versa (Lofland and Skonovd 1985).

These five variations in the experience of joining can and do conjoin in numerous ways. Individual experiences of joining can be (and are) therefore highly varied. Despite a myriad of possible and actual patterns, however, a few are dramatic, extreme, and/or repetitive enough to have prompted identification by researchers. Here are a few of these, summarized (and modified) from longer descriptions by Lofland and Skonovd:

1. *The Mystical Experience.* Prototypically occurring when alone, the person has a rapid, highly aroused experience of personal transcendence and transformation and "blinders falling from the eyes."
2. *The Ecstatic Troop Experience.* For varying reasons, the person begins to participate with SMO members who are ecstatically upbeat about their enterprise and who encourage that enthusiasm in the prospective member. In fullest form, such ecstatic troop experiences are intentionally contrived in order to draw in new members, as have Unificationists, for example. However, equivalent ecstatic troop circumstances are sometimes simply emergent in the course of protest, but produce a similar experience, as among people in Free Speech Movement episodes at the University of California, Berkeley, in the fall of 1964 (Heirich 1971).
3. *Experimental/Incremental Experiences.* The above two patterns are in the classic traditions of dramatic religious conversions, of wrenching, soulful, cosmic discontinuities in life. While there are certainly such experiences, they are likely much less common than slower, incremental, and experimental poking around and tentative and uncertain explorations. Some SMOs, indeed, hold this experience up as the only appropriate one and actively encourage it in prospective members [e.g., the Jehovah's Witnesses, Beckford (1978)].
4. *Focusing Crisis Experiences.* Paralleling causal variable 11 in the formation of SMOs, focal points or crises can be experienced by individuals as major turning points in their lives that foster their SMO participation. Most especially, macrostructural events that penetrate and disturb the immediate life world of a

person—the quotidian—can become orienting experiences, as in economic crashes, war declarations, noxious election results, and personally punishing policy announcements.

There are obviously a great many *additional* kinds of experiences people can have in joining an SMO, but these suffice to suggest the complexity and diversity. [Kilbourne and Richardson (1988) survey a great many others.]

The *underlying* variable to which the above and other experiences point is the degree to which joiners verbally and behaviorally construct their membership as discontinuous with their previous lives. Snow and Machalek (1983) have conceptualized the strongly discontinuous state of this variable as "the convert as a social type." By "social type" these researchers mean that the new member adopts a distinctive (but generic) template of speech and behavior they label "the convert." This template consists of four "rhetorical properties" that make up a change in the "universe of discourse" in which the new convert now participates and which is manifest in her or his "speech and reasoning" (p. 173). This distinctive "convert" speech and reasoning has four main characteristics:

[1] *Biographical reconstruction* [in which the joiner's] biography is . . . reconstructed in accordance with the new or ascendant universe of discourse and its attendant grammar and vocabulary of motives . . . .

[2] *The adoption of a master attribution scheme* [in which] a new or formerly peripheral causal schema . . . or vocabulary of motives . . . authoritatively informs all causal attributions about self, others, and events in the world. Feelings behaviors and events formerly interpreted with reference to a number of causal schemas are now interpreted from the standpoint of one pervasive schema [cf. discussion of "totalistic" beliefs in Section III.B.2 of Chapter 5]

[3] *A suspension of analogical reasoning* [in which converts perceive] their world views as unique. . . . Analogic metaphors are resisted because they violate the convert's belief that his or her world view is incomparable to other competing perspectives . . . .

[4] *Embracement of the convert role* [in which the convert interprets and acts toward] various situationally specific roles . . . from the standpoint of the convert role. [He] or she enthusiastically avows his or her convert identity in nearly all interaction situations. (Snow and Machalek 1984, 173–74; see also Snow and Machalek 1983)

It important to appreciate that these patterns of experiences and the "convert as a social type" are *not*, in and of themselves, causal explanations of joining. Instead, they suggest the complexity and diversity of the dependent variable for which we seek causal accounts.

D. What Is Membership?

SMO members almost always display considerable variation in the *intensity*—the extent—of their participation and in, moreover, the *forms* of participation—the kinds of things they do in the SMO. These variations are dramatic enough to make researchers wonder about the degree to which, as noted above, "one size fits all" in formulating causal theories of joining. That is, some patterns of membership form/intensity may involve different causal factors than others.

Let me report some of the efforts researchers have made to document extent and forms of membership (which is, more broadly considered, the extent and forms of joining). These researches divide into (1) depictions of types within a membership *as a whole* versus (2) a focus on the special class of members who organize, direct, and/or urge the activities of others, the *leaders*.

1. The Body of Members. For the analyst, there are two main types of patterns of membership that an analyst seeks to articulate: (a) the SMO's formal scheme of roles and (b) patterns that are latent (less than fully recognized and intended by members).

a. Formal schemes of roles. The first type is the scheme that people in the SMO may have themselves devised, a set of officially promulgated roles into which members of the SMO are classified. Not all SMOs have such a scheme, and in some SMOs the very idea of such a scheme may be explicitly rejected in the name of values such as equality, androgyny, or cosmic consciousness. But if there is a scheme of formal roles, what it is and how members are distributed in it are among the first objects of the researcher's attention.

In some SMOs, the scheme of roles is less explicitly organizational than one's internal state of achievement or personal evolution. Thus, at one point the SMO Scientology had an enormously elaborate scheme of levels of personal development through which members could rise in the process of becoming "Clear" (Wallis 1977).

b. Analyst articulated patterns. Cross-cutting or independent of any formal scheme of roles put forth by the SMO, researchers often attempt to discern the more informal and de facto patterns of types and extents of participation that can be observed among SMO participants. Among these, let me report Sam Marullo's analysis of this kind on the some one thousand members of the Greater Cleveland Nuclear Weapons Freeze Campaign of the early 1980s. Utilizing his own observation and two surveys of that SMO's membership, Marullo distinguished among and measured the intensity of four ways in which members attempted to change U.S. nuclear weapons policy. In the present terms, he measured "forms" and "intensities" of participation. Labeled "modes of action" in Figure 8.1, the forms are:

[1] *individual participatory actions,* [measured by questionnaire answers on] attending public lectures or films about the arms race, voting for elective official based on their positions on weapons-related issues, attending church peace-group meetings, donating money to peace groups, attending peace rallies or demonstrations, writing or phoning . . . representatives regarding peace issues.

[2] *freeze organizational actions,* [measured by answers to questions on] volunteering in the [Freeze] office, attending meetings, serving on committees, attending national rallies . . . and organizing local events.

[3] *actions to confront nonmovement individuals* [measured by answers to questions on] working on petition drives, doing door-to-door canvassing, phonebanking, voter registration or working with school officials or labor leaders to win support for Freeze activities. . . .

[4] *actions to confront the system directly* [measured by answers to questions] on withholding federal taxes, illegal trespass, and other forms of civil disobedience. (adapted from Marullo 1990, 247–49, emphasis added)

Marullo measured the extent (or intensity) of each member's activity in each of these modes of action by making a composite of their answers to questions pertaining to each. Each member was thus given four scores. The profiles of these four scores varied quite widely, with many members having zero or very low numbers in one or more modes of action. Seeking to specify these high and low differences more sharply, he then classified each member as simply higher or lower on each mode of action. This sharpening results in the eight patterns of membership shown in the left-hand column of Figure 8.1. The four cells in the row next to each member pattern indicate highness or lowness with the label yes or no. Thus, membership pattern number 1 (the adherent) is low or zero on all four "modes of action."

The eight patterns of membership exhibit a progression from little or no activity in the four modes of action to much activity in all four. And as

Figure 8.1. Patterns of membership action in a freeze SMO.

	Four Modes of Action and Intensity ➡				
Membership Pattern ⬇	1. Many individual participatory actions?	2. Freeze organizational actions?	3. Actions confronting nonmovement individuals?	4. Actions confronting the system directly?	Percentage of SMO members
1. Adherents	no	no	no	no	30
2. Weak supporters	yes	no	no	no	14
3. Strong supporters	yes	no	yes	no	8
4. Peripheral members	yes	yes	no	no	13
5. Active members	yes	yes	yes	no	16
6. Core members	yes plus	yes	yes	no	7
7. Partially engaged CD	yes	no	no	yes	3
8. Fully engaged CD	yes	yes	yes	yes	7

Source: Adapted from Marullo (1990:255, Table 17.2, "Ideal-Types of Freeze Movement Participants"). N = 325. The percentages do not add to 100 because of rounding.

breadth and amount of activity increases from pattern to pattern, the proportion of the membership exhibiting the pattern tends overall to decline. Notice, in particular, that the least involved members—the "adherents"—are also the largest percentage of members, some 30 percent. On the other hand, almost half the membership is reasonably involved in the organizational activities of the SMO, in that membership patterns that are yes on Freeze organizational actions? total 43 percent (the total of peripheral, active, and core members and the fully engaged CDers).

Impressionistic reports suggest that the wide variation in involvement that Marullo reports for this SMO is the rule rather than the exception in

SMOs generally. Quite frequently, an SMO—especially the less absorbing ones—are carried on by a core of highly involved people surrounded
by a second layer of somewhat involved people who are themselves
surrounded by a third layer of peripherally involved "members."[3]

  c. *Societal hierarchy and membership patterns.* Whatever may be the
formal or analyst-articulated patterns of membership in an SMO, the
membership can also be viewed in terms of its relation to the categories
of hierarchy and stratification in the larger society. I refer here to the
major bases on which hierarchies are erected in human societies: gender, age, ethnicity, wealth, occupation, physical ableness, education,
geographical region, religion, and the like. The dimensions (and categories of those dimensions) of such societal hierarchies observed in any
given SMO are extremely unlikely to be in proportion to the society as a
whole—to be a random sample of the society as a whole in terms of
societal stratifications. Instead, some categories of some dimensions of
hierarchy are likely to be vastly overrepresented and yet others to be
extremely underrepresented or even absent altogether. Thus, some
SMOs tend to be heavily composed of one gender, one age group, and
one ethnic category (e.g., college-educated white women in their twenties, among numerous other equivalently specialized conjunctions of
particular categories of several dimensions of societal hierarchy).

  These specialized conjunctions of categories of dimensions of hierarchy have suggested at least two lines of research. The first of these
anticipates the report on causes I will give below: What does the specialized demography we see in the SMO suggest about the possible
causes of the SMO and of joining it? Sometimes answers to this question
are fairly obvious and the members of the SMO speak for themselves
quite clearly about it: People of their particular conjunctions of stratifications are exploited or otherwise put upon and, in popular culture language, "are mad as hell and are not going to take it anymore." But also,
sometimes the heterogeneous demography of the SMO makes its meaning less than apparent.

  A second line of research is more pertinent to this immediate context:
What intersections might there be between internal SMO membership
patterns and the wider, societal dimensions of stratification? For example, are all the formal leaders from particular categories of gender, age,
ethnicity, and occupation while all the followers are from different such
categories? Or are the more latent patterns of membership the analyst
articulates engaged in unevenly in terms of societal dimensions of stratification? Thus, for example, are the eight patterns Marullo articulates in
a Freeze SMO engaged in disproportionately by persons of certain occupations, genders, and ages? Any such findings then, of course, raise

questions of why they have occurred (their causes), and what difference they make (their consequences) (see, further, McAdam 1992).

2. The Leaders.   The populations of SMOs (and SMs) are broadly dividable into a class of people who regularly and persistently initiate, organize, goad, and/or urge other people to take SMO-related actions and those who do not. Any member of the former class can be labeled a *leader*, a term it is helpful to define as "one who originates or institutes" or as "one who goads or urges forward" (the phrases are adapted from dictionary definitions of the word *mover*).

Researchers as well as reflective movement participants have distinguished among SMO leaders in several ways using a variety of terms. For survey purposes, let me classify these into the three broadest roles to which elements of the various schemes are variously addressed. These are the generic and ideal-typical roles of the *organizer*, the *speaker*, and the *writer*. I say "ideal typical" in order to signal that I am pointing to pure logical possibilities to which specific people only tend to one or another degree. Thus, while there are "pure" organizers, many other organizers are also speakers and/or writers, and so on for numerous possible and actual combinations of the ideal-typical roles. Nonetheless, in reality, SMO leaders *do* tend to be one more than another of the three. More important, movement people often explicitly *organize themselves* on these distinctions (although they may use different words) and the distinctions therefore have *phenomenological fidelity*.

a. Organizers.   In the research literature as well as in movement strategy manuals, a distinction is commonly drawn between the "nuts and bolts" people, the ones who get practical things done, and the more public personages who may be thought of as "the leaders." Other terms for organizers include "activists," "staff," "administrator," "bureaucrats," and "pragmatic leader" [Blumer (1969a), Roche and Sachs (1955), and Wilson (1975, 216ff.)] In SMOs with formal titles, an organizer might be called an "executive officer," "staff associate," or "program director."

What is called "community organizing" thinking and theory has even elevated "the organizer" to a special and specialized role in the instigation and initial organizing of neighborhood-based SMOs. The inspiration for this model was, of course, Saul Alinsky ([1946] 1969, 1972), who borrowed the idea from union organizing and applied it in the community context. Much of the surprisingly large how-to-do-it literature on social movements is informed by this tradition and written for and by organizers.

As a species of leader, the authority of organizers rests on their technical effectiveness and pragmatic reliability. This is in contrast to speakers and writers whose urgings and goals appeal more directly to morality, idealism, and sense of rightness, or even to charismatic revelation.

b. Speakers. By definition, SMOs and SMs involve sustained *public* articulation of whatever is the moralistic and idealist but excluded or marginal reality (Chapter 1, Section I.C.3). The concrete meaning of this fact is that one or more people have to *stand up* in public and articulate the reality. Historically, this always meant *literally* standing up before a gathering and making reality claims. With the advent of mass media, literally standing may not be required, but it is figuratively still necessary in the sense of "standing up to" the mainstream. (There is still of course much need literally to stand up.)

Other terms often used in speaking of speakers include "leader," "charismatic leader," "agitator," "prophet," "enthusiast," "spokesperson," "delegate," and "representative." In SMOs with named formal roles, they may be called "president," "director," "chair," "founder," "Father," "True Father," "God," "the Lord," or any of many other sometimes equally or more flamboyant appellations.

Speakers share the characteristic of appearing to having a solid understanding of whatever the reality being promoted and are able skillfully to present and defend it before gatherings of various kinds. They differ, though, in their relation to the reality—the beliefs—that they proclaim.

In one pattern, speakers claim only to be applying or expositing a reality whose legitimacy rests in elements derived from tradition or from reason (i.e., from a "rational-legal" basis of authority). John Wilson speaks of such speakers/leaders as "ideological," meaning that he or she "develops, interprets, communicates a set of teachings that are consonant with a given community's interests and aspirations. [P]ower rests, therefore, in . . . imputed skills as an interpreter or disseminator of a vital principle, one which resonates with the needs of a group. . . . The ideology in a sense preexists [the person] who interprets it" (Wilson 1973, 210).

In a very different pattern, the speaker claims a new and special understanding of tradition and reason that derives from her or his unique relation to forces above and beyond both of these. One common framing of this brand new understanding is as "a revelation from God." The speaker and only the speaker has a privileged communication link with supernatural or equivalent forces in which the "really true" and the "really real" have been made known. The claims of tradition and reason can themselves *really* be understood only when viewed through the prism of this shining new understanding that has been given to the speaker. The archetypal expression of revelational injunction that sweeps away tradition and reason is, of course, "It is written but I say unto you" (Wilson 1973, 203).

Speakers who embark on such extraordinary claims are, to be sure, rare, but are no less important for that reason. Likely most often, no one pays such claimers much mind and they remain excluded or marginal. Some are even exiled, imprisoned, or committed to mental asylums.

But such revelatory claims create "charismatic moments" for some listeners—a "compulsive, inexplicable emotional tie linking followers together in adulation of [a] leader" (Zablocki 1991, 63). In this tie, followers believe that the now *charismatic leader* has superhuman powers of perception and ability to discern "the truth." This truth is, indeed, the culmination of human history, as in this declaration about Sun Myung Moon, the "True Father" of mankind in Unificationist eyes:

> Six thousand years of human history have been just for him. . . . His value is more precious than the world. . . . It is only him from whom sinless mankind can start. He is the only man in the universe by loving whom my sin is solved, by loving whom I can be born anew, by loving whom I can be given rebirth and a new life. (Sudo 1975, 155)

As seen in this quote and as stressed by Charles Lindholm (1990) intense *love* for the leader is the central and key element of the charismatic relation, a love that arises in part from the incredible *gift* the leader is thought to have given followers (Weber 1958, Ch. 9; Hall 1987).

c. Writers. By "writers" I mean SMO (and SM) persons who regularly put movement words to paper that are published or otherwise circulated and read seriously. This is critical as both task and role in SMOs (and SMs), but surprisingly underattended by researchers (perhaps because they are themselves scribblers who are therefore like the fish who are the last to discover water).

Organizers and speakers commonly engage in writing, of course, but their efforts are briefer and more limited in aspiration than those of movement writers per se. Writers, in contrast, are dedicated to elaborating complex rationales, collecting exhaustive data, working out criticisms of opposing and competing views, devising new lines of analysis, and sketching innovative lines of action. Such tasks are so involving that many movement writers are not members of particular SMOs. Many others are, however, and some SMOs seem even to be organized to support them in their writing (e.g., in Scientology, L. Ron Hubbard was rarely seen but was highly visible nonetheless in a ceaseless stream of new writing).

d. Generalists and specialists. The research and movement wisdom about these three roles is that specific people are rarely if ever effective in all three. A *few* rare people, even so, might lay reasonable claim to triple proficiency. Leaving aside the substance and morality of his SMO, V. I. Lenin, for example, might have been such a rare "triple threat" in that he was commonly perceived even by his most ardent enemies as a proficient writer ("theoretician"), a persuasive public speaker, and a cunning (ruthless?) organizational strategist.[4]

More commonly though, people's talents and inclinations are more limited and a division of labor arises at both the SM and SMO levels. For example, Thurgood Marshall has remarked of Martin Luther King, Jr., and more generally: "I think he was a great leader [but] as an organizer, he wasn't worth diddly squat. But very few leaders are" (quoted in DeStefano 1993, 1).[5]

So also, in given SMOs, one or more of all three patterns may be present and sometimes become objects of "constant jockeying for pre-eminence," depending on the particular versions of each of the three that are present (Wilson 1973, 195; Roche and Sachs 1955). In the version of two of these roles that Roche and Sachs term the "bureaucrat" (a variation on the organizer) versus the "enthusiast" (a variation on the speaker) in the British Labour party, "the enthusiast was a visionary [, a person] of principle, ruled by emotion and impatient with the petty details of organization. The bureaucrat was the task-oriented official, anxious to establish a secure and stable foundation for the movement and skilled in the arts of administration" (Wilson 1973, 195–96; Roche and Sachs 1955). Such differences in operating tendencies unsurprisingly spawn much tension (cf. Gusfield 1966; Staggenborg 1988).

*　*　*

The complications I have reviewed in this section go to the question, What, exactly, *is* the dependent variable? We want to pursue the question of why people join SMOs, but we now see that the respective meanings of what is joined, what is joining, what is the experience, and membership itself are not homogeneous and clean-cut. Instead, each involves varied matters and these variations probably have correspondingly variable causes.

II. WHY PEOPLE JOIN SMOS:
INDIVIDUAL VARIABLES

Having stated these many complexities and cautions, let me now toss them to the wind, so to speak, and turn to surveying variables re-

searchers have put forth as possibly in part accounting for people joining SMOs.

In reviewing these, the same considerations of *causal logic* I describe in
the previous chapter also apply here: We are examining *variables* that
differ in strength from case to case. Any *particular* variable must therefore always be viewed in the context of the relative strength of *all other*
variables and in terms of their *composite causal force* (Chapter 8, Section
III). The major meaning of this is that joining can be the outcome of
widely different combinations of the strengths of various causal variables. Therefore, in specific cases some of the variables may be extremely weak or even zero in strength. Joining nonetheless occurs
because of sufficient causal strength in yet other variables.

I sort out the variables in this survey along the dimensions of (1)
focusing at the individual versus structural level and (2) operating before
the situation of joining versus in that situation.

1. Regarding the first dimension, researchers distinguish between *individual* and *structural* variables in virtually every survey of causes of
joining (and of kindred matters). The former refers to properties of and
processes in persons per se that are seen as their "attributes" or "characteristics." Persons carry these around inside or on themselves as dispositions and orientations, it is presumed. The research task is to discern the
degree to which these are or are not predictive of joining. "Structural"
variables, on the other hand, refer to features of the circumstances in
which we find people, the contexts in which they have had or are having
certain experiences (McAdam et al. 1988, 705; Snow and Oliver 1995,
577; Machalek and Snow 1993, 57).

2. Regarding the second dimension, variables involved in joining are
often distinguished in terms of their temporal proximity to joining.
Whether individual or structural, a variable that can cause joining may
achieve causal force months or years before the process of possible joining begins. The variable is simply there to begin operation should a
joining possibility arise. As standing states of individuals or of structural
arrangements, these are *background* variables. Other variables, though,
arise and enter into the possibility of joining only at the time when
joining becomes a current possibility. As variables, they may or may not
occur and/or occur in sufficient strength to bring about joining. Because
of their space-time proximity to joining, these are *situational* variables.
(In the previous chapter this same distinction among causal variables
with regard to SMO formation is termed "standing arrangements" versus "situational changes.")

Considered conjointly, there are thus four major types of variables
that researchers have entertained as causes of SMO joining (and/or

Figure 8.2.   Causes of joining SMOs.

	Individual Variables	Structural Variables
Background Variables	1. Biological 2. Deeper motivation 3. Self-concept 4. Belief and socialization 5. Active seeking	8. Macro-structure 9. Organizational membership 10. Prior activism 11. Prior contact/network
Situational Variables	6. Benefit calculation/rational choice 7. Experimentation	12. Suddenly imposed grievances 13. Situational stress 14. Biographical availability 15. Coercive persuasion 16. Affective bonds

causes of an enormous range of other things neighboring SMO joining, such as religious conversion, riot participation, and activism as a generalized role). This conjunction and the four types are displayed in Figure 8.2, Causes of Joining SMOs.

My review of these four types of variables deals first with individual variables. This is also fairly common in summaries of research because dominant strands of inquiry in recent decades have been skeptical of the role of individual variables. These are therefore addressed first in order to "get them out of the way" and to get onto what are thought to be the more important structural variables. I must admit to sharing this bias, but I also recognize that it *is* a bias and I will try to correct for it. In that spirit, a more valid reason to begin with individual variables is that they are phenomenologically prior to structure.

A. Background Individual Variables

Background individual variables draw attention to how "joiners [may] differ importantly from non joiners in terms of personality characteristics . . . cognitive orientation," or other preexisting state (Zurcher and Snow 1981, 449). These variables have also been termed the "convergence approach," in order to call attention to the image that it implies of like-minded people finding one another (Turner and Killian 1987, 19–21). Such variables have also been dubbed the "hearts and minds" approach because of their focus on individuals rather than on social organization and resources (McCarthy and Zald 1987a, 337–38).

Background individual variables vary among themselves in terms of just how "deep" and immutable these matters are thought to be. I begin with the "deepest" and move to the more surface or mutable variables.

1. Biological. Over much of the middle twentieth century, any serious consideration of biological, physical, or organismic variables as causes of SMO joining was defined as decidedly wrongheaded and outside the mainstream. Any credible researcher simply did not raise the possibility—and this reflected a much wider twentieth-century rejection of biological factors in explaining behavior.

This wider rejection has weakened in recent years, however, and with it some forms of this thinking have begun to return to accounts of SMO joining. Drawing on Machalek and Snow's (1993) review, versions of this thinking are seen in such lines of analysis as:

- Stark and Bainbridge's (1987) conceptualization of SMO memberships as providing "compensators," among which are "organismic" deprivations that are compensated.
- Assertion of the existence of a human genome that gives people "powerful psychological needs for group affiliation" for which group membership provides relief (Machalek and Snow 1993, 59).
- Arguing that the evolutionarily based mechanism by which humans recognize kin creates the "behavioral capacity and propensity for" culturally evolved kinlike institutions, some of which are SMOs (p. 59; see also Maryanski and Turner 1992).

Aside from the merits or demerits of the biological content and the specific substance, all these accounts (and others like them) have the drawback of not being variables that distinguish SMO joiners from non–SMO joiners. Instead, such biological variables are universal human propensities that may help us understanding why humans act as they do, but they do not tell us anything in particular about SMO joining—only joining in general.

Recall that the category of "SMO joiners" I describe in Section I consists of various kinds of leaders and not simply the larger body of members. Among the movers, there is the very special personage of the *charismatic leader*. These are unusual people not simply in the extraordin-

ary claims they make about the world and themselves that their followers accept, but also, it is my impression, in their *level of sheer energy*
Not infrequently, such leaders appear to need little sleep and are alert
and physically active over long periods of time that their associates find
exhausting and inexplicable. But more than merely awake and active,
many routinely carry on *active interactional engagement* of other people
over long periods. After only brief periods of rest, they are on the go
again. I know of no systematic studies of this, but my hypothesis is that
such SMO leaders are endowed with especially robust physical bodies
and metabolisms. They come to be the extraordinary leaders they are
thought to be in part because of their unusual and biologically based
high levels of energy. Of course, there are also obviously many high-
energy people who are *not* SMO people. Therefore, variation in energy
level acts as simply one, sometimes contributing causal factor rather than
as a unique causal force.

2. Deeper Motivation.   Although much out of fashion in recent
years, over the middle decades of the twentieth century, variables of a
pervasive, deep motivational sort were prominent in accounts of joining. Looking back over the array of these, Zurcher and Snow (1981)
group them in terms of focus on seven such variables.

[1] *Pursuit of Meaning.* [People] confronted by a chaotic external environment, . . . uninterpretable because of an inadequate frame of
reference, are in a state of suggestibility that renders them susceptible to the simplifying ideology of a movement. . . . [e.g.,
Cantril 1941]

[2] *Authoritarianism.* Individuals who are dogmatic, highly preju-
diced, and insecure are seen as being especially susceptible to
the appeals of movements on the radical left and right . . . [e.g.,
Adorno, Frenkel-Brunswik, Levinson, and Sanford 1950; Lipset
1963] [In one variation on this, Eric Hoffer argues] that submis-
sion to an external cause or authority compensates for feelings
of self-inadequacy . . . and the desire to escape from an unwanted self. [Hoffer writes:] "The permanent misfits can find
salvation only in complete separation from the self; and they
usually find it by losing themselves in the compact collectivity of
a mass movement. . . . " [Hoffer 1951, 15, as quoted by Zurcher
and Snow]

[3] *Search for identity.* Participation in . . . movements . . . is a search
symptomatic of mass society's failure to generate and sustain
meaningful symbols and anchorages, which are seen as a function of rituals. [Participation] experiences in the various institu-

tional domains of life have not provided a sense of personal worth or dignity. [People] are thus seeking a new locus for identify . . . a more satisfactory basis for organizing life. . . . [e.g., Klapp 1969]

[4] *Social isolation or quest for community.* Vulnerability to movement participation is in part a function of being weakly attached or peripheral to existing social networks. . . . Readiness to participate . . . comes from an absence of those conditions that integrate people into the system. . . . With this emphasis on the . . . cohesive . . . functions . . . of movements . . . , movements are viewed as surrogate families and primary groups [that meet] previously isolated participants' needs for social affiliation, a sense of belongingness, and group identity. . . . [e.g., Kornhauser 1959]

[5] *Personal powerlessness.* Subjective powerlessness or little internal control renders the person susceptible to movement appeals and participation. [In a different formulation,] a strong sense of personal control or efficacy, coupled with low social control or system blame, is [said to be] more likely to lead to movement participation. . . . [e.g., Bell 1964]

[6] *Status dissonance . . . inconsistency [, and threat].* "The more frequently acute status inconsistencies occur within a population, the greater will be the proportion of that population willing to support programs of social change." [Lenski 1954, 211 as quoted by Zurcher and Snow] [In the status threat variation on these variables, it is] argued that challenges to the existence and prestige of a life style to which individual are committed can render those individuals candidates for participation in "status politics," and/or "status crusades." . . . [e.g., Gusfield 1963]

[7] *Relative deprivation.* [In] probably the most popular explanation for movement participation . . . the basic idea is that a sense of acute deprivation arises when what people want or think they should have exceeds what they actually have. . . . "Deprivation occurs in relation to desired points of reference, often 'reference groups,' rather than in relation to how little one has" [Morrison 1971, 675 as quoted by Zurcher and Snow; see also Gurr 1970]. When the gap between . . . aspirations and . . . attainments suddenly widens and becomes intolerable, people are . . . especially prone to movement participation. (adapted from Zurcher and Snow 1981, 450–52)

These have been prominent but hardly the only lines of deeper motivational theorizing. Others include linking joining with unresolved oedipal conflicts (Feuer 1969), the quest for cognitive consistency (Rokeach 1968), and serious psychopathology (Kilbourne and Richardson 1988). [Wood and Jackson (1982, Chs. 7 and 8) offer comprehensive reviews.]

In more recent years, background individual variables continue to be recounted as possible causes, but they have not been the subject of much recent research and promotion. There are at least three reasons for this. First, researchers have assessed empirical tests of these kinds of theories as tending, overall, to the negative, or as at least to be "elusive" in supporting or not supporting a theory (McAdam et al. 1988, 705; Snow and Oliver 1995, and the studies and surveys of studies they review or cite). Second, but likely more important than the truth or falsity of any of these variables is their *insufficiency*. Even if a variable *does* contribute to SMO joining, a much, much larger number of people likely exhibit the variable strongly than actually join an SMO. Such variables therefore lack much *predictive utility* (even though, when appropriately researched, they might enhance our grasp of the subjective meaning of joining to particular individuals).

Beyond empirical elusiveness and insufficiency, there is a third reason these kinds of theories/variables have fallen out of favor as factors explaining joining. In one or another way, background individual factors tend to (1) second-guess the motives of participants and (2) impute psychological defects or deficits to them. In the first, researchers are saying they know the "real reasons" for joining and these reasons are not those that the joiners are likely to avow or agree with. The metamessage of these theories is, I know why you joined better than you do. In the second, joining is often construed as a signal of "psychological deficits or pathologies." Being a member is suspect, irrational and/or unhealthy on that account (Snow and Oliver 1995, 577).

These two disparaging metamessages of background individual theories passed unnoticed and accepted when the movements studied were prominently those of the radical left and right, as they were in the middle decades of the twentieth century. But the substantive focus of movement studies shifted to more centrist, moderate, and therefore "good movements" in the 1960s and later—the prime ones being civil rights, anti–Vietnam war, and women's liberation. "Good movements" were, moreover, ones in which many researchers were *themselves* participants and to apply such background individual theories to them was to apply disparaging theories to oneself, hence the shift away from such theories (Morris and Herring, 1987)

The above variables are all addressed to understanding ordinary members, what I term above "the body of members." But how pertinent are these variables to understanding various kinds of "leaders," especially charismatic leaders? At least as they have been studied so far, they are apparently very pertinent, for, psychobiographical analyses of charismatic and other leaders feature many kinds of individual background variables, especially variables of a psychoanalytic and psychodynamic cast. As reviewed by Lindholm (1990), such conceptions include viewing the charismatic as a

> paranoid or schizophrenic scarred by an intense and ambivalent relationship with an unresponsive mother and an absent or passive father. Such individuals never develop an autonomous self, but have a fragmented and fragile identify, full of rage and fear, marked by an inability to accept any difference or distance, maintained largely by grandiose fantasies of omnipotence and domination. . . . Charismatic individuals may find refuge from inner disintegration and recompense for the injuries done in infancy by denying the limitations of reality and the necessary separation between self and surround, constructing instead a total world which they can completely encompass. (p. 64)

3. Self-Concept. To shy away from deeper motivation variables is not, though, to discount all investigation of background individual matters. Many of these matters are relatively "on the surface" rather than "deep," and are part and partial of conscious and normal psychological functioning, even if they vary from person to person. Researchers of diverse interests have looked at such "surface" matters with respect to self-concept (this variable), beliefs and socialization (variable 4) and a person's active seeking (variable 5).

Several researchers have measured the self-concept variable of *personal efficacy*, "the belief that one has the ability to make a difference, especially when coupled with low trust in the existing power structure" (Snow and Oliver 1995, 578). One study finds that more active of SMO members (cf. Section I.D.1.b) were "more dominant, self-confident, energetic, and effective in using their capabilities than [those] who engaged in less activism" (Snow and Oliver 1995, 578, 585; see also Werner 1978; Sherkat and Blocker 1994).

4. Belief and Socialization. Less "deep" than even self-concept variables is the finding that some SMO joiners have attitudes and beliefs consistent with and supportive of joining *long before the joining occasion.* McAdam et al. (1988, 706) boldly (and baldly) generalize:

▶ Activism grows out of strong attitudinal support for the values and goals of the movement.

Quite commonly such attitude/belief prepared "prejoiners" have been socialized to those values in their families and in larger *cultural traditions of activism* based in ethnic, national, and religious traditions (Snow and

Oliver 1995, 579–80). Joining for them is therefore a continuous rather than discontinuous act. Otherwise sometimes termed the "red diaper baby" theory of SMO joining, research has focused, in particular, on how student SMO activists of the 1960s grew up in secure, warm families that "motivated . . . their desire to actualize the political values and attitudes of their parents" (McAdam et al. 1988, 706). Richard Flacks, both a sixties activist and researcher of it, has thus reflected:

> A very narrow stratum of the general American population is differentially socialized to believe in its political efficacy and responsibility—namely, the offspring of the white, upper middle class. It is from this stratum that most political leadership in [the United States] is in fact recruited. . . . There may be other important sources of *chutzpah*, but the fact that one is reared in a climate of comfort and privilege, and more crucially, instructed by family and school experiences to believe that one can and ought to take social responsibility, seem to me to be paramount. Indeed, research several of us did on the social origins of the early New Left established [that they] like other children of the middle class, . . . were encouraged by their parents toward very high intellectual and academic achievement. What differentiated their upbringing from the conventional was the unusual stress parents placed on the moral necessity for dedication to some type of social service rather than personal material gain. These were people who came to feel they could and should be outstanding while simultaneously feeling profound guilt if they experienced themselves as self-serving. (Flacks 1976, 272–73; see also Braungart 1971)

Conceived in terms of cognitive outlooks, people learn broad "rhetorics" of (perspectives on) how to conceptualize and act on social reality. Three major genre of these are the *political*, *religious*, and the *psychological*, focusing, respectively, on changing social systems, changing one's relation to the supernatural, and changing oneself. To the degree that a person uses any one of these cognitive outlooks as a dominant problem-solving perspective, to that degree he or she is apt to be more responsive to SMOs of that genre than to one of the others [Lofland (1985, 134–35); see further Back (1987), Barkan, Cohn, and Whitaker (1993)]. Such pre-established dispositions to define and act in certain rather than other ways thus prompt people to be more sensitive to some SMOs and less sensitive to others.

5. Active Seeking.   Researchers examining how people join religious SMOs have been impressed with the degree to which some and perhaps many such joiners are often quite consciously deliberate and active in their examination of alternative affiliations and their decisions about them. The background to the situation of joining is *not* a "frantic search for a solution to some tension-inducing life problem" (Snow and Machalek 1984, 180). Instead, the more appropriate image is that of "one on a journey for personal and spiritual development and meaning" (p. 180). Kilbourne and Richardson provide this profile of features of such seeking:

> The seeker is generally characterized by . . . : 1) volition, 2) autonomy, 3) search for meaning and purpose, 4) multiple conversions or conversion careers, 5) rational interpretation of experiences, 6) gradual and continuous conversions, 7) negotiation between the individual and the potential membership group, and 8) belief change that follows behavior change, as the individual learns the role of being a new convert. (1988, 2)

The considerable literature reviewed by Kilborune and Richardson documenting this individual background variable makes it clear that at least some people deliberately self-engineer their own personal transformations in conscious quests to do so. This research is thus a corrective to the view that many other variables sponsor, the view that joiners are "passive subjects who have been unwittingly molded by powerful [individual or] external [structural] forces" (Snow and Machalek 1984, 180).

As is true of all the other variables I review, this active seeking variable is itself a function of other variables. It is a dependent variable varying with other independent variables, some of which might even include variables on the list I am reviewing. One research question is therefore and as phrased by Snow and Machalek, "[W]hat predisposes some people to become seekers?" (1984, 180).

B. Situational Individual Variables

Having come into physical contact with the possibility of joining, what individual variables might affect the likelihood of this actually happening?

6. Benefit Calculation/Rational Choice. Aspects of how people actively calculate costs and benefits in some rational-choice fashion have been given particular attention. Recall that in describing the eight generic questions that inform all research, I distinguished between the first seven, which were "passive" in their conception of humans, and the eighth, which is "active" in asking, What is human agency? Adopting the point of view of the actors, how do they go about strategizing and otherwise doing things? Variable 5, "active seeking," (just above) is one version of viewing the causal question of joining as an active agency question as against a driven human construction.

We come now to a second form of reconceiving the causal question of joining as a human agency question. This time, though, we have moved yet closer to the actual situation of joining, and the goal is to decipher the decision-making processes that people may engage in at the time of

joining or *not* joining. There are likely several ways in which this proximate period of decision-making can be conceptualized, but the one that
has been most popular (at least as a model of speculation if not actual
research) is called *rational-choice theory*. This perspective has of course
enjoyed great popularity in economic thinking in recent years and has
been applied in an expanding array of disciplines (Green and Shapiro
1994). Because of its wide fashionableness, we ought not be surprised to
find it applied to movement joining.

Holding aside the theory's problems as applied to joining, the core of
rational-choice theory has the virtue of expanding researchers' awareness of relevant variables in that it draws attention to active, decision-
making persons who calculate *costs* and *benefits* and then act "so as to
maximize net expected benefits" (Stark and Iannaccone 1993, 244). There
are a great many problems endemic to the concepts of calculation, costs,
benefits, maximization, and rational choice—definitional elasticity and
tautology being major among them. But even acknowledging such problems, this approach's demand that we inspect what actors get and what
these *benefits cost* them can lead to much more complete and detailed
understanding. I say "can lead" because, unfortunately, rational-choice
theories of SMO joining are mostly embraced by scholars more interested in abstract modeling and laboratory simulations than in close investigations of actual joining.[6] Therefore, benefit calculation variables
remain more at the level of theoretical speculation than at the level of
empirical investigation (see, though, studies reviewed by Snow and
Oliver 1995, 585).

So, also, the empirical examination of conscious, intentional decisions
featuring cost and benefit assessments has been derailed by a strange
preoccupation with what is called "the free-rider problem." As applied
to movements and reported in the previous chapter, this problem is the
invention of Mancur Olson (1965), who posited:

> True rational actors will not join a group to pursue common ends when,
> without participating, they can reap the benefits of other people's activity
> in obtaining them. If every member of a relevant group can share in the
> benefits . . . then the rational thing is to free ride . . . rather than to help
> attain the corporate interest. (paraphrase by Hechter 1987, 27)

Joining an SMO is thus rendered irrational, while at the same time we
know that people *do* join SMOs. Why, then, do people join SMOs despite the "irrationality" of doing so in this sense?

One answer to this question is to ask if the "free-rider problem" is an
empirically valid situation and question in the first place. The free-rider
problem is made a "problem" by assuming that people's participation is
premised entirely on narrow calculations of future individualistic "free"

benefits. In point of empirical fact, and as nicely put by Turner and Killian, this is a

> short-sighted definition of rationality. A rational person would recognize that the outcome when everyone pursues self-interest in this way has to be failure to produce *any* public good [or benefits for individuals, free riders or not]. By pragmatic test, the rational person would be forced to reject this form of rationality as ultimately irrational. (1987, 333; see also Gamson 1990, 151–55; Klandermans 1984)

As an empirical matter, we know that while "short-sighted" rationality certainly exists, *other* kinds of incentives for participation *also* exist and enter into "benefit calculations." Following James Q. Wilson ([1974] 1995, 33–35), these are commonly conceived as being of

> three broad types . . . : material, solidary, and purposive.
>
> *Material* incentives include salaries, insurance programs, and threats of physical or material retaliation.
> *Solidary* incentives arise from social relations with other participants, such as praise, respect, and friendship shared among coparticipants or shame, contempt, and ostracism in the case of non participants.
> *Purposive* incentives arise from internalized norms and values in which a person's self-esteem depends on doing the right thing. (adapted from Snow and Oliver 1995, 584, emphasis added)

Generalizing about solidary and purposive incentives, Turner and Killian declare:

> Altruism and personal dedication to valued causes [purposive incentives] are real and cannot be entirely reduced to self-interest. And because we are socialized into groups, group advancement [solidary incentive] is as satisfying and important to us as individual advancement once our most basic individual needs are satisfied. (1987, 333)

Believers in the free-rider problem concede at least part of these criticisms by saying that the problem is solved with *"selective incentives—* private goods that reward contributors or coercive measures that punish non participation" (Snow and Oliver 1995, 584, emphasis in the original).

7. Experimentation. There is a second way in which some researchers have conceptualized individual strategizing in the situation of possible joining. This second view is baldly empirical rather than derived or deduced from an a priori model of human functioning such as rational-choice theory. It arises, that is, from the data—with the researcher being with and around new joiners rather than speculating about them from afar.

In this view and at least in SMOs so studied, "joining" has a decidedly *experimental* quality, a trying-it-out motif in which joiners *act* in SMO terms but do so in a tentative way and without embracing whatever the beliefs (Balch 1980; Bromley and Shupe 1979; Beckford 1978; Straus 1979). Some of these studies conceive this as a process of *role learning* in which "joining" in the sense of believing is slow and incremental, if it proceeds at all. In this way, joining an SMO can be similar to how people join and become socialized into groups of more mainstream kinds (Lofland and Skonovd 1985, 165).

In the logic of experimental action, some experiments turn out the way the experimenters expect and some do not. So it is among SMOs. Some experimental associates/joiners remain just that and become *freeriders* in a different sense! They hang around the SMO for whatever the more easily available benefits, but decline to make the harder commitments or to do the tougher work (Stark and Iannaccone 1993, 247–48). [Stark and Iannaccone refer to free-riderism of this kind as, indeed, "the Achilles heel of collective activities," and a "pervasive dynamic [that] threatens all groups engaged in the production of collective goods" (pp. 247–48).]

III. WHY PEOPLE JOIN SMOS: STRUCTURAL VARIABLES

Individual variables seek to specify features of persons that "impel" or "dispose" them toward SMOs and/or cognitive processes involved in decisions to join SMOs. In contrast, structural variables attempt to identify circumstances of individuals that facilitate or inhabit joining. As among individual variables, structural ones can be divided into those that become causally important prior to the situation of joining (and are therefore *background*) and those operating variably in the situation of joining itself (and are therefore *situational*).

A. Background Structural Variables

Background structural variables that researchers have seen as possibly pertinent vary along the macro-meso-micro dimension of scale. Here I report the cluster of *macro*-structure variables often invoked and three more *meso-micro* variables.

8. Macro-Structure. In the view of many researchers, the broad canvas of the society at large and the historical era remain relevant considerations when thinking of the microscopic act of individual joining. One major empirical reason for linking large macro-structure to tiny micro-acts of joining is the fact that SMO joinings come in "waves" or "spurts" (just as do SMO foundings, as indicated in Chapter 7, Section IV.B.12). These waves and spurts are themselves best understood as functions of macro-structural variables.

The macro-structure variables commonly pointed to are similar to or the same as those discussed in the previous chapter as affecting the formation of SMOs. There are, in particular, the macro, standing-arrangement variables (1)–(8) summarized in Figure 7.1, SMO Causes, and which are named (and numbered):

1. social inequality and change
2. political opportunity
3. state penetration of citizen life
4. prosperity
5. geographical concentration
6. prior organization and collective identity
7. cross-cutting solidarities
8. perception/culture of injustice

If we stretch the meaning of "background" versus "situational" structural variables, we might also include the macro-situational variables summarized in Figure 7.1, namely,

9. regime crises and contested political arenas
10. recent decline in amount of repression
11. focal points/focusing crises
12. citizen surge synergy

9. Organizational Membership. The three meso-micro background variables I report, (9)–(11), follow the formulation and terminology of McAdam et al. (MMZ 1988) (which is in turn informed by McAdam 1988b).

The structural counterpart of the self-concept variable of a high sense of personal efficacy (variable 4) is the finding that joiners of *some* SMOs have previously been members of more organizations than nonjoiners have been. MMZ suggest that one among several variables that might explain this finding is the possibility that "those who are organizationally active are more likely to regard activism as potentially effective and therefore worth participating in" (1988, 708). Another and more situational explanation is that participating in organizations "increases a person's chances of learning about movement activity" (MMZ 1988, 708).

I have emphasized the word *some* in reporting this finding because the research on which it is based deals primarily with certain *political* SMOs. There is some evidence that it may apply less strongly to religious and "ego" (personal change) SMOs.

10. Prior Activism.   In this same vein, MMZ report that a "history of prior activism increases the likelihood of future activism" (p. 708). While "activism" is not necessarily SMO joining, the two overlap sufficiently to suggest its pertinence. Indeed, McAdam (1986) finds this relation between prior activism and joining a particular SMO. Joining and prior activism themselves may be related in part because of self-concepts or identities developed in previous activism and because of skills and "know-how" acquired that make a current joining more familiar and comfortable (p. 708). The individual-level counterpart to this more structural variable would appear to be variable (7), "active seeking."

11. Prior Contact.   A third variable to which MMZ point is borderline between background and situational variables, and might be thought of, in fact, as a bridge between background and situational variables. This is the variable (or class of variables) these researchers call *prior contact with a movement member* (MMZ 1988, 707). Other researchers refer to it as "social networks," "network ties," or "preexisting groups and affiliations" (Snow and Machalek 1984, 182; Snow and Oliver 1995, 574).

This is the prior-contact proposition stated in generic form, that is, as applicable to the entire domain of insurgent realities:

⬧ Preexisting social ties or network linkages function to channel the diffusion of all varieties of collective actions. (Snow and Oliver 1995, 574)

In the specifically SMO context, the extremely robust finding is that "prior interpersonal contact [is] the single richest source of movement recruits" (MMZ 1988, 708). Or as put in formal propositional form by Snow, Zurcher, and Ekland-Olson:

⬧ Those outsiders who are linked to one or more movement members through preexisting extra movement networks will have a greater probability of being contacted and recruited into that particular movement than will those individuals who are outside of members' extra movement networks. (1980, 792)

B. Situational Structural Variables

We come, finally, to variables researchers have found to be varyingly operative or inoperative in the immediate circumstances of joining. Researchers have explored five facilitating or inhibiting variables in this proximate surround.

12. Suddenly Imposed Grievances. Edward Walsh (1981) introduced the phrase "suddenly imposed grievances" to point up "those dramatic, highly publicized and often unexpected events—[human]-made disasters, major court decisions, official violence—that serve to dramatize and therefore increase public awareness of and opposition to particular grievances" (MMZ 1988, 706). In addressing the question of SMO formation in Chapter 7 (Section IV.B.11), I reported how researchers speak of such events as "focal points" or "focusing crisis" and explore their relation to SMO *formation*. Here, in contrast, we are interested in their role in SMO *joining*.

Suddenly imposed (or perceived) grievances vary in their intensity, severity and pervasiveness. Even in the lower ranges of these dimensions, we nonetheless find spurts of SMO joining (as well as of SMO formation). Walsh (1981) himself focused on the *relatively* milder suddenly imposed grievance of the Three Mile Island nuclear plant incident of 1979 and he documented a quite dramatic increase in SMO participation attendant to it. Other studies of suddenly imposed grievances in a similar range of intensity, severity, and pervasiveness include Useem (1980), on responses to court-ordered busing as a means to integrate schools racially and Molotch (1975) on responses to an oil spill off the coast of Santa Barbara, California (MMZ 1988, 706–7).

Suddenly imposed grievances in the *higher* ranges of intensity, severity and pervasiveness include deadly epidemics and foreign military invasions that disrupt, discredit, or destroy existing social organization. To the degree a society is subjected to such acute social crises with which existing authorities and groups cannot or will not cope, to that degree people are prepared for SMO affiliation. Or, in the colorful rational-choice language of Stark and Iannaccone as applied to *religious* SMOs (or what they call "firms"):

◆ Anything that causes widespread fear and suffering can undercut consumer satisfaction with the products of the leading religious firms, opening the way for new firms to gain support. (1993, 257)

These authors elaborate this proposition in this fashion:

Crises produced by natural or social disasters often are translated into crises of faith. This is because the disaster places demands on the prevailing religious culture that it appears unable to meet. For example, classical paganism appeared to offer no protection against the two deadly epidemics that swept the Roman Empire in the second and third centuries, nor could it offer an explanation of these terrible events. In contrast, Christianity seemed both to protect again these epidemics and to explain their occurrence. [p. 257; see also Barkun (1974) on "disaster and millennium"]

13. Situational Stress. Many studies of joining *religious* SMOs have highlighted the concurrent presence of private, proximate circumstances that joiners define as stressful or tension-producing. These include "marital strain, the loss of a family member, change or lose of a job, pressures of higher education, or any of a number of other tensions" (Snow and Machalek 1984, 181). However, not all studies, especially those of joining *political* SMOs, find such situational stresses. This inconsistency presents the possibility that situational stress may be a facilitating but not necessary cause in only *some* patterns of joining.

A number of considerations complicate how to interpret the role of situational stress. First, joiners *themselves* sometimes put forth situational stresses as among the reasons for their joining and point to how their SMO membership has, indeed, solved their problems—especially as regards their marriages, jobs, or use of drugs. In having "found the light," they no longer have whatever the particular stresses—what they likely term "problems." While joiner accounts are not, of course, the last word in these matters, they cannot be disregarded either. And in fact, the claims such joiners make about the relation between their former problems and their solutions in SMO membership often have the ring of validity. In some cases, being an SMO member is, in fact, a solution to one or more of many types of situational stresses, exactly as such persons claim their membership to be.

Second, even so, we know that many SMO joiners tend to reconstruct their biographies in ways that "either redefine life before [membership] as being fraught with problems or to allude to personal problems that were either not previously discernible or not troublesome enough to warrant remedial action" (Snow and Machalek 1984, 181).

Third, studies of SMO joiners commonly fail to have a "control" or contrast group with which joiner forms and levels of situational stresses can be compared. If such stresses are much the same in comparable categories of nonjoiners, their causal role is doubtful or at least circumscribed.

14. Biographical Availability. The underlying image of many causal variables tends to be one or the other of two main kinds: push versus pull. For example, suddenly imposed grievances and situational stresses (variables 12 and 13) imply "pushes" to joining. On the other hand, benefit calculation and prior contact (variables 6 and 11) connote "pulls" toward joining. Some variables may, however, not operate in either of these ways. Rather than "push" or "pull," they may simply *permit*—or not permit.

This is the image of casual force underlying what is variously termed "biographical availability," "structural availability," "differential availability," and "absence of countervailing ties" (MMZ 1988, 709; Snow et al. 1980, 794; Snow and Machalek 1984). The focus is on variable ways in which "the biographical circumstances of a person's life may serve to encourage or constrain participation in important ways" (MMZ 1988, 709). To be biographically available is not to have the "personal constraints that may increase the costs and risk of [SMO] participation such as full-time employment, marriage, and family responsibilities" (McAdam 1986, 70). Snow et al. (1980, 794) summarize the research findings in these propositions:

- The fewer and the weaker the social ties to alternative networks, the greater the structural availability for movement participation.
- The greater the structural availability for participation, the greater the probability of accepting the recruitment "invitation."

Researchers find it helpful to think of biographical availability in structural and not simply individual terms. That is, individuals are the analytic units of biographical availability, but strong states of this variable are not distributed evenly across individuals in society and entire societies can differ in their aggregate amounts of it.

There is, first, the structural perspective of the *life cycle*. The very process of living in society produces turning points or critical periods where old roles and involvements terminate and new ones must (or at least can) begin. At such points, the probabilities of SMO involvement appear to increase significantly There is, for example, a quite notable conjunction between late adolescence and involvement in religious SMOs (Machalek and Snow 1993, 62).

Second, viewing societies as composed of different *population segments* prompts the realization that entire segments differ in their biographical availability—the degree to which they are constrained by an array of complex and scheduled obligations or have, in contrast, "discretionary or unscheduled time to explore and participate" (p. 61). In recent times, such *more* biographically available population segments have included students and young adults more generally, autonomous professionals (especially lawyers and professors), and the affluent retired, among other persons of independent means. And all these segments are, in fact, disproportionately represented in SMO memberships.

Third, in conditions of the acute social crises mentioned above as suddenly imposed grievances, large portions of *entire societies* can suddenly become biographically available. Stark and Iannaccone describe this for the case of new religious movements, a pattern that extends to all SMOs:

> When the average member of a group suffers a substantial loss of attachments, social disorganization occurs and conformity to the conventional moral order declines. In this sense, disasters free many members of a group to adopt a new culture [i.e., to join an SMO]. If most of your friends and relatives have perished or have fled, you risk much less when deviating from the conventional religious culture [i.e., from mainstream conceptions of reality]. (1993, 257)

The critical point here is that acute social crises are usually thought of as "push" factors in joining SMOs, and so they can be. But such crises *also* create biographical availability—and biographical availability on a mass scale.

15. Coercive Persuasion. The surge of membership in various "new religions" in the 1970s spurred coercive persuasion or "brainwashing" explanations of joining them—and, by extension, political and ego SMOs. Although embraced by only a few serious scholars of SMOs, this variable has nonetheless been very popular among the public at large, among opponents of new religions, and among mental health professionals whose practices focus on ex-members of these SMOs.

Despite the problem of this variable being false for all but the very smallest number of cases, it does have the virtue of being quite solidly *situational-structural.* That is, in fine sociological fashion, it directly asserts how a recruiting SMO is organized and acts in the ongoing present in ways that result in someone joining that SMO. In this sense, the theory is a situational-structuralist sociologist's dream (but, alas and like other dreams, more often illusion than reality).

What is this alleged organization that is coercive persuasion or brainwashing? Characterized most abstractly, it is "systematic manipulation of powerful social psychological stimuli in a highly controlled group setting" (Kilbourne and Richardson 1988, 12). In such a setting, the individual is "made receptive to new ideas because his or her critical faculties and ego strength have been eroded by information control, overstimulation of the nervous system, forced confessions, and ego destruction, among other factors" (Snow and Machalek 1984, 179).

Classic depictions of coercive persuasion were based on its practice by Soviet and Chinese communists and properly stressed the *literally* coercive aspects that were in fact part of the process: torture, physical debilitation and exhaustion, inadequate diet that reduced weight and stamina. As prisoners who had been arrested or captured, the process also featured total control and isolation, the assumption of guilt but on unclear charges, and systematic humiliation in a context of uncertainly about the future—or uncertainty of any future at all (Schein 1961; Lifton 1963; Somit 1968).

In face of the fact that a recruitment organization with these physically coercive features is virtually never seen among SMOs, more recent formulations have softened the picture to one of "psychological coercion" in which there is "excessive influence" of these kinds:

- isolating members from past and external sources of social support,
- love and support that is contingent upon particular beliefs,
- pressures to maintain group unanimity,
- threat of physical harm,
- threat of psychological punishment,
- eliciting confessions or extensive past histories,
- systematic induction of psychological duress,
- division of the world into "good" and "evil" forces,
- continual verbal and sensory barrage of pro-system information, and
- deprivation of food or sleep (adapted from Kilbourne and Richardson 1988, 13).

This softer version of coercive persuasion or "psychological coercion" does more accurately describe many of the recruitment practices of *some* SMOs at some periods in their history. It is important to point up, however, that such features are *also* found in a number of *mainstream* socialization settings—particularly in elite military units and the monastic religious orders of mainstream religions.

Whether mainstream or excluded, there is certainly pressure to join/ believe and conform and one key question about both is, Are people *voluntarily* involved in these intensive joining/socialization experiences? On this score, researchers who have personally and directly observed these recruitment settings by and large report that participants see themselves as there of their own volition and view the experience as highly positive or even as enthralling. Coercive persuasionists counter that such perceptions are manipulated false consciousness.

This contrast in accepting the participants' consciousness as valid or not reflects a deeper contrast in how joiners are viewed. Are they active, self-aware seekers (variable 5), who are rational people who can make cost-benefit calculations (variable 6), and who can experiment with affiliations (variable 7)? Coercive persuasionist interpreters minimize the presence and strength of all three of these variables, while most researchers tend to see all three variables strongly operating in these high-intensity recruitment settings.

None of this is to say that coercive persuasion never occurs. It seems clearly to have taken place in some few, special cases, among which is likely Patricia Hearst's famous conversion to the radical views of the Symbionese Liberation Army. And like those from whom "conversions" had been extracted in communist coercive persuasion, Ms. Hearst "appeared to return to her earlier sociopolitical beliefs relatively easily and quickly once she was removed from the influence and control of her abductors" (Lofland and Skonovd 1985, 169–70).

So, also, some few joinings brought about in the softer setting of "psychological coercion" might reasonably be construed as a form of manipulated consent. Even so, most joinings arising through these settings appear more enthusiastically voluntarily than zombie-minded compliance. Moreover, a very small proportion of all people who participate in these intense recruitment settings actually join that SMO, suggesting that these setting are not nearly as potent as their critics allege (Barker 1984; Richardson 1993).

In wider perspective, only a tiny fraction of SMOs mount anything remotely resembling even "psychological coercion" programs, much less coercive persuasion on the communist model. I venture to guess, indeed, that the overwhelming mass of SMOs have *no* coherent recruitment efforts or even make scattered, disorganized attempts. Since coercive persuasion or psychological conversion variables are zero in almost all SMOs, they can do little or nothing to account for most joining.

16. Affective Bonds. To say that researchers rarely if ever find coercive persuasion or anything like it in joining is not to say that nothing of causal significance is going on in a possible joiner's relations to members—quite the opposite. Following on from the background-situational *bridging* variable of *prior contact* (11), a large number of research studies document the central role of *positive interpersonal bonds* in bringing about membership. Or, as put strongly by Stark and Bainbridge: "interpersonal bonds are the fundamental support for recruitment" (1980, 1389).

In many cases, such bonds with or ties to SMO members are *preexisting*, as in kinship or work settings, and these loyalties cause a possible joiner to at least pay serious attention to the SMO. Indeed, for many SMOs, the great bulk of new members are recruited through preexisting networks and, central here, are the *affective bonds and personal loyalty and liking* implied by the existence of these preexisting networks. These ties of affection are the subjective, situational-structural meaning of several of the more external, structural variables I reviewed in the previous chapter as pertinent to SMO formation. These are the variables, in particular, of (5) geographical concentration and (6) prior organization and collective identity (6). Both these variables are macro, external, and organizational matters, but a micro, internal, and subjective order of *positive attachments* is implied by and can underlie these structural states. For these reasons, some SMOs enjoy the luxury of *bloc recruitment*, meaning that entire families, work groups, church congregations, neighborhoods, or other geographical concentration, join the SMO all at once in a bloc (Oberschall 1973, 118–37; Stark and Bainbridge 1985, Part IV).

In other cases, the possible joiner is a stranger to SMO members and affective ties must be initiated, a task that some SMOs consciously undertake (and that is apt to cause charges of coercive persuasion). In such a process, the sheer *amount* of interaction assumes causal significance. Other things equal:

▶ The more *intensive* the interaction, the more likely are positive affective bonds and, therefore, the more likely is joining.

Intensive interaction cannot be interaction of simply any sort, clearly. In order to foster affective bonds, such interaction must also be supportive of the self of the possible joiner and, in particular, suggest how the SMO might answer the person's active seeking (variable 5), provide possible benefits (variable 6), afford meaningful experimentation (variable 7), or otherwise address her or his motivations and concerns (variables 1–4). The social psychological dynamic at work here is:

▶ A positive interpersonal tie to one or more groups members can function as an information bridge, increase the credibility of appeals, and intensify the pressure to accept these appeals and corresponding practices (Snow and Machalek 1984, 183).

Turner and Killian catch the spirit of this when they declare that "informal discussion with friends and associates lends interest and reality to topics and ideas that command only superficial attention when presented impersonally" (1987, 330). The upshot is that joining comes to be simply accepting "the opinions of one's friends" (Stark and Bainbridge 1980, 1379). This dynamic is itself premised on the still broader proposition that what a person believes to be true, reasonable, and moral rests in important part on an underlying order of shared group attachments and sentiments (Berger and Luckmann 1967; Harrison 1974; McAdam and Paulsen 1993).

Eric Hirsch (1990) has pressed the analysis of affective bonds forward in specifying how a number of ongoing *group processes* in certain SMOs can function progressively to commit potential joiners to the SMO and its projects. Observing the Coalition for a Free South Africa (CFSA) at Columbia University in 1985, Hirsch identified four evolving and sequential group processes that appeared to function to create commitment to this SMO in the blockade of a university building that ran from April 4 through April 25, 1985:

1. *consciousness-raising* in numerous small group discussions,
2. *collective empowerment* at the initiation of a blockade of a strategic university building,
3. *polarization* and increased commitment in response to the university's threat of disciplinary action, and,
4. *collective decision-making* and the end of the blockade in response to the university's decision to simply wait it out (Hirsch 1990).

Hirsch provides this characterization of how the four processes operated among the several hundred CFSA blockaders:

> [These] were people who had been convinced by CFSA meetings that apartheid was evil, that divestment would help South African blacks, and that divestment could be achieved through protest. They joined the blockade on April 4th because it appeared to offer a powerful alternative to previous impotent demonstrations and because of the example of self-sacrificing CFSA leaders. The solidarity of the group increased after the administrations' escalation of the conflict and because group identification among the protesters was already strong enough so that they responded to the threat as a powerful group rather than as powerless individuals. Protesters remained at the long and risky protest partly because of the democratic decision-making processes used by the group. (p. 252)

IV. CAUSAL LOGIC REITERATED

These sixteen types of variables and single variables are *candidates* for causal significance in joining. Because of the heterogeneity in what is joined, what joining means to different researchers, and how it is experienced that I reviewed at the outset, no one of these variables seems strongly operative in *every* instance of joining. Indeed, some of them may be operative in very few cases. Closer inspection of pertinent data might even show some of them to be entirely wrong, in the sense that they help to account for *no* cases in which the data are properly assembled and understood.

This leaves us then with a storehouse or inventory of possible causes rather than with a tight statement of "why people join SMOs." But do not despair. This is itself an achievement. At minimum it means that researchers have moved beyond simplistic monocausal accounts to the more sophisticated level of multiple and contingent causes (cf. Lieberson 1992). Even through the causal going gets rougher from here, it can also be more accurate.

One route to greater accuracy is, I think, to press forward toward *causal process models* of joining. The two categories of "background" and "situational" variables into which I have classified the sixteen candidate causes are a rudimentary first step in the direction of such models. *Within* the background and situational categories—or within some more refined temporal formulation—specific candidate causes likely occur or are activated in diverse temporal sequences that facilitate or inhibit joining. In addition to specifying yet additional causes, the task is to identify their *order* of causal operation as well as *differential paths* in processes of joining.

The spirit of such causal process models is expressed well by Stark and Bainbridge in reflecting on the causal role of affective bonds (variable 16) in joining, a variable they believe to be "the fundamental support for recruitment:"

> Despite the importance of interpersonal bonds for . . . recruitment, we cannot reject the complementary deprivation [variable 2] and ideological appeal [variable 4] position. Any complete theory of recruitment . . . must include both these elements. However deprivation and ideological compatibility seem unable to serve as more than very general contributory conditions in any satisfactory theory of recruitment. Although they do limit the pool of persons available for recruitment, they do not limit it very much in comparison to the very small number of such persons who actually join. Many people are deprived and are ideologically predisposed to accept [an SMO's] message. But in explaining why so few of them actually join, it is necessary to examine a number of situational variables. (1985, 323)[7]

V. MEMBERSHIP MAINTENANCE

One reasonably safe empirical generalization about SMO membership is that turnover or defection runs from fairly to quite high among a large portion of them. Many if not most SMOs more than seven or eight years old probably have more *former* than current members.[8] People may join, but they also quit and they do so at high rates.

While affiliation may bring rewards and happiness, it also brings new problems—just as in any other relationship. The character and intensity of these problems vary across SMOs and over time in given SMOs, but the following are among the more common:

- As marginal or excluded realities, membership carries at least stigma and perhaps even active repression. These can cause weariness, to say the least (Coles 1964).
- SMOs are often not at all (or not very) successful in achieving their goals. How long does one strive to achieve seemingly "impossible dreams"? Taking just these two problems together, Wollman, Wexler, and Priddy observe about political SMOs that "political activism is extremely demanding: emotions run high, immediate rewards may be few, and confrontation and conflict must be dealt with. . . . The activist can be thought of as a . . . salesperson whose product involves thinking in new ways. Few salespeople have a product more volatile, a marketing area less structured and a personal reward less tangible" (1994, 12).
- Conversely, the major goal of the SMO is sometimes achieved (e.g., Messinger 1955). What, then, is the point of further participation?
- The goals and programs of the SMO may shift in ways with which the member does not agree and cannot change. How can one support an SMO doing things one disapproves?
- Aspects of the beliefs and programs of the SMO not known before joining have now come to light and these are highly objectionable to the member. Can one continue to be a member of an SMO with such newly known noxious features?
- Allegations of the illegal or immoral behavior of SMO leaders and others come to light. What if those charges are true?
- The hours of work may be very long and the work conditions burdensome.
- Living circumstances may be spartan and the diet even more so.
- Certain factions in the SMO disapprove of you and/or the faction with which you are aligned and they are obstructing you and your faction. Why not quit rather than put up with this?
- Obligations a member has to family or other significant people may not be met, with a consequent sense of guilt.
- A number of the member's aspirations are not met within the SMO and are not realizable within it (e.g., a stable job and career).
- The insurgent reality that was once believed to be a brilliant new path to perfect human life now, in the light of certain events, seems absurd and bizarre.

In view of these and other problems that are endemic to SMOs (and to other associations as well), the wonder might be that SMOs retain members at all. But they do, clearly, and the research question is, What variables affect the degree to which membership is maintained and maintained, in particular, with a high or low level of morale and esprit de corp? [Blumer (1969a, 102–10). See further Simmons (1969) and Snow and Machalek (1982).]

Because of the multiple problems that continually beset affiliation, researchers find it helpful to conceive membership as something that must continually be reproduced or achieved. Rather than a once-and-for-all established thing, it is a fragile and ever-new production dependent upon many supportive factors for its continued reproduction (Turner and Killian 1987, 329).

Researchers have explored two main classes of variables as affecting membership maintenance and morale: those that are *managerial*—meaning focused on immediate situations—those that are *broader*—meaning focused on the SMO as an entity and its contexts.[9]

A. Managerial Variables

People in SMOs are often not obtuse, of course, and problems of the above and other kinds may be openly discussed and conscious efforts to deal with them devised. Terms commonly used in these discussions include *weariness* (Coles 1964) and *burnout* (a term also referring to mainstream job stress). Indeed, movement how-to-do-it manuals increasingly feature burnout as a problem on a par with strategic problems per se. Prominent among what can be thought of as managerial recommendations are explicit injunctions such as these:

- Take more time off. Do not spend all your work or spare time on SMO work.
- Organize and participate in renewal workshops where morale problems are discussed.
- Become process oriented; focus on the rewards of the work itself rather than its outcome.
- Think in the long-term perspective rather than in terms of simply the present.[10]

The degree to which such items of managerial advice and action bolster morale and maintain membership or not is unclear.

B. Broader Variables

Observers of SMOs in wider perspective—as holistic entities—have put forth two variables that are broader than managerial recommendations as affecting membership maintenance.

1. Succession of Success-Hopeful Projects. SMOs differ in the extent to which members' expectations are organized around what is perceived as a large and important near-term project that will be successful. Leaders of SMOs that maintain membership are adroit in inventing and fielding a *succession* of such projects—and/or they are fortunate in having *external events* provide occasions in terms of which to organize projects. Regarding the latter, though, even the most fortunate external events have to be *defined* by leaders as such and action organized in terms of them.

The leadership problem with large and important projects is that these must be *victories* in order to sustain morale. If failures, they can be more disastrous for membership than no projects at all. While it is certainly the case that spectacular project failures can and do depress SMO memberships (and crush SMOs themselves sometimes), there remains a large *zone of ambiguity of outcome* in which victory and success can plausibly be claimed and thus serve to maintain membership. The more precise formulation of this proposition is, therefore:

▶ The succession of large and important projects should be ones for which a range of likely outcomes can be defined as success or victory even if they are failures in given respects.

The *history* of a membership-maintaining SMO is, in this proposition, one characterized by one large and important project after another, each of which is credibly evaluated as a great victory or success. At any given time, the membership is preoccupied by "it"—a campaign, undertaking, impending event, or whatever.

In this kind of membership maintenance work, SMOs with charismatic or otherwise authoritarian leaders have the advantage of rapid acceptance and action by the membership. Rather than dawdle through endless democratic debates on possible projects, such leaders can make inspired announcements and thrust forward with the project immediately—an immediately that is claimed to be *urgent* and *imperative*. The history of the Unification Church led by the charismatic Sun Myung Moon is quite spectacular in this way in being a series of one-after-the-other full-tilt projects of highly varied kinds (see, e.g., Bromley and Shupe 1979; Benford 1993a). Of course, defining every project as a success and victory is much assisted by Moon being able to reckon the results in terms of a hidden providential history that operates on the "spiritual" plane of reality and not merely in current effects in the "material" world. Even the leader of an early 1960s missionary band of the Unification Church executed this successive project principle well in the face of a failure to make converts despite this being their central goal.

Over the course of the first four years of this pioneering cadre, its leader mounted these successive projects that served to maintain (and even slightly enlarge) membership:

- decamp the entire membership and migrate en masse to a new location (a rather common strategy in religious SMO history),
- announce the imminent but unspecified arrive of Moon in the United States, an arrival that required elaborate preparations,
- define present time as preparatory, planning, and organizing time (as in editing and printing the group's book), after which goals will *really* be achieved,
- geographically disperse members on missionary quests, creating a sense of expansion from new places and newly encountered people even if the membership did not change much (summarized from Lofland [1966] 1977, Ch. 12).

2. SMO Culture.   As was described in Section V of Chapter 5, SMOs vary in the extent or magnitude of their cultural development. The proposition given there is pertinent here:

▶ The greater the degree of cultural development, the higher are participant morale and, therefore, commitment and tenacity in the face of adversity, and retention of movement participants.

Blumer and others have hypothesized that among the many dimensions of cultural development, strong degrees of *informal fellowship* and *ceremonial behavior* are especially important to esprit de corps and morale (Fine and Stoecker 1985; Neitz 1987).

Informal fellowship refers to occasions on which members "have the opportunity to come know one another as human beings instead of as institutional symbols" and to "develop a common sympathy and sense of intimacy which contributes much to solidarity. Thus, [in developed SMO cultures] we . . . find many kinds of informal and communal association. Singing, dancing, picnics, joking, having fun, and friendly informal conversation are important devices of this sort" (Blumer [1939] 1969a, 107).

Examples of formal *ceremonial behavior* and ritual include

meetings, rallies, parades, huge demonstrations and commemorative ceremonials, [which involve a] psychology of being on parade. The . . . participant experiences the feeling of considerable personal expansion and therefore has the sense of being somebody distinctly important, [a feeling that] comes to be identified with the [SMO]. Likewise, the paraphernalia of ritual . . . serves to foster feelings of common identity [and in fuller development] consists of a set of sentimental symbols, such as slogans, songs, cheers, poems, hymns, expressive gestures, and uniforms. (pp. 107–8; see also Berger 1981; Blood-Patterson 1988; Zablocki 1980)

VI. MEMBERSHIP CONSEQUENCES

The consequences that SMO membership may or may not have for people depends, of course, on what they were members of, in what way, for how long, and what specifically happened. Such heterogeneity makes for corresponding heterogeneity in various possible consequences treated as dependent variables. Propositions about the consequences of SMO membership must therefore always be contextualized in the sense of appreciated as only about consequences of some delimited variety of SMO membership rather than about membership in general.

In particular, studies of the consequences of SMO participation have tended to focus on ex-members of high intensity, all absorbing, "high-risk, high-cost" SMOs and episodes of activism (Sherkat and Blocker 1992, 2). Such memberships and the consequences for their participants may well be quite atypical relative to the universe of all SMO members and membership consequences. Extreme caution must therefore be exercised in assessing the generality of consequences for all SMO members based on such samples.

Within this cautionary delimitation, researchers have pursued two primary types of propositions about the consequences of SMO membership: psychological and life course.

A. Psychological Consequences

For reasons I leave aside for the moment, quite a few researchers of *religious* SMOs have been preoccupied with their consequences for the mental health of members. This preoccupation is of note because virtually no researchers pursue this question regarding *political* SMOS, although, in the sheer logic of the matter, mental health consequences are surely as pertinent to political as to religious SMOs (perhaps more so).

Be this curious imbalance as it may, psychological researchers divide on the question of whether or not religious SMOs "contributes to mental illness and are an obstacle to the development of a healthy personality" (Saliba 1993, 99). Surveying the research literature, John Saliba concludes that it "does not offer an unequivocal answer to the . . . question of whether cults [religious SMOs] are adverse or beneficial to individual mental health" (p. 110). Limitations of samples, measurements, and research designs, as well as conflicts among perspectives on human behavior, render existing studies inconclusive. The one safe generalization that can be offered is that credible but debatable data and cases can be marshaled for both positive and negative effects on mental health.

B. Life Course Consequences

A more sociologically focused stream of research has focused on the *life course* consequences of SMO and movement involvement.[11] Among several ways to think about these consequences, perhaps the most common question has been, What, in the perspective of decades, are effects of youthful SMO involvements? Types of effects so scrutinized have included, as summarized in one study:

(1) political participation and orientation,
(2) social psychological dispositions,
(3) religious orientation and participation,
(4) status attainment and occupation,
(5) residential mobility and homeownership, and
(6) family structure and solidarity (Sherkat and Blocker 1992, 1).

Not surprisingly, the samples employed in most researches have been ex-members of 1960s-era SMOs. Among these studies, Doug McAdam's 1983–1984 follow up of participants in the 1964 Mississippi Freedom Summer voter registration project is especially noteworthy because, unlike many other studies, it has before-after measures of several variables and a plausible "control group" in terms of which to assess changes.[12] In his interviews some twenty years later, McAdam found (among many other things):

- Participants remained significantly more active in political matters than people who applied to and were accepted into the Freedom Summer project but who did not actually go.
- "[T]he project seems to have initiated an important process of personal change and political resocialization and the beginnings of a kind of activist career" (McAdam 1989, 753).
- Likely as a concomitant of such activist careers, at the time of the follow-up interviews participants had lower incomes and were less likely to be married than accepted applicants who did not actually participate in the Freedom Summer project (McAdam 1988a, 1989, 1992).

Placed in broader perspective, it is clear that some high-intensity and dramatic movement/SMO involvements, especially in youth, stamp their participants' biographies for life. Sometimes this is the foundation of an activist career (a succession of SMO memberships), the form that McAdam documents. But it can also simply be a lifelong badge that a person wears quite apart from future SMO participation, as in the cases of 1960s personages Jerry Rubin and Eldridge Cleaver, who remained famous as *former* SMO people (the Youth International Party and the Black Panther Party, respectively) who "went mainstream." Or, without "going mainstream," having been a member—an *important* member—of an SMO at a given time can be a lifelong badge of honor (or dishonor, depending on your religion or politics) that the person wears. Thus, even in the absence of any further notable movement activity:

- Rosa Parks was honored for life as the person whose refusal to sit in the back of a bus occasioned the Montgomery Improvement Association in December 1955.
- Mario Savio was forever known as the eloquent "firebrand" of the Free Speech Movement at Berkeley in the fall of 1964.
- Some thirty years after his Black Panther Party days, a campus conference could bill Bobby Seale "a living legend in American history."[13]

For people youthfully involved in high-risk/high-cost SMOs there can be the *nostalgia effect*, by which I mean periodic occasions in later life in which the veterans get together and review what are retrospectively constructed as wonderful, warm times of peak and risky high drama— "the best years of our lives" (see, e.g., Hayden 1988). The nostalgia effect is certainly not confined to SMO veterans. It follows in the wake of all high-risk/high-cost involvements. Participation in war is perhaps the best-known instance of this generic collective experience, and war veterans' associations are importantly about sponsoring *nostalgia occasions*. SMOs also spawn such occasions, as witness their proliferation on the twentieth, twenty-fifth, and thirtieth anniversaries of 1960s SMO actions.

The above types of data point to long-term SMO consequences for people whose life courses are importantly or mostly mainstream in character. Some people, though, join SMOs and stay in them—or in movement activism more generally in a succession of SMOs. Their central life interests and organization are, that is, framed and shaped by an SMO (or a series of them). What might be said of such lives as regards their consequences?

Among several lines of analysis, researchers have asked this question: What have members' SMO lives been like *relative to* what we can plausibly project them to have been had they *not* joined a particular SMO? I am prompted to pose this question as a consequence of reflecting on the life courses of early American converts to the Unification Church (UC) whom I first met in 1961 and whose careers I have seen develop in the UC over a period of more than thirty years. Almost a dozen of these very early joiners I knew (from among a not terribly larger total membership in the early 1960s) went on to positions and careers of considerable importance in the UC. Musing on this with me, Rodney Stark, who also studied and knew these same people, remarks that there is "much to be gained from taking part in such a movement—[they] have had lives far more exciting than most (or than they would have had if they had not become [UC members] and have earned a deep sense of worth and achievement. [They] are famous pioneers."[14] These reflections are themselves prompted by a UC volume devoted to laudatory life stories of these earliest converts, a publication casting them as revered elders.[15]

Some people argue that there are many negative larger consequences of totalistic ideologies such as that of the UC and of the intransigent factionalism of SMOs espousing such beliefs. These consequences and concerns may well be valid, but they should not blind us to the personal gains of meaningful, exciting, and worthwhile lives (in the participants' eyes) that such SMOs can also provide. Indeed, if mainstream social policy is to deal realistically with SMOs that give people meaningful and exciting careers, it must come to grips with the likelihood that the people embracing these life-meaning opportunities are often those who otherwise have little access to them [cf. causal variables (5) and (6), above].

Indeed, in structural terms every new SMO of any breadth, aspiration, and longevity offers new and quite challenging career opportunities—opportunities, moreover, of the entrepreneurial sort so ardently urged on everyone by free-market mavens. Given the restricted and declining number of such opportunities in the American mainstream (Riley et al. 1995), enterprising SMOs may be the growth industry of the future. The wages and working conditions are often not all that great, but these limitations may be offset by engaging challenges, meaningful projects, and comradely respect.

VII. RECRUITMENT

By definition, SMOs are collectively proclaiming an insurgent reality that is believed to be true and therefore one that other people should accept. In this broad sense, all SMOs recruit. We need, however, to distinguish between (1) efforts to win agreement with SMO positions and (2) efforts to get people to join an organization. The first is *general outreach* or promotion, while the second is *recruiting*. Virtually all SMOs do at the least some of the former but many less set about the latter systematically. That is, recruiting new organizational members in a conscious and organized way is a *variable* on which SMO differ greatly.

A. Recruitment Strategies

Researchers frequency think of recruitment as composed of the two sequential phases of *contact* and *cultivation*. The contract or access phase of recruitment refers to means by which sheer, initial communication with a prospective member—a prospect—is established and interest aroused such that a subsequent contact becomes likely.

This interest-aroused subpopulation of all contacts is then subject to *cultivation* strategies, the broad second phase of recruitment, which can itself be broken into subphases (cf. Turner and Killian 1987, 329). Having "hooked" a prospect into a second or further contact with the SMO, nurturing and tending efforts strive to bring her or him along to belief, participation, and membership.

I am mindful that the terms "contact" and "cultivation" are contentious. This is because people opposed to the recruitment practices of certain SMOs view their practices as much more malevolent and deceptive than is captured by these terms. Such opponents are likely to think that terms such as *seduction, bewitchment, entrapment, lure,* and *brainwashing* more accurately depict those recruitment practices. In selected instances, this might be true. But since such terms are far from appropriate for SMO recruitment activities as a *generic* category, it is better to reserve them for whatever subcategories they may best label.

1. Contact Strategies. In reflecting on the full array of SMOs in terms of "general outreach and engagement channels that movements can exploit for . . . recruitment" Snow et al. suggest the following two central and underlying dimensions:

[1] [T]he various sociospatial settings in which movements and potential participants can come into contact [vary] in terms of a continuum ranging from public to private places. . . .

[2] [T]he variety of generally available modes of communication through which information can be imparted [which] can be conceptualized . . . in terms of whether they are face-to-face or mediated. (Snow et al. 1980, 795)

Treating these two dimensions as dichotomies and cross-classifying them yields four generic types of "general outreach and engagement channels," that is, contact strategies:

Figure 8.3. Recruitment contact strategies.

		Spatial Setting	
		Public	Private
Mode of communication	Face-to-face	Face-to-face leafleting, petitioning, and proselytizing on sidewalk; participation in public events, such as parades; staging events for public consumption, such as sit-ins, protests, movement-sponsored conventions, and festivals	Door-to-door leafleting, petitioning, and proselytizing; information dissemination and recruitment among familiar others along the lines of promoter's extramovement interpersonal networks.
	Mediated	Recruitment via radio, television, and newspapers.	Recruitment via mail and telephone.

Source: Adapted from Snow et al (1980, 790, Figure 1).

[1] recruitment efforts among strangers in public places by face-to-face means;

[2] institutionalized, mass-communications mechanisms;

[3] recruit[ment] among strangers in private places by such means as door-to-door canvassing;

[4] recruit[ment] through members' extramovement social networks. (p. 795, adapted)

These are displayed graphically and additionally elaborated in Figure 8.3, "Recruitment Contact Strategies."

These two dimensions resulting in four basic strategies appear to map the broadest possibilities. Within them, many further variations are possible and observed. Contact strategies of the Unification Church, for example, have varied along these additional dimensions:

- the particular type of place employed (e.g., religious versus secular),
- the social status of people contacted (e.g., "ordinary" folks versus institutional office-holders, students versus workers),
- mainstream people versus members of other SMOs,

- ascriptive categories (e.g., selected conjunctions of categories of age, ethnicity, and gender, as in young, white, females),
- making one's beliefs initially clear or not—being overt or covert in one's contact presentations (Lofland [1966] 1977, 66 and Part II).

2. Cultivation Strategies. When engaged in at all—and many to most SMOs appear not to do so—cultivation strategies may be conceptualized as moving along the three main lines of the behavioral, cognitive, and affective. Any given strategy will feature elements of the other, obviously, but the differential stress of each requires separate attention.

Behavioral strategies stress concocting *something* that a now interested prospect will show up for or engage in. The strategic sentiment is to keep the prospect on the line with almost "whatever it takes," playing against the day of her or his intellectual enlightenment and/or emotional engagement. Thus:

- Like parties? Well, let's have one.
- Need a loan of money, a ride someplace, to borrow an object? No problem (see, e.g., Lofland [1966] 1977, Part II).
- Need a job? Well, let's go see (pp. 307–9).

Cognitive strategies feature formal efforts to explain the SMOs belief system to prospective members. Organized forms of this include what might be billed as lecture series, debates, study groups, or discussion circles.

Affective strategies center on what Turner and Killian (1987, 239) term "the cultivation of new social ties." As we have seen before, these authors suggest that these ties serve two key functions in recruitment:

[1] [They] provide the intrinsic satisfaction of a vital interpersonal relationship. . . .

[2] [They] facilitate communication [and] informal discussion with friends and associates [that] lends interest and reality to topics and ideas that command only superficial attention when presented impersonally. (pp. 229–330).

Such ties can be cultivated in varied ways, including flattery and solicitude. In more fully developed cultivation programs, SMO recruiters are given detailed instructions on exactly how to stimulate affective ties. For example, in one period, recruiter-members of the Unification Church (UC) were told to ask prospects, "What do you feel most excited about?" and to *"write down* their hooks [things that excite prospects] so that the whole center knows in follow up" (quoted in Lofland [1966]

1977, 308, italics in the original document). The principle here, of course, is to try to get prospects to like SMO members because they seem interested in what the prospects care about.

Beyond interaction-scale gambits such as just illustrated, a few SMOs organize entire specialized subunits that have the single-minded task of creating and cultivating interpersonal, affective ties with new prospects. One form of this is the geographically remote *cultivation camp* to which groups of prospects are taken for weekend or longer periods of intense camaraderie and the affective embracement that UC members call "love bombing." As mounted by the UC in its most successful period in using this strategy, several dozen prospects paired with a like number of UC members would sweep through an enthralling "whirlwind round of singing, chanting, hand-holding, preaching, and diffuse, loving camaraderie" (Lofland and Skonovd 1985, 168). Social-psychologically, UC cultivation camps represented a marked

> transition from a relatively mundane world to a dynamic environment of ecstatic youth. . . . All aspects of the training session blend together with exhilarating momentum [in which the UC members'] enthusiasm requires prospects to invest their entire beings in the participatory events. (Taylor 1978, 107, 153)

* * *

Herbert Blumer provides an appropriate sensitizing image for researchers to use in continuing studies of SMO cultivation strategies:

> The gaining of . . . members rarely occurs through a mere combination of a pre-established appeal and a pre-established individual psychological bent on which it is brought to bear.
>
> Instead, the prospective . . . member has to be aroused, nurtured, and directed, and the so-called appeal has to be developed and adapted.
>
> This takes place through a process in which attention has to be gained, interests awakened, grievances exploited, ideas implanted, doubts dispelled, feelings aroused, new objects created, and new perspectives developed.
>
> To repeat, this comes not from mere contact of appeal and psychological disposition: it occurs from contact of person with person, in a structured social situation wherein people are interacting with one another. The so-called appeal has to compete with other appeals and further has to contend with the resistance and indifference set by the existing social structure. These have to be overcome.

Thus, realistically it is not the mere appeal that counts; instead, it is a *process of agitation* that is important. (Blumer 1957, 148, emphasis in the original)

B. Questions about Recruitment Strategies

We now see some of the main ways in which contact and cultivation strategies vary among SMOs. In terms of the eight generic questions, these are answers to question (1): What are the aspect's types (i.e., ways in which it varies)? The answer is that there are two "types" (phases) of recruitment (contact and cultivation) that vary in the ways indicated (i.e., each has its own "types").

With these depictions of the types (variables) before us, we can attend to other of the eight generic questions. These will be the questions of the *magnitude* of recruitment efforts per se and of the *causes* and *consequences* of certain types of such efforts [generic questions (3), (6), and (7)].

1. Magnitude of Recruitment Effort and Its Causes.   As variables, the above quantitative and qualitative differences in contact and cultivation strategies raise the question, Why are some SMOs so very much more organized, energetic, and inventive in how they go about bringing in new members than are others?

Researcher's have given most attention to three variables that might account for this variation: **(a)** the degree of discrepancy between the prospect's and the SMO's beliefs, **(b)** the degree to which the SMO seeks to absorb the prospect into SMO activity and transform her or his beliefs and everyday life, and, **(c)** the degree to which the SMO beliefs seek to transform society totally. The three are, of course, related but analytically distinct nonetheless. Let us look at each of these.

a. Most basically, there is the question of the *degree* to which the SMOs insurgent's beliefs *are* insurgent, that is, the degree to which they vary from the mainstream and/or from the preexisting beliefs of whatever prospects may be at hand (the two discrepancies are not necessarily the same, depending on the pools in which is the SMO is fishing). Snow et al. (1986) have used the language of "frame" and "frame alignment" in thinking about the degree of this discrepancy. By "frame" they mean "'schemata of interpretation' that enable individuals 'to locate, perceive, identity, and label' occurrences within their life space and the world at large" (p. 464; quotes within the quote are from Goffman 1974, 21). (Researchers otherwise call these "beliefs," among other terms; see Chapter 5). By "frame alignment" they mean "linkage of individual and SMO interpretative orientations such that some set of individual interests, values, and beliefs and SMO activities, goals, and ideology are congruent and complementary" (Snow et al. 1986, 464).

As insurgent realities, SMOs face the problem of their frame and those of the public at large and prospective members *not* being in alignment, of their frames being *discrepant*. Snow et al. delineate *four degrees* to which SMOs and prospects can be out of alignment:[16]

1. In some cases, the prospect and the SMO are already in "frame alignment" but they have no contact with one another. The task here is merely to "get the word out," or in the slang phrase "round up the usual suspects" for SMO involvement. This is frame *bridging,* in which "ideologically congruent but untapped and unorganized sentiment pools" are contacted (p. 468). For such prospects, rudimentary contact strategies and less intensive cultivation tactics can suffice for recruitment.

2. In a second pattern, prospects may already agree with the SMO but the salience and strength of those beliefs is weak. The task here is therefore one of *frame amplification*, "the clarification and reinvigoration of an interpretive frame" (p. 469). In contact and cultivation, therefore, recruitment themes seek to strength prospects' sense of the *seriousness* of some problem, the *specificity of the causes* of this problem, the new actions of *antagonists* that must be countered, the likely *efficacy* of prospect SMO action, and the *propriety* of new involvement (p. 470).

3. Frames or belief systems differ in the degree of their elaboration on given topics. Many have *elaborational gaps* such that they may not seem "especially salient" to given prospects rather than something with which they disagree. In this case, the SMO task is that of *frame extension*, in which prospect frames are grafted onto or incorporated into the SMO frame. One such ongoing effort that has never achieved this has been peace movement SMOs' efforts to extend their frames to appeal to members of disadvantaged minorities.

4. In the pattern of greatest discrepancy, the SMO frame "may . . . appear antithetical to" prospect frames and *frame transformation* is therefore required (p. 473). In frame terminology, this involves a new *keying*, the systematic alteration of the meaning of things in moving from one frame to another. In this, these former things are now "seen by the participants to be something quite else" (p. 474, quoting Goffman 1974, 45). One prominent form of this "keying" (or rekeying) in SMO joining is a shift in "attributional orientation" from "fatalism or self-blaming to structural-blaming, from victim-blaming to system-blam-

ing" (p. 474). Also referred to as the "adoption of an injustice frame," in some of these attributional shifts, a previously accepted "status, pattern of relationships, or a social practice is redefined as inexcusable, immoral, or unjust" (p. 475).

This is the proposition relating SMO-prospect frame discrepancy to degree of organized contact and cultivation in recruitment:

▶ The greater the discrepancy between the SMO and the prospect's frames (beliefs), the more elaborate will be (and must be) an SMO's contact and cultivation efforts.

More qualitatively and quantitatively modest contact/cultivation strategies suffice to populate SMOs with *bridging, amplification,* and *extension* prospect situations, but more elaborate recruitment work is required in frame *transformation*.

b. As described in Chapter 6 (Section II.B) SMOs differ in the degree to which they seek to absorb and reorder the lives of members. Linked to recruitment as the dependent variable, the proposition is:

▶ The greater the degree of proposed SMO absorption, the more elaborate will be the SMO's contact and cultivation measures.

Casting this as a hypothesis about recruitment effectiveness rather than strategy, Turner and Killian provide this parallel proposition:

▶ Cultivation of interpersonal ties within the movement is more critical in recruitment to a total absorption movement than in recruitment to a segmental movement. When a movement requires total involvement, ties within the movement tend to become the only vital network available to the recruit. (1987, 330)

c. And, as described in Chapter 5 (Section III), SMOs vary in the degree to which their beliefs are totalistic and seek to change the entire society or completely to remake the individual. Such beliefs are likely to be quite discrepant with existing prospect frames/beliefs and therefore to involve frame transformation. The proposition is therefore:

▶ SMOs that seek "total change of society across all institutions" and therefore involve frame transformation are more likely to devise elaborate contact and cultivation programs (Snow et al. 1986, 476).

These three generic variables help to shed light on the seeming tendency of religious SMOs to field more elaborate recruitment programs than political SMOs. This difference may not be a function of the religious-political difference in beliefs per se, but in how these two types of SMOs also tend to differ in the above three ways. That is, religious tend more often than political SMOs to (1) field prospect-discrepant "frames," (2) absorb recruits more, and (3) envision more radical and sweeping social changes (see, further, Rochford 1982).

2. Causes and Consequences of Types of Recruitment Efforts. Sheer magnitude of recruitment efforts tells us little (but not nothing) about substantive variations in them and their associated causes and consequences.

Looking again at Figure 8.3, we see that some main substantive variations in contact are recruiting face-to-face versus mediated and recruitment of strangers in public places versus "familiar others along the lines of the promoter's extra-movement interpersonal networks" (Snow et al. 1980, 790). What causes an SMO to concentrate on one or another of these and what differences (if any) do differing concentrations make?

As already reviewed above regarding causes of SMO joining (Section III.A.11), in a great many studies prior contact and network variables have been shown to be quite powerful in the process of joining. Here is how various authors have stated this finding as a proposition about causes and consequences of this kind of contact (and, by implication, cultivation) strategy:

- "Groups with procedures that tend to recruit social isolates . . . have a very slow growth rate" (Stark and Bainbridge 1985, 323; 1980).
- "The network channel is the richest source of movement recruits" (Snow et al. 1980, 790).
- "The successes of movement recruitment efforts . . . will vary with the extent to which movements are linked to other groups and networks via members' extramovement ties" (and vice versa) (Snow et al. 1980, 797).
- "Those outsiders who are linked to one or more movement members through preexisting movement networks will have a greater probability of being contacted and recruited into that particular movement than will those individuals who are outside of members' extramovement networks" (p. 792).

Variations in SMOs regarding the degree to which they demand intense and exclusive participation are also apparently linked to type of recruitment strategy selected and its actual success. Snow et al. provide this summary of the relation:

♦ "Movements requiring exclusive participation by their members in movement activities will attract members primarily from public places rather than from among extramovement interpersonal associations and networks" (and visa versa). (1980, 796)

Turner and Killian put the same generalization in the obverse: "preexisting social ties are more important in recruitment to segmental involvement movements than to total absorption movements" (1987, 330). Researchers currently guess that there are two underlying dynamics here: (1) Total absorption SMOs tend to "use up," and/or rupture extra-SMO networks. In this structural isolation, public places become these SMOs' only face-to-face option. Hence, one finds them there. (2) Less considered, people who are responsive to recruiters in public places may themselves be more likely to be network isolates—or at least more "biographically available" [causal variables number (14)].

*   *   *

This is a long and complicated chapter because movement researchers have spent a great deal of time trying to answer the question, Why do people join SMOs? (or some variant on this phrasing) as well as the other questions reviewed. Even at this length and complexity, I have not reported work on answers to several other quite interesting questions related to members, among them, What are the *processes* of SMO careers? and What are *strategies* of member participation?

Be this as it may, it is time to change the unit of analysis from the individual back to the SMO per se. In the same way we looked at SMOs holistically regarding their beliefs, organization, and causes in Chapters 5, 6, and 7, let us now proceed to examine how, as entities, they pursue their goals. This is the question, What are SMO strategies? and it is addressed in the next chapter.

NOTES

1. In addition, a person's report that she or he has undergone a profound and transforming religious/psychological experience that has made her or him a new and better person may be a *conversion* and may or may not accompany SMO membership (cf. Snow and Machalek 1983).

2. Cf. McAdam 1988b. Snow and Oliver propose that "more dramatic changes" appear "under the following conditions": "movement ideology and practices are culturally idiosyncratic, [the] movement is stridently oppositional and defined as threatening or revolutionary, [the] movement is more 'exclusive'

in terms of membership eligibility and requirements [the] movement is more 'greedy' in terms of membership depends" (1995, 581).

3.   See further, Turner and Killian (1987, 225ff.), whose distinctions include sympathizers, adherents, and activists, and McCarthy and Zald (1987b, 23ff.).

4.   See, for example, the unsympathetic account offered by Volkogonov, who also observes that Leon Trotsky was "an outstanding organizer, orator and writer," the exact triple of roles and functions reported here (1994, 252).

5.   It is of note that Marshall employs the common movement contrast between the terms "leader" and "organizer."

6.   In an interview with the *Chronicle of Higher Education*, Ian Shapiro, coauthor of the Green and Shapiro (1994) critique of rational-choice theory in political science, declares: "There's a profound sense in which the tail is wagging the dog. . . . Their work is theory-driven rather than problem-driven" (quoted in Coughlin 1994, A9). On this same theory- versus problem-driven defect in movement studies, see Lofland (1993b) and Section VI of Chapter 13 in this volume. (Another phrasing for "problem-driven" is *question-driven*, which is the strategy employed in this guide.)

7.   On causal order and differential paths, see also Snow and Machalek (1983, 184–85), Rambo (1993), Cable, Walsh, and Warland (1988), McAdam (1988), Sherkat and Blocker (1993, 1994), Hirsch (1986).

8.   This is a hypothesis rather than an established frequency/magnitude proposition. Suggestive data include, though, Barker (1984), Schwartz and Paul (1992), Lemert (1951, Ch. 7).

9.   I here highlight an organizational approach to membership maintenance, thus slighting the individualistic approach to what is commonly called "defection" or "apostasy." Studies and reviews of studies of individual "leaving" include Toch (1965, 157–81), Skonovd (1981), Wright and Ebaugh (1993), Goertzel (1992), and Rochford (1989).

10.   Themes gleaned from a variety of movement publication articles on "burnout." See also Lofland ([1969] 1977, 244–45) on verbal devices—or "rhetorical mechanics"—of members in an SMO dedicated to making converts but who were unsuccessful at it. More broadly cast than "rhetorical mechanics" and perhaps a major analytic category of its own is Hunt and Benford's (1994) treatment of what they term identity talk among SMO members. For these researchers "identity talk" is conversation among members about "four moments of identity construction: becoming aware, active, committed, and weary" (p. 492). It is talk, that is, about how they came to be in the movement; points of disillusionment; times of witnessing "inhumane and immoral happenings"; ways in which they had been guided and inspired by others; and the horrendous effects of violence and injustice, among other topics. Hunt and Benford classify such identity talk into the six categories of "associational declarations, disillusionment anecdotes, atrocity tales, personal is political reports, guide narratives, and war stories" (pp. 486–88). The proposition of relevance here is:

♦ Identity talk functions to help maintain participation in an SMO.

11.   It is important to maintain a distinction between the (1) consequences of an SMO/movement identity and (2) the consequences of an identity per se

separate from any SMO/movement. Thus, Taylor and Raeburn (1995) trace stig-
matizing and other negative consequences of open lesbian, gay, and bisexual
identities, but these reactions were not necessarily to *SMO/movement* identities.

12.   In addition, his findings are consistent with other studies of 1960s high-
risk/high-cost activism. Other studies and reviews include Sherkat and Blocker
(1992), Braungart and Braungart (1991), Fendrich and Lovoy (1988), Whalen and
Flacks (1989).

13.   Handbill announcing a conference titled "My Reality, Your Perception,"
University of California, Davis, January 27–30, 1992.

14.   My thanks to Rodney Stark for permission to quote a letter from him to
me dated March 19, 1991.

15.   Winter 1987 theme issue, "Beginnings in America," *Blessing Quarterly: An
Educational Journal for the Blessed Families of the Unification Movement.*

16.   Their analysis strives to embrace both general outreach and prospect
recruitment, but I focus on recruitment alone here. How frame alignment works
in general outreach is considered in the next chapter, the treatment of SMO
strategies.

9

What Are SMO Strategies?

The topic of strategies is the next logical item in the sequence of matters we have examined. Thus:

- Based on given *beliefs* (Chapter 5),
- SMOs *form* (Chapter 7),
- devise an *organization* (Chapter 6),
- and people *join* (Chapter 8)
- in order to work toward goals associated with the beliefs.

This chapter is directed to the last item on this list: the central matter of working toward goals. This is otherwise often termed *strategy*, a word defined as "a method devised for making or doing something or attaining an end." Its synonyms include *plan, scheme*, and *project*. Closely related concepts include *means, method*, and *way*. Central to all these terms is the idea of *ends* (or goals) for which one devises *means*.

Pertaining to SMOs and beginning with generic question (1), the question is, How do SMOs go about achieving whatever their goals? What are their strategies—their ends-means modes of action?

    I.   In order to answer this question, we need first to specify what is or is not an instance of a "strategy." What is *central*, goal-attainment action as opposed to other action? This is the topic of Section I.

   II.   Within this clarification and specification, in Section II I report how various researchers have gone about answering the pivotal question of this chapter, What are SMO strategies?

  III.   Answers to this question provide, of course, the dependent-independent-variable platforms on which researchers stand in order then to ask questions about the *causes* and *effects* of strategies. Conceiving strategic variations as *dependent* variables, in Section III I review answers to the causal question, Why are some rather than other strategies selected by SMOs? Put differently, What *causes* various strategies?

IV.   Then, conceiving strategic variations as *independent* variables, in Section IV, the consequences question is, What are the *effects* of various strategies? The most famous version of this question is, obviously, What strategies are successful?

V.   The above questions address only three of the eight generic questions (1, 6, and 7). In Section V, I briefly review some other generic questions applied to strategy.

I. WHAT SMO STRATEGIES ARE: SIMILARITIES

In broadest compass, anything any SMO does can be seen as a strategy. Or, at least, all actions are "strategic" in the sense that they can be presumed (or guessed) to be in *some* way goal oriented and ends-means calculative. While all action may be strategic in this broad sense, SMO researchers nonetheless tend to restrict the concept to actions consciously undertaken to achieve an SMO's *stated, major goals*.

Ordinarily, it is not difficult to identify stated major goals and strategies for attaining them. As insurgent change-oriented realities, what people are doing and why they are doing it is very much on everyone's minds, leaders and followers alike. Leaders are commonly and often constantly exhorting the members with regard to them. The researcher has therefore only to be attentive.

Of course, SMOs have problems and needs beyond those explicitly a part of the stated major goals. Most especially, every SMO requires financing and therefore a strategy of financing. And every SMO must have some division of labor and therefore strategies of achieving and maintaining it. Ordinarily, such strategic matters are *secondary* or *support* goals and strategy. Such secondary matters must, of course, be successfully managed if the major goals are gong to be achieved. But their successful management does not in itself constitute major goal achievement. It only helps make major goal achievement more possible.

Although it is easy in the abstract to distinguish between major and support goals, in practice in many SMOs, the distinction is quite murky and contentious. Indeed, one key form of conflict within many SMOs is over whether or not a given activity is a major versus a support goal and what priority it ought therefore be accorded it.

SMO members often lament two kinds of support goals and strategies as having supplanted the major "true" goals to which the SMO is formally committed. One of these "insidious" supplanters or major goal defectors is what David Garrow labels "media madness," which is the "widespread, often implicit assumption that obtaining news coverage is a substantive achievement in and of itself [which can lead SMOs] to mold their efforts with more of an eye to winning the media's short term attention than to producing longer range political results" (1985, 15). The other form of allowing a secondary to become a major goal is "preoccupation with internal affairs and organizational functioning that results in . . . devoting far more . . . time and energy to 'institutional maintenance' than to political outreach and substantive organizing work" (p. 15).

The tricky thing about these two and other forms of "defection" from major goals is that *some* "media-chasing" and organization maintenance may actually be necessary in order to achieve the major goals. The difficult task is judging when proper secondary goals have displaced major goals.

SMO researchers have not employed it very often, but there is a long tradition of distinguishing three levels of thinking in goal strategizing in conflict situations: *policy, strategy, and tactics*:

- Decisions taken on the level of *policy* are ones that define a group's objectives, determine what price may be paid for them, what an acceptable outcome may consist of, when to commence the conflict, and when to stop fighting.
- It is at the level of *strategy* that plans for securing the objectives are adjusted to real-life, real-time circumstances. Strategic decisions coordinate all of a group's resources and actions to pursue described outcomes in a fluid process of interaction with opponents.
- On the next level down, *tactical* decisions govern behavior toward the opponents and their agents in specific encounters (adapted from Ackerman and Kruegler 1994, 7).

As these authors mention, all three are commonly referred to as "strategy," but, as can be seen, the three are quite different. Nonetheless, SMO researchers have tended to gloss over these distinctions (and I tend to do so here).

II. WHAT SMO STRATEGIES ARE: DIFFERENCES

Researchers vary in their conceptualizations of how SMO strategies differ. This diversity presents the temptation to choose one or a few variations, to present it or them as the best, and to downplay or ignore many others. Each, however, can be useful for different purposes (e.g., for relating to different, other variables) and I therefore resist the temptation seriously to expunge. Paralleling the inventory approach I employ in other chapters, I here list a range of ways in which students of SMO strategies have distinguished among them.

The schemes of strategic variations researchers have put forth differ in (1) the *scope* of variation among SMOs they strive to capture, (2) the *unit scale* of social organization at which strategy is conceived, and (3) their focus on traditional, sociological substance versus the dimension of "dramaturgy," the style rather than the content of action.

- By *scope* I mean the degree to which a research effort seeks to specify the entire gamut of strategic possibilities among SMOs versus showing only possibilities within some more delimited type of strategy.
- By *unit scale* I mean the combined (1) scale of social organization presumed to execute the strategy, (2) the order of magnitude of the number of people involved in mounting it, and (3) the time-period over which the strategy plays out. Terms for organizational units of strategies that imply very different unit scales include speech practice, gathering, event, workshop, teach-in, convocation, convention, action, confrontation, campaign, project, organization, battle, war.
- By *dramaturgy* I mean the style of staging and acting as opposed to its substance. The word *dramaturgy* is taken from the planning of plays on stages, an activity that has its own principles of production that are separate from the content of any specific play that is produced (Goffman 1959; Benford and Hunt 1992). In "dramaturgic" analysis, this distinction is applied to all of social life, with attention to the "dramaturgic."

Often, researchers' depictions of strategies are not clear as regards their scope, the unit scale of which they speak, and the degree of dramaturgic focus. I have nonetheless made rough assessments of various efforts and I use these assessments to determine the order in which I present schemes. I begin with those of broader scope and larger unit scale and work toward those of more restricted scope and smaller unit scale. I then report analyses highlighting the dramaturgy of strategy. Last, I call attention to SMO "strategic medleys."

A. Larger-Scope or Scale-Substantive Differences

The seven schemes of wider scope I inventory move from the truly broad, generic, and simple to the narrower, substantive, and complex.

1. Main Objectives. At (or at least close to) what we can think of as the broadest or most fundamental level of SMOs, there is the question,

What is the main objective? Different answers to this question both constitute basic strategy and set up propensities for or against a wide variety of other strategies. Adopting and adapting Turner and Killian's answer to this question, there are four basic ways SMOs answer this question:

[1] Is the better world to be instituted by changing social institutions or by changing the hearts and minds of people? [The former is] *societal manipulation* and [the latter is] *personal transformation*. [Taking personal transformation as the first possible main objective, societal manipulation divides into three others.]

[2] If a group of people seek a changed way of life, they can work toward that objective by using the power at their disposal to get persons in authority to make the desired changes. [This is the strategy of] concessions.

[3] [Or, they can seek] to take control of the community or society so that they can institute whatever changes they wish. [This is the strategy of] *control*.[1]

[4] [And,] by using their power to establish and protect a separate existence free from outside control and interferences [they can pursue a strategy of] *separation*. (adapted from Turner and Killian 1987, 292, emphasis in the original)[2]

2. Overt versus Covert. At a similar level of fundamentalness or "broadness" is the question of whether to adopt strategies that are overt versus covert. Overt strategies are "taken in the full light of publicity, while [in] covert strategies a dominating concern [may be] to keep the existence or objectives of the movement, the identities of the adherents, or other aspects secret" (p. 92).

Complex mixtures of overt and covert strategies are, of course, possible and have been fielded by such diverse SMOs as the Communist party in several countries (Goldberg 1991, Ch. 5) and the Unification Church (Lofland [1969] 1977; Bromley and Shupe 1979).

3. Frontal Assault versus Attrition. Last at this extremely broad level of variation and drawing from military thinking about strategy, it is sometimes helpful to distinguish between *frontal assault* and *attrition*. In the former, quick and massive campaigns of direct attack are mounted "in the hope of gaining a quick victory" (Turner and Killian 1987, 291). In contrast, with the latter, the effort is to "wear . . . down the opposition by a long-continued series of encounters, each of which may be won by the opposition, but whose cost is so great as to force eventual surrender" (p. 291).

4. Contentiousness. SMO strategies vary in terms of their *contentiousness*, three degrees of which are often identified:

- Politeness of action—civil, restrained, and circumspect efforts to press a point or program of change or resistance to change. Forms of mainstream *and sometimes* SMO polite action include electioneering and lobbying. The ideals of this civility are codified in works such as Robert's *Rules of Order* and Emily Post's *Etiquette*.
- *Protest of action*—ostentatious, dramatic, and ambiguously legal or illegal nonviolent efforts. This is also often termed nonviolent or direct action (and is discussed in Section III.B.3).
- *Violence of action*—efforts that injure or destroy property or humans (Lofland 1985, Ch. 12; 1993a, Ch. 5)

The particular effort of this trinity of forms is to isolate the "in-between" form of action called variously *protest, direct action,* or *nonviolence.* Or in yet another rendition of this scheme, Waskow refers to the politics of order, violence, and disorder:

> In the politics of order, people divide their attention between the changes to be accomplished and the accepted rules of society about the "legitimate" ways of bring about change.
>
> In the politics of violence, people divide their attention between the changes to be accomplished and those powerful people who get in the way of change—the enemy.
>
> In the politics of disorder, people tend to reduce greatly their interest in both the given rules and the enemy; instead they focus very strongly on the changes to be accomplished. . . .
>
> In the politics of order, [people] follow the rules, in the politics of violence, they attack their enemies; in the politics of disorder, they pursue change. (Waskow 1966, 277–78).

5. Tactical Mechanisms. At this same level of comprehensiveness and high abstraction and also attuned to the amount of force involved, several authors have proposed *persuasion, bargaining,* and *coercion* as the most basic and logically exhaustive types of strategies.[3] Turner and Killian conceive the variable underlying these three to be differences the "mechanism" by means of which the behavior of a target will be modified:

- In *persuasion,* the advocate strives to make a target aware of a condition and to appeal to her or his moral sensibilities and values as a basis on which to act in ways the SMO wants. Persuasion is "strictly symbolic manipulation, uncomplicated by the offer of substantial rewards or punishment" (Turner and Killian 1987, 297).

- While retaining the trinity of persuasion, bargaining and coercion, Turner and Killian insert the mechanism of *facilitation* between persuasion and bargaining. By this they mean "offering help to make it possible for the target group to act in support" of the SMO's proposals (p. 298). Like persuasion, this mechanism assumes that the target group is kindly disposed to the SMO, or at least not strongly opposed to it.

- In the SMO context as well as elsewhere, *bargaining* refers to the process of negotiating an exchange of valued goods of some kind and actually concluding such exchanges. Bargaining presumes, of course, that each entity has something the other wants. In the case of SMOs, interestingly, it is often the case that such entities have little or nothing the targets want—which is part of the reason some SMOs form in the first place. Hence the use of other tactical mechanisms.

- "*Coercion* is punishment or the credible threat of punishment in case the target group does not support" the SMO's proposals (p. 298). These range in intensity from *nuisance* through *disruption* tactics. Turner and Killian view the myriad *tactics of nonviolence* I report on below as mostly falling somewhere between nuisance and disruption in their intensity. Terrorism, kidnapping, bombings, and the like are, of course, among the most intensive forms of coercive disruption.

Turner and Killian usefully distinguish between bargaining and coercion in terms of how well off the SMO and the target anticipate being after their engagement. In theory at least, bargaining is "win-win," in that an exchange leaves both parties with something of value they did not previously possess. Each is better off. Coercion, in contrast is "negative bargaining," in the sense that the best the target can hope for is not to be worse off than at the start. The threat is to worsen the target's situation unless proposals are complied with.

6. Target, Force, Implementer Combinations. The foregoing schemes are wide in scope and encompassing in unit scale. They are therefore relatively unspecific about how several strategic dimensions might *combine* into patterns of strategies, for example, (1) who is acted toward (the target) with (2) what amount of force or coercion, and (3) who is charged with implementing whatever the change sought.

These are, indeed, three variables that Robert Lauer has thought about in terms of how variations in them might intersect to form basic SMO strategies. Before looking at the intersections, here is an expanded description of the variables themselves:

[1] *The Target of Change:* Does the SMO target "changes in the social conditions in which individuals find themselves" or "changes in individuals"? (Lauer 1976, 92, quoting Coleman 1971).

[2] *Amount of Force Required:* Can the change be achieved with persuasion and bargaining—nonviolence, using the term generally rather than technically—or must coercive or violent methods be used?

[3] *Who Implements the Change:* Does the SMO itself undertake to initiate the change (i.e., its beliefs are *exemplary*) or does it pressure the larger society to make the changes (i.e., *adversary* beliefs)? (Exemplary versus adversary beliefs are described in Section III.B of Chapter 5).

Along with notes that explain and give examples of each type, Figure 9.1 shows how these three dichotomized dimensions intersect to form six major kinds of strategies.

*7. **Strategic Organizational Postures.*** SMOs taken holistically as the unit scale have been classified in terms of the most prominent kind of persuasive, advocacy activity they commonly engage in. One such scheme suggests that seven main kinds of strategic patterns can be geared to promoting an insurgent reality (or other realties for that matter). Captioned as advocacy social roles connected to SMOs, these are:

1. *transcenders*—promote rapid shifts of consciousness in glitzy, high-tech presentations,
2. *educators*—communicate facts and reasoning,
3. *intellectuals*—produce new facts and reasoning,
4. *politicians*—undertake political electioneering and lobbying,
5. *protesters*—force issues by noncooperation and disruption,
6. *prophets* —affect deep moral regeneration,
7. *warriors*—engage in violent action (Lofland 1993a, Ch. 1, 196)

The activities of an SMO are not, of course, confined to only one of these. Most, indeed, engage in more than one. Even so, a great many SMOs are quite specialized. In particular, a great many SMOs are *educators* in the sense that their major activity is the production and dissemination of their reality as "news." So scrutinized operationally, hard-left sects of the Trotskyite variety, for example, are dominantly educator SMOs because their most prominent activity is the publication and distribution of a newspaper and associated printed items (e.g., O'Toole 1977).

Figure 9.1. **Lauer typology of strategies.**

Dimensions of Variation ↓	Type of Strategy →					
	Educative	Conversionist	Bargaining	Separatist	Disruptive	Revolutionary
1. Target	individuals	individuals	social structure	social structure	social structure	social structure
2. Force	nonviolent	nonviolent	nonviolent	nonviolent	coercive/violent	coercive/violent
3. Who Implements	society	movement	society	movement	society	movement
Description	Changes will be won through rational public discussion and decision-making.	Programs of recruitment and personal change (such as reported in Section VI of Chapter 8) are the key.	Garden variety SMO strategy in democratic societies; described above as "polite action" (Section A.4.) and bargaining (Section A.5.).	Withdraw into exemplary enclaves or liberation lifestyles, e. g., "clandestine urbanites" (Lauer 1976:91).	Rational persuasion— the educative strategy — is not enough; disruption is additionally required. Methods of it are shown in Figure 9.2.	An SMO vanguard of dedicated revolutionaries must lead the uplifted masses in violently smashing the state (e.g. Chapter 6, Sections IV and V).

Source: Adapted from Lauer (1976:93).

SMOs that are superficially dissimilar to such political sects can, in fact, be fundamentally similar to them at the level of organizational posture. Thus, at this level, the Nation of Islam, for example, is very much like a political sect because of the prominent part its newspaper and associated publications play in its organizational life.

B. Smaller-Scope or Scale-Substantive Differences

Narrower-scope and lower-in-scale conceptualizations of strategies have (among other matters) focused on (1) a special cognitive theme (such as "framing"), (2) the spectrum of activities of a special type of SMO, (3) a distinctive type of action (such as nonviolence), or (4) staid mainstream forms of action. Let us examine each in turn.

1. Framing Issues. As a species of insurgent reality, SMOs are in the business of producing and maintaining *meaning* for constituents, antagonists, bystanders, media, elites, and others. In a "politics of signification," SMOs seek to have "certain meanings and understandings gain ascendance over others, or at least move up in some existing hierarchy of credibility" (Snow and Oliver 1995, 587).

Conceived as a generic activity, this is the strategic process of *framing*, a process already discussed in the previous chapter (Section VI.B.1) with regard to recruitment and, specifically, the degree of discrepancy between an SMO and a prospective member's frame. Repeating the definition given there, a frame is a "'schemata of interpretation' that enable individuals 'to locate, perceive, identity, and label' occurrences within their life space and the world at large" (Snow et al. 1986, 464, citing Goffman 1974, 21).

In contrast to the previous consideration of framing in *recruitment*, we here focus on it as a strategy of *general outreach*. Both a noun and verb, *framing* in general outreach is a "process of reality construction [that is] active, ongoing and continually evolving. . . . It entails agency in the sense that what evolves is a product of joint action by movement participants in encounters with antagonists and targets; and it is contentious in the sense that it generates alternative interpretive schemes that may challenge existing frames" (Snow and Oliver 1995, 587).

In this fashion, framing is a *variable* rather than a constant, a process that has diverse forms. In what are by definition more sophisticated SMOs, framing is a topic of conscious and extensive strategizing. For example, Ryan (1991) reports how leaders in a hotel employee union she studied consciously avoided framing their issues as "money." Instead, these leaders held that you have to "organize people over ideas. . . . We talk about non-negotiable issues, like dignity, respect on the job, social justice" (quoted in Gamson 1990, 150). Commenting on this case, Gamson observes that, more generally, unions tend to be framed by the media and the public more generally (especially when they strike) as "disrupting orderly life" and as "special interest groups, grubbing for financial gain" (p. 150).

In the case Ryan reports, the union strove to forestall and outflank such a negative framing with *counterframe* goals cast in a universalistic language that had broader appeal. Issues of money were muted and questions of "dignity, respective on the job, social justice" were made central. The union

> chose to highlight issues of racial and language discrimination, unfair job practices, harassment of women workers. Economic issues were presented from a justice perspective, the right of workers to a living wage and health benefits, the right to support their families in dignity. (Ryan 1991, quoted in Gamson 1990, 150)

Gamson observes that "by articulating their goals in this fashion" the union "was attempting to activate larger collective identities that members shared with others in their communities—identities of gender, class, race, and ethnicity" (Gamson 1990, 150).

Although Ibarra and Kitsuse (1993) speak of their work on social problems claims-making as a rhetorical analysis of "moral discourse," their analysis can also be viewed as a depiction of variations in issue framing. Their centerpiece concept is the "rhetorical idiom," by which they mean a related set of words that define some problematic condition in a distinctive moral way. Ibarra and Kitsuse elucidate five clusters of what they also term "thematic complexes" and "narrative tool kits." For SMO researchers, these are *frames*.

[1] [In the *loss* frame one central image] is that of humans as custodians or guardians of some unique and sacred thing or quality. . . . Positive terms composing the idiom's moral vocabulary [include] innocence, beauty, purity, nature, clarity, culture . . . cleanliness. . . . Negative terms [include] sin, pollution, decadence, chaos. . . . The concept of protection assumes a central position, . . . evoking the heroism of the rescuer [as in] "save the planet" . . . and . . . "save the schools. . . . "

[2] [The *entitlement* frame] emphasizes the virtue of securing for all persons equal institutional access. . . . Its negative terms are emblematic forms of discrimination: intolerance, oppression, sexism, racism, ageism, and even specieism. [Its] positive terms stem from its relativist philosophy: lifestyle, diversity, choice, tolerance, empowerment. . . .

[3] [The *endangerment* frame] is applied to condition-categories that can be expressed as threats to the health and safety of the human body. [It] is a relative of entitlement discourse inasmuch as the presumption is that individuals have a right to be safe from harm, to have good health and to be sheltered from . . . types of bodily risk. [Its positive terms include] hygiene, prevention, nutritiousness, fitness. . . . Negative terms pinpoint the processes that warrant fear: disease, pathology, epidemic, risk, contamination, health threat. . . .

[4] [The *unreason* frame highlights] concerns about being taken advantage of, manipulated, "brainwashed," or transformed into a "dupe" or "fool." [This frame] posits an idealized relationship between the self and the state of knowing, and then locates an instance where that proper relationship is being distorted. . . . Certain categories of persons are understood to require greater vigilance [and are] said to be trusting, naive, innocent, uneducated, uninformed, desperate, [and] can be "taken advantage of" as easy prey.

[5] [The *calamity* frame] is distinguished by . . . metaphors and reasoning practices that evoke the unimaginability of utter disaster. . . . Claimants using this idiom [i.e., frame] will recognize the existence of other claims-making activities, . . . yet cast these into perspective by demonstrating how these other moral objects are contingent upon the existence of "their" condition-category. [The calamity frame is] a way of countering centrifugal tendencies by bringing a variety of claimants under a kind of symbolic umbrella, hence providing a basis for coalition building. (Ibarra and Kitsuse 1993, 32–37, emphases omitted)

One key feature of these packages of ways of thinking about conditions/situations is their *portability* or *transferability*. A frame or idiom that began with application to one problem can be packaged up, so to speak, and carried over and applied to yet other problems. For example, cigarette smoking has historically been framed as an *endangerment* problem. But, in more recent times, SMO entrepreneurs began to reframe it as an *entitlement* problem, as something that interfered with the rights to others to have equal institutional access (as well as an endangerment to nearby nonsmokers).

The image here, then, is that of a *variety* of *framing packages* or possibilities among which SMO strategists browse in search of new ways of framing conditions whose current frames are not successful in general outreach and occasions of conflict (cf. Capek 1993; Koopmans and Duyvendak 1995; Simmons 1981; Simmons, Mechling,, and Schreier 1985).

Differing and opposed frames put forth on the same issue by an SMO and its opponents become *frame contests*. From the SMO researcher's perspective, the key matter of interest is not the substantive aspects of the issues per se, but instead, Whose frame—whose meaning—prevails for what reasons and with what consequences?

2. Local Amelioration. The subset of SMOs attempting to ameliorate some fairly specific, proximate, and localized social condition tends to "one or some mix of three general strategies: public education, direct service and structural change" (McCarthy and Wolfson in press).

[1] Public education involves attempts to bring social conditions to wide audiences while attempting to convince those audiences to take some action. A wide variety of tactics may be used in pursing this general strategy. . . .

[2] [Direct service] involves providing direct aid to the victims of the social conditions. . . . Sometimes this is seen as an end in itself . . . , while for other groups it is seen as a palliative while efforts to bring about structural change are simultaneously pursued. An exclusive attachment to this strategy is sometimes labeled a "soup kitchen approach."

[3] Movement leaders may directly pursue structural change by attempting to change laws, authorities and/or regimes. This is the strategy most commonly associated with social movements—especially when "unruly tactics" are used.

3. Nonviolent Action. The terms "protest" and "nonviolence" are labels for major categories of strategy in the wide-scope schemes reviewed above. Some analysts have singled out nonviolent action for special and detailed treatment. Most notably, in his classic and monumental *The Politics of Nonviolent Action* (1973), Gene Sharp elucidates nonviolence as a special type of action with myriad manifestations.

Following Sharp's conception, Ackerman and Kruegler present the distinctive earmarks of nonviolent action as:

[1] It does no bodily harm.
[2] It involves direct action (as opposed to [institutionally approved "polite" action].
[3] It requires no particular [i.e., specific] ideological commitment.
[4] . . . if successful, [the action constitutes] a sanction by adding to the costs of pursuing [the action to which the nonviolent actionists object]. (Ackerman and Kruegler 1994, 19)

The third earmark of "no particular ideological commitment" is especially pertinent in the empirical study of strategic or pragmatic nonviolence. This is because some people espouse nonviolence as a *philosophy* of conflict or of life that involves

> a commitment to transforming the process of conflict itself from a win-lose proposition into a win-win exercise. By enduring suffering rather than inflicting it, the nonviolent protagonists melt their opponents hearts and lift the contest onto a completely different, and more human, level of interaction, where victory is less important than the quality the process that produces it (p. 14).

For the philosophically nonviolent, this is the only "true" nonviolence; mere strategic or pragmatic nonviolence is not "really" nonviolence.

As a social fact about some nonviolent actionists, philosophical nonviolence is beyond doubt important and the fact of that existential commitment must be reckoned in any analysis. Such a commitment is, though, a *variable*, the contrast being with *pragmatic* nonviolence. And it is empirically the case that pragmatic use of nonviolence is vastly more common than philosophical nonviolence (p. 14).

One of the better-known aspects of Gene Sharp's *Politics of Nonviolent Action* is the list of 198 "methods" that he compiles and that comprise an entire volume in the three-volume edition of that work. This book of methods is, indeed, found on the bookshelves of many an SMO and is consulted for inspiration when thinking about future "actions." I am tempted to reproduce the one-page version of the 198 methods that also circulates in SMO and movement researcher circles, but in the interest of space and simplicity I give only Ackerman and Kruegler's abbreviation of it appearing in their *Strategic Nonviolent Conflict* (1994). Shown here as Figure 9.2, the forty-two "methods" Ackerman and Kruegler select or consolidate from Sharp's list of 198 answer this question: What, exactly, does one mean by nonviolent action?

The three categories into which the methods are classified in Figure 9.2 are also those of Sharp. Here is an explanation of them:

- Recognizing that the categorization of any method depends in good part on how authorities respond to it, *protest and persuasion* methods tend nonetheless to be the least disruptive and they overlap a good deal with simple "polite" (mainstream) politics. Three prime forms of protest and persuasion methods are the procession (e.g., marches, parades), the assembly (e.g., the rally), and diverse public acts (e.g., picketing) (Lofland 1985, 263).
- *Noncooperation* methods involve refusal to provide actions necessary for a social arrangement to continue. Sharp suggests that nonviolent actions are "overwhelmingly" of this sort and 103 of

Figure 9.2. Methods of nonviolent action.

Protest and Persuasion	Noncooperation	Intervention
mass demonstration	civil disobedience	overloading facilities
petitions	strikes (all types)	sit-ins
protest funerals	economic boycotts	creating parallel institutions
walkouts	tax withholding	nonviolent blockades
renouncing honors	credit withholding	teach-ins
picketing	legal obstruction	seizure of assets
mock awards	providing sanctuary	alternative markets
fraternization	rent withholding	guerrilla theater
vigils	diplomatic noncooperation	counterfeiting
speeches/advocacy	resignation of posts	forcible exposure of identity
mock elections	draft refusal	nonviolent invasion
symbolic public acts	social boycotts	nonviolent sabotage
parades and marches	nonrecognition of appointed officials	seeking imprisonment
"haunting" officials	judicial noncooperation	dumping commodities

Source: Ackerman and Krueger (1994:6, Table 1.1).

the 198 he details are so classified. The strike is the most familiar form. Others include the slowdown and the boycott.

* *Intervention* methods may "disrupt or even destroy established behavior patterns, policies, relationships, or institutions which are seen as objectionable" (Sharp 1973, 357). Compared to the other two classes, these methods "pose a more direct and immediate challenge." Four patterns of intervention are of particular note:
    1. *Harassment,* in which the objectionable activities of a person are continually called attention to in some extraordinary manner.
    2. *System overloading,* in which too large an amount of whatever an arrangement processes is injected.
    3. *Blockade,* in which protesters temporarily impede the movement of objectionable people and/or materials.
    4. *Occupation,* in which people "enter or refuse to leave some

place where they are not wanted or from which they have been prohibited" (Sharp 1973, 371; Lofland 1985, 265).

4. Staid, Conventional Activities.   While it is necessary and appropriate to recognize and stress SMO cognitive and/or behavior *insurgency*, this appreciation should not distract attention from the fact that many if not the bulk of the strategies of many if not most SMOs *are merely the strategies used by mainstream groups.* Certainly, many SMOs *do* engage in illegal, quasi-illegal, "unruly," impolite, or otherwise colorful strategies and tactics. The familiarity of the popularity of the forms of nonviolent action described immediately above is clear testimony to the association of such actions with social movements.

But even so, SMOs *also* ordinarily engage in many if not most of the strategic activities of garden variety mainstream groups that seek to bring about or prevent prosaic social changes. There are five central forms of such staid, conventional action (actions, indeed, that movement how-to manuals commonly provide instructions on doing).[4]

a. Media-managing.   Even SMOs focused inwardly on personal transformation rather than outwardly on societal changes often find it necessary to deal with the media of mass communications—the print and electronic organizations that regularly disseminate words and pictures on a mass scale. Such "dealing" divides into the two directions of *proacting* to get one's messages into the media and *reacting* to media-initiated messages about the movement or its issues. In either case, as insurgent realities laboring under marginality or exclusion, SMOs commonly see themselves in an uphill battle to get heard at all, much less fairly heard—a topic on which I will elaborate in the next chapter.

In this inauspicious situation, SMOs nonetheless commonly strive to "play the media game" in some fashion. As quite accurately reported in a great many movement how-to manuals, the basics of this "game" involve meeting and cultivating people in the media, understanding media "framing" practices and other routines, learning to write effective press releases, and otherwise developing "media savvy."

The oft-mentioned irony about SMOs dealing with the media is that many SMOs that are fundamentally critical of how the media operate must nonetheless construct themselves in the media's terms in order to use them. In so doing, SMO people are in danger of becoming what they least want to be—figures molded and presented in noxious media formats.[5]

b. Educating.   Although I have not systematically counted the relative frequency with which SMOs engage in the categories of strategy I review in this chapter, I venture to guess that *the* single, most common SMO strategic activity is mundanely *educational*. By "educational" I mean, first and construed narrowly, gathering people together for the purpose of listening to a speaker or panel or otherwise simply discussing a topic. Such gatherings have many names: talks, panels, forums, public meetings, rallies, teach-ins, convocations, conferences, conventions.

Second and more broadly, educational strategies consist of appearing on radio or television programs; doing radio or television series; writing and publishing op-ed pieces; informational tabling in public places and at auspicious gatherings of other groups; putting out newsletters or newspapers; writing, publishing, and distributing leaflets, brochures, and pamphlets; producing and distributing video programs or books.

As reported in Section II.A.7 some SMOs adopt a specific strategy as its central *strategic organizational posture*. Education as I have just described it is quite common as such an SMO "strategic organizational posture." It is one, also, that advocates of other strategies tend to criticize as wholly inadequate to the task of achieving many kinds of fundamental changes. As a strategy, education rests on the assumption that reasoned argument is sufficient to convince people of the need for given changes (or that it is at least helpful in changing people's minds). Such an educational effort and premise was embodied in, for example, the Southern Conference for Human Welfare and its successor the Southern Conference Educational Fund, two civil rights SMOs that operated widely in the south from the thirties through the sixties. One careful assessment of their efforts concludes that "neither . . . accomplished many concrete results" (Lawson 1992, 1621, reporting Reed 1991). "The credit for the destruction of Jim Crow must go to" SMOs that had different strategic postures: the litigation of the National Association for the Advancement of Colored People and the active nonviolence of the Southern Christian Leadership Conference, the Student Nonviolence Coordinating Committee, and the Congress of Racial Equality (Reed 1991, 1621) (also see Section IV.C on confrontation and crisis).

Nonetheless, even though education as a strategy or strategic organizational posture is not enough, it can function to "keep . . . alive a vision of . . . justice during [periods] of political pessimism," as did the two educational SMOs mentioned above (Lawson 1992, 1621, reporting Reed 1991). And, also, they can provide vital written and visual materials that can greatly assist more militant SMOs acting in times of crisis and confrontation (cf. Thorne 1975).

c. Researching. As one component of an SMO's strategy, research refers to finding information on one's issues or targets that supports the

SMO's demands. Somewhat broader, an SMO may assemble information on an area, company, or other entity in order to assess *exactly which* would be the best issues or targets among several possibilities.

Although information useful for this kind of research can sometimes be found on the shelves of ordinary libraries, perhaps more commonly various kinds of *public records* are more rewarding resources: real estate transactions, disclosure reports filed by businesses, financial holdings of public officials. Corporations of various kinds must, in particular, file many kinds of reports that are publicly available. [Specifics are given in Villarejo (1980) and Staples (1984, Ch. 6).] In moving along these lines, such researching has a certain resemblance to investigative journalism and private detective investigations. Indeed, skills and routines presented in SMO how-to research manuals are similar to manuals in these two other fields (see, e.g., Ullmann and Colbert 1991; Anderson and Benjaminson 1976; Weir and Noyes 1983).

SMOs of the community organization variety are among the more intensive users of research of the kinds I have just described. Based on their 1993 survey of 325 such groups in the United States, McCarthy and Castelli conclude that research was "a major tool" for these SMOs. Among other topics, it had been used to "identify . . . redlining in banking and insurance, . . . problems facing working women, low rates of child support enforcement, and . . . health issues" in local communities (1994, vi).

As with education, research can also be a "strategic organizational posture"—the central and main or only task of the SMO. The social landscape of Washington, D.C., is, for example, not only littered with *mainstream* research centers or "think tanks," but, as counterpoint to them, a great many that do mission-research guided by realities that are more insurgent. Within that milieu, Ralph Nader is likely the all-time champion inventor and funder of them (although the realities promoted are more merely contentious or marginal than excluded).

d. Politicking. Together with educating, politicking is, of course, the officially approved mainstream strategy of working for or against social change. Its two main forms are *election campaigning* for or against candidates and other items on ballots and *lobbying* of officeholders regarding their votes on legislative or administrative ("ministerial") decisions. Of course (and for quite varied reasons), many SMOs hold politicking in contempt, some reasoning that "if voting mattered, they wouldn't allow it."

Politicking in the mainstream-approved fashion nonetheless remains a lure even for SMOs whose realities are at the same time very much excluded. One major dilemma for such SMOs is whether to become part of a mainstream political force and "work within it" or to go it alone as a separately identified party. This is, of course, the "third-party" problem of American politics, a problem that has no obvious answer since either decision extracts a significant price and engenders important dangers (Gilespie 1993).

Much more narrowly and episodically than the third-party problem, community-organizing SMOs quite commonly engage in the special kind of lobbying that features fielding *crowds* at legislative and administrative hearings. Called "crowd" or "people's" lobbying, the strategy is to impress officeholders with the size and passion of a body of ordinary citizens who are here *now* (Lofland 1985, Ch. 14).

e. Litigating. In many movement circles, the idea of seeking social change through the courts is the polar opposite of everything that "movement" means and stands for. Litigating is slow, polite, methodical, hair-splitting, and mainstream-framed. "Movement," in contrast is exactly that: fast, confrontational, radical, insurgent. Therefore, a lawsuit is among the very last strategies an SMO wants to think about.

While this is one view—and one that is credible *in some contexts*—it is not the only view. Recall that the defining feature of "movement" is *insurgent reality*, a reality marginal to or excluded from the mainstream. For some SMOs, the question, How can we best press our excluded reality into mainstream credibility? is answered, By the continuous and relentless use of the courts. This answer is, of course, premised on the belief that the law is in one's favor and that the courts will see that fact once it is effectively presented to them. The assumption must be that one's now excluded reality is not excluded for any proper reason that can be found in the law. Once so recognized, the reality will move from exclusion to the mainstream. Sound implausible and impossible? Well, at least one SMO has pulled it off: The NAACP Legal Defense Fund regarding the citizenship of African-Americans resulting in a pivotal Supreme Court decision in May 1954 (Greenberg 1994). And since that litigation's success in moving a reality into the mainstream, many other marginal and excluded realities have likewise been encouraged to employ such a strategy.

C. Dramaturgic Differences

Orthogonal to dimensions of substantive strategic variation such as those above are variations in the *dramaturgy* (or rhetorical) structure of strategies. As indicated previously, the term "dramaturgy" calls attention to the *manner* in which or *style* with which strategy is executed as apart from its sheer substance.

1. Dramaturgic Dimensions.   One approach to dramaturgy is to focus on how an *image of the power* of an SMO is constructed and displayed. The central interest is therefore in *dramaturgic techniques* used to show power in scripting, staging, performing, and interpreting. Benford and Hunt (1992) elaborate these concepts in this fashion:

[1]   Scripting

Scripting refers to the development of a set of directions that define the scene, identity actors and outline expected behavior. . . . Scripts are built upon "frames" that provide a collective definition of the situation [and] begins with the development of dramatus personae [which include] identities and roles for antagonists, victims, protagonists, supporting cast members and audiences. . . .

[S]ustaining the cast's involvement . . . is contingent in part on . . . convincing individuals . . . that they have the capacity to affect power relations [through] vocabularies of motive [that] supply adherents with compelling reasons . . . for taking action. . . . Scripting also provides direction for appropriate performances. . . .

[2]   Staging

Staging refers to appropriating, managing and directing materials, audiences and performing regions. [Problems regarding these include] developing and manipulating symbols [,] audience segregation and backstage control. . . .

[3]   Performing

Performing involves the demonstration and enactment of power. . . . Presenting a movement performance that effectively communicates power . . . requires the coordination of a variety of dramatic techniques [which include the following].

Dramaturgical loyalty refers to . . . performers [acting] as if they have accepted certain moral obligations. . . .

Dramaturgical discipline . . . involves sustaining self-control so as to behave in ways that maintain the movement's affective line: avoiding involuntary disclosure of secrets, having the presence of mind to "cover up on the spur of the moment for inappropriate behavior." (Goffman 1959, 216)

Dramaturgic circumspection [is] the ability to prepare for performances in advance and to adapt an ongoing performance to unforeseen circumstances. . . .

[4]   Interpreting

Interpreting [is] the process of . . . making sense out of symbols, talk, action and the environment, or, more succinctly, determining what is going on. [It] is an never-ending social activity that makes movement scripting, staging, and performing possible. . . . Interpretations . . . are

> the . . . object of [movement] performances [in seeking to] affect audiences' interpretations of reality. . . .
> [Yet] factors beyond the control of social movements can . . . distort or otherwise modify the desired interpretation of the intended audiences. [In particular, movement interpretations are often] filtered by media agents [and others] in the reality construction business. (adapted from Benford and Hunt 1992, emphasis added)

2. Dramaturgic Ingratiation. The insurgent reality of an SMO is, by definition, at least somewhat suspect in the eyes of mainstream power holders, the public at large, and other parties. People in a given SMO are, of course, aware of these suspicions and react to them in diverse ways. Some, in the slang expression, "couldn't care less." But other SMOs have practices and goals that prompt them to undertake *accommodative strategies* that seek to assure the mainstream that the SMO is acceptable despite its also suspicious aspects. David Snow reports that the Nichiren Shoshu of America (NSA) has been such an accommodative SMO, one that developed a strategy of *dramaturgic ingratiation*.

Aspects of the NSA its members think the public might look askance at include:

> (1) the repetitive changing of Nam-Myoho-Renge-Kyo to the Gohonzon (a small replica of a scroll [the original of which is] regarded as the most powerful object in the world);
> (2) the daily performance of morning and evening Gongyo (a liturgical prayer in which the member recites chapters of the *Lotus Sutra* in Japanese before the Gohonzon); and in
> (3) the unrelenting practice of Shakubuku or the act of spreading the word and bringing others into contact with the Gohonzon and the key to unlocking its power—Nam-Myoho-Renge-Kyo. (Snow 1979, 28)

These activities make up part of the "one way" by means of which humans can move toward happiness and a "human revolution," a revolution requiring *all* persons to adopt the above practices and "building a new culture" (p. 27). This "spiritual regeneration of all people will lead to that elusive utopian dream of peace and happiness among all . . . , to . . . a 'Third Civilization' (the union of spiritualism and materialism, capitalism and socialism, in accordance with the principles and practices of Nichiren Shoshu)" (p. 27).

By dramatic or **dramaturgic ingratiation** Snow means "the process of strategically attempting to gain the favor and blessing of others by conducting and presenting oneself in a manner that projects an image that is reflective of fitting in and deferential regard for certain values, traditions, and properties perceived to be important to those whose favor is being courted" (p. 30). NSA "practices or tactics . . . employed in its effort to render itself respectable and legitimate in the public eye [have included]":

> 1. *[T]he tactic of articulating a linkage between its mission and values and the values and traditions of the larger society.* [For example,] participating in . . . public parades, . . . prominent . . . displays of the American flag, [proclamations that NSA] is the reincarnation of [the] early pioneer spirit and tradition, [and that its meetings] are in keeping with the 'town meetings of old' and epitomize what Democracy is all about. . . .
>
> 2. *[T]he practice of instructing members to be "winners" in all domains of social life.* [For example,] the following directives appear . . . as article titles [in the NSA newspaper:] *Become a Victorious Person, Doing the Utmost Work . . . Seek Perfection in Work and Daily Activities . . . Become Best Examples in Contemporary Society. . . .*
>
> 3. *[T]he practice of celebrity ingratiation and endorsement seeking.* [NSA] court[s] the favor and seek[s] . . . the endorsement of various celebrities or public figures, all of whom have achieved the status of a "winner" in their own respective occupations. . . .
>
> 4. *[T]he practice of instructing members to conduct themselves with propriety and deference when in the public eye.* [In addition to many general instructions in NSA literature, such as articles with titles like "Consideration of Neighbors Leads to Understanding of NSA," members are admonished to be courteous in] various and sundry situations [as in] "always be mannerly and courteous to the waitress [in a restaurant], because they will judge NSA by our actions." (adapted from pp. 31–35, emphases added).

Snow interprets—explains—this strategy of dramaturgic ingratiation as an effort to build *idiosyncrasy credit.*

> NSA is confronted with the problem of reducing or neutralizing the stigma attached to [it] in order to facilitate its recruitment efforts. . . . Hence, the strategic practice of attempting to build idiosyncrasy credit by attempting to render itself respectable and legitimate. . . . By emphasizing that it is carrying out the unfinished work of America's founding fathers and pioneers, by respectfully deferring to various American traditions and customs, and by actively encouraging members to become "winners" on the job who are "respected and loved by everyone," NSA has been attempting, in part, to build up its credit or balance of favorable impressions [so] that outsiders will tolerate or overlook the more idiosyncratic aspects of its philosophy and ritual practices and grant it a certain amount of respectability and legitimacy. [It is] a strategic attempt to buy license to engage in the business of propagating its beliefs and practices. (p. 38)

3. Personal Bearing.   As we move down the scales of scope and "unit scale" we come to the relatively microscope level of the personal bearing, demeanor, tenor, general appearance, and sensibility of the concrete people executing a strategy (Ibarra and Kitsuse 1993, 45). Here, also, Ibarra and Kitsuse have been very helpful in identifying such holistic, dramaturgic variations as what they term "claims-making styles." The range of these they discern is attuned to social problems, but their relevance to SMOs is also evident.

[1] [In the] *scientific style* . . . the frame of reference . . . includes certain typifications: a bearing that is "disinterested;" a tone that is "sober;" and a vocabulary that is "technical" and "precise." [Being] "too rhetorical," "political," or "poetic" can be taken to be . . . a departure from the hallmark of the style. . . .

[2] [The] *comic style* [includes] those practices . . . which foreground absurdities in certain positions, highlight hypocrisies of claimants . . . , or draw upon some measure of irony or sarcasm to point up a particular moral. . . . Caricature might be used to fashion a counterclaim by ad absurdum extension of claims. . . .

[3] The *theatrical style* [makes] a point of illustrating the group's moral critique in the very way in which the claim is represented. . . . "Actions," such as "die-ins," are dramatizations of the issue being contested. . . . Operation Rescue demonstrations against abortions have featured such actions as symbolic mass funerals. . . .

[4] The *civic style* [has] what we might call "the look of being unpolished." [It] is based on being "honest," "sincere," "upright," "unstylized." . . . To appear too well organized or "too slick" is to be part of an "interest group." [It trades] off an ideal of the "common, decent folk."

[5] The *legalistic style* is premised on the notion that the claimant is in fact speaking on behalf of another party . . . and that the merits of that party's case are consistent with rights and protections embodied in law.

[6] Various segments of society—whether self-defined by class, race, ethnicity, gender, sexual orientation, or geographical location—tend to evolve unique or "local" . . . ways of commenting on the larger social world. [As a set, there is a] *subculture style*. (pp. 45–49, emphases in the original)

These of course provide but an orientation to the rich area of possible research along these lines. Among other reports on personal bearing, consider:

- Wolfe (1970) on "mau-mauing the flak catcher."
- Neil (1990) on the studied professional demeanor of Physicians For Social Responsibility in opposing nuclear weapons.

- Lofland (1993a, 117–23) on "persona" in the American peace movement of the 1980s

4. Speech Practices.   At the microscopic level, some researchers have carried out detailed dissections of the rhetorical structures (strategies) of the speech texts and speaking styles of SMOs. One of the classics is Alfred McClung Lee's and Elizabeth Briant Lee's (1939) delineation and application of what they term the "tricks of the trade" of the "propagandist." They derived these seven "tricks" from study of the speeches of Father Charles E. Coughlin, a Catholic priest of fascist sympathies who made widely followed radio broadcasts spanning several years in the middle and late 1930s. While based on the speeches of this "radio priest," the "tricks" are themselves quite generic and, as Lee and Lee say: "They are workable. Anyone can use them" (p. 22, emphasis omitted).

Name calling—giving an idea a bad label—is used to make us reject and condemn the idea without examining the evidence.

Glittering generality—associating something with a "virtue word"—is used to make us accept and approve the thing without examining the evidence.

Transfer carries the authority, sanction, and prestige of something respected and revered over to something else in order to make the latter acceptable; or it carries authority, sanction, and disapproval to cause us to reject and disapprove something the propagandist would have us reject and disapprove.

Testimonial consists in having some respected or hated person say that a given idea or program or product or person is good or bad.

Plain folks is the method by which a speaker attempts to convince his [or her] audience that he [or she] and his [or her] ideas are good because they are "of the people," the "plain folks."

Card stacking involves the selection and use of facts or falsehoods, illustrations or distractions, and logical or illogical statements in order to give the best or the worst possible case for an idea, program, person, or product.

Bandwagon has as its theme, Everybody—at least all of *us*—is doing it. With it, the propagandist attempts to convince us that all members of a group to which we belong are accepting his [or her] program and that we *must therefore* follow our crowd and "jump on the band wagon." (pp. 23–24)

Other useful studies of speech practices include Michael Blain's (1988) analysis of Adolph Hitler's "hyperbole" practices.

D. Strategic Medleys and Campaigns

The array of schemes for typifying and classifying strategies and tactics I portray above tends to the "pure type" in conception. That is, their author's are trying to depict one or another distinctive pattern or set of them as abstract generics. While efforts of this kind are important in the research work of articulation and clarification, the reality of specific SMOs tends to be more complicated and messier.

The genius of the leaders of some SMOs is, indeed, manifest in the untidy and improbable combinations of strategies and tactics they creatively improvise in pursuit of SMO goals. Consider this observation on the "bizarre medley" of strategies and constituencies assembled by United Farm Worker leader Caesar Chavez:

> He invented a type of organizing that synthesized the tactics of the civil rights and anti-war movement, cooperatives, labor unions, community organizing and religious ministries. Everyone in the union was uncomfortable with at least one aspect of this bizarre medley. But he got us all to live with each other because the union needed every one of these tactics and constituencies. . . . He didn't care whether he had to march 1,000 miles or set up a shrine outside a vineyard—if it worked, we were going to do it. (Gardner 1993, 19)

Strategic genius is by definition uncommon, but even less inspired leaderships not infrequently cobble together inventive strategic medleys.

As the level of the strategic medleys of particular SMOs, researchers sometimes use the idea of the *campaign* as a way to organize their inquiries into strategies. By "campaign" I mean a near-term focus and set of goals and associated activities that provide direction and integration over the space of weeks, months, or seasons. Often campaigns are geared to a sequential set of seasons running a year or somewhat more [cf. Marwell and Oliver (1984) on "collective campaigns"].

III. FACTORS AFFECTING SELECTION AND CHANGE OF STRATEGIES

Viewing any or all of the above strategic possibilities as *dependent variables*, the question is, What independent variables cause the selection (or invention) of one rather than another strategy?

Efforts to answer this question divide into (1) sensitizing images of the situation of an SMO, (2) general schemes for thinking about the entire range of causal factors involved, and (3) more specialized and detailed studies of why specific strategies are adopted or abandoned.

A. Images for Thinking about
   SMO Strategizing

Any inquiry must begin with some root mental picture of the nature of the object or subject at hand. Such a picture is a *sensitizing image* that serves to focus a researcher's attention in certain ways (as well as prevent it from focusing in yet other ways) (cf. Blumer 1969b). This image is not yet an analysis or even a specific scheme of concepts with which to perform an analysis. Instead, it is a way of visualizing and thinking that will structure further inquiry and detailed analysis. Let me report two such sensitizing images of how SMOs select strategies.

1. Strategic Dilemmas. The first of these images evokes the situation of the SMO as one of a complex field of forces and possibilities in which all the strategic choices have not only benefits but significant *costs* as well. No matter what is done, it incurs significant disadvantages along with whatever advantages may come. This is commonly termed the situation of the *strategic dilemma*. Doug McAdam, John McCarthy, and Mayer Zald provide a concise summary of this sensitizing image:

> SMOs find themselves confronting a wide range of organizations with very different interests vis-à-vis the movement. Some, representing countermovements or segments of the elite, would like to see the movement destroyed or at least tamed. Other groups may be allies of the movement. Still others have yet to take a decisive stance either for or against the movement. The media are often among these "neutral third parties."
>
> These groups play a decisive role in shaping the choices SMOs make regarding goals and tactics. In choosing between all tactical and programmatic options open to them, SMOs typically weigh the anticipated responses of these various groups and seek through their choices to balance the conflicting demands of the organizational environment in which they are embedded. . . .
>
> SMOs must [also] balance the need to respond . . . to pressures from other organizations with . . . the need to maintain the strength and viability of the organization. It matters little [for example] if one has attracted media attention, if in the process, one has antagonized support and jeopardized the flow of resources to the organization. . . .
>
> Any number of such strategic dilemmas confront SMOs as they seek both to adapt to and shape the ongoing macro and micro environment they confront. (1988, 728)

2. Tactical Interaction. A second sensitizing image centerpieces the SMO as a probing and flexible creature that is responsive to target reactions and innovative in continuously (or at least periodically) revising its strategies as a function of target reactions. In reality, of course, SMOs differ greatly in their degree of tactical innovation and adaptation.

Many, indeed, are strategically frozen and slog on irrespective of target and other responses. But the degree of tactical flexibility actually observed in any SMO can at least be made a question, and the sensitizing image of *tactical interaction* serves that end.

Doug McAdam has provided the most influential formulation of tactical interaction as a sensitizing image. Although a social movement rather than an SMO is the unit of his analysis, the guiding vision is applicable to SMOs:

> The pace of . . . insurgency [is] an ongoing process of *tactical interaction* between insurgents and their opponents.Lacking institutional power, challengers must devise protest techniques that offset their powerlessness. This [is] a process of *tactical innovation.* Such innovations, however, only temporarily afford challengers increased bargaining leverage. In chesslike fashion, movement opponents can be expected, through effective *tactical adaptation,* to neutralize the new tactic, thereby reinstating the original power disparity. To succeed over time, then, a challenger must continue to search for new and effective tactical forms. (McAdam 1983, 752, emphases in the original)

B. General Schemes of Causes

The several oft-recounted general schemes of factors affecting selection of strategies overlap but still differ in their particular cast or emphasis. I therefore report each separately rather than attempting to synthesize them into a single, comprehensive account.

1. Causes of Repertoires of Collective Action. The broadest scheme pertinent to explaining SMO strategic selection is arguably not actually pertinent. This is because the dependent variable it seeks to explain is not necessarily *SMO* strategy, but *collective action* strategies in general observed in any *population.* The concept of "collective action" is much more inclusive than SMO strategic action and encompasses what I described in Chapter 1 as "crowd/mass insurgencies" as well as social movements. However, collective action can also include SMO action/strategy, and this scheme, proposed by Charles Tilly (1978, Ch. 5), is therefore informative even though much more general.

Tilly suggests that any population exhibits a *repertoire of collective action* (a collection of social movement, crowd mass insurgence actions) that

[1] includes only a handful of alternatives. . . .
[2] generally changes slowly [and]
[3] seems obvious and natural to the people involved. (p. 156)

One key question, Tilly declares, is: "How . . . does such a repertoire come into being?" "The answer," he says, "surely includes at least these elements":

1. *[T]he standards of rights and justice prevailing in the population* . . . govern the acceptability of the components of various possible types of collective action. . . . For example, a group which [thinks that] persons directly producing an object . . . has a prior right to its consumption is likely to condone some kinds of forcible resistance to [these objects'] expropriation. . . . This is the implicit rationale of the modern European food riot and tax rebellion.

2. *[T]he daily routines of the population* . . . affect the ease with which one or another of the possible forms of action can actually be carried on. The strike became feasible when considerable numbers of people assembled to work in the same location. The notable shift of collective action away from routine assemblies such as markets and festivals toward deliberately called gatherings as in demonstrations and strikes resulted in part from the residential dispersion of occupational groups and others who shared a common interest. . . .

3. *[T]he population's internal organization* [which is] hard to distinguish [from] daily routines [because they] overlap. The three [historical] stages [in Europe] correspond approximately to pure craft organization, the organization of proletarianizing trades, and the full-fledged proletarian structure. . . . The shifts in organization interact with changing daily routines to make different forms of collective action feasible and advantageous. . . .

4. *[T]he accumulated experience with prior collective action* . . . includes both the contender's own successes or failures and the contender's observations of other similar groups. We see that blend of previous practice and observation in the rich street theater that grew up in the American colonies from the Stamp Act crisis of 1765 to the Revolution. Mock trials, parading of effigies [and] tarring and feathering of Loyalists accompanied petitions, declarations, and solemn assemblies. . . . The particular form and content of these gatherings were new. But their principal elements were already well-established ways of dealing with declared enemies of the people. The prior experiences of urban sailors, artisans, and merchants shaped the revolutionary repertoire of collective action. . . .

5. *[T]he pattern of repression in the world to which the population belongs* . . . makes a large difference in the short run because other powerful groups affect the relative costs and probable returns

of different forms of action theoretically available to a particular group. It also matters in the long run because that sort of cost setting tends to eliminate some forms of action as it channels behavior into others. The widespread legalization of the strike in the 1860s and 1870s [in Europe] so increased its attractiveness relative to direct attacks on employers and on industrial property that the latter virtually disappeared from the worker's repertoire. (pp. 156–58, adapted and emphases added)

2. Limiting Factors in Selecting Strategies. A second way to think about SMO strategic choice is in terms of factors that limit or constrain action. As conceived by Turner and Killian in tandem with their distinctions among the "tactical mechanisms" of coercion, bargaining, and persuasion (Section II.A.2), such limiting factors include the following:

[1] *The values and interests of [SMO] constituencies* [,] the larger category of people for whom the movement claims to speak and from whom it recruits its adherents. Religious or humanistic values sometimes inhibit the use of coercion as an unacceptable strategy. Extreme democratic idealism may lead to excessive reliance on persuasion . . . and a blindness to the possibilities of bargaining. Persuasion is downgraded among some groups as an indicator of weakness. . . . Bargaining strategies incur the risk that . . . leaders may be viewed as having sold out. . . .

[2] *The values and interests of potentially concerned publics* [have] been a recurrent factor limiting the use of coercive tactics and augmenting reliance on persuasive tactics. . . . Although violence and coercion have been recurring features of social change in America, they have seldom been assigned major parts in the strategies of . . . reform movements. The pressure of cooptable humanitarian elements [of concerned publics] has likely been the major factor accounting for the number of movements that . . . rely on persuasive . . . tactics. . . .

[3] *The nature of the relationship between movement constituencies and the target group.* . . . The two key variables in the constituency-target relationship are *dependency* and *interpenetrating relationships*. The least restraint against the use of coercive and bargaining strategies applies [for example] to movements such as the cargo cults and other nationalistic developments in colonial countries. The presence of a relatively self-sufficient community able to sustain its members along traditional lines regardless of the presence or absence of colonial rulers and having very few personal relationships with the ruling group, makes any fear of damaging relationships a trivial consideration. [In contrast,

groups] directly dependent upon the favor of specific [members
of a ruling group are] not freed from restraints upon using bargaining and coercion. [For example] the decline of special [and
dependent African-American] forms of employment and [their]
dispersion into the larger impersonal labor force have under-
mined. . . . [the] sense of dependency, fostering greater reliance on bargaining and coercion. (pp. 299–300, adapted and
emphases added)

3. Factors Affecting Strategic Options.   The schemes just described
are addressed to struggles in a population quite generally (Tilly) or to
social movements in the abstract (Turner and Killian). A third scheme of
note is, in contrast, thought out explicitly in terms of the SMO as the
unit. This is the model of Jo Freeman, a formulation she in fact labels "a
model"—or, more precisely, "a model for analyzing strategic options of
social movement organizations" (1983b, 193).
    Freeman's model is divided into the "four major elements" of

[1] mobilizable *resources,*
[2] *constraints* on these resources,
[3] *SMO* structure and internal environment,
[4] expectations about *potential targets.* (p. 195, adapted and emphases
        added)

In her publications on this model, Freeman presents a diagrammatic and
flow-chart visualization in which the four terms I italicize just above are
displayed in a left to right sequence, which is:

Resources   Constraints   SMO   Potential Targets

The image is that of a situation beginning (on the left) with (1) resources
that are then (2) constrained and processed through (3) an SMO and (4)
affected by expectations and reactions of targets. Said differently and
physically, the strategic action moves from left to right through the
model so visualized (Freeman 1979, 171; 1983b, 194).
    Schematic "pictures" of each of these four elements are given above
their respective captions. Thus:

Above resources: three clusters of small circles represent conscience,
    beneficiary, and institutional constituencies, respectively.
Above constraints: a single large circle with filterlike internal markings
    represents a narrowing of options.
Above SMO: a rectangular maze represents the SMO into which con-
    strained resources go and tortuously make their way through and
    out the other side and toward the target.

Above potential targets: a large circle represents this element, with two thick arrows pointing back toward the SMO, one labeled "feedback" and the other labeled "expectations."

Lines representing the flowing, channeling, constraining, and shaping of resources connect resources and constraints, constraints and SMOs, and SMOs and potential targets (Freeman 1979, 171; 1983b, 194).

Here are some of the main points that Freeman makes about each of the four elements.

Mobilizable Resources

The most obvious distinction among the varieties of resources available to organizers is between the tangible and the intangible. . . .

[1] [T]angible resources [are] primarily money, space, and a means of publicizing the moment's existence and ideas.

[2] People are the primary intangible resource of movements, and . . . a major distinguishing [feature of] social movements [is a low level of] tangible resources, especially monetary, but strong on people resources. . . . The many different resources people can contribute can be divided into three categories. . . .

[a] Specialized resources . . . are possessed by only a few participants. These . . . include expertise of various sorts, access to networks through which other resources can be mobilized, access to decision makers relevant to the movement, and status. . . .

[b] Time [is] the unspecialized resource needed to perform necessary labor and to sit through meetings. . . .

[c] Commitment is the willingness to take risks or entertain inconvenience.

Whenever a deprived group triumphs over a more privileged one without major outside interference, it is because their constituencies have compensated with a great deal of time and commitment. . . .

Constraints

All resources . . . have constraints on their uses. [There are at least] five different categories of constraints. . . . Their filtering function can best be explored by applying them to the two branches of the women's liberation movement. . . .

[1] Early participants in the younger branch [held *values* that] led easily to the idea that hierarchy was bad [and resulted in] leaderless, structureless groups. [In contrast, the values of the older branch led to] well-run organization. . . .

[2] The more *immediate [past] experiences* of the early participants . . . also had an effect on their initial choice of tactics. . . .

[3] The [*reference group*] standards new feminists wanted to meet were very different for the two branches. Women in the younger branch . . . considered themselves *radical* women. [Women in the other branch used a reference standard of] effectiveness. . . .

[4] The *expectations* of the women in the two branches [differed]. For young women, the goal was revolution. . . . Older branch women . . . expected changes to be slow and gradual. . . .

[5] [For the older branch], the *targets* were concrete and identifiable. . . . In the younger branch, the first major debate was over just who the target was. . . .

SMO Structure

Neither branch of the movement deliberately created a structure specifically geared to accomplish its desired goals. Instead, the founders of both branches drew upon their previous political experiences. Women of the older branch . . . were familiar with national associations, and that is what they created. Women of the younger branch inherited the loose, flexible, person-oriented attitude of the youth and student movements. . . .

Once these different structures were created, they in turn molded the strategic possibilities. [For example, because of] "the tyranny of structurelessness" . . . the activities that could be developed by [the younger] branch were limited to those that could be performed by small homogeneous groups without major divisions of labor.

Expectations about Potential Targets

As an SMO searches for effective actions there are three factors it must consider about potential targets and the external environment. . . .

[1] *The structure of available opportunities for action.* . . . The success of a . . . movement is often determined by its ingenuity in finding less obvious leverage points from which to pressure its targets. . . .

[2] *Social-control measures that might be taken.* . . .

[3] *The effect on bystander publics.* . . . As a general rule, movements try to turn bystander publics into conscience constituencies. (adapted from Freeman 1979; 1983b, 193–209, emphasis added)

C. Specific Strategies and Cases

Specific empirical inquires about SMOs strategies have tended to address one of these two questions: (1) the causes of a particular type of strategy or tactic as a generic class across many cases, and (2) the reasons a specific SMO/social movement selected the strategy or strategies it did.

1. Causes of a Type of Strategy. The effort in the first type of research is to isolate some wider or narrower type of strategy and to try to specify factors that account for its presence or absence as a general matter.

The "resort" to violence is likely the strategy most commonly focused on in this way. Historically, violence as an aspect of crowd and group insurgencies has been of more interest than violence strategized by SMOs.[6] But there is also a considerable body of work using SMOs as the unit, a literature tending to label such violence "terrorism." The question is then, Under what conditions do SMOs adopt violence/terrorism as a strategy?

As might be anticipated, causal answers vary. They do so in part in terms of other features of the SMOs being analyzed. In particular, SMOs in the third world that are guerrilla armies bent on ousting colonizers elicit rather different causal accounts than do clandestine violent SMOs in the first world composed of middle-class educated youth bent on destroying the capitalist class. In the former case, one key theme is intransigent foreign elites driving the natives to violence because of lack of other avenues of redress. In the latter case, more is made of transient, generational socialization that produces isolated pockets of out-of-touch revolutionaries.[7]

2. Causes of Strategies in a Case. In the second form of studying strategies more specifically, the researcher begins with a particular SMO and traces the historical succession of its strategies, attempting also to specify causes of those strategies. Thus, Sheldon Messinger (1955) traces the Townsend movement's change *from* public education and structural change *to* direct service strategies (see Section II.B.2). He argues that this shift was caused by the Townsend movement having achieved its major goal—that of government pensions for the elderly. [Several additional examples of "explain[ing] the choice of particular tactics . . . on a case by case basis" are provided by Turner and Killian (1987, 287–91). See also White (1989).]

IV. EFFECTS OF STRATEGIES AND SMO SUCCESS

Of perennial interest is, of course, the question, What strategies are successful? Or, slightly more complicated, Which ones work, when, and why?

Alas (perhaps), there are no simple and agreed-on answers to the question of which strategies are successful under what circumstances. We have, instead, myriad observations suggesting that given strategies are sometimes associated with success and *also often* with failure.

The main reason for the conflicting results of many strategies is that an SMO's actions are only *one* component of very complex fields of forces that are outside the control of the SMO. These external, beyond-

SMO-control forces are *also* at play in determining effects of strategies, including success and failure. Therefore, SMO success or failure in given instances is not merely or solely a function of SMO strategy. All manner of other influences most often make up the mix of causal elements.

These larger fields of forces are extremely complex, rapidly changing, and different from case to case. They are so kaleidoscopic that researchers have not been yet been able with confidence to grasp them *and* the role of particular strategies within them as they change from case to case. The best that can therefore be said about almost any strategy is that it is successful sometimes, but we are very uncertain about the features of the successful versus unsuccessful "sometimes."

Recognizing that an SMO is but one entity in a complex field of forces allows us to see that the question of when SMOs are successful is not the same as the question of the effects of SMO strategies. The question of success is a broad causal question, while that of strategic effects is a narrow consequences questions. This difference is depicted visually in Figure 9.3.

Indeed, most studies of the effects of strategies (panel A in Figure 9.3) are actually studies of the causes of success (panel B). In these studies, success is the dependent variable and researchers look to whatever independent variable might account for variations in it. Such independent variables may be SMO strategies in the sense defined at the beginning of this chapter. But, then again, important determinants of success and failure may *not* be such conscious SMO strategies—and often are not.

The prominent analyses of strategies I report below use one or both of these modes of conceptualization—and sometimes go back and forth between them.

A. Combat Willingness and Readiness

The modern, classic effort to specify determinants of success is William Gamson's (1974, 1975, 1990) quantitative comparisons of fifty-three randomly selected SMOs that were challenging, insurgent realities in the United States between 1800 and 1945. Gamson employed two summary measures of success:

[1] whether other power holders came to accept the groups as valid representatives of legitimate interests. . . .
[2] whether the group gained new advantages for its constituents and beneficiaries and accomplished its goals. (p. 37)

Treating these two as dichotomies, there are four possible outcomes and the 53 groups distributed with the percentages shown by each outcome:

    complete success (new advantages and complete success)   38%
    co-optation (no advantages but acceptance)   9%
    pre-emption (advantages but no acceptance)   11%
    failure (neither advantages or acceptance)   42%

What independent variables might account for this variation in the dependent variable? Gamson coded and correlated "39 organizational, tactical, and goal-oriented parameter for each group" (Goldstone 1980, 1018), producing a very complicated set of findings of which only the several most central (and controversial) will concern us here.

Gamson's finding on the relation between violence and success are perhaps *the* most discussed result of his research—and for good reasons:

Figure 9.3.   Effects of strategies versus causes of success.

Panel A: Effects of strategy

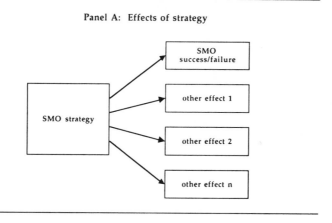

Panel B: Causes of success/failure

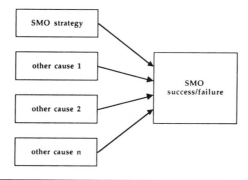

Most of the groups had no violence at all in their history but 15 of them participated in some kind of violent exchange. . . . We divided [these] groups into two types—eight activist groups who, whether or not they initiated a fight, were willing to give and take if one started. The other seven were passive recipients; they were attacked and could not, or simply did not, fight back. . . . The activist groups that fought back, or in some cases initiated violence, had a higher than average success rate; six of the eight won new advantages and five of the six were eventually accepted as well. The nonviolent recipients of attack, however, lost out completely. None of them met their goals, although one . . . was co-opted (Gamson 1974, 37)

Gamson concludes that "in the case of violence, it appears better to give than to receive if you want to succeed in American politics" (1974, 37).

Violence is one form of the broader category that Gamson variously terms "high-pressure," "forceful," and "unruly" tactics, which include such measures as "strikes, boycotts, and efforts to humiliate or embarrass . . . antagonists" (p. 37). What is the relation between using or not using such forceful tactics and success? Gamson reports:

Forceful tactics are associated with success, as violence is. Eight of the 10 groups that applied such pressures were [complete successes], a percentage that is twice as great as the percentage for groups that avoided such tactics. (p. 37–39).

Gamson interprets these findings on violence and unruliness as meaning that "the successful group in American politics is not the polite petitioner who carefully observes all the rules. It is the rambunctious fighter, one with limited goals, that can elbow its way into the arena" (p. 39).

Having shown that the *willingness* to fight makes for success, Gamson then asks, Does being *able* to fight matter? He elaborates "being able" as composed of the two dimensions of "a *bureaucratic structure* to help become ready for action, and *centralized power* to help in reaching unified decisions" (p. 39, emphases added).

He measures *bureaucratic structure* in terms of an SMO having or not having three characteristics:

[1] a constitution or charter that states the purpose of the group and rules for its operation;

[2] . . . a formal list of its members, which distinguishes from mere sympathizers.

[3] at least three internal divisions, e.g., executives, chapter head, rank and file. (p. 39)

And he finds on this measure of bureaucratically "being able": "Twenty-four of the groups met all three criteria, and these were more likely than nonbureaucratic groups to win acceptance (71 to 28 percent) and new advantages (62 to 38 percent)."

Centralized power, the second dimension of "being able," is measured as "power resided in a single leader or central committee, and local chapters had little autonomy. Slightly more than half of the groups, 28, had such a centralized structure" (p. 39). Centralization is also associated with success (Gamson 1975, 93).

While, says Gamson, each of these two makes a contribution, "it is the combination that really does the trick. Groups that were both bureaucratic *and* centralized had the best chance of achieving their goals; 75 percent of them were successful. Groups that were neither bureaucratic nor centralized had very little change of winning anything" (Gamson 1974, 39).

Putting these findings together they mean, to Gamson, that "the meek don't make it," the bold typeface tag title used in his 1974 *Psychology Today* popularized capsule of this research. "Challengers do better when they realize they are in political combat situation. They don't need to look for a fight, but they had better be ready to participate in one if the occasion arises. They must therefore be organized like a combat group—with willing, committed people who know what to do, and a command structure that can keep its people out of the wrong fight at the wrong time" (p. 41).

Other Gamson findings that have been of particular interest to researchers include:

- single-issue SMOs had higher success rates than groups that pursued many goals (Gamson 1975, 44–46).
- groups whose goals required the "displacement of antagonists" were less likely to be successful than those whose goals did not (pp. 41–46; McAdam et al. 1988, 761).

Gamson published the raw codings of the fifty-three groups on the thirty-nine variables as an appendix in the 1975 report of his study. As he observes, "in effect, this extended an invitation to other scholars to have a go at analyzing these cases in other ways to see whether they would arrive at the same conclusions" (Gamson 1990, 181). And so they did, creating what two later analysts of these data called a "growth industry" (Foley and Steedly 1980). Some applied different kinds of statistical procedures and techniques and some questioned many of the codings and even recoded good portions of the original data. The upshot has been

sometimes quite sharp disagreement on the truth of Gamson's propositions. While Gamson and others continue to think his basic propositions
survive later analyses, others do not.

To his enormous credit, Gamson not only published his raw dataset in
his 1975 book, in the 1990 republication of it he included the main
reanalyses of those data. The entire affair is therefore conveniently available for scrutiny.[8]

B. Radical-Flank Effects

As reported in Chapter 3, the SMOs of many social movements can be
arrayed on a moderate to radical continuum running *from* the more
conservative SMOs who are closer *to* the mainstream, to the more militant and radical SMOs who are further to the extreme "left," "right," or
merely "out" (whatever the case may be). Within movements featuring
such a spectrum of SMOs, the strategic dynamic of the *radical-flank effect*
can arise. This is the dynamic in which the more extreme and militant
SMOs frame the parameters of social movement demands and have
either *negative* or *positive* radical-flank effects (Haines 1984).

In *negative* radical-flank effects, intense fear provoked by the most
militant of SMOs in the social movement precipitates reactive repression
of the entire movement, setting back if not destroying the cause. This, at
least, is a concern commonly expressed in the more moderate SMOs of
movements.

While negative radical-flank effects certainly occur, *positive* radical-
flank effects are also possible. In this pattern, "the bargaining position of
moderates is strengthened by the presence of more radical groups"
(Haines 1984, 32). As analyzed by Herbert Haines:

> This happens in either (or both) of two ways. The radicals can provide a
> militant foil against which moderate strategies and demands are redefined
> and normalized—in other words treated as "reasonable." Or, the radicals
> can create crises which are resolved to the moderate's advantage. [It is
> likely, for example, that] mainstream reformist women's organizations
> would have been dismissed as "too far out" during the late 1960s and the
> early 1970s had it not been for more radical groups: lesbian feminists and
> socialist feminists appear to have improved the bargaining position of
> such moderate groups as the National Organization for Women. [So, also,]
> demands by the labor movement for an eight-hour day and collective
> bargaining became negotiable only after the emergence of serious socialist
> threats in the early 20th century. [And, it would appear that] the emer-
> gence of black militants in the 1960s helped to increase white acceptance of
> nonviolence tactics and integrationist goals. (p. 32)

Such positive or negative radical-flank effects can, of course, move along many dimensions—of state repression, pubic opinion, media coverage, and so forth. In developing the idea of a radical-flank effect, Haines traces the effects for the dimension of *funding* of the 1960s civil rights movement. Specifically, he sought to determine if the emergence of black militancy and rioting slowed funding or restricted the range of its sources. Reviewing dollar figures on amounts and sources of civil rights funding, he concludes that militancy had, in fact, the *opposite* effect: "radicalization of segments of the black community had the net effect of improving the resource bases of moderate civil rights organizations by stimulating previously uninvolved parties to contribute ever increasing amounts of financial support" (p. 31).

The moderate-radical SMO spectrum of a movement is not a strategy in the stricter or narrower sense in which I use the term here, but it is nonetheless a variable that enters into the likelihood of success. Thus recognized, radical-flank effects can presumably be something that are, indeed, consciously strategized by SMOs!

C. Confrontation and Crisis

One implication of taking seriously the idea that SMOs maneuver in a complex and ever-changing field of forces is that, for success, SMOs *sometimes* need to be strategically *confrontational, flexible,* and *multitactical.*

Aldon Morris's analysis of such strategic confrontation, flexibility, and multiplicity in the Birmingham civil rights confrontation of April–May 1963 is an especially acute depiction of these variables as they relate to success. Although publicly represented by an outside personage—Martin Luther King, Jr.—the key organizational actor in this struggle was a local SMO, the Alabama Christian Movement for Human Rights (AC-MHR). At the time of the Birmingham confrontation, it had already "amassed a wealth of experience in mobilizing, organizing, and preparing large numbers of people to engage in collective action" (p. 634).

As reported by Morris, the goal of the ACMHR in Birmingham (and of the SCLC of which it was an affiliate), was to "generate a crisis of such magnitude" that national and local white establishments "would have no option but to capitulate" (Morris 1993, 624). The means to this end were "large-scale economic and political protests" in Birmingham that would hopefully become a model for use in other cities.

The ideas of *confrontation* and *crisis* are central to understanding this strategy. Many movements are plagued by mainstream pleas that the movement must go slow or that the time for vigorously pressing demands is not quite right. If one only waits—a few weeks, months, or whatever—*then* one can press harder for one's demands. But not right now. Give the forces of reason and moderation a fair chance to work before escalating one's tactics. On the movement side there can come the realization—among *some* leaders—that the time will *never* be right. Reason and moderation will always want more time. Hence, confrontation and crisis are necessary. This is the realization that the civil rights SMO leaders had—fitfully and ambivalently—in *plotting* strategy for the Birmingham campaign many months earlier *and* in the period of confrontation, April 3 through May 8, 1963 (Branch 1988, 688–92).

The distinction sometimes drawn between *loosely* and *tightly coupled* conflicts is helpful in understanding the strategy of confrontation and crisis. Many conflicts are loosely coupled in the sense that two parties disagree on social arrangements but those arrangements are so pervasive and built into the fabric of everyday life so thoroughly that it is hard to pick out or pinpoint any particular one as something that must be changed. Those responsible for the noxious arrangements are everywhere, rendering them (as targets) nowhere. Thus, who exactly segregated the work force and lunch counters in the American South? The answer is everyone and therefore no one in particular. The relation between the parties in such a conflict is "loosely coupled" in the diffuseness of responsibility and of ambiguity of appropriate *specific* targets.

In contrast, to target *particular businesses* of downtown Birmingham with direct action demands for *specific* change *now* is to create a *tightly coupled* conflict. Such specificity creates a taut relation between the SMO and the target. Each reacts to the moves of the other in day-to-day— even hour-to-hour or minute-to-minute—responsiveness (which includes intransigent nonresponse to which the SMO responds).

Let us, then, examine transformation of a loosely into a tightly coupled conflict—the creation of confrontation and crisis featuring escalating and flexible, multiple tactics.

1. Initiation: Economic Boycott Begins, April 3–11. The initiating and centerpiece tactic in the overall strategy was an economic boycott of downtown Birmingham businesses that began on April 3, 1963, just less than two weeks before Easter Sunday, April 14. This period was selected because it was a "prime shopping season" and a boycott therefore put all the more pressure on downtown business. Economic rather than political elites were targeted for desegregation demands because, at that time, blacks "lacked voting strength," but they "had sufficient buying power so that withdrawal could make a difference" (King 1964, 56, quoted in Morris 1993, 626).

Each afternoon was marked by a march downtown and was accompanied by picketing and sitting in. The boycott began to take hold and the number of daily protesters was credible but not large.

2.   *Escalation and Lull: Injunction Violation, Other Tactics, April 12–May 1.*   Downtown business people refused to negotiate and city authorities obtained a court-ordered injunction against the daily marches and protests. Many ACMHR leaders wanted to obey the injunction and call off the marches and associated protest acts. But King decided to march in defiance of the order. Accompanied by Ralph Abernathy and only forty others who had agreed to be arrested, all were arrested and jailed. At least one thousand onlookers present, however, made an impressive protest scene.

"King and Abernathy remained in jail until April 20. However, . . . support for the movement increased, as did demonstrations. . . . Throughout April, picketing and sit-ins continued in the downtown business district" (Morris 1993, 628).

"[But] by early May, neither local economic elites nor national elites had shown any willingness to concede to the demands of the movement. At this point, movement leaders intensified the struggle by making good on the promise to create widespread social disorder. The time had arrived to implement the plan for mass arrests that would fill the jails and stage mass demonstrations that would disrupt the economic and social activities of the city" (p. 629).

3.   *Children's Escalation, Violent Confrontation, May 2–7.*   The opening move in this strategy of escalation was to have previously trained and organized school age children march to the downtown on "D Day," **Thursday, May 2.** Seven hundred were arrested, filling up the jails.

More children marched on **Friday, May 3,** and, because the jails were full, authorities attempted to disperse rather than arrest them, using high-velocity water hoses and police dogs. About one thousand were arrested, nonetheless. A large number of national media were now on the scene and pictures of the water hosings and police dogs attacking were major, national news stories on Friday, May 3, and Saturday, May 4. In particular, an especially shocking picture of a fifteen-year-old boy being "whirled . . . into the jaws of a German Shepherd" appeared on the front page of the *New York Times* (and in other papers) and came instantly to "symbolize Birmingham: a white policeman in dark glasses grasping a Negro boy by the front of the shirt as his other hand gave just enough slack in the leash for the dog to spring forward and bury its teeth in the boy's abdomen" (Branch 1988, 760).

The shocking still and moving pictures of children so treated flashed across the nation and marked the turning point. At last, "the Birmingham movement was taking off. The burden of inertia was shifting" (Branch 1988, 762). Also, movement-supportive celebrities of several sorts began arriving in Birmingham, notably, Dick Gregory and Joan Baez.

The **Saturday, May 4,** march began to meet with violence and was aborted, although 150 marchers were arrested.

"On **Sunday, May 5**, the mass march continued without arrests" (Morris 1993, 630). At this time, businessmen began to meet with black leaders, but with no agreement.

"A monumental march designed to intensify the developing crisis" went forth on **Monday, May 6th** (Morris 1993, 630). It featured complex units and waves of children, some two thousand of whom were arrested along with about five hundred adults. Labeled the "largest single day of nonviolent arrests in American history . . . [,] the movement was becoming a tempest" (Branch 1988, 771). The black community of Birmingham was now thoroughly energized by the campaign and numerous evening mass meetings were overflowing. At one of these meetings this Monday evening, King declared: "There are those who make history. There are those who experience history. . . . You are certainly making history, and you are experiencing history. . . . Never in the history of this nation have so many people been arrested for the cause of freedom and human dignity" (King quoted in Branch 1988, 773).

Branch (p. 777) refers to **Tuesday, May 7,** as "Birmingham's nonviolent Bastille Day." Despite strenuous police efforts to seal off the downtown, by numerous ingenious means devised by key organizers, thousands of "young Negroes broke . . . into the downtown enclave [and] jammed the sidewalks and streets in wild celebration of triumph and possession, paying little attention to the august businessmen who were obligated to go around them or, coming upon a patch of sidewalk literally carpeted with sit-ins, to step over them. [There were what] King proudly called 'square blocks of Negroes, a veritable sea of black faces.' Newspaper estimates of their number would run upward from three thousand. Joyous, weaving procession burst out of segregated stores, then back in again. . . . Wincing [police] commanders explained to the business leaders that they were making no arrests because the jails would hold no more, and they could not otherwise clear the area without teargassing or shooting up the downtown sanctum itself" (Branch 1988, 777).

Branch characterizes the tumultuous events of May 7th as striking the downtown business people "with revolutionary force." Under pressure from many and diverse sources—including even President John Kennedy—key business people this day "empowered a committee to negotiate a settlement" (Branch 1988, 780). Working through the night, agreement was achieved and announced the next day, **Wednesday, May 8.**

Morris's analysis of this episode is framed as a refutation of the frequently encountered thesis that movement leaders set out to provoke police violence in Birmingham (which they knew would not be difficult in that violence-inclined city often also called "Bombingham") and they succeeded in doing so. This nationally shocking police violence led to various pressures on local elites, forcing them to capitulate to the movement.

Morris's counterthesis is that movement leaders set out, instead, to create "the total breakdown of the business community and [to] create widespread social disorder." It was "social disorder, not violence [that] provided the leverage for success" (Morris 1993, 631). His evidence for this counterthesis consists of a detailed documentation of the increasingly *varied* and *intense* tactics that were devised and executed on the principle that "everything must build" (p. 626; Branch 1988, 689). Morris gives particular attention to the innovative complexity and scale of the tactics employed on the climatic day of May 7, the day designed "to accomplish the total breakdown of the business community and [to] create widespread disorder." The extremely complex plan, which in fact came off successfully, went, in part, as follows.

The movement's main task was to have thousands of demonstrators reach the business district without being blocked by police, dogs, tear gas, or high pressure water hoses. Several measures accomplished this.

- First, the demonstrations were to begin at noon rather than the usual one o'clock starting time. Not only would the new starting time be a surprise, but many police would be at lunch doing the noon hour. . . .
- Second, small groups of protesters would serve as decoys to attract police attention, while hundreds of demonstrators from various points across the city headed for the business district. . . . Once the police began chasing the decoys and demonstrators, a final burst of hundreds of demonstrators would stream from the original church, now left virtually unguarded.
- Moreover, . . . designated activists throughout the city would sound false fire alarms to draw the attention of social control agents and embellish the crisis with wailing alarms. (adapted from Morris 1993, 631–32)

As described above, the downtown of Birmingham was paralyzed the afternoon of May 7 and, Morris reports, "the business community realized they could no longer tolerate the crisis and would have to negotiate a settlement. . . . This had not been [their] view . . . that morning" (p. 632). But astounded by the multitudes, the businessmen, according to King, "realized that the movement could not be stopped" (King 1964, 104, quoted in Morris 1993, 632).

Morris thus concludes that "the evidence clearly suggests that the crisis produced by the economic boycott, massive demonstrations, mass arrests, picketing, defiance of the injunctions, and sit-ins forced the settlement" (1993, 633).

Precise assessment of the relative influence of several causal variables in unique historical cases is not only difficult, it is, in the logic of the matter, impossible to do with much certainty. Even so, it is also likely the case that no one independent variable is unambiguously dominant in determining an outcome such as movement success. Instead, multiple factors are more plausibly determinants of success. In the case at hand, Morris is probably correct in faulting researchers who have thought of official violence and its external pressure consequences as *the main* variable causing success in Birmingham. But, on the other hand, I think it is equally one-sided for Morris to propose movement strategic mobilization as *the main* variable in that success. Instead, there is the obvious and more credible third possibility that both kinds of variables—violence and mobilization—contributed to success, each in its own way and at different times.

D. Great Turns and Periods of History

The variables affecting SMO success or failure reviewed immediately above focus on relatively mesoscopic or even microscopic matters: organizational characteristics (Section A), position in a spectrum of radicalness (Section B), scale and breadth of strategic mobilization (Section C).

Above and beyond all such variables, though, are the large and imponderable matters of the major forces of and turns in history on the grand scale. In the same way that immense earthquakes, fires, and storms literally crush, burn, or blow away even the most robust human plans and projects, large periods in and turns of history can stifle or kill SMOs—as well as sweep them to victory. Consider this example of stifling:

Active at and after the turn of the century, the radical labor union the Industrial Workers of the World (IWW or "Wobblies") was, by all estimates, not especially successful in organizing American workers, but at least it slogged along and survived with some vigor. As a declared opponent of capitalism and all it stood for, the union had, of course, many enemies, but also substantial pockets of labor support. But then, in 1917, two great turns of history caught the Wobblies. These were the American declaration of war on Germany in April and the Bolshevik coup in Russia in October. The IWW condemned the war and the public came increasingly to define the union as unpatriotic and as "sinister and alien" (Goldberg 1991, 60). Sympathetic with the revolutionary changes then going on in the new Soviet Union, IWW members were also denounced as revolutionary subversives. The upshot was that, in the context of the red scare of the period, Wobblies were physically attacked in various ways, many leaders arrested and deported, and "by 1922, nineteen states had outlawed membership" in the union (Goldberg 1991, 62). While the IWW would likely have failed for many more meso-microscope reasons [as Gamson (1975) documents], these great turns of history pushed it lower than mere failure and into virtual extinction.

In recoding the Gamson dataset I describe above in Section A, Jack Goldstone has argued that, indeed, such *overwhelming exogenous factors* of history seem to him more important than the organizational factors that Gamson studied. In fact, Goldstone finds that Gamson's successful SMOs cluster in six periods of time in which they were successful rather than being evenly distributed over the years of their operation (1800–1945). He argues that these six clustering periods of success were *also* periods of "broad crises" in American society. Therefore, the "near-perfect match between periods of [SMO] success and periods of broad crises" suggests that "the incidence of large-scale crises, rather than organizational or tactical efforts of particular [SMOs], determines the timing . . . of success" (Goldstone 1980, 1040, 1042).

*　*　*

Of course, myriad factors other than those above enter into the effects of SMO strategies and SMO success. Particular vulnerabilities of the targets selected are among these (Walsh 1986; Nelkin and Poulsen 1990; Geschwender 1983; Mirowsky and Ross 1981; Shlay and Faulkner 1984; Stark 1987).

V. OTHER QUESTIONS AND ANSWERS ABOUT STRATEGY

In this chapter I have given prime attention to only three of the eight generic questions that guide researchers:

Generic question (1), What are the aspect's types? addressed in Sections I and II as similarities and differences in SMO strategies.
Generic question (6), What are the aspect's causes? addressed in Section III as factors affecting section of strategies.
Generic question (7), What are the aspect's consequences? addressed in Section IV as effects of strategies and SMO success.

Generic questions not addressed are, of course, those of frequency, magnitude, structure, process, and agency. Of these, I want briefly to point up the importance of the two questions of process and agency.

1. Answers to the question of "what are SMOs' strategic processes?" move in at least two directions. The first is a depiction of the internal phases or stages of a given strategy. The summary of Aldon Morris's analysis of the Birmingham campaign I give in Section IV.C illustrates such a dissection of a process in terms of its internal stages.[9] The second form of process analysis is "external," in focusing on the succession of strategies through time (McAdam 1983). Such strategic change or succession is commonly in reaction to other entities in the SMO environment. Because of this, succession is appropriately considered in the next chapter as an aspect of the topic of "reactions" to SMOs.

2. The generic question of agency focuses our attention on SMO strategizers as exactly that: strategizers. One form of this focus is on what such thinkers have themselves to say about strategizing. It happens that many of them have set their thoughts on paper and these reflections have become even quite famous documents of strategy that have been and still are read by real and would-be movement leaders for enlightenment and inspiration. These are among the more famous and historically influential:

Michael Bakunin, *Catechism of the Revolutionist*[10]
Vladimir Illyitch Lenin, *What Is To Be Done?*[11]
Adolph Hitler, *Mein Kampf*[12]
Mao Tse-tung (Zedong), *Quotations From Chairman Mao Tse-tung*.[13]
Saul D. Alinsky, *Reveille for Radicals*[14] and *Rules for Radicals* (1972)

These and the many other reflections of their kind are not dispassionately social scientific, but such documents nonetheless merit careful study for at least two reasons. One, many express theories of action that their writers successfully carried out in reality. Such practical success suggests that at least some of what they claim may well be true. Two, fully to understand why people act as they do, one must understand how they define their situation. Empirically valid or not, reflections like those listed are more or less accurate reports of what the writers thought they were doing and why. To fathom their authors and their SMO actions, we must comprehend their cognitive constructions. This alone is not enough, of course, but it is an important stop on the road to understanding.

* * *

So far in this guide, we have focused on (1) the SMO or an aspect of it or (2) the SMO's point of view.

- From the first vantage point we have thus examined organizational structure (Chapter 6), causes of SMO formation (Chapter 7), and individual joining (Chapter 8).
- From the second, we have attended to beliefs (Chapter 5) and strategies (Chapter 9) in a way that looked over the shoulder of the SMO.

Both these vantage points are fine and necessary, but each also neglects at least one additional and major focus: the point of view of *reactors* to SMOs together with their varied *reactions*. This is the vantage point to which we turn in the next chapter.

NOTES

1. In his analysis of fifty-three challenging SMOs, Gamson (1974, 41–45, 28–37) labels "control" a "displacement" goal and "concession" is termed "new advantages."

2. Although I do not it report it in Section II, after the analysis I summarize above, Turner and Killian go on to offer a theory of when concessions, control, or separation will be adopted as a main strategy, as the "main power objective."

3. Etzioni (1961), Gamson (1968), who uses the terms constraints, inducements, persuasion, and Boulding (1989), who speaks of the "three faces of power."

4. These are among movement how-to manuals that provide step-by-step instructions on each of the five: Staples (1984), Kahn ([1982] 1991), Bobo, Kendall, and Max (1991), Brockway (1992), McEachern (1994).

5. In addition to the chapter-length activist analyses of media cited in the previous note, Ryan (1991) is an excellent full-scale treatment of the media from a movement/SMO view. In addition, see Gamson (1990, Ch. 10; 1995), Gamson and Wolfsted (1993).

6. Causal accounts of collective violence conceived as competing theoretical schools are surveyed by Rule (1988). On objections to conceiving causal accounts as theoretical schools, see Lofland (1993b) and Section VI of Chapter 13 in this volume.

7. Laqueur (1987), White (1989), della Porta (1992). Other statements of factors conducing given types of strategy include Turner and Killian (1987, 303–6) on the causes of nonviolence.

8.   And, there is at least one additional reanalysis: Frey, Dietz, and Kalof (1992). Brill (1971) provides a case study that might be seen as an in-depth example that supports Gamson's generalizations.

9.   In addition, process-cast depictions of strategy appear frequently in how-to manuals. These suggest what to do before, in, and after "actions" and "campaigns" on a specific issue. Thus, in Staples's guide (1984, 155–63), John Beam's depiction of "actions from start to finish" suggests the process phases of reconnaissance, covering the bases, preparing the participants, in action, debriefing.

10.   Written in 1866 and multiply published since then. Often also attributed to Sergei Nechayev and even presently published under his name (e.g., Nechayev 1989). This dispute about authorship is discussed in Gross (1974, 134, 159).

11.   Published in Germany in 1902 and republished in many languages and numerous countries. See, e.g., Lenin ([1902] 1989).

12.   Published as two separate volumes in 1925 and 1926 and subsequently combined. Numerous editions and translations, including Hitler ([1926] 1962).

13.   Several editions and languages including the 1966 first English edition (Mao 1966). This is also called "the little red book" because of its pocket-size dimensions and red plastic cover. Like some other bibles, this edition also has a string page marker (in red, of course).

14.   Originally published in 1946, republished 1969. Springer and Truzzi (1973) provide a very useful compendium of the strategic thinking of a wide variety of historically important revolutionaries of varied political leanings.

10

What Are Reactions to SMOs?

I use the term "reactions" to refer to the space- and time-proximate ways in which outsiders take action with regard to an SMO. Herbert Blumer captures this aspect well when he declares that a movement "has to carve out a career in what is practically always an opposed, resistant, or at least indifferent world" (1957, 147). As (recall) *insurgent* realities, the social going for SMOs is bound to be rough in many ways. As Blumer suggests, the reaction may be indifference, at best—a response that does not jibe well with moralism and idealism. More likely, reactions run to the actively negative along any number of dimensions. But despite this more dismal side, some SMOs also nonetheless elicit positive reactions and, over time, their reality-claims may even become "everyone's" beloved mainstream commonsense.

The purpose of this chapter is to review varied responses to SMOs, from whom particular responses are likely to come, and for what reasons. Before proceeding, though, we need to understand main provisos and perplexities that attend the concept of "reactions" and to specify and clarify them. Like most other ideas, that of "reactions" is clear enough on first viewing, but gets murkier when looked at more closely.[1]

I. THE CONCEPT OF REACTIONS

Reactions as an area (or aspect) of SMOs requires specification and clarification along at least six lines.

A. SMOs versus Reactors as Vantage Points

First, outsider responses to an SMO *could* be conceived as *effects* or consequences of the SMO. While one *can* conceptualize outsider reactions this way, I prefer not to do so because of the difference in vantage point invoked by each. Reactions viewed as SMO effects adopts the vantage point of the SMO. This is what we did at the end of the previous chapter in speaking of the effects of SMO strategies and SMO success. And we will do so again in the next chapter, which addresses SMO effects as I will now define them.

Both of these efforts are fine, but they use the SMO vantage point in terms of which to construct analysis—as the "unit" of analysis. An *additional* vantage point that we also need is that of *outsiders* to the SMO. Adopting this vantage point, we examine outsider lines of action from their point of view—from over their shoulders. As an intellectual operation this parallels what we did for SMOs regarding strategies in the previous chapter. Indeed, "reactions" of outsiders might also be labeled strategies of outsiders—and in places below I will do so.

The trickiness or slipperiness in this vantage point distinction is that researchers sometimes tend to move from one to the other (or back and forth) in a way that confuses discussion. Therefore, care must be exercised consistently to maintain a single vantage point—or clarity as to the one used at any time.

B. Reactions versus Effects

Reactions as a unit of analysis requires specification and clarification, *second*, because of difficulty in deciding which outsider responses are space and time *proximate* and which are not. Some responses are clearly proximate in that the reactors are interacting with the SMO in close-in space and in ongoing "real time." But just how soon in time and close in space should a reactor respond reasonably to be thought of as having relevantly responded? Does a response from the other side of the globe and decade after the SMO's demise count as a reaction? The trickiness here is that the more distant a reaction in space and time, the more likely researchers are to conceive it as an *effect*. Thus, the list of space- and time-distant effects of movements I review in the next chapter is in one sense also all reactions. However, these are placed in the next chapter and analyzed as effects rather than reactions because they are at considerable distances in space and time from the SMOs and movements in question. But, again, how long and how far must this be?

C. Reactions versus Reactors

Reactions are tricky and require specification, *third*, because of the need to distinguish between *reactions* and *reactors* and to deal with them conjointly and systematically in analysis. A *reaction* is a reactor's pattern of action oriented to an SMO. A *reactor*, on the other hand, is some extra-

SMO person, organization, category of actors, or other "grouping" doing the reacting. At the simplest level—the *case* level—the reactors are simply specific people and organizations. A researcher can make a list of them and describe their activities. But in quest of generic propositions, researchers want to go further and to conceptualize (to categorize) such specific people and organizations at the *generic* (generalized) level (Chapter 4, Section I.B).

A first major challenge at this level is to devise an accurate and fruitful set of generic categories of reactors. At this time, however, there is no such agreed-upon scheme. Indeed, there are relatively few efforts even to formulate one. However, putting comprehensive schemes aside, several generic or generalized categories of reactors have been proposed with some frequency and a few have even been studied. Drawing together diverse sources, these generic reactor categories include:

- *Ruling elites*—policymaking and associated strata targeted by an SMO in an effort to achieve or resist social change or otherwise to promote an insurgent reality.
- *Dissident elites*—elite strata who doubt the wisdom of the actions of the ruling elites regarding an SMO and who support the SMO in some fashion. This grouping includes *elite funders*, persons or organizations of significant discretionary wealth who fund SMOs.
- *media*—the means of mass communication, including television, newspapers, magazines, books, videotapes.
- *Similar SMOs*—SMOs in the same or different social movement whose beliefs and actions create the presumption of possible mutual support, aid, alliance, or coalition in one or more ways.
- *Counter-SMOs*—citizen forces mobilized expressly to counter a particular SMO or movement more broadly.
- *Beneficiary constituents*—people perhaps not participating in the SMO but in whose name it speaks and who are asserted to benefit from the SMO's actions.
- *Conscience constituents*—people not thought directly to benefit from the SMO but who are sympathetic with it and who, taken collectively, form a field of allies for the SMO.
- *The public*—the mass of the spectator public whose positive or negative opinions are often objects of contest between SMOs and other interaction partners.
- *Bystander publics*—that portion of the public primarily concerned with the risks and inconvenience an SMO may be creating for them (rather than with the issues in dispute) and who demand that authorities "do something" to end their risk and inconvenience.

Again, this is a rough and provisional list of reactors and not an elegant depiction of the social landscape in which SMOs function.

D. Reactions versus Reactors in Organizing Analysis

Fourth, the distinction between reactions and reactors presents us with two axes of variation in terms of which researchers organize investigations. On the one hand, researchers inspect *reactions* as a generic and irrespective of particular reactors. The result is a statement of reactions per se, with only subsidiary reference to how each reaction is associated with particular reactors.

On the other hand, researchers can focus on *reactors* and inspect the reactions of each of them. The result is a statement of who the reactors are, with subsidiary reference to how each has reacted.

These two possibilities for organizing analysis are shown in Figure 10.1, which cross-classifies these two dimensions. Reactions are shown vertically (the columns) and reactors are shown horizontally (the rows). In focusing on reactions, analysis proceeds from left to right in terms of categories of reactions. Alternatively, in focusing on reactors, analysis proceeds from top to bottom through the rows in terms of categories of reactors.

In a world of infinite information, time, and other resources, the ideal course of action might well be to do both of these and even to do both simultaneously. Alas (perhaps), no one lives in such a world. Instead, researchers make hard choices and, for the most part, have elected to examine responses within categories of reactors rather than reactions as

Figure 10.1.   Two ways to organize analysis: reactions versus reactors.

		Reactions			
		1	2	3	n
Reactors	1				
	2				
	3				
	n				

a generic category. This being the case, I am likewise constrained in how I review research on reactions. Because the existing literature is organized by "reactor reactions" rather than by reactions per se, I employ that mode of organization in this chapter. Moreover, the several categories of reactors listed in Section I.C have not been investigated with equal degrees of thoroughness, and my review is therefore further constricted by a lack of much in terms of empirically grounded generic propositions to report regarding some of them.

E. Reactions versus Interactions and Relationships

Fifth, there is yet an additional vantage point that might be the central unit of analysis: the *interaction* between an SMO and its several reactors. Instead of looking over the shoulders, so to speak, of the SMO or reactors, the researcher focuses on the interaction and *relationship between* these two units (the SMO and the reactors). While little research has explicitly employed interaction or relationship as the unit of analysis, some has. Because this is an especially promising unit of analysis, I include instances of it below and point up their significance. And in Section V, I focus on interaction processes per se.

F. Scope, Scale, and Dramaturgy of Reaction

Last, I used the three dimensions of scope, scale, and dramaturgy to organize a review of SMO strategies in the previous chapter. In the sheer logic of analysis, these same three dimensions are equally pertinent to analyzing outsider reactions. Unfortunately, the literature is so heavily organized by reactors instead of reactions that has proved too difficult to apply these dimensions in any thorough way. Within categories of reactors, I do, though, point up scope, scale, and dramaturgy differences where these can be seen with clarity.

II. PRIMARY REACTORS AND TYPES OF REACTION

As I say above, researchers have attended to some reactors more than to others. I reflect this here in devoting one section each to five of them that are "primary" in both the degree of attention they have been accorded and in their importance. Following explanations of these, I briefly describe some additional categories of reactors.

A. Ruling Elites

I use the term "ruling elite" to designate whatever mainstream group-ing an SMO targets for action or otherwise identities as "the opposi-tion." Quite often (and perhaps increasingly) such elites are government officials at some level. But in the logic of the matter, they need not be. For example and quite prominently, insurgent workers may identity the managers or owners of enterprises for which they work as the relevant "ruling elites." Or, where unions are entrenched and corrupt, workers may identify union leaders as the pertinent "ruling elites" against whom SMO insurgency is undertaken.

Among religious or egocentric (personal transformation) SMOs, rul-ing elites may be conceived in vague or abstract ways such as the "prin-cipalities of this world" or "oppressive society." In such conceptions, "ruling elites" are encompassing, omnipresent, and diffuse.

The orienting conception of elites I have just given is "phenome-nological," meaning that it uses *SMO depictions* to identity pertinent elites. This might be fine and sufficient for many purposes, but it may be insufficient for others. Among these other purposes, researchers often also need an independent assessment of who is "elite" in order to be able to talk about those elites that are *not* targeted by SMOs, but who *might* be and which elites are and are not targeted for what reasons. Such questions require *structural* rather than only phenomenological conceptions or criteria of elites.

Structural criteria for identifying elites vary among themselves in terms of their narrowness or broadness. Toward the narrower end of this variation, some researchers are comfortable thinking of elites as only a "finite number of people relatively proximate to state power" who are "an inner circle making or benefiting from the political order" (Meyer 1990, 94). Many other researchers, though, prefer a broader conception of elites as "people with a disproportionately large share of political resources, including status, money, and political access, who can aid or constrain a movement's development" (p. 94).

The broader and narrower structural conceptions of elites are useful or not as a function of what the researcher is trying to do. Thus, in the three schemes for thinking about ruling elite reactions I recount below, the reference is sometimes one and sometimes the other and each high-lights different matters.

1. Basic Forms of Reaction. Thinking in terms of the broadest sweep of possibilities for reacting, Roberts and Kloss (1979) have propounded the following five patterns of what they call "negating the negation" or "elite controls of social movements." The first three focus more on manipulating the symbolic environment—*framing* the movement—and the last two stress the use of physical force to "destroy or render harmless" an SMO.

[1] **Studied Ignorance.** Likely the most common and even effective response in many situations is for ruling elites (or other targets) studiously to ignore an SMO and its efforts. Because an SMO likely has limited resources for mobilization, the elites hope that those resources will be depleted and the SMO will collapse before a response is required. The elite fear (and often the reality) is that a reaction can be used by the SMO as an energizing and resource mobilizing new target. Therefore, elites try to deprive the SMO of any such target by not reacting.

[2] **Ridicule.** If a reaction is elected, ridicule in the forms of demeaning and dehumanizing characterizations of the insurgents is one early form of attempt to discredit a movement. Thus, feminists have been subject to labeling such as "ladies lib," "bra-burners," and "femi-nazis." This is "trivialization of movements through manipulation of symbols" (p. 192).

[3] **Co-optation and Minimal Reform.** Co-optation is the strategy of solicitously offering SMO leaders opportunities and favors of various kinds in the hope that such advantages will cause them to scale down their demands and thus separate them from their memberships. "Bribes such as the ones offered Emiliano Zapata are the most overt examples of such a ploy. Yet more subtle pressures and appeals can be made as well" (p. 192).

Cordial foot dragging is among prominent forms of co-optation and minimal reform. In this, elites declare their sympathy with the demands of the SMO, say that these demands must be studied, and undertake to conduct elaborate elite-SMO joint investigations. Elites deploy their investigative resources to develop materials that make the situation ever more complex and difficult to fathom. Time drags on and on, SMO resources decline, and the matter peters out in a mire of complexity and a welter of conflicting factual and value claims.

From a movement viewpoint, an even more insidious elite response is what movement skeptics label *pseudoembracement through neutralizing reinterpretation*. Elites publicly proclaim to have come over to the movement view and are prepared to accept the demands and to incorporate them into its practices. From the movement's perspective though, what is embraced and accepted is superficially what was demanded but changed in significant ways and even gutted. Thus, some such analysts suggest that the mainstream acceptance of Martin Luther King, Jr., and the citizen ideals he represents is only of him as an idealistic "dreamer" rather than as the hard-headed radical leftist about power and race that he actually was (Rockwell 1992). The theme of the pseudoembracement thesis is, indeed, similar to if not the same as the common charge that Christmas is more about commerce and greed than about the message of the carpenter from Nazareth. In the environmental arena, the term *greenwash* is used to identify such pseudoembracement by corporations and other ruling elites with regard to environmental actions. These elites vigorously proclaim their commitment to the environment, but, so say movement skeptics, the actions of these same elites belie their professions.

[4] **Surveillance, Agent Provocateurs, Assassination.** Ruling elites with their own surveillance and police or security forces have with considerable frequency deployed them to (1) infiltrate, observe, and report on SMOs; (2) recruit informers among SMO members; (3) infiltrate and entice SMO people to engage in violent or violence-provoking strategies (a role termed *agents provocateurs*): and (4) murder or arrange for the murder of SMO leaders.

The point of surveillance is, of course, to gather information that can be used, among other ways, to demoralize or discredit SMO leaders. Among the most infamous of such efforts has been the extensive efforts of the FBI to "neutralize" Martin Luther King, Jr., by threatening to publicize information it thought discredited him (Roberts and Kloss 1979, 194).

Surveillance and infiltration has on occasion taken on bizarre proportions. In his detailed analysis of the role of the agent provocateur, Gary Marx (1974) has observed, for example, that "in the early 1960s about 1,500 of the estimated 8,500 members of the United States Communist Party were F. B. I. agents" (quoted in Roberts and Kloss 1979, 194).

[5] **Unofficial and Official Violence.** Less directly and pointedly organized than the pattern just described, by inaction and subtle approval ruling elites may seek to create an environment in which antimovement mob and other *unofficial* violence is encouraged in such forms as lynch mobs. Members of the Industrial Workers of the World are historically notable recipients of several forms of such unofficial violence (Goldberg 1991, Ch. 4). [See also Evans (1983) on the climate of inaction and sympathy that encouraged the Ku Klux Klan to engage in unofficial violence.]

Official violence, in contrast, is undertaken openly by the police or military agents of the ruling elites. Although often framed by elites as unauthorized, a tragic error, or an unfortunate and dire necessity, the fact that officials have done it nonetheless sends a movement-chilling message. Historically notable instances in the U.S. experience of the 1960s and 1970s included police/military killings of students at Southern University, Jackson State, and Kent State (Roberts and Kloss 1979, 196). Members of the Black Panther Party were objects of a quite complex set of episodes of such official violence.

2. Government Efforts to Damage or Facilitate. Roberts and Kloss display some basic responses of ruling elites at a relatively general level. Focusing less broadly and on *government* as a type of ruling elite, Gary Marx (1979) has documented an array of inhibiting actions undertaken in the 1960s against SMOs and their leaders by agencies of the U. S government and local governments. While these data are specific to that period, the patterns Marx identifies are generic in character and are therefore of interest to us here.

[1]   Creation of an Unfavorable Public Image

Public labeling of a social movement . . . is affected by what [government] leaders say about it. . . . Image-damaging information may be given friendly journalists [and] may involve passing on information about arrest records, associations, life-styles and statements of the targeted person or group that are thought likely to hurt the movement. . . . In the case of the New Left, FBI agents were [instructed by their superiors] that "every avenue of possible embarrassment must be vigorously and enthusiastically explored."

[2]   Information Gathering

The largest single activity of control agents with respect to social movements has probably been information gathering. . . . In roughly descending order [techniques of this] include:
Collection of news items, movement documents, membership lists.
Informers. . . .
Attendance at public meetings and demonstrations.
Still photography and videotape.
Background investigations using public and private records and interviews. . . .

[3]   Inhibiting the Supply of Resources and Facilities

Social movement organizations need money, means of communication, services and supplies, and physical space. Government actions may be taken to restrict a movement's access to these. . . . The government may seek to discover the source of an organization's funding. Efforts of varying degrees of legality may then be carried out to dry up larger sources of contributions. . . . The tax-exempt status of social movement organizations or those contributing to them may be chosen for auditing on strictly political grounds and then revoked. . . . Those renting offices or providing office or meeting space to a movement may be encouraged not to do so.

[4] Derecruitment

Beyond trying to stop a movement from expanding, the government may try to reduce the movement's size and weaken the morale and degree of commitment among those currently active. . . . [E]mployers, parents, neighbors, friends, or spouses may be contacted, sometimes anonymously, in the hope of encouraging them to dissuade or threaten activists. . . . Activists may encounter direct appeals from government agents who point out the risk they face, argue matters of ideology, give them damaging information about others in the movement, and threaten them. . . .

[5] Destroying Leaders

Because social movement leaders are symbolically and instrumentally important, movement-damaging activities often focus on weakening them as the most visible and presumed central part of a movement. . . . They may be subject to . . . surveillance, harassment, assaults, and threats. They may face a variety of legal sanctions, such as injunctions against demonstrating, grand jury inquiries of a fishing expedition nature, arrest on false or vague conspiracy charges, and excessive bail and sentences. Tax difficulties may be created for them. . . . Co-optive efforts may be undertaken. There may be efforts to displace them, as the government infiltrates its own people into the movement who become leaders or build up a rival group. The campaign against Martin Luther King included most of these tactics . . . and Communist, Klan, black militant, and New Left leaders have faced similar efforts.

[6] Internal Conflict

A major aim of domestic counterintelligence activities has been to create internal conflict by encouraging factionalism, jealously, and suspiciousness among activists. Schisms based on disagreements over tactics, goals, or personalities may be created and encouraged. . . . Key activists or those known to be violent may be anonymously and falsely accused of being informants or set up to make it appear that they are, in the hope that they will be attacked, isolated, or expelled.

[7] Encouraging External Conflict

Conflict between the movement and groups in its environment may be encouraged in the hope of damaging and diverting it from the direct pursuit of broader social change goals. In extreme cases, this strategy involved the encouragement of armed conflict. . . . Action aimed at preventing coalitions and cooperative actions may be undertaken. . . . A related tactic involves creating alternative social movement organizations.

[8] Sabotaging Particular Actions

Movements often have a loose and shifting nature, are geographically dispersed, and frequently lack specialized internal resources. When national or regional meetings or demonstrations are held, out-of-town members must be housed and fed. Goods and services must be obtained from secondary sources. Strangers are brought together ostensibly in cooperative action but without the usual means of verifying identify. These factors make public social movements vulnerable to disruption. Those seeking to disrupt a movement are offered a rich field for intervention. Tactics of misinformation have been used to notify members falsely that events were canceled, that they were being held elsewhere, or that times had been changed. (Marx 1979, 96–105)[2]

Although Marx concentrates on ways in which U.S. governmental elites have tried to inhibit or damage specific SMOs and broader movements, he acknowledges and also discusses the fact that, on occasion, these elites undertake to *facilitate* at least certain forms and kinds of SMOs. Before 1960, "the major beneficiaries of facilitative efforts were right-wing, anti-civil rights, and management groups [that have] tended to involve countermovements and often vigilante-like action" (1979, 106). In the 1960s, "the federal government legitimated the civil rights movement and put resources into voter registration and initiated the War on Poverty and community action, and [in] the 1970s . . . women's rights gained considerable support" from the government (p. 106).

In addition, ruling elites may seek simply to *manage* rather than to damage or facilitate insurgent realties. McCarthy, McPhail, and Crist (1995) have documented this response in terms of the "public order management system" that several national governments have devised over the last two centuries.

3. Counterframes. Recall from Chapter 9, Section II.C.1, that how issues are *framed* is an important variable in SMO strategy. Now, on the other side, mainstream elites (and other reactors) must decide how to respond to such claims, should they elect overtly to respond at all. As reported above, "studied ignorance" combined with various covert efforts to damage the movement may be the preferred courses of action.

But if elites elect to come up with a public and "reasoned" response to claims made in SMO frames, they need *counterframes* or, in the terms of Ibarra and Kitsuse, "counterrhetorical strategies" (1993, 38).

As conceptualized by these analysts, these counterrhetorical strategies "fall into two classes":

> (1) *sympathetic* counterrhetorics, which accept, in part or whole, the problematic status of [the matter addressed] but which . . . block the request for remedial activities; and
>
> (2) *unsympathetic* counterrhetorics which countenance neither the proposed characterization and evaluation nor the suggested remedies. (p. 39, emphasis added)

Ibarra and Kitsuse describe five *sympathetic* counterframes:

> [1] *Naturalizing* is a move that accepts the assessment proposed while rejecting the call for action. . . . Well, what did you expect? Of *course* society is violent. . . .
>
> [2] [In] *the costs involved* [the matter] must be lived with rather than remedied . . . because "two wrongs do not make a right," or . . . the "benefits" do not outweigh their "costs" [as in, for example, eradicating] racism in the workplace might involve "reverse discrimination"; pornography is the "price" of free speech. . . .
>
> [3] [In] *declaring impotence* [the counterframer registers] moral sympathy while pointing to an impoverishment of resources at hand. [For example, a counterframer may say,] Yes, racism is a problem, but it is futile to try and do away with it until class oppression is countered. . . .
>
> [4] [In] *perspectivizing* . . . the claim is characterized as an opinion. In the locution, "You're entitled to your opinion . . . " [the counterframer] avers the [framer's right to participate] while simultaneously placing a check on that participation by implying that the [counterframer] need not, as a matter of opinion, subscribe to . . . the same view or the call for remedies. . . .
>
> [5] *[T]actical criticism* . . . accept[s] the characterization of [the issue], but demur[s] in the means the claimants employ. "Yes, women are oppressed, but do those feminists have to be so militant and strident about publicizing the fact?" is an example here. (pp. 39–40)

Unsympathetic counterframes or rhetorics oppose the characterization of the issue given in the SMO frame and, therefore, whatever remedy is put forth. Ibarra and Kitsuse describe four forms of this.

> [1] *Antipatterning* holds that the claim has not [provided evidence of being] a full-scale social problem . . . , but rather is focused on . . . "isolated incidents." This was a characteristic response to charges of sexual harassment on college campuses in the 1980s. [Antipatterning issues a] challenge for the claimant to verify the magnitude of the

[matter at issue] or specify the meaning of terms being used [as in] "what counts as sexual harassment?" . . .

[2] [T]he *telling anecdote* presumes to invalidate a claim by virtue of citing an instance . . . illustrating that the generality of the analysis offered by claimants is suspect. . . . To the charge that smoking is a problem since it causes cancer can come the response, "My grandfather smoked a pack a day and lived to be a good eighty years and then some." The telling anecdote thus [holds the frame] accountable to invariability instead of likelihood. Therefore, claims couched [as] scientific generalization are particularly susceptible to the usage of this strategy. . . .

[3] In . . . the *counterrhetoric of insincerity* [the SMO framer] is suspect because of a "hidden agenda" [, variations on which are career advancement and] securing or gaining power, status, or wealth. . . . Thus [for example], prolife men are involved in the movement to reassert masculine privilege. [This theme is] often delivered in the shape of "sincerity tests"; if prolifers really care about children, then why don't they do something about malnutrition or children in poverty?

[4] [T]he *counterrhetoric of hysteria* [suggests] that the moral judgment of the claimant is not based on a "sound" assessment . . . but is under the influence of "irrational" or "emotional" factors. Thus, . . . the involvement of "Hollywood liberals" in efforts to "save the Amazon rain forest" is yet another demonstration of their susceptibility to "faddish causes." [Reactors] are instructed to note that the claims display (cultlike) features of the claimants' subcultures, rather than matters of concern to the "mainstream" of society. (pp. 41–42)

Ibarra and Kitsuse stress that effects of any of these counterframes or rhetorics are very much dependent on the specific contexts in which we find them used. One key research task is therefore investigation of "the kinds of uses these strategies are good for, and the kinds for which they fall flat" (p. 42).

B. Dissident Elites

The patterns of reaction I report as often observed among "ruling elites" are primarily unsympathetic, to say the least. While such reactions are commonly observed, they are, taken alone, frequently a skewed view. This is because *some* sectors of societal elites may react more sympathetically. As groupings, these elites are sometimes labeled "dissident" or "patronizing," as in "elite patronage."

From among the eight generic questions a researcher might ask about these elites, I here focus on the questions of their variations (their types), the causes of their dissidence, and this dissidence's consequences.

1. Types.   Dissident elite reactions vary in terms of offering support and encouragement of various kinds as distinguished from taking up actual SMO membership as a rank-and-filer or leader. I elect here to confine discussion to the former type of reaction because joining per se is discussed in Chapter 8 and the variables listed there also apply to elites who join SMOs (as well to other joiners).

However, this distinction between giving support and encouragement from outside an SMO and being a member of an SMO or a movement is a tricky one. Sufficient, persistent support and encouragement can become, in a way, membership, at least in a movement if not in a specific SMO.

Within dissident elites as a category or "grouping" it is sometimes important to give separate attention to the form of elite organization called "the foundation," which is a tax-advantaged fund established to give money to what are defined as worthy projects. Taken as a class, in American society such foundations—such *funding elites*—have had significant influences on many SMOs and the larger movements of which they are a part (as I will report below).

2. Causes.   The Nuclear Weapons Freeze movement of the 1980s had quite considerable dissident elite support and encouragement, which David Meyer has elucidated in terms that are helpful in thinking about generic causes of the "defection of the elites" (1990, Ch. 6).

> First, by definition, elites are privileged in education, income, leisure, positive sense of self, and sense of efficacy. Having no concern with primary needs such as food, clothing, and shelter, such persons can afford to take a broad and empathetic view of the situations of other less well situated people and to concern themselves with the large policy issues facing society (as in, for example, foreign policy). Many elite persons are not so "broad visioned," of course, but, even so, many elite persons *do* demonstrably form a more generous and compassionate view of people less fortunate than themselves and of social policies that are mean-spirited and belligerent. Sheer elite privilege and auspicious, socially responsible socialization, then, can be factors prompting elite dissidence (Flacks 1976, 1988).
>
> Second, and in a "more cynical view," elites may be privileged in various ways, but they are not all equally privileged and they sometimes jockey among themselves to *protect* existing privileges that are threatened, *enlarge* existing privileges relative to other elite sectors, or *restore* privileges that have been lost or are slipping away. In this sense, dissident elites may be using an SMO (or movement more generally) as an element of a *strategy of struggle among elite groupings*.

In this view, elites are rarely if ever united and stable. They are differentially affected by social changes, and some sectors are rising while others are falling. Insurgent realities may be seen as useful corporate actors to manipulate as pawns in these intra-elite struggles. Thus, in the case of the Freeze, Meyer suggests that the dissidence of some elites was a "rear-guard action against a new ascendant group, designed not to empower new groups but to prevent the entrenchment of a new elite. . . . Many of the architects of U.S. defense policy for the 20 years before Reagan's presidency attacked the new administration's policies. [This] old guard, while ostensibly allied with those demanding radical changes in U.S. defense posture, was far more concerned with restoring previous foreign and military policies" (1990, 95).

Third, elites may simply disagree on how best to becalm an insurgent reality. Most centrally, elites need to decide whether it is best to strike a hard line or to be conciliatory in getting control of an SMO or movement. This and other decisions like it are exceedingly difficult to make because of the inherent uncertainty involved in predicting the consequences of alternative courses of action. Therefore, elites with equal interests in maintaining the status quo can in all good faith radically disagree on exactly what actions best advance their shared objectives of becalming a social movement. What appears to be dissidence, then, may simply be tactical disagreement over how best to deal with insurgency. As Meyer puts it, "an apparent transfer of allegiance or a defection may actually be something quite different" (1990, 96).

3. Consequences. The following are among the varied possible consequences of elite support and encouragement that Meyer (Ch. 6) mentions in his discussion of elite support for a nuclear freeze and that I have drawn from other sources:

- Members of the SMOs at issue can be heartened or even inspired by the emergence of elite support. The strength and resolve of the SMO as an entity may thus be strengthened
- The fact of elite support may be constructed as "news" and therefore the object of news coverage. As discussed below, this can advance an SMO by giving it "standing," even if the coverage involves neither preferred framing or sympathetic treatment (Section C).
- Third parties not otherwise inclined to see an SMO or its demands as legitimate are persuaded otherwise by the example of sympathy offered by dissident elites. Initially indifferent or hostile par-

ties are prompted by the example of dissent elites to "take another look" at the SMO and even to change their minds.

- By definition, elites of all sorts have more resources than other citizens, including, especially, access to monetary and political resources. Support and encouragement sometimes translate directly into such resources.
- The desire to gain, maintain, and/or enlarge dissident elite support can prompt SMO strategizers to frame their issues and select their strategic actions in ways that will not offend elites. In this way, elites can have a becalming or constraining effect on SMOs. Specifically, the lure of elite support tends to cause them to shy away from disruptive actions because, Francis Fox Piven and Richard Cloward argue, "in their search for resources to maintain their organizations [organizers are] driven inexorably to elites, and to the tangible and symbolic supports that elites [can] provide" (1977, xxii).
- Although perhaps not intended by elites, some researchers have argued that their monetary support of SMOs—especially in the forms of foundation grants—has a becalming effect on wider insurgency through selective funding of SMOs that are more moderate. Craig Jenkins and Craig Eckert have attempted empirically to evaluate this proposition with data on the civil rights movement of the 1960s. They come to the cautious conclusion that while elite financial support "may have accelerated movement decay," it "did not transform movement goals or tactics" (1986, 812). Rather than supporting a strong "social control" or "co-optation" thesis regarding elite funding, Jenkins and Eckert counsel a "channeling" metaphor: "The social control effects of patronage . . . are more subtle and indirect than a simple cooptation thesis would assume. . . . Quite clearly, it channeled the movement into professionalized forms. But it did not divert the movement from the black power agenda or unruliness" (p. 828).
- And, effects of elite support are even more complicated and changing from circumstance to circumstance. Thus, in another study also involving Craig Jenkins, this time with Charles Perrow, the proposition is that in yet other circumstances success in organizing a successful SMO presence is facilitated by elite support. The circumstances under study were efforts to unionize California farm workers. Efforts to do this failed before the success of Caesar Chavez's United Farm Workers (UFW). Jenkins and Perrow asked themselves how the UFW effort differed from earlier ones in ways that might explain UFW success. Their answer is summed up in this proposition:

▶ A major cause of successful union organizing among California migrant agricultural farm workers in the 1970s was new and broad support among elite sectors of the society.

Raised to the generic level of abstraction and generalization, the proposition is:

▶ As the degree of support by elite sectors for a disadvantaged group increases, the chances of successful organizing among that group increases.

The above is my propositional "gloss" of the Jenkins and Perrow study, which is not phrased in such elite-pointed terms. Their language is, instead:

> What produced the sharp difference in outcome was the difference in political environment encountered. [A major previous effort] received token contributions, vacillating support for its boycotts and confronted major acts of resistance by public authorities. In contrast, the UFW received massive contributions, sustained public support for its boycotts and encountered a more "balanced," neutral official response. (Jenkins and Perrow 1977, 266)

C. Media

The term "media" is shorthand for "media of mass communication" and it is a label for the set of large organizations that collect and disseminate words and pictures to large numbers—"masses"—of people. Most prominently, these mass communicators are newspapers, television, radio, and magazines. As collectors, selectors, and disseminators of words and pictures—of *frames of meaning*—the media are the quintessential location of the *mainstream*. In fact, their contents are among the first things any SMO researcher wants to look at in answering the question, What *is* the mainstream? in the sense of what is the current reigning view of what is true, reasonable, and moral.

Consonant with the concept of the "mainstream" I employ in this guide, Gamson and Wolfsfeld have referred to the media as speaking "mainstreamese," that is, a discourse of cultural codes that is in large part uncontested, "a realm where the social constructions rarely appear as such to the reader and may be largely unconscious on the part of the writer as well. They appear as transparent descriptions of reality, not as interpretations, and are apparently devoid of political content" (1993, 119).

From among the larger set of possibilities, I here report on two questions that have especially preoccupied SMO researchers regarding the media:

(1)   How do media react to SMOs? This is a variable, of course, and media react differently to different SMOs and to the same ones over time. Even so, certain dominant tendencies in reactions are also apparent, researchers claim.

(2)   What factors enter into explaining why the media exhibit some rather than other reactions to SMOs?

1. Trends and Variations in Media Reactions.   As regards the first question and answers to it, Gamson and Wolfsfeld (p. 11) have suggested three ways in which media reaction—or what they call "coverage"—importantly varies:

(1)   *standing,* that is, the extent to which the [SMO] is taken seriously by being given extensive coverage, regardless of content;
(2)   *preferred framing,* that is, the prominence of the group's frame in media discourse on the issues of concern; and
(3)   *movement sympathy,* that is, the extent to which the content of the coverage presents the group in a way that is likely to gain sympathy from relevant publics. (p. 11, emphases added).

Viewed in terms of this profile of variables, researchers have observed, first, that major media organizations tend to deny even *standing* to most SMOs on most matters, must less preferred framing or sympathetic coverage. Recall that, above, Roberts and Kloss refer to this reaction from ruling elites as "studied ignorance," the decision to act as though an insurgent reality does not exist even though it is known about. Thus modern societies abound in an increasingly rich and complex array of insurgent realities that the mass of citizens simply never hear about if they only attend to the mainstream media of mass communication (Croteau and Hoynes 1994).

If, through a turn of events or SMO strategizing,[3] media elect to do coverage, researchers observe that the content tends not to provide the SMO's preferred framing or to be very sympathetic [variables (2) and (3)]. Instead, media framing tends to feature what Todd Gitlin terms *deprecatory themes,* such as these devices that he observed used in early 1965 national television's newscast framing of the Students for a Democratic Society:

•   *trivialization* (making light of movement language, dress, age, style, and goals);

- *polarization* (emphasizing *counter*demonstrations, and balancing antiwar movement against ultraright and neo-Nazi groups as equivalent "extremists");
- *emphasis on internal dissension;*
- *marginalization* (showing demonstrators to be deviant or unrepresentative);
- *disparagement by numbers* (undercounting);
- *disparagement of the movement's effectiveness.* (pp. 27–28, emphases in the original)

Gitlin additionally reports that anti–Vietnam War protest "turned to more militant tactics" later in 1965 and, in response, television coverage added "new themes and devices" such as these:

- reliance on statements by government officials and other authorities;
- emphasis on the presence of Communists;
- emphasis on the carrying of "Viet Cong" flags;
- delegitimizing use of quotation marks around terms like "peace march";
- considerable attention to right-wing opposition to the movement, especially from the administration and other politicians. (p. 28, emphases omitted)

The three tendencies not to give SMOs standing, their preferred framing, or sympathetic coverage are, of course, exactly that: *tendencies,* albeit rather strong or even overwhelming ones in many if not most cases.

Nonetheless, *some* insurgent realities *do* manage to break through to standing, preferred framing, and sympathetic coverage. The civil rights movement and its component SMOs of the 1960s are among conspicuous, successful instances in these three terms. Indeed, as the first major *televised* social movement in human history, such supportive reactions of television itself are reckoned by many observers to have been among major variables contributing to the degree of success that movement achieved.

In addition, there is the irony that for many SMOs and their movements, the variable of *standing* has a "spigot" quality: It is either turned completely off or suddenly it is turned completely on. From *not* (or barely existing) in media consciousness, some collection of SMOs is abruptly the central object of media attention. Jo Freeman (1975, Ch. 5) has likened this sharp change to the rapid, overnight emergence of mushrooms, thus terming it. *the mushroom effect.* Freeman discusses the mushroom effect as it worked in the women's movement of 1970, but it has also been documented for a number of other movements as an element of a larger *interaction process* of synergy in the surge of many SMOs simultaneously (Lofland 1992, Part II). (As but one component of such a process, I will return to media as an element in interaction processes in Section V.B.)

2. Causes of Varying Reactions.   If media coverage varies in terms of (1) standing, (2) preferred framing, and (3) sympathetic treatment, what are causes of these variations?

Discussions of the causes of variations in these three aspects of media reactions often focus on their movement-negative states: failure to give an SMO standing, the framing it desires, and sympathetic treatment. Research and theory is so focused, of course, because these three treatments are thought to be far more common than their opposites. Indeed, there is a fairly large literature dedicated to understanding negative media treatment of movements. In her *Prime Time Activism*, Charlotte Ryan summarizes this literature as focusing on three classes of variables that help explain this movement-negative dominant tendency of media (1991, Ch. 1).

The *first* set of these variables deals with the internal workings of the media as organizations whose workers develop daily routines that disfavor SMOs. Often also termed *gatekeeper* variables, attention is focused on, as the name suggests, news gathering and reporting as a highly selective process that opens the media "gate" only to certain "credible" and routine "sources." Thus, news organizational practices, such as a *selected* set of "beats" that reporters cover routinely while other possible "beats" are ignored, massively mitigate against covering a great many SMOs (much less preferred framing or sympathetic coverage).

A *second* set of variables calls attention to "larger structures shaping news production" (p. 9). Sometimes termed the *propaganda model*, the central thesis is that the rich and powerful own the media and purchase its ongoing control by means of advertising, thereby ensuring that insurgent realities will not be covered or will be covered in unsympathetic ways. In their *Manufacturing Consent*, Edward Herman and Noam Chomsky conceive this effect as the product of a series of *filters* that operate to "filter out the news fit to print, marginalize dissent, and allow the government and dominant private interests to get their messages across to the public" (1988, 2). These authors point to four major levels of such filters:

> (1) the size, concentrated ownership, owner wealth, and profit orientation of the dominant mass-media firms;
>
> (2) advertising as the primary income sources of the mass media;
>
> (3) the reliance of the media on information provided by government, business, and "experts" funded and approved by these primary sources and agents of power;

(4) "flak" as a means of disciplining the media. . . .

These elements interact with and reinforce one another. The raw materials of news must pass through successive filters, leaving only the cleansed residue fit to print. They fix the premises of discourse and interpretation, and the definition of what is newsworthy in the first place, and they explain the basis and operations of what amount to propaganda campaigns. (Herman and Chomsky 1988, 2, as quoted in Ryan 1991, 15)

A *third* set of variables "focus[es] on the role of the news in the dialectic between social being and social consciousness" (Ryan 1991, 9). Conceived at this broad and abstract level of "being" and "consciousness," media are seen as but one factor in the larger effort of dominant institutions—the mainstream—to determine how people construct reality. The broad and diffuse action of this effort has been referred to as the *process of hegemony*, which is a system of

if not usurping the whole of ideological space, still significantly limiting what is thought throughout the society. The notion of hegemony . . . is an active one: hegemony operating through a complex web of social activities and institutional procedures. Hegemony is done by the dominant and collaborated in by the dominated. (Antonio Gramsci quoted by Ryan, 18)

Broader than organizational and power-holder independent variables, this third class of determinants draws attention to unspoken, simply assumed *cultural codes* or cultural mind-sets that mainstream dominant institutions hegemonically sponsor and the mass of the population collaborate in by accepting.

Referring to these cultural codes or mind-sets as the "dominant realm of discourse," Todd Gitlin's depiction of the "fundamental and inescapable dilemma" of movements captures the all-pervading nature of the cultural hegemony that helps to explain media non- or unsympathetic coverage:

If [an SMO] stands outside the dominant realm of discourse, it is liable to be consigned to marginality and political irrelevance; its issues are domesticated, its deeper challenge to the social order sealed off, trivialized, and constrained. If, on the other hand, it plays by conventional political rules in order to acquire an image of credibility—if, that is, its leaders are well-mannered, its actions well-ordered and its slogans specific and "reasonable"—it is liable to be assimilated into the hegemonic political world view; it comes to be identified with narrow (if important) reform issues, and its oppositional edge blunted. (Gitlin 1980, 290–91)

Taking these three classes of variables together, they suggest this proposition:

‣ Media coverage of an SMO (and larger movement) is
    (a) small or nonexistent,
    (b) not the SMO preferred framing, and

  (c) unsympathetic
to the degree that the SMO activities and beliefs
  (a) do not mesh with the organizational routines of the media,
  (b) challenge the interests of dominant power-holders, and
  (c) go against the dominant cultural codes (the "dominant realm
      of discourse").

In also asking the question of determinants of media coverage of movements, Gamson and Wolfsfeld offer this additional hypothesis, one that is consistent with Gitlin's observations given just above:

▶ The narrower the movement's demands, the more likely it is to receive coverage that presents it sympathetically to a broader public. (1993, 123)

In his path-marking essay titled "Media and Movements," Harvey Molotch (1979) very usefully frames the relation between SMOs and the media as an instance of the much broader phenomenon of "doing news" in any situation, not simply in the media of mass communication. Specifically, virtually everyone "does news" in their daily lives and especially with people with whom they are acquainted but not intimate. Thus, it is common and even obligatory in everyday life to ask an again-encountered associate, What's new? Think, then, about how we—all of us—"do news" with the people we meet in daily life. Molotch rightly suggest, I think, that we do not report just "anything" or a random assortment of things as news. Instead, we tailor the news we give to "a sense of relevancies derived from our" life in common with the person to whom we are giving news. We take account of our associate's known interests, our shared and separate biographies, our own interests, and many other matters. Thus, in encountering a faculty colleague, Molotch reports of himself:

> I may answer with talk about a paper I am writing, a student who passed an exam, a piece of dirt on an administrator we both dislike. Although I am called upon to talk about "anything," I *know* that not anything will do. I do not, for example, tell my colleague about my love life, my most recent meal, my sister's operation, or my growing dislike of my colleague's best friend. Yet all these details might, in a different context, be the appropriate and called-for reply to the question "What's new?" (p. 74)

Molotch is careful to point up that in tailoring our new-giving, we are *not* simply being cynical and "telling half-truths, withholding information, or distorting the facts" (p. 74). Instead, we are striving to be "responsive to the goal of being *interesting*."

And what strikes one as interesting emerges from the context surrounding both the speaker and listener. Ordinarily, a piece of information that does not facilitate my own goals is less interesting to me than one that does. The fact that a highway I use on my way to work is closed to traffic is more interesting than the fact that another, "irrelevant" highway is closed. My listener has an analogous set of *news needs,* and my ability to provide for those needs is the degree to which I am interesting to him. The skilled conversationalist apprehends things as "interesting" based on these two criteria. (p. 75)

Molotch therefore reasons that "two things are hence at work when I do news."

[1] I must provide replies that suit the relevancies and news needs of the other; and

[2] I must strive to provide self-serving particulars that will enhance my own goals or at least be neutral to them (p. 75).

He concludes that

News is, accordingly, *purposive behavior,* and doing news is important survival work. Certain people are more skilled than others because they have more talent, are structurally located in an advantageous power status, have greater access to knowledge of particulars and alternative schemes of relevance, and . . . have easier access to media, which provide an opportunity to serve the news needs of others while simultaneously enhancing goals of one's own. (p. 75, emphasis added)

In thus viewing "news" as something we *all* do for the purposes of being interesting while also advancing our own goals, it is perhaps easier then to understand that the media of mass communication are doing exactly the same things. They want to be interesting but they also, like the rest of us, want to advance their own goals or at least to protect their own interests. It follows that in the same way we tailor our face-to-face news-giving, the media tailor theirs (Croteau and Hoynes 1994). Given that prominent media goals are corporate profit and advertising revenue, treatment of SMOs consistent with those goals ought not surprise us. Instead, inquiring minds should to be surprised if it were any other way.

D. Similar SMOs

On a naive first viewing, it might seem that SMOs with similar beliefs and strategies would be quite friendly with and mutually assistive of one another in their common or shared fight against the mainstream. The empirical facts of the matter are virtually the opposite. While conflict and cooperation form a *variable,* the state of this variable moves as much or more often in the direction of conflict as of cooperation. In their discussion of conflict and cooperation among similar SMOs, Zald and McCarthy offer this proposition as to when such relations move in the conflict direction:

> ◆ Under conditions of declining availability of marginal resources, direct competition and conflict among SMOs with similar goals can be expected to increase. (Zald and McCarthy 1987, 164)

In addition to "declining . . . marginal resources," it needs to be appreciated that similar SMOs are often competing for much the *same* resources with an SMO "product" that is only marginally different from its competitors. This very similarity makes such SMOs threats to one another: their products are competing in the same market (and for) the same "buyers." In contrast, markedly different SMOs are much less of a threat because they do not compete for the same clientele. Hence this ironic proposition:

> ◆ The most bitter and even deadly conflicts are often between those SMOs that distant outsiders can barely distinguish in terms of beliefs, organization, and other major features (cf. Benford and Zurcher 1990).

(The broader and more generic proposition underlying this one is that the most intense conflicts arise in relations of close interrelation and dependence, as discussed in Kriesberg 1982 and Pruitt et al. 1994.)

Nonetheless, in some circumstances, cooperation does occur even among similar SMOs. Zald and McCarthy formulate this proposition about such circumstances:

> ◆ Social control [e.g., state repression] produces increased cooperation among SMOs when the social control efforts threaten the very existence of a number of SMOs. (1987, 172)[4]

This is the SMO-specific version of the well-known generic proposition that a common enemy makes friends of foes, i.e., "my enemy's enemy is my friend."

E. Counter-SMOs (CSMOs)

Some researchers use the term "countermovement" to designate reactions to movement bearing these earmarks:

1. relatively organized and enduring efforts,

2.   arising specifically to oppose—to "counter"—an initial SMO,
3.   that are themselves insurgent realities.

By means of the first of these earmarks, broad, diffuse, and atomized "backlash" against broad social movements in a society are excluded as countermovements and best treated as public-at-large reactions, or in terms of the particular groups reacting (e.g., the media, entertainment industry). Thus, in *Backlash*, Susan Faludi (1991) reviews themes of popular culture, intellectual discourse, and mainstream political action over the 1980s that can be seen as "backlash" reactions to the women's movement that arose in the 1970s. While the broad and diffuse backlash activities Faludi delineates are certainly important, they are not countermovements per se (cf. Mottl 1980).

Pertinent to the second earmark, a portion of Faludi's survey nonetheless includes SMOs devised specifically to oppose feminists SMOs and their proposals. In this way, Faludi also treats "countermovements" in discussing, for example, the Concerned Women for America and the Eagle Forum. Key to this second earmark, these SMOs oppose specific feminist SMOs rather than some nonmovement/mainstream social grouping or social circumstance.

Therefore, in the context of SMO study as distinct from the broader topic of social movements, the core countermovement case is that of an SMO formed specifically for the purpose of countering another SMO or set of them. More precisely speaking, these are "counter-SMOs" (and can be abbreviated CSMOs) (Mottl 1980).

Clarence Lo provides these examples to further clarify the difference between CSMOs and other reactions: "An anti-pornography crusade is not a countermovement, because pornography stems not from a social movement but rather from small businesses. Movements to teach a creationist theory of human origins or to prohibit sex education are not countermovements because the opponents are not social movements but professions" (1982, 119).

The realities organized to oppose initially insurgent realities are themselves, by definition, also highly contentious, marginal, or excluded from the mainstream. This "by definition" earmark is necessary because of the importance of distinguishing countermovements from the actions of ruling elites, dissident elites, media, or yet other mainstream groupings. To the degree that efforts opposing an SMO use a mainstream construction of reality and are carried on by mainstream groupings, researchers focus on them as such. Here, instead, we want to isolate the CSMO "dark twin," so to speak, that SMOs sometimes generate.

Because researchers have focused so heavily on "progressive" or "left" movements, there has been a tendency to equate countermovements with conservative or right-wing reactions to left movements. But as

McAdam, McCarthy, and Zald observe, "such labeling serves little analytic purpose and may be contradicted in fact" (1988, 721). For example,
some of the most active and successful CSMOs are ideologically left and
dedicated to discrediting and otherwise undoing radical right, especially
neo-Nazi, SMOs. The champion such CSMO in the recent United States
is, of course, the Southern Poverty Law Center, which has effectively
used the courts to harass and even annihilate neo-Nazi SMOs.

It follows from the above that a key image of (or template for) thinking
about CSMOs is that of an "interacting pair" (Lo 1982, 119), which is
engaged in an "interactive dance." In this "chesslike interactive dance"
(Zald and Useem 1987), CSMOs spend their time "attempting to undo
the effects" of the initiating SMO or SMOs (McAdam et al. 1988, 721;
Bromley and Shupe 1993).

Following the instructive analysis of Zald and Useem (1987), the
phrases "interacting pair" and "interactive dance" ought not, though, be
construed as suggesting a "tightly coupled" relation of conflict between
the SMO and the CSMO. Drawing from general theories of conflict, by
"tightly coupled" Zald and Useem mean conflict relations in which the
feuding parties are in close physical and/or informational proximity,
such that each party has rapid and rich knowledge of the actions of the
other and believes it is necessary quickly to respond to the actions of the
other. This tight coupling produces a pace and intensity of exchange that
is prone to escalation.

While some few SMO-CSMO relations are on occasion tightly coupled
in this fashion, more commonly the conflict is "loosely coupled." The
antagonists operate at some physical distance from one another; information on the other's actions travels slowly and less than fully; and
immediate, hurried, or crisis responses are not usually thought necessary. At this distance there are also time and inclination to attempt to
draw in various sorts of third parties as allies or pawns, a possibility that
is more difficult in the close encapsulation of tightly coupled conflicts.

1. CSMO Formation. CSMOs may be the "dark twins" of initiating
SMOs, but every SMO (or movement more generally) does not necessarily have one or more of them. Like SMOs, CSMOs are themselves a
variable: Sometimes they form and sometimes they do not; or some
SMOs generate more of them than do others. One question then is,
Under what conditions do CSMOs appear (or not appear) and with what
rapidity, frequency, and magnitude?

Of course, the same factors that account for initial SMOs are likely also
involved in accounting for CSMOs. If that is true, we need only apply to
CMSOs the eighteen causes of SMOs reviewed in Chapter 7. But in the
same fashion that not all of the eighteen variables reviewed in that

chapter are equally and always pertinent to every SMO, a specialized profile of *more* pertinent causes might apply to CSMOs. In that spirit, Zald and Useem (1987) have proposed four variables that may be among the more relevant in understanding CSMO "mobilization," the term they use to mean formation, magnitude, and frequency taken together.

Zald and Useem label the *first* of these variables *movement success*, which refers to the degree to which the initial SMO and its larger movement are rapidly and thoroughly achieving their goals. Their hypothesis is that early signs of possible success, without success yet, encourages CSMO formation. *But* the relation is curvilinear: if the initial movement "wins a huge, crushing victory" with some rapidity, possible CSMOs are "paralyzed as supporters see little chance of success" (p. 254). Viewed in terms of the variables reported in Chapter 7, this is a version of variable (18), "the degree of belief in the necessity and effectiveness of forming."

Zald and Useem label their *second* variable *appropriate ideology*. This refers to "the development of an ideology that arouses enthusiasm and creates commitment" (p. 255). Being a variable, opponents of an initial SMO/movement may lack a "frame" that aligns with potential members and larger publics [variable (17) in Chapter 7]. In its absence, mobilization is retarded. These authors suggest that such a deficit likely accounts for the rather slow crystallization of antiabortion CSMOs following the Supreme Court decision legalizing it in the United States: "Only with the development of an ideology about the relationship of abortion to family life and the role of women in society was the antiabortion movement able to draw on a broader constituency" (p. 255).

CMSOs like other SMOs depend on the availability of "discretionary recourses to invest in collective action," a *third* variable that Zald and Useem label *availability of resources* (p. 255). In Chapter 7, I reviewed the degree of presence and absence of such resources as the variables of (4) the degree of prosperity, (14) the degree of communication networks and similar resources, and (16) the degree of situational availability, among others. Potential CSMO formers and members are often *not* fortunately situated in terms of such resource variables. When they are not, CMSOs are retarded.

Fourth and last, Zald and Useem suggest that "the public agenda may or may not 'permit' the emergence" of CSMOs (or SMOs) (p. 256). Labeling this the variable of *constraints and opportunities*, they point to how "wars, depressions, the existence of other movements, and the focus on other events [may] crowd the [public agenda] space" for CSMOs (as well as for SMOs) (p. 256). In Chapter 7, I reported on this as variable (2) the degree of political opportunity. In addition to the degree to which the public agenda is already crowded, political opportunity refers to how "political structures vary in the opportunities they provide to movements" (p. 256).

2. Astroturf CSMOs and Counter-Counter-SMOs.   The above discussion of CSMOs assumes that they—like SMOs—are "true" movements in the senses that they have their own "mobilized membership, organization, and leadership" (Lo 1982, 119). The main alternative possibility is, of course, that the CSMO has been funded and organized by ruling elites and is really and merely a front for elite efforts to counter given SMOs (as mentioned in Section II.B).

While this ruling-elite strategy has a long history, there is some suggestion that such CSMOs have increased in numbers in recent years. Befitting their use of new technologies, some wags have labeled them "astroturf" movements, striking a technological contrast with "real" or *grass roots* movements, that is, with SMOs with their *own* "membership, organization, and leadership" (p. 119). From among hundreds of recent instances consider, for example, the Coalition for Equal Access to Medicines. Describing itself as an "'ad hoc volunteer organization' composed of poor people, minority members and public health advocates," *In These Times* recounts a *New York Times* report that this organization was "actually created and financed by the prescription drug industry" ("Corporate Grassroots" 1993, 7).

The initial SMOs targeted by these burgeoning astroturf CSMOs have, of course, wondered exactly who is after them. They have done research and the result is the hypothesis that astroturf CSMOs are, as mentioned, on the rise. Indeed, one response to the rise of these and other kinds of corporate front groups is a new class of SMO, the *counter-counter-SMO* (CCSMO). Making up a third level of organization (SMO/CSMO/CCSMO), these entities monitor CSMOs (grassroots and astroturf) opposing initial SMOs, as well as carry on broader monitoring activities. The Center for Media and Democracy, publisher of *PR Watch,* is one of the more prominent and active CCSMOs. In addition, some SMOs have internal units or projects specializing in monitoring CSMOs and publicizing their existence. Products of these efforts include Public Citizen's *Masks of Deception: Corporate Front Groups in America* (Public Citizen 1991) and Greenpeace, USA's *The Greenpeace Guide to Anti-environmental Organizations* (Deal 1993).

III. OTHER REACTORS

As reported, there have been few attempts generically to depict types of reactors to SMOs, and extant efforts have an ad hoc and disjointed quality. The five "primary" reactors I have reviewed above—ruling elites, dissident elites, media, similar SMOs, and counter SMOs—have some currency in research. But beyond them, proposed categories of reactors are sketchier, murkier, inconsistently defined, and overlap the five reactors reported on above. Such additional candidate reactor groupings include the ideas of "beneficiary constituents," "conscience constituents," the public at large, and "bystander publics" (McCarthy and Zald 1987b, 21–24; Turner and Killian 1987, 225–26).

In a rendering that straddles McCarthy and Zald's and Turner and Killian's differing treatments just cited, *beneficiary constituents* can be defined as people for whom the SMO claims to speak and who would presumably benefit by SMO successes (as well as suffer from its failures). Depending on whose usage one follows, beneficiary constituents may or may not be members of the pertinent SMO.

Conscience constituents consist of persons who do not stand directly to gain from SMO efforts but who provide support and encouragement for the SMO and who, in McCarthy and Zald's usage, might also be members of the SMO. Of course, this category overlaps with that of dissident elites, all of whom are conscience constituents, but not all conscience constituents are dissident elites.

Distinguishing between beneficiary and conscience constituents helps researchers to see that SMOs can have variable and even ironic relations between and among who is acting and who is claimed to benefit from that action. Thus, a society can develop a quite sizable strata of affluent people who can be conscience constituents of a wide variety of SMOs dedicated to causes from which they do not stand to benefit in direct ways. As Zald observes: "children, whales, and dogs are the object of concern of foundations, voluntary associations, professional groups, and professional schools" (quoted in Gamson 1987, 7). Indeed, these examples illustrate how it is possible for an SMO not to have *any* beneficiary members and to be speaking for a beneficiary constituency who is ignorant of or even opposed to the SMO.

Although they do not use a vocabulary of beneficiary and conscience constituency, Adamson and Borgos are making this distinction when they juxtapose "grass roots protest" SMOs and "left-wing political" SMOs in *This Mighty Dream* (1984), a lively treatment of farmer, labor, African American civil rights, and urban tenant movements in American history. These four movements—complex collections of SMOs—share the characteristics of acting on "specific and immediate grievances experienced by masses of people at the bottom of society" who were *themselves* collectively responding to those grievances to further their *own* interests (p. 13). Such acting *themselves for themselves* on *proximate* grievances makes them "grass roots protest." In contrast, historical "left-wing political" movements, which perhaps even "enshrined the 'working class,' in practice recruited their membership from all economic and occupational strata" (p. 14). And members of these SMOs engaged in ideological discussion of the state of society in general more than in action on the immediate work and everyday life grievances of their members. In the present terms, American left-wing SMOs have had more conscience than beneficiary constituents.

The concept of the conscience constituency begins to point to the wider (and widest?) reactor of all: people in general in a society—a "unit" of reaction variously labeled the "public," "public at large," or "mediating public" (Turner and Killian 1987, 205). To the degree that SMOs and the primary reactors take public-at-large reactions seriously and therefore seek to influence them, the interaction among these groupings is a contest over what *public definition* or image of a movement will prevail.

A first step in understanding public definitions or images of SMOs is to specify what appear to be the several major types of these definitions or images. Turner and Killian's effort to portray such types proposes that "the public views movements in four different ways":

[1] *respectable-nonfactional*, as in "many charitable movements, reli-
    gious movements like the Billy Graham crusades, the move-
    ment to 'support your local police,' and earthquake and other
    emergency preparedness movements. . . . They receive wide-
    spread lip service from respectable community leaders and
    little, if any, organized opposition."
[2] *respectable-factional*, which are "competing movements offering dif-
    ferent solutions to the same problems."
    Both of the two above types are respectable in that their "leaders
    can appeal for financial contributions and other resources from a
    wide spectrum of people and organization and recruit adher-
    ents and supporters broadly and openly."
[3] A movement publicly defined as *revolutionary*, in contrast, "will be
    met with public intolerance and often with violent government
    suppression. Movement advocates will be denied normal access
    to institutional and governmental decision-makers."
[4] "Between respectable and revolutionary movements there is an-
    other category of movements viewed as odd, queer, or *peculiar*.
    [Many] 'crackpot' schemes to change the world are more pecu-
    liar than threatening so long as they lack political clout and
    attract few adherents and sympathizers. Although they de-
    nounce. major values in society, they are thought to be harmless
    and consequently are tolerated and granted considerable access
    to legitimate means for promoting their objectives. They are

opposed largely through ridicule, isolation, and ostracism of
their members rather than repression or violence" [Turner and
Killian (1987, 256–58, adapted; see also Richardson (1992)].

A *first* key sociological proposition about public images or definitions is:

▶ Public definitions have an existence that can and should be empirically ascertained separately from whatever an SMO "really" is as
assessed by researchers or other observers.

So focusing on public images as having their own reality and life, researchers are then alert to how SMO labeling may change (or remain
constant) as a function of factors that relate only in part to how an SMO
may or may not be changing. Thus, Turner and Killian observe that "the
difference between a revolutionary and peculiar [public] definition is
often simply a matter of apparent strength or weakness. [A] change
from one label to the other is [therefore] frequent" (p. 257). That is, how
an SMO is publicly characterized may be a function of what is believed
about it rather than of how it has itself changed (cf. Best 1989). And
public images of SMOs can change because of historical events unre-
lated to the SMO rather than because of changes in the SMO. In describing "great turns and crises of history" in Section IV.D of Chapter 9, I
recounted one well-known instance of such great turning and its effect
on the Industrial Workers of the World (as well as on many other socialist SMOs) in the "red scare" of the late teens and early twenties. In that
case, the onset of World War I and the occurrence of the Russian Revolution, both in 1917, precipitated a radical shift in how left-wing SMOs
were publicly defined quite apart from the behavior of those SMOs.

A *second* key sociological proposition about public images/definitions
relates them to how SMOs are organized and function in a broad range
of ways. Tuner and Killian posit a very strong link between pubic definition and SMO organization and functioning:

▶ How . . . [an SMO] is publicly understood and defined will have
more effect than the views and tactics of typical adherents on the
sources from which it can recruit adherents and accumulate resources, the type and tactics of opposition and official control with
which it must cope, and the degree to which it can operate openly
through legitimate means. (1987, 256, emphasis omitted)

As this proposition is stated, it is close to a thesis that public definition is
the all-determining causal factor in the state and functioning of almost

all aspects of SMOs. Put differently, if we want to explain why an SMO is organized and otherwise works the way it does, we only have to look how it is publicly defined.

Indeed, Turner and Killian go on even to incorporate the famous and generic *self-fulfilling prophecy* proposition into the above proposition. A movement *not* what it is currently labeled can *become* what it is labeled as a consequence of that label:

> ▶ The label of revolutionary attached to a movement can be a self-fulfilling prophecy. (p. 256)

In having to adopt illegitimate means as a consequence of being labeled revolutionary, such actions provide evidence that the revolutionary label was right in the first place and strengthens the public definition of the SMO as revolutionary.

Last with respect to "other reactors," Turner and Killian have identified the *bystander public* as that segment of the population that has "no stake in the outcome" of an SMO in conflict with whoever the reactors, but who are "in danger of being injured so long as the conflict continues" (p. 216). "The bystander public defines the primary issue as restoration of order and elimination of danger and inconvenience by bringing *any* end to the conflict. The bystanders' slogan is 'a plague on both your houses'" (p. 217, emphasis in the original).

Turner and Killian hypothesize that when SMO-target conflicts are disorderly and drawn out, bystander publics focus their attention on *authorities* responsible for maintaining public order and increase their demands on them rather than on parties in the conflict itself. Under this pressure, authorities then fear that the public will define them (the authorities) as incompetent in maintaining order, thereby jeopardizing their positions. This fear prompts authorities to increase their involvement in the SMO-target conflict in the hope of bringing it to a quick end. When and how they so intervene often has decisive effects—such as prompting concessions or repressing one or both of the parties. Sometimes, heavy-handed, repressive treatment of SMOs in this intervention can itself become a prime issue that wins new allies for the SMOs.

IV. POTPOURRI OF OTHER REACTIONS

The foregoing focus on reactors and their reactions neglects many reactions that are not specific to particular reactors or that are may be found among many reactors. Let me list at least some of the more important or intriguing of these:

- *Consistent, Widespread, and Open Repression.* One at least theoretical possibility is that of virtually all the elements of mainstream society cooperating in consistent, unabashed, and planned repression of the insurgent reality and any SMOs that bears it. Contemporary reactions to pedophile SMOs might, for example, come close to exemplifying this pattern. In the former Soviet Union, a wide variety of possible SMOs appeared to have labored under such a response. In some periods of American history, the efforts of American workers to form unions were subject to something approaching consistent, widespread, and open repression (Sexton 1991; Griffin, Wallace,, and Rubin 1986; Fantasia 1988).

- *Sporadic Repressive Campaigns ("Scares").* Many of the reactions described above have bureaucratic, grinding-away qualities that are often undertaken in secret. In contrast and on occasion, elites and several other categories of reactors become openly and highly agitated and reactive about an SMO or class of them that are defined as posing an immediate and serious threat. In collective-behavior language, (a) the societal situation is defined as out of the ordinary, (b) emotions of fear and hostility run strong, and (c) extraordinary control action is publicly undertaken (Lofland 1985, 37–38). Collective behaviorists label such episodes "scares" (or, sometimes, "witch-hunts"). In American history, one of the most famous is the "red scare" of 1919–1920 (Murray 1955). In this period, the government, along with diverse citizen groups and countermovements, engaged in varied public and collective activities to repress left-wing SMOs. As mentioned just above and in Chapter 9 (Section IV.D), the Industrial Workers of the World, a radical union, was the special object of this fear and hostility, although this scare was by no means confined to it.

- *Preemptive Siphoning-off in Organizational Alternatives to SMOs.* In the period of active struggle for unions among American workers, in addition to espionage, physically brutal strikebreaking and other coercive or violent measures, employers sometimes undertook "open-shop" propaganda campaigns. Key here, they set up employee organizations intended to compete with unions as avenues for redressing worker dissatisfactions. Commonly called "company unions," these were unions in name only because they were created and controlled by employers. As Fantasia observes though, many such "unions" and the reforms associated with them *did* provide "important benefits to workers. . . . But lest workers develop too keen a taste for reform, companies . . . often simultaneously engaged in coercive and repressive anti-union campaigns" (1988, 29–30) More broadly, some social historians have argued that the spread of the lodge (e.g., the Moose, the Elks) as a form of cross-class social organization among adult males at the time of rising unionism was an orchestrated effort to draw working-class males away from union militancy by offering them lodge-based, cross-class sociality and social "bonding" (Voss 1993). (In the terminology of SMO causes, these associations were efforts to create "cross-cutting solidarities" that would inhibit union formation. See, further, Section IV.A.7 of Chapter 7.)

- *SLAPP: Strategic Lawsuits against Public Participation.* For more than a decade, sociologist Penelope Canan and law school professor George Pring, both of the University of Denver, have been tracking and analyzing what they term "strategic lawsuits against public participation," or SLAPPs. SLAPPs are tort actions brought by housing developers, land speculators, and a variety of other economic enterprises against citizens and citizen groups who publicly oppose one or another of their actions by such means as circulating petitions, sending letters to a public officials, filing complaints with pertinent government agencies, or organizing boycotts.

  In the United States, a person or company cannot "legally sue persons for exercising their political right to petition and participate in the political process" (Canan and Pring 1988, 511). Therefore, companies have begun to counter political action by seeking to "recast the offending political behavior as common torts and thereby mask the original nature of the dispute. Six legal claims [have appeared] most frequently: defamation, business torts, conspiracy—and secondarily—judicial process abuse, constitutional rights, and nuisance" (p. 511). By this means, companies seek to "transform the dispute topics (e.g. zoning becomes libel) and move the forum of dispute from the city hall to the courtroom. To invoke the courts, [companies] represent a political difference as a judicially cognizable claim of injury. They seek to reprivatize and contain a political conflict made public by the citizens' grievance" (p. 515).

  There is both good and bad news for SMOs about this growing trend. On the good news side, courts have mostly discerned this tactic for the perversion of politics that it is. In analyzing some six hundred cases, "Canan and Pring [have] found that more than 77 percent of SLAPPs are won in court by those who were sued" (Nye 1994, 15). Yet other cases were settled before court judgment. But still, 10 percent have been won by companies. So, the news is not all good. But, on the bad news side, mainstream citizens and SMOs alike must face the prospect of SLAPP suits, and as knowledge of them spreads, this likely will have a chilling effect on citizen/SMO action. Even if one wins when subjected to a SLAPP, the process of seeing it through is time-consuming, anxiety provoking, and expensive. Even if SLAPP filers have not and will not prevail in court, the fear and intimidation they have created—and continue to create—is in itself an important victory for them.

The SLAPP story is an evolving one. Every tactic tends to create a countertactic and in this case the emerging new level of action is the *SLAPP-back*: a countersuit for "violation of . . . constitutional or civil rights, malicious prosecution, abuse of process, political and emotional injury, or outrageous conduct" (Nye 1994, 18).

V. A THIRD VANTAGE POINT: INTERACTION

In this chapter we switched *from* looking over the shoulders of the SMO (the dominant viewpoint in previous chapters) *to* looking over the shoulders of various reactors. Put differently, we have previously adopted (1) the point of SMOs or (2) of those reacting to them. These are, respectively, *actions* and *reactions*. But there is yet a *third* view that researchers can and do adopt. They stand outside both SMOs and reactors and examine the *interaction* between the two. This vantage point is developed in two main directions: schematics of interaction fields and dissections of interaction processes.

A. Schematics of Interaction Fields

In the former direction, researchers conceive the SMO and the various reactors as forming a set of "nodes" among which there are complex lines of influence, feedback loops, and other reverberating effects. In the language of Miles and Huberman (1994), such depictions are "displays" of all the key social entities making up an interaction field. The entities are visually interrelated by lines of different kinds representing varying directions and forms of action and relationship. In Figure 10.2, I present a simple example of such an interaction field. It's "nodes" are the SMO and several categories of reactors I have described in this chapter. The lines among the nodes illustrate some two-way relations of influence.

Michael Lipsky's schematic of the "process of protest by relatively powerless groups" in his famous article "Protest as a Political Resource"

Figure 10.2.   Schematic of an SMO-reactors interaction field.

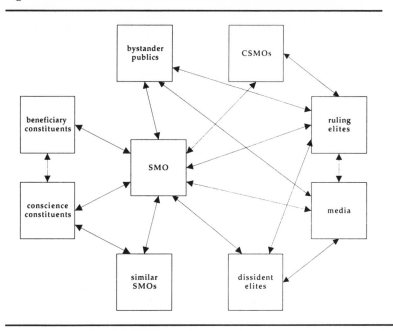

is perhaps the best-known schematic of an interaction field involving an SMO (1968, 1147, Figure 1).

B. Interaction Process

Displays of interaction fields such as illustrated by Figure 10.2 are static in the sense that the acting units are fixed in visual space and researchers describe activities moving among them. In contrast and in a second direction, researchers focus on a process of interaction itself as the unit and as it operates over time.

As of the present, researchers have put forth such process analyses as a goal and an image more frequently than as actual accomplishment. Prominent in moving toward such accomplishment, though, is Doug McAdam's work on "the pace of insurgency" in the civil rights movement of the 1960s—an analysis that focuses on the movement's changing, dominant strategies. These are the successive strategies of (i) the bus boycott, (ii) the sit-in, (iii) the freedom-rider and (iv) the community campaign. He ties this sequence of strategies together into a process with the proposition that each tactic arose in response to the neutralizing responses of authorities. These neutralizing responses included mass arrests by the police, the passage of state or local anti-trespassing ordinances, the permanent closure of the lunch counters, and establishment of various biracial negotiating bodies to contain or routinize the conflict. (1983, 745)[5]

These and other neutralizing responses are not, though, treated in counterpunctual detail, as cycles, circuits, spirals, or other possible processes of interaction. Instead, we only know that some such process was (or processes were) transpiring.

Lest my assessment that McAdam's analysis lacks processual detail seem overly demanding, let me be equally if not more demanding of my own efforts, which have the same shortcoming. In inspecting the activities of the U.S. peace movement of the 1980s as it interacted with other entities, Sam Marullo and I were impressed with its character as an *upward spiraling and expanding synergetic* interaction process. We identified eight classes of events interacting in this process, each of which mutually monitored and interacted with all the others: (1) ruling elite goading events, (2) local dissenting events, (3) dissident elite legitimizing events, (4) national dissenting events, (5) coalescing (SMO formation) events, (6) media events, (7) funding events, (8) public opining events. We asserted that simple cause-effect interaction linkages were an inadequate way in which to conceptualize of all those mutually influencing categories of events. Instead, each of the eight

> is in a synergistic or feedback fashion responding to the others. Many are very often feeding off each other and mutually causing enlargement of the others. [All are] operating on the other simultaneously, or at least in numerous and complicated feedback loops that we can glimpse in the available data but for which we do not have detailed documentation. (Lofland and Marullo 1993, 241)
>
> [In this synergistic process] we make no prior designation of exogenous variables that explain a discrete outcome. Instead, the surge outcome is itself a confluence of events that continuously and simultaneously cause each other. (p. 235)

Thus, like McAdam, we evoke an image of a particular kind of interaction process—an upward-spiraling synergy—rather than trace it in detail. But also like McAdam, even though our effort is short of the actual analysis of process, we think we have moved in the right direction.[6]

There has been, though, at least one effort actually to trace—to dissect—interaction processes in a generic way. This is Max Heirich's monumental study of the 1964–1965 Free Speech movement and conflict on the Berkeley campus of the University of California. The key SMO player in this conflict was the Free Speech movement (FSM) and Heirich treats it as one entity in a complex, moving field of diverse groupings that are acting and reacting.

But the FSM and the other "players" in this conflict over student speech rights are not the central units of Heirich's analysis. Instead and as befits interaction process as a third view, Heirich focuses on twenty-six episodes of conflict spread over the 1964–1965 school year and the factors affecting how the players acted in each episode and moved to the next one. His goal was to understand why and how each major party acted as it did from episode to episode and, as a consequence, the overall sequence of episodes. In Heirich's words, his analysis

> does not analyze the dynamics of a movement, but deals instead with the dynamics of *conflict.* Thus only secondary attention is given to coalition formations or to the strategies of elites, although what they did and the rationales by which decisions were reached are recorded. The account has tried to capture some of the more influential rhetoric used during the controversy, but makes little attempt to interpret the larger world view that lay behind it or to describe aspects of the life style of Berkeley radicals beyond the immediate controversy. (Heirich 1970, 397, emphasis in the original)

Heirich's focus on conflict episodes results in an extremely complex, generic analysis of interaction processes. It is so complex, in fact, that movement researchers have so far found it too daunting to cope with and to learn from. As a consequence, his analysis has been neglected over the now quarter of a century since its publication. A lesson to be learned here might therefore be that analysis can become *too* complicated for future researchers to deal with.[7]

So the task of researchers addressing interaction processes in SMOs and social movements would seen to be that of moving beyond mere images such as offered by McAdam and Lofland and Marullo, but not as far beyond as Heirich.

VI. OTHER QUESTIONS

In the foregoing I have focused mostly on forms of reactions (i.e., "types of" or "variations in" reactions) found among varied "reactors" Viewed in terms of the eight generic questions, this is a focus on only the first of those questions, What are the aspect's types? (Chapter 3, Section II). Detailed treatment of the other seven questions pushes us far beyond the scale of this guide. Let me therefore simply list the other seven questions as applied to reactions.

Frequencies: How frequent are given reactions to SMOs specifically and movements more generally?

Magnitudes: How do reactions vary in their scale, size, or strength, as in the number of people involved, the amount of money spent, and investment of other resources?

Structures: What are detailed structures of reactions?

Processes: What processes or phases of reactions are observed? (This can otherwise be thought of as processes of action and reaction and treated as interaction and relationship along the lines indicated in Section V.B.)

Causes: What factors enter into reactors adopting one rather than another form of reaction? One kind of causal answer to this question was outlined in the discussion of media, in Section II.C, and in discussion of dissident elites in Section II.B.

Consequences: What are the effects of various kinds of reactions? This question parallels, on the reactor side, the question of SMO effects and success discussed at the end of the previous chapter.

Agency: What are strategies of reactors? To the degree that categories of responses are consciously strategized by reactors, they display human agency rather than simply responsive behavior. Paralleling the movement leader strategizing I reported at the end of the last chapter, there is, on the reactor side, a growing literature written for and by defenders of the mainstream detailing how to foil insurgent movement realities (e.g., Harrison 1993).

* * *

Recall that in Section I.B, I distinguished between *reactions* and *effects* in terms of degrees of space and time proximity to SMOs. Reactions are defined there as responses to SMOs that are spatially and temporally *close* or near to SMOs. Effects, in contrast, are responses or consequences that are space and time *distant* or remote.

Having addressed reactions (and interactions) in this chapter, we now turn to effects—the more distant consequences of SMOs (and of social movements).

NOTES

1. My amalgamation of various "reactors" into "reactions" is informed by the concept of "societal reaction" as long applied in the sociological specialty labeled "deviance." The active history of the idea of "societal reaction" begins with Lemert (1951). The idea of "social control" provides an alternative way to think

about this aspect. In Smelser's formulation, for example, social control is the sixth of his six major "value-added . . . determinants" (1962, 13–15). Like Lemert, though, I think an image of social control imputes to the mainstream more unity and capacity for corporate response than is empirically warranted. The more disjointed implications of the concepts of "reactors" and "reactions" strike me as fitting the data better. Social conflict is a third concept that may yet prove superior to the ideas of either reactions or social control in thinking about these matters.

2.   Marx focuses on covert efforts to damage, but elites can also obviously proceed quite overtly, as in public prosecutions such as depicted by Barkan (1985a). See further Glick (1989) and Sexton (1991).

3.   On "turns of events" in such forms as "accidents" and "scandals," see Molotch (1975) and Molotch and Lester (1974). On other factors affecting sheer coverage, such as size of public demonstration, see McCarthy, McPhail, and Smith (in press).

4.   Cooperation in the form of coalitions is considered in Staggenborg (1986). Benford (1993b) addresses the prior question of the generic forms of disputes among similar SMOs. In his analysis, "three generic types of disputes" are "diagnostic, prognostic, and frame resonance" (Benford (1993, 677). See further Barkan (1985b).

5.   In addition, these several strategies were fielded by a variety of different and differing SMOs. McAdam"s process analysis is therefore of a movement rather than of given SMOs per se.

6.   And also like McAdam, our unit of analysis is a movement and its reactors (the classes of events) rather than an SMO and its reactors.

7.   Cf. Davis (1971) and Obserschall (1993). Other analyses moving in promising interaction-process directions include Hirsch (1990) (on a student protest at Columbia University, summarized in Section III.B.16 of Chapter 8) and Morris (1993) (on the 1963 Birmingham confrontation, summarized in Section IV.C of Chapter 9). Pertinent to both these analyses and other close-in inspections of strategic processes is Light's neglected but important formulation of *the law of passage advantage*, which is:

> ◆ If the authorities are passive, the protesters will be defined as aggressors and thus start at a disadvantage [and continue to lose ground if the authorities create a"stand-off" in which] the authorities refuse to take action against [the protesters], but they also refuse to yield to the demands made. . . . The longer the stand-off lasts, the more ground the protesters lose. (Light 1969, 81; cf. Hirsch 1990)

11

What Are Effects of SMOs?

The seventh and last question I feature in this guide is, What are the effects or consequences of SMOs? The central task of this chapter is to report an array of these effects that researchers have propounded.

I. THREE SPECIFICATIONS

In order best to do this, I must begin with three specifications of the status of the inventory that follows.

A. Previously Reported Effects

The first of these specifications is the recognition that we have—as a logical matter—already asked and answered the question of effects about aspects of the SMO *other than* the SMO itself taken as an entity. Thus, I have reported effects of varying kinds of beliefs, forms of organization, kinds of participation, and so forth.

Further, in the previous chapter I reported *reactions* to SMOs taken as holistic entities. As previously indicated, these reactions are, logically speaking, simply effects of SMOs. But in desiring to distinguish between effects in the ongoing present and the longer term, I focused on the former in the previous chapter.

B. Narrow and Broad Conceptions of Effects

The distinction between temporally and spatially close versus distant effects of SMOs can otherwise be thought of as a narrow versus broad conception of effects. In a narrow conception, one asks, Did SMO participants achieve the goals they set out to achieve? This conception is narrow because it centers on

1. the short term,
2. effects participants desired, and
3. the degree to which those goals were achieved.

While researchers certainly want to know about effects of these sorts (and these were discussed in Section IV of Chapter 9), this conception casts the identifying net too narrowly. Looking more broadly, researchers also want to know:

1. effects in the long term, in the time perspective of decades and generations, and not simply days, months, or years;
2. effects on a wide variety of matters not found in SMO goal statements and effects that are not intended or recognized by SMO actors.

C. SMO-Centric and Cause-Centric Effects Frames

Researchers use two different framing images in thinking about the effects/consequences of SMOs: the SMO-centric and the cause-centric. Both are valid and useful, but they are different and each serves as a corrective for limitations of the other.

In SMO-centric framing, the researcher focuses on the SMO and seeks to enumerate all the possible consequences it has had. This is shown graphically in panel A of Figure 11.1

In contrast, in cause-centric framing, the researcher selects an effect and asks, What are all the variables that have had some role in bringing it about? This alternative is depicted in panel B of Figure 11.1.

Movement researchers tend to use an SMO-centric frame and this is fine, except that it also tends to underemphasize the degree to which *other variables* are also at play in causing any effect of an SMO. It is these "other variables" that the cause-centric model brings forcefully to our attention, as shown in panel B of Figure 11.1.

In this chapter I employ the SMO-centric frame for the purpose of laying out a range of matters on which SMOs sometimes have effects. All these statements must, however, be tempered with the realization that in every case there is always the question of *other variables*, as depicted in panel B of Figure 11.1.

To complicate matters further, there are not only other causal variables of a variety of kinds, SMOs themselves differ and these differences affect the degree and kinds of effects that they have. For example, and recalling previous chapters, SMOs vary in such matters as beliefs, forms of organization, financing, characteristics of members, and strategies.

Figure 11.1.   SMO-and cause-centric effects frames.

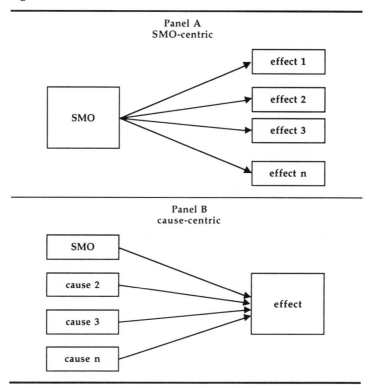

These and other variations are undoubtedly important in causing different effects.

Taking these several specifications (and complications) into account, my report of effects is cast in a highly qualified manner. It is an inventory of the *range* of outcomes that have *occurred at least once* or perhaps a few times, but are *not* always effects of any specific SMO—or broader movement. From the point view of someone researching an SMO, the effects I report provide an inventory of possibilities to be evaluated for the degree of their presence or absence in a particular case.

II. SMO EFFECTS: WORKING INVENTORY

Without at all suggesting that this list is exhaustive, let me point to a range of sometime consequences of SMOs, effects often also involving, of course, a great many SMOs in larger SMs.

A. Changes in Governments, Laws, Policies, Policy Systems

While varying in frequency, some SMOs have indisputably played major roles in—or *the* major role in—changes of governmental systems (as in revolutions), the downfall of particular ruling elites within governments, and the adoption of laws and policies desired by a movement. For example, in the United States the familiar and prosaic laws, regulations, and government bureaucracies relating to labor relations, ethnic and gender rights, and the environment are all—in part—products of the fervor of SMOs in, respectively, the thirties, sixties, and seventies.

One of the more interesting effects at this institutional level is what are called "policy systems," which are large and informal networks of people involved with government who have a special interest in an area. Not existing prior to the surging of given and multiple SMOs, these policy systems crystallize in the wake of SMOs and endure thereafter. [The rise of one such system attendant to the women's movement is described in Freeman (1975, 226ff.).]

B. Winning Acceptance

Even if many of the specific laws or policies sought are not achieved, the issues raised by the SMO/movement can come to be more or less permanently "on the agenda." Or, as phrased in a different policy jargon, the SMO/SM gets "a place at the table." This may be accompanied by "shifts in public perceptions of social issues" more generally (McAdam et al. 1988, 727). Effects of this more diffuse sort at this institutional level have otherwise been termed "winning acceptance" (Gamson 1990).

C. New or Enlarged Movement Establishment

As reported in Chapter 7 (Section IV.B.12), many SMOs are born in the ferment of "citizen surge synergy"—periods when SMOs are proliferating on all sides and stimulating one another's formation. This soaring surge peaks and declines and many surge-born SMOs go out of business. But a great many persist and form a new kind of *movement establishment*. It may be much smaller than at the peak of the movement surge, but it is nonetheless a larger, stable "movement" presence than before the surge (Mauss 1975; Lofland 1993a).

D. New Items of Mainstream Culture

Some few SMOs and their encompassing SMs are successful in creating enduring ideas and events that become part of the society's cultural mainstream. The SMOs of the civil rights movement of the sixties have been among the more successful at this in recent times, with the creation of a federal holiday named for Martin Luther King, Jr., and the yearly commemoration of key events of the civil rights surge.

Continuing mainstream homage may be in such forms as putting the pictures of leaders on postage stamps or their busts in the equivalent of the National Portrait Gallery (in which gallery Rosa Parks was installed in 1983, for example) (Dowdy 1987, 218).[1] The Christian movement establishment growing from Christian SMOs and the establishment resulting from American secessionist SMOs (which included guerrilla troops) rank among the most effective of SMOs in mainstream cultural consequences. That is, days (and seasons) such as Christmas, Easter, and the Fourth of July are commemorations of signal events in the lives of their respective SMOs/movements. Much the same is also true of major cultural aspects of every modern nation. (An irony, of course, is that many of the piously religious or patriotic folks who most enthusiastically celebrate such cultural days seem less than fully to appreciate that they are paying homage to once disreputable, treasonous, or even terrorist SMOs.)

E. Shifts in Norms, Cultural Images and Symbols

More broadly, SMOs and waves of them in SMs may set in motion shifts in how major categories of the population conceive of one another and assess their respective rights, duties, and capacities. Thus, in the United States, it is likely that the sixties-seventies surge of feminist SMOs help set in motion a general shift in "understanding[s] of what women are capable of doing and [this shift has] also [altered] the opportunities for political action on the part of women" (McAdam et al. 1988, 728).

Looked at the other way around, some varieties of previously acceptable cultural images and institutional practices may be rendered improper and discontinued. Public entertainments that demean particular ethnic, gender, or physical ability groupings have been the particular subjects of such alterations in recent cultural images and symbols.

F. Changes in the Interaction Order

People do not live merely in "society." Instead, their immediate social worlds consist of people with whom they are in direct, face-to-face interaction. Sociologist Erving Goffman (1983) dubs this the "interaction order," and documents the myriad ways in which it operates in terms of its own dynamic rules of systemic functioning. In the interaction order, given slang terms, forms of address, and bodily gestures are considered correct, "taken for granted," and even unnoticed. A surging array of SMOs can, however, render improper, or at least problematic, interaction practices previously unthought about, unperceived, or though too "obvious" to even mention. Thus, recently in many parts of the United States, a previously "unnoticed" interactional practice such as calling an adult female a "girl" is now likely to disrupt the interaction order. Or the previously taken for granted interaction practice of a man opening and holding a door for a woman becomes, in some circles at least, a moment that is sticky and difficult to manage (Walum 1978).

G. The Shape of Strata Structures

People in more recent human societies are structured into layers of differential economic standing, political power, and degrees of deference or prestige. Within these social "layers," people are not distributed evenly or randomly in terms of their ascriptive attributes. Instead, some rather than other ethnic groups, sexes, ages, and such tend to be higher in economic standing, political power, and prestige and deference. Such inequalities and the sometimes attendant sense of injustice are often the targets of SMO goals, such as the aims to:

1. *abolish* the strata shape of societies altogether,
2. provide *parity* among ascriptive categories in terms of economics, politics, and prestige, or
3. *reverse* the order of inequality while retaining economic, political, and prestige inequality.

Some very few SMOs, some very few times, achieve (or claim to achieve) one or another of these three changes/effects. Thus, communist SMOs in Russia embraced the first aim listed as its goal and program, devised the USSR as its means of implementation, and had strata structure effects that are well known. More commonly, SMOs embrace the second aim. Considerable research effort has gone into assessing the degree of ascriptive parity achieved following major SMO surges in the United States as well as in other countries. Parity has proven difficult to assess, however, importantly because of disagreements on exactly what parity might mean and how fast it can or should be achieved. Gains can sometimes be shown, while persisting important inequalities can also be shown. The assessment becomes a matter of judging whether the glass is half empty or half full; that is, there are key differences in perspective that cannot be resolved with empirical study alone. This is seen keenly in the case of assessing the degree of parity achieved by African-Americans and other ethnic groupings in the recent United States. There are many indicators of increasing parity, but yet other indicators have not changed, or have become even more unequal since periods of surging SMOs/movements.

H. Cultural Clarification and Reaffirmation

Some analysts of human social organization argue that the vitality of and commitment to core cultural values are not self-sustaining. Instead, the meaning and value of beliefs and practices grow dim and uncertain over time as people with the original animating experiences die off and are replaced by their progeny, who do not have those experiences. Occasions of calling core values centrally to attention and reassessing and reaffirming them are therefore required in order for commitment to them to remain vigorous.

Caught up in their mundane lives, it is difficult to persuade people seriously to undertake such clarification and reaffirmation. Moments of crisis and challenge, however, *do* serve to bring values centrally to people's attention and to suggest the consequences of not vigorously maintaining them. In dramatic acts and in surges of them, SMOs can be *one* prominent form of crisis and challenge. (Functionally equivalent crises and challenges include economic disaster and external military attack.) Spectacular SMO episodes or a surge of SMOs can require people to think again and to think seriously about the meaning of such values as democracy, equality, education, freedom, and economic security. It is out of the fray of the drama of crisis and challenge that people are prompted to clarify and recommit themselves to revised and refined conceptions of such values.

I. Entertainment and Spectacle.

Effects I have so far enumerated tend to be on the upbeat, enlightenment side of things. Winning acceptance, shifting pubic conceptions of categories of people, new items of culture, and the like are variations on a theme of rational, educated, and "progressive" social change. This is the "light" (or "enlightenment") side of effects.

Some analysts point, in addition, though, to darker sides. SMOs sometimes function as just one more form of spectacle, dramatic entertainment, or amusement. Especially as framed by television, SMOs can be mere blips in the unending cascade of popular spectacles and amuse-ments—situation comedies, Olympic Games, Super Bowls, World Se-ries, World Cups, natural disasters, lightning military interventions, space explorations, political scandals, and genocidal wars. They all come and go in Huxleyian *Brave New World* fashion, serving as moments of amusement, disgust, and distraction before going down Orwell's Mem-ory Hole. In being so tolerated and forgotten, such tolerance is in this way repressive, some observers have argued (Debord 1983).

J. Violence and Tyranny

And even more darkly on this dark side, *some* SMOs/movements spawn holocausts (including *the* Holocaust), genocidal campaigns and wars, tyranny, and totalitarian regimes. As I said at the outset regarding beliefs (Chapter 5, Section I), insurgent realities are not necessarily ei-ther "good" or "bad" by virtue of their marginal or excluded standing. Movement beliefs, like mainstream beliefs, come in myriad varieties and some are decidedly more bloodthirsty than others. Movements may be major means by which social change comes about, but the changes some of them bring are far from necessarily benign or progressive.

K. Scholarly Trade.

In affluent, complex societies, virtually every form of problematic hu-man activity gives rise to circles or even social worlds of intellectuals and other scribblers who specialize in thinking, writing, and publishing on whatever "the problem." The topics of SMOs and social movements are no exception. Their continuing upwellings create interest in preventing, mollifying, promoting, and otherwise responding to them. Sustained scholarly treatments are thought by intellectuals (and the elites who pay them) to be among relevant, long-term postures toward SMOs. Hence, the book you are holding is one among a myriad of intellectual products that are consequences of SMOs/movements. At the level of particular movements, we even get such specialized worlds as the Historians of American Communism and the Peace History Society—among other elements of the trade I described in Chapter 2.

L. Models for Later SMOs.

Implied in the discussions of SMO causal variables (8) and (17) in Chapter 7—the "sense of injustice" and "frame alignment"—is the fact that people's conceptions of what is owed them and how they can act are in part framed by their knowledge of previous movements. Such previous moments of asserting what is just and acting in an SMO can enter the consciousness of a wide variety of other people who use those episodes as *models* for their own new SMO. By the term "model" I do not mean that they copy history exactly or in a slavish fashion. Although there may be an element of this, previous experience is adapted at the same time that it is inspirational. This is sometimes termed a "diffusion" of, especially, tactical models of movement action. Civil rights SMOs of the sixties appear, in particular, to have served as something like "master models" or "master frames" for SMOs in subsequent decades (Snow and Benford 1992; Meyer and Whittier 1994).

Moreover, the effect of previous SMOs/movements on later movements is sometimes more direct and tangible than simply ideational "models." Thus, Taylor (1989) has shown quite direct, supportive relations between the U.S. women's movement in "abeyance" in the 1950s and 1960s and the onset of a new surging women's movement in the late 1960s and early 1970s.

III. CAUSES OF EFFECTS

Recalling the distinction between SMO-centric and cause-centric framings of effects shown graphically in Figure 11.1, researchers are humbled by the realization that any SMO effect must be presumed to have *multiple causes*. This is the cautious presumption shown as "cause-centric" in panel B of Figure 11.1. This caution attaches to each and every effect I have described immediately above.

Moreover and as has been abundantly illustrated, SMOs vary a great deal in many ways. Pertinent here, SMO variations differentially effect the kinds of outcomes inventoried above. For example, William Gamson's (1990) well-known study of SMOs has at least tentatively established that SMOs (1) whose beliefs seek partial rather than total changes in societies, (2) that are organizationally more centralized and bureaucratic, and (3) that are prepared to be involved in "unruly tactics" are more likely to achieve changes or at least to win acceptance "at the table" of policy (effects A and B above). SMOs lacking these features are less likely to have these effects.

The tasks of researchers are therefore and also to explore (1) non-SMO causes of effects and (2) how SMO variations make for different effects.

*   *   *

This concludes my guided tour of seven main questions that researchers often ask about SMOs. However, our junket has not quite
ended. Like excursions of other kinds, this one has a postclimax—wind-
ing-down—phase. For an overview of it, simply turn this page to the
"part page" that introduces the two short chapters comprising Part III.

NOTE

1.   The actions of the National Portrait Gallery provide a sensitive and useful
"tracer variable" in the task of assessing social movement effects and what has
(or has not) become "mainstream." (United States Postal Service decisions on
postage stamp subjects are useful for the same reason.)

III

Perspectives:
Dissections and Contexts

We have finished looking at the big exhibits in the main hall and we are leaving. But there are still some important items to be to be seen on the way out and in the souvenir shop by the exit gate. These are assembled in the two short chapters of Part III. In them, I strive to provide two kinds of *perspective*.

In Chapter 12, I suggest a way in which an inquiring mind can strengthen her or his mastery of the questions and concepts of this guide. This chapter might, indeed, be thought of as the souvenir shop in that it shows one how to analyze a published report on a social movement organization, thereby acquiring a personal memento.

In Chapter 13, I draw together and draw out a number of themes that provide several contexts for movement studies—that treat some larger issues in which movement studies are situated.

12

Dissecting Research Reports

A person's understanding and mastery of an activity is best increased by actually engaging in that activity rather than by simply reading about it. As is rightly opined in folk wisdom, "practice makes perfect." However, actually engaging in an activity is often not practical or feasible. Assiduous learners therefore turn, as a working substitute, to the close, analytic study of *examples* of the activity that displays the array of contingencies and skills involved. Of course, the searching study of examples is not a substitute for doing, but it does move the learner beyond the abstract contemplation of generalizations and approaches by showing how they operate in concrete cases.

In this spirit of grounding generalizations in cases and thereby enlarging understanding of them, I have in this chapter recast my reports of case study *procedures* (Part I) and sociological *propositions* (Part II) as a guide to dissecting published reports of research.

While primarily intended to be of learning assistance to people who do not plan to do their own case study of an SMO, it can obviously also be helpful to people who *do* have such plans. For the same reasons that fledgling painters, writers, and other artists are not idling away their time when they scrutinize the masters, fledgling researchers can, in part, learn their craft by dissecting exemplars.

I divide aspects of dissecting research reports into *format and procedures* and *dissection questions*.

I. FORMAT AND PROCEDURES

Operationally, the task is that of answering the following questions about a research report one has selected and read.[1] In some course, seminar, or study group situations, the answers might be written out in outline or text and distributed to fellow participants.

A. Articles versus Books

The "dissection questions" enumerated in Section II can be applied to an article or book. Of course, books are roughly the equivalent of five to ten articles and thereby provide many more points to analyze (as well as require more work).

B. Research Reports

In order to be most useful in terms of this guide, a research report selected for analysis should have many if not most or all of the following features. Put differently, it should be a *report* of serious *research*:

1. The report should be literally that—a *report* of data—rather than a theoretical essay, review of the literature, or similar formulation.
2. It is helpful but not absolutely necessary that the data be on one (or a few) SMOs and employ qualitative data rather than on a large number of them treated quantitatively.
3. The report should display the ordinary apparatus of scholarship. The following are some earmarks of that apparatus as seen in serious books. The more a book has of them, the more likely that it is a serious work of scholarship.

   • It has a serious table of contents, one that avoids "cute" and metaphorical titles.
   • It has footnotes, a bibliography, and an index.
   • In the introductory chapter or chapters, the author or authors try to relate their work to what other people have written about the SMO and whatever the *aspects* (or units) of analysis, *questions*, and *propositions* about social movements or SMOs.
   • The chapters are internally subdivided with headings that communicate lines of analysis
   • There is a concluding chapter in which what has been accomplished is summarized and directions for future work are set forth.

Except for a table of contents, articles should display essentially the same features. In place of a table of contents, look for an abstract (which functions as a table of contents).

C. Locating Research Reports

There are literally thousands upon thousands of books and articles on SMOs (and on social movements, as well) that display the above features of serious reports of research. Procedures for identifying reports have been described in Section III of Chapter 2. Prior even to that, one can peruse the reference list at the end of this guide.

One must be cautious in selecting a book or article, because there are *also* thousands upon thousands of books and articles on SMOs (and social movements) that are *not* serious reports of research. Instead, they are sensationalistic journalism, countermovement attacks, or kindred productions that are not based on serious efforts to collect data and judiciously to analyze them in terms of sociological aspects, questions, and propositions.

When in doubt about the degree to which a report is "serious" in the above senses, show the report to other people involved in these matters and ask their views.

II. DISSECTION QUESTIONS

The dissection I suggest is formulated as a set of questions to ask and to answer in the process of reading and re-reading a report and then reflecting on it. The answers to some questions will be found in one or just a few places in the report, but others require looking back over the document as a whole and assessing its overall qualities.

If the answers are worked up as a written report, one format is simply to organize the materials in terms of the headings given below and to present them in the same order as used here.

A. Identification

Of books: What is the name of the author, the full title of the book, publisher, and year of publication? Indicate any complications of publication history such as a reissue by another publisher, an enlarged edition, or a translation.

Of articles: Give the full citation of the article.

B. Social and Personal Matters

Some data involve much more complicated social relations and personal matters than do others. If interviewing or observational data were used, the following questions are especially pertinent, although at least some of these questions arise with other kinds of data as well. Where a question is not pertinent because of the kind of data used, report that fact and the reasons why. If the report does not contain information that answers a particular question, so state.

1.   What does the author say motivated the study? Who paid for it?

2.   Where, geographically, was the research done? What "populations" or social organizations were studied?

3.   In what ways was initial access to the data and/or the site problematic, if at all? Financial? Ethical? Practical? Personal? Other?

4.   How were such problematic aspects (question 3) managed in order to get started?

5.   What type of social role did the researcher occupy or assume in the research and what limitations and advantages did it have?

6.   What were special stresses in the social relations involved, if any? How were these managed? What did the research "do" to the researcher (as in getting converted or the like)?

7.   Were there, in particular, issues of confidentiality, disguised observation, other undercover data collection, and informed consent? Describe them. If none, explain why.

8.   In what ways might the actions of the researcher have influenced either the people at the sites involved (and hence the "data") or the character of the data collected?

9.   What were especially helpful and positive aspects of researcher-researched relations? (For example, were there special informants?)

10.   What is your overall assessment of the ways in which and the degrees to which the researcher may or may not have been biased or less than objective in the data collection? Enumerate and document the ways and degrees.

C. Data Matters

1.   Using the discussion in Chapter 2, above, as a guide, what techniques of data collection were used? (Recasting aspects of Chapter 2, possibilities include published accounts, historical archives, quantitative datasets, survey questionnaires, observation, interviewing, life histories.)

2.   What was the relative "balance" and "mix" of sources of data?

3.   If pertinent, indicate the number of people observed or interviewed (and for how long), the period of time over which the study was conducted, and the number and nature of other sources located and scrutinized.

4. What technical, physical, or other devices did the author employ in moving from collected data to written analysis (for example, personal computers, unusual filing systems, special workplaces and practices, particular forms of coding, theoretical memoing, computer programs for data analysis)?
5. If there are several and diverse "cases," how were these selected?
6. Overall, how convinced are you that the author has collected data adequate to the matter at hand? What additional data, if any, should reasonably have been collected?

D. Aspects Addressed

1. In the list of *aspects* of analysis given in Figure 3.3, which ones are addressed? Or are aspects not on that list addressed?
2. What are the less abstract versions of these or other aspects that the author formulates?
3. Count the number of pages devoted to each more specific aspect you have enumerated and compute the percentage of pages of the report devoted to each. For this calculation, take the total number of pages in the report as your base, count pages no shorter than half a page, and round all percentages to the nearest whole number. Set up as a vertical column with summary labels for each aspect, and report the results of your calculations.

E. Questions Asked

1. In the list of eight generic questions (Chapter 3, Section II. B), which ones are addressed?
2. What are the less abstract versions of these questions that the author formulates?
3. Count the number of pages devoted to answering each of these more specific questions and compute the percentage of pages of the report devoted to each. As above for aspects, use the total pages in the report as your base, count pages no shorter than half a page, and round to the nearest whole number. Set up as a vertical column with summary labels, and report this calculation.

F. Propositions Propounded

1. Enumerate and state the proposition or propositions the author offers regarding the aspects and questions, that is, the answers to the questions posed.

2. Count the number of pages where these propositions are discussed directly (as distinct from data and the like leading up them) and compute the percentage of pages of the report so devoted to each proposition. Set up as a vertical column with summary labels, and report these percentages. (Once more, use the total pages as the base and round to whole numbers.)
3. For aspects, questions, and propositions, what techniques of concept charting are used, if any (Chapter 4, Section IV.C)? How effective are any such techniques?

G. Literature Context

1. Into what theoretical, conceptual, or kindred context does the author place her or his propositional answers to questions about aspects?
2. What claims about the advancement of knowledge, the disproof of mistaken theory, or other assertions does the author make to justify the report?

H. Data Presentation

1. What is the percentage relation between text that presents quantitative or qualitative data, on the one hand, and analytic text, on the other hand? Using whole pages as your smallest unit, count the pages devoted to each (data versus concepts) and compute and report the percentage devoted to each.
2. Focusing only on the pages presenting data, what percentage are quantitative data (i.e., present and discuss numbers) and what percentage are qualitative data (i.e., provide prose reports of what was studied)?
3. To what degree does the author move back and forth between presentation of data and conceptual discussion of them? Extreme possibilities in this are (a) the first and last sections are conceptual, but everything in between is data with no analysis; (b) every section right down to the paragraph level moves back and forth between data and concepts. (This "moving back and forth" is discussed in Section VI of Chapter 4.)

I. Overall

1. Overall, how clearly and logically organized is the report? Is it easy or difficult to grasp as a whole? Why?

2. How convinced or unconvinced are you by whatever is propounded by the author? Why?
3. In what ways does the work either inhibit or facilitate future work on the same or larger topics? In particular, is the report set in a theoretical context sufficient to make its current and future relevance clear?
4. What are some such future relevances (question I.3, just above)?
5. What consequences has the report had for the author, the SMO studied, enemies of the SMO studied and others involved with it, and the wider social and political world? In different words, what are (or might be) the political and social meanings of this report? It is difficult to know these consequences for many reports, but some sense of them can be inferred from tracing citation histories in such sources as the *Social Science Citation Index*. For books, there are also reviews that can be read (and these can also be found through the *Social Science Citation Index*, as well as through indexes of book reviews).

* * *

For the intellectually curious, dissections of this sort are fascinating adventures in discovery. Like other puzzle solvers, the dissector seeks to discern whatever underlying order may lurk in the materials. Beneath the glossing melange of words forming the visible body of the report, what is the stark and bare structural skeleton that holds it up? Once stripped bare, how strong is that skeleton in relation to the fleshy casing of words in which it is embedded?

Indeed, in this broader perspective of order discerning per se, dissecting reports is cognitively much like the task of researching SMOs themselves. In both cases, the quester seeks to identify essentials, to perceive order, and to assess the accuracy of how each of these is depicted. There is therefore a great deal of cognitive continuity between dissecting reports and researching SMOs. People with a taste for one have a taste for the other (and vice versa, perhaps).

NOTE

1. Some of the text and topics that follow are adapted from Lofland and Lofland (1995, 231–36).

13

Contextual Themes

For the sake of simplicity and clarity, in previous chapters I have kept in the background a number of important issues and topics that attend the study of social movements. In concluding, I want to reverse ground and to bring a number of these matters into the foreground. Put differently, a number of issues that form contexts of movement studies that I have left implicit in the foregoing will now become explicit.

I begin with the wider and more abstract of these contextual themes and move by degrees to those that are narrower and more concrete.

I. AN OMNIBUS INTELLECTUAL TOOL KIT

This is a specialized volume in the sense that it is about "SMOs"—entities that abound in the world but that are not part of everyone's everyday lives. However, this guide is specialized only in this sense. In two other senses, its contents are very general and of vital relevance to anyone's ordinary life.

The first sense in which the content is ubiquitously pertinent has to do with the generic character of the intellectual scheme that organizes it. In briefest terms, this scheme consists of the ideas of

1. using *case study immersion-induction* to
2. ask *generic questions* about
3. *aspects* of things in order to
4. formulate generic *propositional answers* to questions.

These items make up an *omnibus intellectual tool kit* that can be applied to virtually any topic. People who master the several tools in this kit have equipped themselves with powerful means of making sense of anything. Confronted with the disorderly confusion of a circumstance, persons so prepared know how to collect, sort, order, and analyze data and thereby better to understand their options for action.

A first contextual theme has therefore been that while I have addressed specialized matters, the manner of doing this employs fundamental and omnirelevant canons of inquiry.

II. AN IMPLICIT GUIDE TO MORAL PHILOSOPHY

The second sense in which this guide is generically informative even though about a specialized topic pertains to the distinctive relation between SMOs and morality.

By their very nature in being "insurgent realities," SMOs raise the profound existential issues of what we—any and all of us—ought to believe and how we ought to live. Each of the many variations in beliefs, organization, membership, strategies, and reactions to SMOs that I report are *not* simply, merely, or only neutral ways in which SMOs vary about which we can be neutral or indifferent. Instead, each presents—to the SMO *and* to each of us as aware moral beings—an *existential* choice that must be made, a *philosophical/religious* selection that needs to be grappled with, a *moral* decision that must be pondered. Thus:

- Are totalistic, apocalyptic, and kindred beliefs ever reasonable?
- Should one vilify one's opponents?
- Is all-embracing, "rich" culture a good thing?
- Can the high absorption of members in SMOs be justified?
- Should associations be democratic or oligarchic?
- Are professional social movement organizations morally proper?
- Is charismatic leadership a good or bad thing in human life?
- Is civil disobedience moral?
- Can violence as a strategy of social change be justified?
- Which responses of elites to movements are moral and which are immoral?

This is but a sampling of the existential/philosophical questions that inexorably emerge from asking, How should life be lived? about each of the variations I have reported.

In larger perspective or at the next level of meaning then, this book is about morality and moral choice. While I have (mostly) not advocated one or another choice, by stressing variations I have highlighted matters about which such choices must be made and major options regarding them. Read with the aim of answering the question, How should life be lived? a serious moral inquirer can indeed develop key provisional elements of a philosophy of life.

III. A LEITMOTIF OF ANALYTIC ETHNOGRAPHY

In assembling this guide to research on SMOs, I have made a special effort to include empirical inquires that exhibit a certain complex of methodological features, one termed *analytic ethnography*. However, my special effort to include such researches does not mean that I have disfavored or excluded inquires of different methodological leanings. Instead, I have simply made rather more effort to roster analytic ethnographies. Given the fact that such studies are present as a "leitmotif" of this guide, it is incumbent on me to explain what analytic ethnography is and why I favor it.

In Chapter 2, I reviewed eight "sources of data and types of methods," the eighth and last of which is "interviewing and observation." Analytic ethnography is one prime form of this eighth "source of data and type of method"—a form that its partisans such as myself like to think of as *the* prime and best form of interviewing and observation. Be that claim as it may, analytic ethnography as a way to perform an empirical study refers to research processes and products in which, to a greater or lesser degree, an investigator

1. attempts to provide generic propositional answers to questions about social life and organization;
2. strives to pursue such an attempt in a spirit of unfettered or naturalistic inquiry;
3. utilizes data based on deep familiarity with a social setting or situation that is gained by personal participation or an approximation of it;
4. develops the generic propositional analysis over the course of doing the research;
5. strives to present data and analyses that are true;
6. seeks to provide data and/or analysis that are new; and,
7. presents an analysis that is developed in the senses of conceptually elaborated, descriptively detailed, and concept-data interpenetrated (adapted from Lofland 1995a, 30).

This package of seven features of analytic ethnography is a leitmotif of this guide because all seven of its features have, in fact, been explained (albeit sometimes in different terms) in the discussions of data collection and analysis given in Part I and, as said, applied in selecting studies for review in the chapters of Part II.

Alas, despite my fondness for analytic ethnography, it is much more common in other areas of inquiry, especially in the analysis of everyday life, than in the study of SMOs/movements (Lofland 1995a). Among the some five hundred items in the bibliography of this guide, a little more than three dozen are (or contain) an analytic ethnography, although numerous other studies listed also move in that direction. As a supplemental exercise and treasure hunt for those interested, I have inserted the letters AE after each item in this guide's list of references that I think is a reasonable example of analytic ethnography.

IV. DISCIPLINE AND EMPOWERMENT
IN THE SMO FOCUS

In Chapter 1 and in other chapters, I note the fact that SMOs are but one of three major foci in the domain of insurgent realities, the other two being crowd and mass actions ("waves" of collective action) and social movements.

Although I have not taken up the matter in this guide, the SMO as a focus in fact *competes* with these other two foci of research attention and intellectual development. Indeed, over the last two decades or so SMOs have competed somewhat weakly against these other two. Instead, social movements and crowd and mass actions (collective action) as major historical configurations have been the main objects of attention (e.g., Tarrow 1994).[1]

While these more macrohistorical units of analysis are certainly valid, they also have at least two limitations that an SMO focus serves to balance and correct.

The first of these limitations is that since they are sprawling and indefinite upwellings—*ambiguous objects*—analysts and participants alike have a good deal of *leeway* in what they can plausibly claim to "be" a "social movement," "mass protest," or other macrohistorical construct, and its various features. While there are clearly *some things* out there, what they are exactly and how they should be cognitively constructed is not compellingly clear. This leads, indeed, to contending constructions of exactly what any "it" is or "they" are.[2]

This fundamental ambiguity opens the way for a wide variety of equally contentious assertions about given " movements," "protest cycles," or other macrohistorical unit. Not least among these contentious constructions is viewing a "movement," in particular, as a unified corporate actor with motives, intentions, and the capacity to strategize. The upshot is the spinning of cognitive constructions that gloss movements as persons or organizations, which they clearly are not. And, undisciplined by clear empirical referents in many other regards, movements are, I think, erroneously and even fictionally portrayed with some frequency.

SMOs, in contrast, *do* more compellingly impose the discipline of clear (or at least clearer) empirical referents. They *are* more definitely corporate actors and because of the clarity of their memberships and leaderships and their functioning, they can be more reasonably be viewed as having motives, intentions, and strategies. Most important, the greater clarity of their empirical boundaries allows researchers more easily to test their cognitive constructions against reality.

Consider in this context such a seemingly benign undertaking as an undergraduate student setting out to write a course paper on—let us say—"the men's movement." So framed, the student goes about locating and collating a variety of sources on its beliefs, causes, reactions to it, and the like. A great many degrees of cognitive *formation freedom* are central in this process. In going over the scattered and inchoate materials under the rubric "men's movement," our researcher is as much in a position of creating or assembling a picture of the movement as being constrained by facts accurately to describe and analyze it. Starting with a vague abstraction and some preconceptions about it, he or she can dip miscellaneous bits from the simmering broth of factoids to assemble a satisfying dish. As Herbert Blumer has so well warned us: "we necessarily view any unfamiliar area of group life through images we already possess" and the more ambiguous the object itself, the more likely it is that our preexisting images will "become a *substitute*" for the object of study (1969b, 36–37). (Indeed, I am reminded of findings of starvation experiments in which the volunteers are shown extremely ambiguous drawings and the hungrier they are the greater is the likelihood they will perceive even the fuzziest of blobs as forms of food.)

Of course, using the more definitely visible SMO as one's unit of inquiry is no guarantee against such exercises in elaborating preexisting images. Nonetheless, the SMO imposes at least *some* greater degree of constraint.

The second limitation of macrohistorical focus on the large formations called social movements and "collective actions" is their *disempowerment metamessage*. Upwelling movements and mass protests are vast, impersonal, and *surprising* occurrences that elude any particular human intentions and planning. These features imply that the best a person can do is either wait quietly or even in despair for the "next wave." The implied answer to the human moral question, What can I do? is, Not much, really.

Focus on SMOs, in contrast, carries the metamessage that people are engaged in insurgent realities at a great variety of times and with important effects quite aside from the current state of mammoth movements and immense crowd and mass upwellings. Sometimes all three coincide to create momentous historical moments, but often they do not. But the insurgent realities of SMOs go on and make many differences nonetheless, quite aside from large movements and mass actions.

I want to be careful not to seem exclusionary in pointing up these two important limitations of focusing on larger movements and mass collective actions. I argue limitations rather than fatal flaws. In that spirit let me acknowledge a major limitation of the SMO focus. The greater intellectual discipline and focus accompanying an SMO focus is purchased at a price. SMOs are, in fact, often parts of larger movements and sometimes coincident with waves of collective behavior. These two contextual facts are integral to understanding them. But, the very fact of focusing on the SMO tends to direct attention away from these larger movements and waves of collective actions. SMO-focused researchers are hence prone to purchase empirical discipline at the price of adequate contextualization.

V. VARIATIONS IN PROPOSITIONAL RICHNESS

I tend to rank the eight generic propositions/answers I have used in organizing discussion of various aspects of SMOs in terms of what I think of as their "richness." By "richness" I mean the degree to which a propositional answer provides an orderly and generic dissection of the ongoing substance of an SMO. Here is a passage I have adapted from a 1957 article by Herbert Blumer that captures the idea of "richness," a passage I have returned to again and again in order to regain my bearings in movement studies:

> A *movement has to be constructed* and has to carve out a career in what is practically always an opposed, resistant, or at least indifferent world. Thus conscious movements have to depend on
>
> - effective agitation,
> - the skillful fomentation and exploitation of restlessness and discontent,
> - an effective procedure for the recruitment of members and followers,
> - the formation of a well-knit and powerful organization,
> - the development and maintenance of enthusiasm, conviction, and morale,
> - the intelligent translation of ideology into homely and gripping form,
> - the development of skillful strategy and tactics, and, finally,
> - leadership which can size up situations effectively, time actions, and act decisively.
>
> These are the ingredients of successful movements. To ignore them through preoccupation with the "causes" of movements leads to inadequate and distorted knowledge. (adapted from Blumer 1957, 147, emphasis in the original)

Attuned to the idea of richness as so skillfully evoked by Blumer, my ranking of the eight propositions goes like this, placing the "richer" propositions higher on the list:

1. Structures
2. Processes
3. Agency
4. Types/variations
5. Effects
6. Causes
7. Frequencies
8. Magnitudes

In simplest terms, I am inclined to group the top four together as "richer" on the whole than the bottom four. Further, the top four are, as a group, more *qualitative* in character than the bottom four, which are more *quantitative*. That is, the first four encourage orderly *textual* reports, while the bottom four clearly call for *numerical* reports (if done properly and seriously).[3]

Scanning back over the seven chapters of Part II, the reader can easily see that I have stressed answers to the four top-ranked questions/propositions, (even though the received literature has required that I devote almost all of Chapters 7 and 8 to the causal questions of SMO formation and joining).

Let me explain my fondness and preference for the four qualitative propositions—a fondness that does not, nonetheless, reject or exclude quantitative propositions.

First, I hold that researchers must have a clear conception of what it is they want to talk about before they can sensibly attempt to adduce its causes, effects, frequencies, or magnitudes (or to answer other yet other questions). This declaration is obvious and simple but it is also widely ignored. Rushing to whys and hences, researchers bound blithely over the qualitative "whats" that need study in order most accurately to engage the four quantitative types of propositions.

In my view, answers to questions that arise from ill- or even unconsidered "whats" tend to be more fantasy than reality. As Herbert Blumer as properly cautioned in his declaration that merits requotation from just above: "we necessarily view any unfamiliar area of group life through images we already possess" and in the absence of careful scrutiny, these images "become a *substitute*" for more accurate views that can result from careful scrutiny (Blumer 1969b, 36–37, emphasis in the original).

Viewing this point more broadly, I think that an enormous task of *myth-dispelling* is required in all social science inquiry as regards what things "are." Researchers, along with most everyone else, approach subjects with preconceived notions of "what" they are looking at. Without carefully pausing and inspecting the "what" it is very easy to, as Blumer says, substitute what one thinks is to be seen for what is actually there. We wind up with mere self-fulfilling prophecies. Therefore, all preconceived notions must be examined carefully and one way to do this is to begin by asking, What, really, *is* this? How does its vary? What *varieties* (types) of it do we observe? How is it structured? How does it operate as a process? How do people do it?

Second, I am not convinced that questions of causes and effects—of why and hence—can ever be answered with any reasonable degree of confidence—although researchers should certainly continue to try. I do, though, think that accurate depictions of "what" in the senses of types/variations, structures, processes, and agency are more possible. Given the roles that accurate "whats" otherwise play (stated immediately above), it behooves researchers to give serious attention to them.

VI. VARIABLES NOT SCHOOLS; ANSWER-IMPROVING NOT THEORY-BASHING

Starting in the early 1970s, many movement scholars began to construe movement studies as composed of opposing "schools," "theories," "models," or "perspectives" as regards (mostly) the causes of social movements and joining them. Because one or more of these "schools" was viewed as wrong, or at last as importantly defective or woefully incomplete, the task of the researcher was that of using some cache of data to "prove" such wrongness, defectiveness, or incompleteness. Often, the researcher's task was *not* that of *improving* a causal (or other type of) account, but of overthrowing and eliminating wrongheaded schools.

I have elsewhere elaborated the view that this way of intellectually constituting movement studies is fundamentally misconceived and has had seriously debilitating effects on the development of the sub-discipline (Lofland 1993b). The "schools" that these researchers thought they perceived "out there" were more in their minds than in reality.

Rather than promoting full-blown "schools," "perspectives," or the like, researchers accused of constituting one or another "school" were in fact and for the most part simply pointing to one or another *variable* as likely pertinent in a causal account. A variable, or even a few of them, do not make a "school" (perspective, or whatnot) or pretend to comprehensive truth in the way that the school-minded were wont to allege. Sadly, though, researchers who attacked what they construed as defective "schools" of thought began then to think of themselves as representing their own new school! A proliferation of what I regard as fictive "schools" ensued—schools mostly built merely on fondness for some mere *variable* as opposed to some other, equally if not more pertinent other variable.[4]

In this guide I have attempted to "deschool" causal accounts of movements and of people joining them, as well as other topics. In particular, in Chapters 7 and 8 I have striven to assemble viable *variables* from whatever "school" and to think about the complexity of the possible interplay of any and all of them in given cases, types of cases, and SMOs as a general class. As I try to exemplify in Chapters 7 and 8, the proper task is to *improve answers to questions*, not to bash fictive theories that are mere framing foils and betray a profound intellectual laziness.[5]

VII. CUMULATION AND ITS PROBLEMS

Concomitant with my rejection of the "school" construction of movement studies, I hold to the old-fashioned notion that social science should strive to be a "linear, cumulative undertaking . . . controlled and directed by deductive systems" (Gusfield 1978, 123). One of my main purposes in assembling this guide is to make this possibility more of a reality for at least the study of social movement organizations.

As Gusfield's characterization indicates, cumulation requires a framework into which inquiries fit—contexts that tell us what already exists and what therefore might exist. In this guide, I have tried to formulate such a framework at a fairly high level of abstraction that is guiding but not coercive. This framework is, of course, the matrix of topics formed by the intersection of several *aspects* of SMOs and eight *generic questions* about those aspects (Chapter 3). Within this framework, less abstract and more specified formulations of both aspects and questions lead in myriad directions. In this way, the framework carves out relevance while it is at the same time open-ended.

A. Cumulating Quantitative and Qualitative Research

Taking this framework as our context, I think that cumulation of research takes different forms depending on whether a proposition is "qualitative" or "quantitative," as I have made this distinction above in this chapter.

The character of cumulation as regards quantitative propositions— those of causes, effects, frequencies, and magnitudes—has been more commonly treated historically and is therefore perhaps not especially problematic. A given quantitative estimation of whatever specific causes, effects, frequencies, and magnitudes stands as tentatively accepted knowledge until a next study either confirms or competently refutes, revises, or otherwise improves one or more existing studies. The criteria used in these assessments are technical in the sense that study designs and numerical data are compared and assessed. Judgments of likely truth—of causality, effects, frequency, and magnitude—are made.

Qualitative propositions present a different situation. These are qualitative generic depictions of types/variations, structures, processes, and strategies that seek to portray kinds of things. Each stands as a generic characterization of something that is likely best thought of in the perspective of naturalist or field biology rather in the perspective of quantitative proposition testing.

Consider, for example, these two classic studies: Rothschild and Whitt's generic picture of the "collectivist-democratic" SMO (1986) and Hank Johnston's portrayal of the "marketed" SMO (1980) (both recounted in Section III of Chapter 6). These authors are propounding that given, distinctive, but generic types of SMOs exist "out there." In cases such as these two, the question of cumulation and succession revolves around the degree to which the researchers got their observations right in the first place and came up with the correct number and content of generic features. Their findings presumably stand as tentatively accepted knowledge until new researchers who restudy the cases (or study new cases of the same thing) dispute (1) the observations or (2) the generic constructions that have been made of them.

Viewed in the wide perspective of grasping social movements, I regard qualitative studies such as those by Rothschild and Whitt and Johnston in the same way I regard field reports on species done by field biologists: as indispensable identifications of types of creatures "out there" in nature. As in field biology, if the observers got their observations and generic inferences right, the results of their studies are essentially forever (e.g., Peterson 1990; Hickman, Roberts, and Larson 1993). As in field biology, the thing identified need not even exist anymore in order to endure—to cumulate—as a pertinent item of human knowledge. Indeed, the very fact of extinction (or of extreme rarity) can render research knowledge of it all the more important—all the more in need of cumulation.

This assessment rests on my still broader view that a much greater portion of social science ought to be conducted on the model of field biology and its associated focus on generically informed taxonomies of creatures. While questions of frequencies, magnitudes, causes, and effects are surely also important, in the beginning are the whats: the types/variations, structures, processes, and human agency. It is to *these* that a field biological mind-set directs our attention.

B. Problems in Cumulating Qualitative Research

Believing qualitative research/propositions to have the special importance I have just described, I have of course striven to cumulate them in this guide. In so doing I have become aware of some difficulties that arise in so striving.

By their nature, the conceptual structures of qualitative research reports are complex and these structures are intertwined with rich qualitative data, at least some of which must be retained in cumulation. This is decidedly different from quantitative researches and propositions, which are reducible to mathematical formulations or at least to one or a few declarative sentences.

In contrast, the accurate but still parsimonious cumulation of qualitative studies—as in this guide—involves:

1. extensive paraphrasing (which tends by its nature to violate the original study),
2. severe editing (which sprinkles texts of an inelegant shower of dots, as in " . . . "), and/or
3. quotation that rapidly exceeds the bounds of current and mistakenly restrictive construals of the fair use provisions of U.S. copyright.

Cumulated qualitative research with such features departs from some existing conceptions of appropriate expositional forms and copyright fair use. I think, though, that if we are to cumulate qualitative research properly, we need to revise and expand our ideas of how research studies are best synopsized and inventoried in the corpus of social scientific knowledge.

VIII. INQUIRY IS ALWAYS UNFINISHED

Scientific inquiry is in its nature always tentative and incomplete. This book—or any book—of empirical investigation is always in essence a first draft, an unfinished and unfinishable effort to answer questions. At any particular point in time, the incompleteness and weakness of our data bearing any question are quite clear. The defects of our perception of key variations in variables, of causes, of effects, or of other matters are evident.

For those who desire final solutions, this is a situation of despair. But for those who like wrestling and stretching with puzzles, it is a circumstance of exhilaration and enlargement. It is in the latter spirit that I regard the assembly of items making up this guide as, truly, a first draft. While this volume is "finished" in the physical sense of being a book, in the perspective of the intellectual tasks of inquiry, it is but a beginning.

I am mindful, moreover, that even though I have assembled a large amount of SMO research, this guide remains conspicuously incomplete. The reasons for this are the usual ones of finite space and time and the limits of my knowledge and diligence.

Happily, however, this conspicuous incompleteness also creates some possibilities and opportunities for SMO researchers. These include:

1. identifying existing and better research on given topics that I have overlooked (and taking me to task for my inexplicable and inexcusable ignorance, of course!);
2. creating synthesis statements on topics where there are as yet only several and diversely framed analyses that I have simply listed (e.g., the inventories of strategies and reactions given in Chapters 9 and 10 versus the syntheses of causes seen in Chapters 7 and 8);
3. conducting new research that supersedes the existing formulations I report by improving on them;
4. pioneering research on important topics that researchers have so far neglected (as regards, for example and especially, the *processes* of any SMO aspect).

I am hopeful, indeed, that this guide will be received positively enough to justify a next edition that is revised and evolved in these four ways (as well as in other ways). In that spirit and in addition to using public means of scholarly interaction, I welcome direct suggestions from SMO researchers. (My postal address is the Department of Sociology, University of California, Davis, California 95616 and my e-mail address is <jflofland@ucdavis.edu>.)

NOTES

1. Thought of as the three societal levels of macro, meso and micro, one would say that the "macro" (social movements and mass actions) has received much more influential attention than the "meso" (SMOs). So conceived, we can then more readily see that the "micro" has gotten the shortest stick of all. I have in mind, specifically, Gamson's brilliant but virtually ignored study of "encoun-

ters with unjust authority" (Gamson et al. 1982). (In this case, personal factors are nicely sorted out by the greater attention given Gamson's more macro and meso work.)

2. See, for example, Lofland (1993a, 88) on fourteen diverse and competing names for the American "peace movement" of the 1980s.

3. I am aware that the first four types of propositions can be (and are) treated quantitatively, as in such techniques as network analysis (structure), event history analysis (process), game and rational-choice theory (agency), and, measurement itself (types/variations). But because one *can* do something does not mean one *should* always do something.

4. Thus, among myriad examples, one school-minded researcher framed his task as that of "defining a general theoretical alternative to the collective behavior and resource mobilization perspectives on social movements" (Hirsch 1990:253). In "school-mania," abstracts and first paragraphs of reports are littered with names of deficient approaches, as in this one featuring five schools/theories/perspectives/models in the space of seven sentences: "frustration or grievance theory . . . the challenger perspective . . . political opportunity theories . . . institutionalist perspective . . . polity model" (Amenta and Zylan 1991, 250; see also Koopmans 1995, Chs. 1 and 5). Perhaps saddest of all, some of the initial scholars accused of being a "school" *accepted* the accusation—the cognitive construction of them as such—and set about defending this enemy-created entity against its critics! Specifically, several school entrepreneurs massaged a mere assortment of topics and variables labeled "collective behavior" into a "school" ("theory," "perspective," "approach"). Unhappily, influential researchers associated with this label took the bait (as in Turner and Killian 1987, Chapter 12) and the game was afoot. I discuss this brouhaha (and provide a bibliography on it) in Lofland (1993b). See further Aguirre (1994), Curtis and Aguirre (1993), Goode (1992), L. Lofland (1990), John Wilson (1995).

5. As John Wilson has engagingly put it: "One generation simply kills its forebears, only for those ancestors to be exhumed and reanimated, and newly labeled, by the next generation of contenders" (1995, 1634).

References

Aberle, David F. [1962] 1982. *The Peyote Religion among the Navaho* (2nd ed.). Chicago: Aldine.

Ackerman, Peter, and Christopher Kruegler. 1994. *Strategic Nonviolent Conflict: The Dynamics of People Power in the Twentieth Century*. Westport, CT: Praeger.

Adamson, Madeleine, and Seth Borgos. 1984. *This Mighty Dream: Social Protest Movements in the United States*. Boston: Routledge & Kegan Paul.

Adler, A. R. 1990. *Using the Freedom of Information Act: A Step by Step Guide*. Washington, DC: American Civil Liberties Union.

Adorno, T., E. Frenkel-Brunswik, D. J. Levinson, and R. N. Sanford. 1950. *The Authoritarian Personality*. New York: Harper.

Agee, V., J. Bertelsen, R. J. Holland, and C. Wivel. 1985. *National Inventory of Documentary Sources in the United States* (compiled for the National Historical Publications and Records Commission). Teaneck, NJ: Chadwyck-Healey.

Aguirre, Benigno E. 1994. "Collective Behavior and Social Movement Theory." Pp. 257–72 in *Disasters, Collective Behavior, and Social Organization: Essays in Honor of Enrico Quarantelli*, edited by R. Dynes and K. Tierney. Newark: University of Delaware Press.

Alinsky, Saul D. [1946] 1969. *Reveille for Radicals*. New York: Vintage.

———. 1972. *Rules for Radicals: A Practical Primer for Realistic Radicals*. New York: Vintage.

Amenta, Edwin, Bruce Carruthers, and Yvonne Zylan. 1992. "A Hero for the Aged? The Townsend Movement, the Political Mediation Model, and U.S. Old-Age Policy, 1934–1950." *American Journal of Sociology* 98(2, September):308–39.

Amenta, Edwin, and Yvonne Zylan. 1991. "It Happened Here: Political Opportunity, the New Institutionalism and the Townsend Movement." *American Sociological Review* 56(April):250–65.

Anderson, David, and Peter Benjaminson. 1976. *Investigative Reporting*. Bloomington: Indiana University Press.

Ayvazian, Andrea. 1986. *Organizational Development: The Seven Deadly Sins*. Amherst, MA: Peace Development Fund. (AE)

Babbie, Earl R. 1990. *Survey Research Methods (2nd ed.)*. Belmont, CA: Wadsworth.

———. 1995. *The Practice of Social Research* (7th ed.). Belmont, CA: Wadsworth.

Back, Kurt W. [1972] 1987. *Beyond Words: The Story of the Sensitivity Training and Encounter Movement* (2nd ed.). New Brunswick, NJ: Transaction.

379

Bailey, Robert. 1974. *Radicals in Urban Politics: The Alinsky Approach*. Chicago: University of Chicago Press. (AE)

Bainbridge, William Sims. 1984. "Cultural Genetics." Pp. 157–98 in *Religious Movements: Genesis, Exodus, and Numbers*, edited by R. Stark. New York: Paragon House.

Baker, Andrea J. 1982. "The Problem of Authority in Radical Movement Groups: A Case Study of a Lesbian-Feminist Organization." *Journal of Applied Behavioral Science* 3(3):323–41. (AE)

Baker, Therese L. 1994. *Doing Social Research* (2nd ed.). New York: McGraw-Hill.

Balch, Robert W. 1980. "Looking Behind the Scenes in a Religious Cult: Implications for the Study of Conversion." *Sociological Analysis* 41(2):137–43. (AE)

Barkan, Steven E. 1979. "Strategic, Tactical and Organizational Dilemmas of the Protest Movement Against Nuclear Power." *Social Problems* 27(1, October): 19–37. (AE)

———. 1985a. *Protesters on Trial: Criminal Justice in the Southern Civil Rights and Vietnam Antiwar Movements*. New Brunswick, NJ: Rutgers University Press.

———. 1985b. "Interorganizational Conflict in the Southern Civil Rights Movement." *Sociological Inquiry* 56:190–209.

Barkan, Steven E., Steven F. Cohn, and William H. Whitaker. 1993. "Commitment Across the Miles: Ideological and Microstructural Sources of Membership Support in a National Antihunger Organization." *Social Problems* 40(3, August):362–73.

Barker, Eileen. 1984. *The Making of a Moonie: Choice or Brainwashing?* Oxford: Blackwell.

Barkun, Michael. 1974. *Disaster and Millenium*. New Haven, CT: Yale University Press.

Barzun, Jacques, and Henry F. Graff. 1977. *The Modern Researcher* (3rd ed.). New York: Harcourt Brace Jovanovich.

Becker, Howard S. 1963. *Outsiders: Studies in the Sociology of Deviance*. New York: Free Press of Glencoe.

Beckford, James A. 1978. "Accounting for Conversion." *British Journal of Sociology* 29(2, June):249–60.

Bell, Daniel. 1964. *The Radical Right*. New York: Doubleday.

Benford, Robert D. 1993a. "'You Could Be the Hundredth Monkey': Collective Identity and Vocabularies of Motive in the Nuclear Disarmament Movement." *Sociological Quarterly* 34:195-216. (AE)

———. 1993b. "Frame Disputes Within the Nuclear Disarmament Movement." *Social Forces* 71:677–701. (AE)

Benford, Robert D., and Scott A. Hunt. 1992. "Dramaturgy and Social Movement: The Social Construction and Communication of Power." *Sociological Inquiry* 62(1, February):36–55.

Benford, Robert D., and Louis A. Zurcher. 1990. "Instrumental and Symbolic Competition Among Peace Movement Organizations." Pp. 125–39 in *Peace Action in the Eighties*, edited by S. Marullo and J. Lofland. New Brunswick, NJ: Rutgers University Press. (AE)

Berelson, Bernard, and Gary Steiner. 1964. *Human Behavior: An Inventory of Scientific Findings*. New York: Harcourt, Brace & World.

Berger, Bennett M. 1981. *The Survival of a Counterculture: Ideological Work and Everyday Life Among Rural Communards.* Berkeley: University of California Press. (AE)

Berger, Peter L. 1963. *Invitation to Sociology: A Humanistic Perspective.* Garden City, NY: Doubleday.

Berger, Peter L., and Thomas Luckmann. 1967. *The Social Construction of Reality.* Garden City, NY: Doubleday.

Best, Joel. 1989. *Images of Issues: Typifying Contemporary Social Problems.* Hawthorne, NY: Aldine de Gruyter.

Best, Joel, and David F. Luckenbill. 1994. *Organizing Deviance* (2nd ed.). Englewood Cliffs, NJ: Prentice-Hall.

Buitragg, Ann M., and Leon A. Immerman. 1981. *Are You Now or Have You Ever Been in the FBI Files? How to Secure and Interpret Your FBI Files.* New York: Grove.

Bittner, Egon. 1963. "Radicalism and the Organization of Radical Movements." *American Sociological Review* 28(December):928–40.

Blain, Michael. 1988. "Fighting Words: What We Can Learn from Hitler's Hyperbole." *Symbolic Interaction* 11(2):257–76.

Blee, Kathleen M. 1995. "Review of Nancy MacLean, behind the Mask of Chivalry." *Contemporary Sociology* 24(3, May):344–47.

Blood-Patterson, Peter. 1988. *Rise Up Singing: The Group-Singing Song Book.* Bethlehem, PA: Sing Out.

Blumer, Herbert. 1957. "Collective Behavior." Pp. 127–58 in *Review of Sociology: Analysis of a Decade,* edited by J. B. Gittler. New York: Wiley.

———. [1939] 1969a. "Collective Behavior." Pp. 65–121 in *Principles of Sociology* (2nd ed.), edited by A. M. Lee. New York: Barnes and Noble.

———. 1969b. *Symbolic Interactionism: Perspective and Method.* Englewood Cliffs, NJ: Prentice-Hall.

Bobo, Kim, Jackie Kendall, and Steve Max. 1991. *Organizing for Social Change: A Manual for Activists in the 1990s.* Washington, DC: Seven Locks.

Boulding, Kenneth E. 1989. *Three Faces of Power.* Newbury Park, CA: Sage.

Branch, Taylor. 1988. *Parting the Waters: America in the King Years, 1954–63.* New York: Simon and Schuster.

Braungart, Margaret M., and Richard G. Braungart. 1991. "The Effects of the 1960s Political Generation on Former Left- and Right-Wing Youth Activist Leaders." *Social Problems* 38(3, August):297–315.

Braungart, Richard G. 1971. "Family Status, Socialization and Student Politics: A Multivariate Analysis." *American Journal of Sociology* 77:108–29.

Breines, Wini. 1980. "Community and Organization: The New Left and Michels' 'Iron Law.'" *Social Problems* 27(April):419–29.

Brill, Harry. 1971. *Why Organizers Fail: The Story of a Rent Strike.* Berkeley: University of California Press. (AE)

Brink, T. L. 1982. "Review of *The Hitler Movement* by J. Rhodes." *American Historical Review* 87:483–84.

Brockway, Sandi. 1992. *Macrocosm USA: An Environmental, Political, and Social Solutions Handbook with Directories.* Cambria, CA: Macrocosm USA.

Bromley, David G., and Anson D. Shupe, Jr. 1979. *"Moonies" in America: Cult, Church, and Crusade.* Newbury Park, CA: Sage. (AE)

———. 1980. "Financing the New Religions: A Resource Mobilization Approach." *Journal for the Scientific Study of Religion* 19:227–39.

———. 1993. "Organized Opposition to New Religious Movements." *Religion and the Social Order* 3A:177–98.

Brown, Huntington. 1966. *Prose Styles: Five Primary Types*. Minneapolis: University of Minnesota Press.

Buhle, Mari Jo, Paul Buhle, and Dan Georgakas. 1990. *Encyclopedia of the American Left*. New York: Garland.

Burek, Deborah M., and Martin Connors. 1992. *Organized Obsessions: 1,001 Offbeat Associations, Fan Clubs, and Microsocieties You Can Join*. Detroit, MI: Visible Ink.

Cable, Sherry, Edward J. Walsh, and Rex H. Warland. 1988. "Differential Paths to Political Activism: Comparisons of Four Mobilization Processes after the Three Mile Island Accident." *Social Forces* 66(June):951–69.

Calhoun, Craig (ed.). 1994. *Social Theory and the Politics of Identity*. Cambridge, MA: Blackwell.

Canan, Penelope, and George Pring. 1988. "Strategic Lawsuits against Public Participation." *Social Problems* 35(5, December):506–19.

Cantril, Hadley. 1941. *The Psychology of Social Movements*. New York: Wiley.

Capek, Stella M. 1993. "The Environmental Justice Frame: A Conceptual Discussion and Application." *Social Problems* 40(1, February):5–24.

Carroll, Andrew, and Christopher Miller. 1991. *Volunteer USA: Comprehensive Guide to Worthy Causes That Need You*. New York: Fawcett Columbine.

Carson, Rachel. 1962. *Silent Spring*. Boston: Houghton Mifflin.

Carter, Lewis F. 1990. *Charisma and Control in Rajneeshpuram: The Role of Shared Values in the Creation of a Community*. New York: Cambridge University Press. (AE)

Charmaz, Kathy. 1983. "The Grounded Theory Method: An Explication and Interpretation." Pp. 109–26 in *Contemporary Field Research: A Collection of Readings*, edited by R. M. Emerson. Boston: Little, Brown.

Chernow, Barbara A., and George A. Vallasi (ed.). 1993. *The Columbia Encyclopedia* (5th ed.). New York: Columbia University Press/Houghton Mifflin.

Chronicle of Higher Education. 1992. "Footnotes." *Chronicle of Higher Education* (22 January 22):A7.

Cloward, Richard A., and Frances Fox Piven. 1984. "Disruption and Organization: A Rejoinder to Gamson and Schmeidler." *Theory and Society* 18:587–99.

Cohn, Norman R. 1961. *The Pursuit of the Millennium: Revolutionary Messianism in Medieval and Reformation Europe and Its Bearing on Modern Totalitarian Movements* (2nd ed.). New York: Harper Torchbooks.

Cohn, Steven F., Steven E. Barkan, and William H. Whitaker. 1993. "Activists Against Hunger: Membership Characteristics of a National Social Movement Organization." Sociological Forum 8(1): 113-131.

Coleman, James S. 1971. "Conflicting Theories of Social Change." *American Behavioral Scientist* 14(May/June):633–50.

Coles, Robert. 1964. "Social Struggle and Weariness." *Psychiatry* 27 (November):305–15.

Colwell, Mary Anna. 1989. *Organizational and Management Characteristics of Peace*

Groups. Working Paper Number 8, Institute for Nonprofit Organization Management, University of San Francisco.

"Corporate Grassroots." 1993. *In These Times* (August 9):7.

Coughlin, Ellen K. 1994. How Rational is Rational Choice? *Chronicle of Higher Education* (7 December):A8–A9, A16.

Croteau, David, and William Hoynes. 1994. *By Invitation Only: How the Media Limit Political Debate*. Monroe, ME: Common Courage.

Cuba, Lee J. 1988. *A Short Guide to Writing about Social Science*. Dallas: HarperCollins.

Curtis, Russell, and Benigno Aguirre (eds.). 1993. *Collective Behavior and Social Movements*. Boston: Allyn and Bacon.

Curtis, Russell L., and Louis A. Zurcher. 1973. "Stable Resources of Protest Movements: The Multi-Organizational Field." *Social Forces* 52:53–61.

———. 1974. "Social Movements: An Analytical Exploration of Organizational Forms." *Social Problems* 21(3): 356-370.

Darnay, Brigitte T., and Janice A. DeMaggio. 1990. *Directory of Special Libraries and Information Centers, 13th Edition*. Detroit, MI: Gale Research Inc.

Davis, E. S. (compiler). 1988. *Holdings List of U.S. National Archives Records Administration*. Chicago: Center for Research Libraries.

Davis, Murray S. 1971. "That's Interesting! Toward a Phenomenology of Sociology and a Sociology of Phenomenology." *Philosophy of Social Science* 1:309–44.

Deal, Carl. 1993. *The Greenpeace Guide to Anti-Environmental Organizations*. Berkeley: Odonian.

Debord, Guy. [1967] 1983. *Society of the Spectacle* (first published in French). Detroit: Black & Red.

della Porta, Donatella (ed.). 1992. *Social Movements and Violence: Participation in Underground Organizations* (International Social Movement Research, Volume 4). Greenwich, CT: JAI.

DeStefano, Anthony M. 1993. "Seal Broken on Marshall Tapes." *Sacramento Bee*, May 25, 1.

Dowdy, Dru. 1987. *National Portrait Gallery: Permanent Collection Illustrated Checklist*. Washington, DC: Smithsonian Institution.

Downey, Gary L. 1986. "Ideology and the Clamshell Identity: Organizational Dilemmas in the Anti-Nuclear Power Movement." *Social Problems* 33(5, June):357–73.

Downs, Anthony. 1972. "Up and Down with Ecology—The 'Issue-Attention Cycle'." *The Public Interest* 28(Summer):38–50.

Edwards, Bob, and Sam Marullo. 1995. "Organizational Mortality in a Declining Movement: The Demise of Peace Movement Organizations in the End of the Cold War Era." *American Sociological Review* 60(6, December):908–27.

Edwards, Bob, and John D. McCarthy. 1992. "Social Movement Schools." *Sociological Forum* 7(3):541-50.

Eisinger, Peter K. 1973. "The Conditions of Protest Behavior in American Cities." *American Political Science Review* 67:11–28.

Epstein, Barbara. 1985. "The Culture of Direct Action: Livermore Action Group and the Peace Movement." *Socialist Review* 82/83:31–61. (AE)

————. 1991. *Political Protest and Cultural Revolution: Nonviolent Direct Action in the 1970s and 1980s*. Berkeley: University of California Press.

Etzioni, Amitai. 1961. *A Comparative Analysis of Complex Organizations*. New York: Free Press of Glencoe.

Evans, Ernest. 1983. "The Use of Terrorism by American Social Movements." Pp. 252–61 in *Social Movements of the Sixties and Seventies*, edited by J. Freeman. New York: Longman. (AE)

Eyerman, Ron, and Andrew Jamison. 1991. *Social Movements: A Cognitive Approach*. University Park: Pennsylvania State University Press.

Faludi, Susan. 1991. *Backlash: The Undeclared War Against American Women*. New York: Crown.

Fantasia, Rick. 1988. *Cultures of Solidarity: Consciousness, Action and Contemporary American Workers*. Berkeley: University of California Press. (AE)

Felshin, Nina. 1995. "Introduction." Pp. 9–29 in *But Is It Art?: The Spirit of Art as Activism*, edited by N. Felshin. Seattle, WA: Bay Press.

Fendrich, James Max, and Kenneth L. Lovoy. 1988. "Back to the Future: Adult Political Behavior of Former Student Activists." *American Sociological Review* 53(October):780–84.

Ferree, Myra Marx, and Patricia Yancey Martin (eds.). 1995. *Feminist Organizations: Harvest of the New Women's Movement*. Philadelphia: Temple University Press.

Ferree, Myra Marx, and Frederick D. Miller. 1985. "Mobilization and Meaning: Toward an Integration of Social Psychological and Resource Perspectives on Social Movements." *Sociological Inquiry* 55:38–61.

Feuer, Lewis. 1969. *The Conflict of Generations: The Character and Significance of Student Movements*. New York: Basic.

Fine, Gary Alan. 1993. *Talking Sociology* (3rd ed.). Boston: Allyn and Bacon.

Fine, Gary Allan, and Randy Stoecker. 1985. "Can the Circle Be Unbroken: Small Groups and Social Movements." *Advances in Group Processes* 2:1–28.

Flacks, Richard. 1976. "Making History vs. Making Life: Dilemmas of an American Left." *Sociological Inquiry* 46(2–4):263–280.

————. 1988. *Making History: The American Left and the American Mind*. New York: Columbia University Press.

Fogarty, Robert S. 1980. *Dictionary of American Communal and Utopian History*. Westport, CT: Greenwood.

Foley, John W. and Homer Steedly. 1980. "The Strategy of Social Protest: A Comment on a Growth Industry." *American Journal of Sociology* 85(6, May):1426–28.

Freeman, Jo. 1975. *The Politics of Women's Liberation: A Case Study of an Emerging Social Movement and Its Relation to the Policy Process*. New York: David McKay.

————. 1979. "Resource Mobilization and Strategy: A Model for Analyzing Social Movement Organization Actions." Pp. 167–89 in *The Dynamics of Social Movements: Resource Mobilization, Social Control, and Tactics*, edited by M. N. Zald and J. D. McCarthy. Cambridge, MA: Winthrop.

————. [1970] 1982. *The Tyranny of Structurelessness*. London: Dark Star. (Since 1970 numerous "movement" presses have issued it, or as Dark Star Press says, "ripped [it] off.")

————. 1983a. "On the Origins of Social Movements." Pp. 8–30 in *Social Movements of the Sixties and Seventies*, edited by J. Freeman. New York: Longman. [Enlarged from an article in *American Journal of Sociology* 78(4, January 1973):792–811.]

————. 1983b. "A Model for Analyzing the Strategic Options of Social Movements." Pp. 193–210 in *Social Movements of the Sixties and Seventies*, edited by J. Freeman. New York: Longman. (AE)

Frey, R. Scott, Thomas Dietz, and Linda Kalof. 1992. "Characteristics of Successful American Protest Groups: Another Look at Gamson's Strategy of Social Protest." *American Journal of Sociology* 98(2, September):368–87.

Friedan, Betty. 1963. *The Feminine Mystique*. New York: Norton.

Friedman, Debra, and Doug McAdam. 1992. "Collective Identity and Activism: Networks, Choices, and the Life of a Social Movement." Pp. 156–73 in *Frontiers in Social Movement Theory*, edited by A. D. Morris and C. M. Mueller. New Haven, CT: Yale University Press.

Gage, John T. 1987. *The Shape of Reason: Argumentative Writing in College*. New York: Macmillan.

Gagnon, Eric. 1995. *What's on the Internet*. Berkeley, CA: Peachpit.

Gamson, William A. 1974. "Violence and Political Power: The Meek Don't Make It." *Psychology Today* (July):35–37, 39–41.

————. 1975. *The Strategy of Social Protest* (1st ed.). Homewood, IL: Dorsey.

————. 1987. "Introduction." Pp. 1–7 in *Social Movements in an Organizational Society*, edited by M. N. Zald and J. D. McCarthy. New Brunswick, NJ: Transaction.

————. 1990. *The Strategy of Social Protest* (2nd ed.). Belmont, CA: Wadsworth.

————. 1992a. *Talking Politics*. New York: Cambridge University Press. (AE)

————. 1992b. "The Social Psychology of Collective Action." Pp. 53–76 in *Frontiers in Social Movement Theory*, edited by A. D. Morris and C. M. Mueller. New Haven, CT: Yale University Press.

————. 1995. "Hiroshima, the Holocaust, and the Politics of Exclusion." *American Sociological Review* 60(1, February):1–20.

Gamson, William A., Bruce Fireman, and Seven Rytina. 1982. *Encounters with Unjust Authority*. Homewood, IL: Dorsey.

Gamson, William A., and Emilie Schmeidler. 1984. "Organizing the Poor: An Argument with Francis Fox Piven and Richard A. Cloward, Poor People's Movements: Why They Succeed, How They Fail." *Theory and Society* 13: 567–85.

Gamson, William A., and Gadi Wolfsfeld. 1993. "Movements and Media as Interacting Systems." *Annuals of the Academy of Political and Social Science* 528(July):114–25.

Gardner, John. 1993. "Seeds of Justice." *In These Times* (May 17):18–20.

Garner, Roberta. 1996. *Contemporary Movements and Ideologies*. New York: McGraw-Hill.

Garrow, David. 1985. "Don't Fall for Media Madness." *Democratic Left* (May–June):15.

Georgakas, Dan. 1990a. "Vanguard Party." Pp. 813–14 in *Encyclopedia of the American Left*, edited by M. J. Buhle, P. Buhle, and D. Georgakas. New York: Garland.

———. 1990b. "Preparty Formations." P. 596 in *Encyclopedia of the American Left*, edited by M. J. Buhle, P. Buhle, and D. Georgakas. New York: Garland.

———. 1990c. "Front Group." P. 248 in *Encyclopedia of the American Left*, edited by M. J. Buhle, P. Buhle, and D. Georgakas. New York: Garland.

———. 1990d. "Factions and Tendencies." P. 215 in *Encyclopedia of the American Left*, edited by M. J. Buhle, P. Buhle, and D. Georgakas. New York: Garland.

George, John, and Laird Wilcox. 1992. *Nazis, Communists, Klansmen, and Others on the Fringe*. Buffalo, NY: Prometheus.

Gerlach, Luther P., and Virginia Hine. 1970. *People, Power, Change: Movements of Social Transformation*. Indianapolis, IN: Bobbs-Merrill.

———. 1983. "Movements of Revolutionary Change: Some Structural Characteristics." Pp. 133–45 in *Social Movements of the Sixties and Seventies*, edited by J. Freeman. New York: Longman. (AE)

Geschwender, James A. 1983. "The Social Context of Strategic Success: A Land-Use Struggle in Hawaii." Pp. 235–51 in *Social Movements of the Sixties and Seventies*, edited by J. Freeman. New York: Longman. (AE)

Gillespie, J. David. 1993. *Politics at the Periphery: Third Parties in Two-Party America*. Columbia: University of South Carolina Press.

Gitlin, Todd. 1980. *The Whole World Is Watching: Mass Media in the Making & Unmaking of the New Left*. Berkeley: University of California Press.

Glick, Brian. 1989. *War At Home: Covert Action against U.S. Activists and What We Can Do About It*. Boston: South End.

Goertzel, Ted. 1992. *Turncoats and True Believers: The Dynamics of Political Belief and Disillusionment*. Buffalo, NY: Prometheus.

Goffman, Erving. 1959. *The Presentation of Self in Everyday Life*. Garden City, NY: Doubleday.

———. 1974. *Frame Analysis: An Essay on the Organization of Experience*. New York: Harper and Row.

———. 1983. "The Interaction Order." *American Sociological Review* 48(1):1–17.

Goldberg, Robert A. 1991. *Grassroots Resistance: Social Movements in Twentieth Century America*. Belmont, CA: Wadsworth Publishing Company.

Goldstone, Jack A. 1980. "The Weakness of Organization: A New Look at Gamson's The Strategy of Social Protest." *American Journal of Sociology* 85(March):1017–42. (Reprinted in Gamson 1990.)

———. (ed.). 1986. *Revolutions: Theoretical, Comparative, and Historical Studies*. New York: Harcourt Brace Jovanovich.

Goode, Eric. 1992. *Collective Behavior*. Fort Worth, TX: Harcourt Brace Jovanovich.

Green, Donald P., and Ian Shapiro. 1994. *Pathologies of Rational Choice Theory: A Critique of Applications in Political Science*. New Haven, CT: Yale University Press.

Green, Marguerite. 1986. *Peace Archives: A Guide to Library Collections of the Papers of American Peace Organizations and of Leaders in the Public Effort for Peace*. Berkeley: World Without War Council.

Greenberg, Jack. 1994. *Crusaders in the Courts: How a Dedicated Band of Lawyers Fought for the Civil Rights Revolution*. New York: Basic.

Griffin, Larry, Michael E. Wallace, and Beth A. Rubin. 1986. "Capitalist Resistance to the Organization of Labor before the New Deal: Why? How? Success?" *American Sociological Review* 51(April):147–67.

Gross, Feliks. 1974. *The Revolutionary Party: Essays in the Sociology of Politics.* Westport, CT: Greenwood.

Gunderloy, Mike, and Cari Goldberg Janice. 1992. *The World of Zines: A Guide to the Independent Magazine Revolution.* New York: Penguin.

Gurr, Ted. 1970. *Why Men Rebel.* Princeton, NJ: Princeton University Press.

Gusfield, Joseph R. 1963. *Symbolic Crusade: Status Politics and the American Temperance Movement.* Urbana-Chicago: University of Illinois Press.

———. 1966. "Functional Areas of Social Movement Leadership." *Sociological Quarterly* 7:137–56.

———. 1978. "Historical Problematics and Sociological Fields: American Liberalism and the Study of Social Movements." Pp. 121–49 in *Research in Sociology of Knowledge, Sciences and Art: An Annual Compilation of Research* (Volume 1), edited by R. A. Jones. Greenwich, CT: JAI.

———. 1981. "Social Movements and Social Change: Perspectives of Linearity and Fluidity." *Research on Social Movements, Conflicts and Change* 4:317–39.

Haines, Herbert H. 1984. "Black Radicalization and the Funding of Civil Rights: 1957–1970." *Social Problems* 32(1, October):31–43.

———. 1992. "Flawed Executions, the Anti-Death Penalty Movements, and the Politics of Capital Punishment." *Social Problems* 39(2, May):125–38.

Hall, John R. 1978. *The Ways Out: Utopian Communal Groups in an Age of Babylon.* Boston: Routledge & Kegan Paul. (AE)

———. 1987. *Gone From the Promised Land: Jonestown in American Cultural History.* New Brunswick, NJ: Transaction.

———. 1988. "Social Organization and Pathways of Commitment: Types of Communal Groups, Rational Choice Theory, and the Kanter Thesis." *American Sociological Review* 53(5):679–92.

Harrison, E. Bruce. 1993. *Going Green: How to Communicate Your Company's Environmental Commitment.* Homewood, IL: Business One Irwin.

Harrison, Michael. 1974. "Preparation for Life in the Spirit: The Process of Initial Commitment to a Religious Movement." *Journal of Contemporary Ethnography* 2(4, January):390–401. (AE)

Hayden, Tom. 1988. *Reunion: A Memoir.* New York: Random House.

Heberle, Rudolf. 1951. *Social Movements: An Introduction to Political Sociology.* New York: Appleton-Century-Crofts.

Hechter, Michael. 1987. *Principles of Group Solidarity.* Berkeley: University of California Press.

Heirich, Max. 1970. *The Beginning: Berkeley, 1964.* New York: Columbia University Press.

———. 1971. *The Spiral of Conflict: Demonstrations at Berkeley 1964–1965.* New York: Columbia University Press. (AE)

Herman, Edward, and Noam Chomsky. 1988. *Manufacturing Consent: The Political Economy of the Mass Media.* New York: Pantheon.

Hickman, Cleveland P., Larry S. Roberts, and Allan Larson. 1993. *Integrated Principles of Zoology* (9th ed.). St. Louis, MO: Mosby.

Hilgartner, Stephen, and Charles Bosk. 1988. "The Rise and Fall of Social Problems: A Public Arena Model." *American Journal of Sociology* 94(July):53–78.

Hill, Michael R. 1993. *Archival Strategies and Techniques*. Thousand Oaks, CA: Sage.

Hirsch, Eric L. 1986. "The Creation of Political Solidarity in Social Movement Organizations." *Sociological Quarterly* 27(3):373–87. (AE)

———. 1990. "Sacrifice for the Cause: Group Processes, Recruitment, and Commitment in a Student Social Movement." *American Sociological Review* 55(April):243–54. (AE)

Hirschman, Albert. 1970. *Exit, Voice and Loyalty: Responses to Decline in Firms, Organizations and States*. Cambridge, MA: Harvard University Press.

Hitler, Adolf. [1926] 1962. *Mein Kampf* (Sentry edition, translated by Ralph Manheim; first published in German). Boston: Houghton Mifflin.

Hobsbawm, E. J. 1965. *Primitive Rebels: Studies in Archaic Forms of Social Movements in the 19th and 20th Centuries*. New York: Norton.

———. 1969. *Bandits*. Middlesex, England: Penguin.

Hoffer, Eric. 1951. *The True Believer: Thoughts on the Nature of Mass Movements*. New York: New American Library.

Hofrenning, Daniel J. B. 1995. *In Washington But Not of It: The Prophetic Politics of Religious Lobbyists*. Philadelphia: Temple University Press.

Holmes, Robert L. (ed.). 1990. *Nonviolence in Theory and Practice*. Belmont, CA: Wadsworth.

Howlett, Charles F. 1991. *The American Peace Movement: References and Resources*. Boston: G. K. Hall.

Hunt, Scott A., and Robert D. Benford. 1994. "Identity Talk in the Peace and Justice Movement." *Journal of Contemporary Ethnography* 22(4, January):488–517. (AE)

Ibarra, Peter R., and John I. Kitsuse. 1993. "Vernacular Constituents of Moral Discourse: An Interactionist Proposal for the Study of Social Problems." Pp. 21–53 in *Reconsidering Social Constructionism: Debates in Social Problems Theory*, edited by J. A. Holstein and G. Miller. Hawthorne, NY: Aldine de Gruyter.

Inter-university Consortium for Political and Social Research. 1994. *Guide to Resources and Services, 1993–1994*. Ann Arbor, MI: Author.

Jackson, Maurice E., Eleanora Peterson, James Bull, Sverre Monsen, and Patricia Richmond. 1960. "The Failure of an Incipient Social Movement." *Pacific Sociological Review* 3(1, Spring):35–40. (AE)

Jacobus, Lee A. 1989. *Writing As Thinking*. New York: Macmillan.

Jaeger, Gertrude, and Philip Selznick. 1964. "A Normative Theory of Culture." *American Sociological Review* 29(5):653–69.

Jasper, James M. 1990. *Nuclear Politics: Energy and the State in the United States, Sweden, and France*. Princeton, NJ: Princeton University Press.

Jasper, James M., and Dorothy Nelkin. 1992. *The Animal Rights Crusade: The Growth of a Moral Protest*. New York: Free Press.

Jenkins, J. Craig. 1983. "The Transformation of a Constituency into a Movement: Farmworker Organizing in California." Pp. 52–70 in *Social Movements of the Sixties and Seventies*, edited by J. Freeman. New York: Longman.

Jenkins, J. Craig, and Craig M. Eckert. 1986. "Channeling Black Insurgency: Elite ment of the Black Movement." *American Sociological Review* 51(6, December):812–29.

Jenkins, J. Craig, and Charles Perrow. 1977. "Insurgency of the Powerless: Farm Worker Movements (1946–1972)." *American Sociological Review* 42(2):249–68.

Johnston, Hank. 1980. "The Marketed Social Movement: A Case Study of the Rapid Growth of TM." *Pacific Sociological Review* 23(3, July):333–54. (AE)

———. 1991. *Tales of Nationalism: Catalonia, 1939–1979*. New Brunswick, NJ: Rutgers University Press.

Johnston, Hank, and Bert Klandermans. eds. 1995. *Social Movements and Culture*. Minneapolis: University of Minnesota Press.

Kahn, Si. [1982] 1991. *Organizing, A Guide for Grassroots Leaders* (revised ed.). Silver Spring, MD: National Association of Social Workers.

Kanter, Rosabeth M. 1972. *Commitment and Community: Communes and Utopias in Sociological Perspective*. Cambridge, MA: Harvard University Press.

———. 1973. *Communes: Creating and Managing the Collective Life*. New York: Harper & Row.

Katsiafricas, George. 1987. *The Imagination of the New Left: A Global Analysis of 1968*. Boston: South End.

Kerbo, Harold R. 1982. "Movements of Crisis and Movements of Affluence: A Critique of Deprivation and Resource Mobilization Theories." *Journal of Conflict Resolution* 26(4, December):645–63.

Kerr, Clark, and Abraham Siegel. 1954. "The Interindustry Propensity to Strike—An International Comparison." Pp. 189–212 in *Industrial Conflict*, edited by W. Kornhauser. New York: McGraw-Hill.

Kick, Russ. 1995. *Outposts: A Catalog of Rare and Disturbing Alternative Information*. New York: Carroll and Graf.

Kilbourne, Brock, and James T. Richardson. 1988. "Paradigm Conflict, Types of Conversion, and Conversion Theories." *Sociological Analysis* 50(1):1–21.

Killian, Lewis M. 1980. "Theory of Collective Behavior: The Mainstream Revisited." Pp. 275–89 in *Sociological Theory and Research: A Critical Appraisal*, edited by H. M. Blalock. New York: Free Press.

———. 1984. "Organization, Rationality and Spontaneity in the Civil Rights Movement." *American Sociological Review* 49:770–83.

King, Florence. 1995. "Review of *Edison: Inventing the Century* by Neil Baldin." *American Spectator* 28(5):70–71.

King, Lisabeth A. 1994. *Directory of Electronic Journals, Newsletters and Academic Discussion Lists*. Washington, DC: Association of Research Libraries.

King, Martin Luther, Jr. 1964. *Why We Can't Wait*. New York: New American Library.

Kitschelt, Herbert P. 1986. "Political Opportunity Structures and Political Protest: Anti-Nuclear Movements in Four Democracies." *British Journal of Sociology* 16:57–85.

Klandermans, Bert. 1984. "Mobilization and Participation: Social-Psychological Expansions of Resource Mobilization Theory." *American Sociological Review* 49(October):583–600.

———. (ed.). 1989. *Organizing for Change: Social Movement Organizations in Europe and the United States* (Volume 2 in the International Social Movements Research Series). Greenwich, CT: JAI.

Klandermans, Bert, Hanspeter Kriesi, and Sidney Tarrow (eds.). 1988. *From Structure to Action: Comparing Social Movement Research across Cultures* (Volume 1 in the International Social Movements Research Series). Greenwich, CT: JAI.

Klandermans, Bert, and Dirk Oegema. 1987. "Potentials, Networks, Motivations, and Barriers: Steps toward Participation in Social Movements." *American Sociological Review* 52(August):519–31.

Klapp, Orrin. 1969. *Collective Search for Identity*. New York: Holt, Rinehart and Winston.

Klehr, Harvey. 1988. *Far Left of Center: The American Radical Left Today*. New Brunswick, NJ: Transaction.

Kleidman, Robert. 1993. *Organizing for Peace: Neutrality, the Test Ban, and the Freeze*. Syracuse, NY: Syracuse University Press.

———. 1994. "Volunteer Activism and Professionalism in Social Movement Organizations." *Social Problems* 41(2, May):257–78.

Klein, Kim. 1988. *Fundraising for Social Change* (2nd ed., revised and expanded). Inverness, CA: Chardon.

Knoke, David, and David Prensky. 1984. "What Relevance Do Organization Theories Have for Voluntary Organizations?" *Social Science Quarterly* 65(Spring):3–20.

Koopmans, Ruud. 1995. *Democracy from Below: New Social Movements and the Political System in West Germany*. Boulder, CO: Westview.

Koopmans, Ruud, and Jan Wilem Duyvendak. 1995. "The Political Construction of the Nuclear Energy Issue and Its Impact on the Mobilization of Anti-Nuclear Movements in Western Europe." *Social Problems* 42(2, May):235–51.

Kornhauser, William. 1959. *The Politics of Mass Society*. New York: Free Press.

Kossy, Donna. 1994. *Kooks: A Guide to the Outer Limits of Human Belief*. Portland, OR: Feral House.

Kriesberg, Louis. 1982. *Social Conflicts*. Englewood Cliffs, NJ: Prentice-Hall.

Krit, Robert L. 1991. *The Fund-Raising Handbook*. Glenview, IL: Scott Foresman.

Lakey, George. 1994. "From Superman to Empowerment: Two Models of Intervention." *Peacework* (245, October):8–9.

Lang, Kurt, and Gladys Engel Lang. 1961. *Collective Dynamics*. New York: Thomas Crowell.

Lannon, John M. 1986. *The Writing Process: A Concise Rhetoric* (2nd ed.). Boston: Little, Brown.

Laqueur, William. 1987. *The Age of Terrorism*. Boston: Little, Brown.

Larana, Enrique, Hank Johnston, and Joseph R. Gusfield (eds.). 1994. *New Social Movements: From Ideology to Identity*. Philadelphia: Temple University Press.

Lauer, Robert H. 1976. "Ideology and Strategies of Change: The Case of American Libertarians." Pp. 85–96 in *Social Movements and Social Change*, edited by R. H. Lauer. Carbondale: Southern Illinois University Press.

Lawson, Ronald. 1983. "Origins and Evolution of a Social Movement Strategy: The Rent Strike in New York City, 1904–1980." *Urban Affairs Quarterly* 18(3, March):371–95.

Lawson, Steven F. 1992. "Review of *Simple Decency and Common Sense* by Linda Reed." *American Historical Review* 97 (December):1620–21.

Lee, Alfred McClung, and Elizabeth Briant Lee. 1939. *The Fine Art of Propaganda*. New York: Harcourt Brace.

Lemert, Edwin. 1951. *Social Pathology*. New York: McGraw-Hill.

Lenin, Vladimir Ilyitch. [1902] 1989. *What Is to Be Done*? London: Penguin. [Initially written in Russian and published in Germany, it has been republished in many translations in numerous countries.]

Lenski, Gerhard. 1954. "Status Crystallization." *American Sociological Review* 19:405–13.

Liberty, John. 1981. *Journals of Dissent and Social Change: A Bibliography of Titles in the California State University, Sacramento, Library*. Sacramento: Library, California State University.

Lieberson, Stanley. 1992. "Einstein, Renoir, and Greeley: Evidence in Sociology." *American Sociological Review* 57(1, February):1–15.

Lifton, Robert J. 1963. *Thought Reform and the Psychology of Totalism: A Study of "Brainwashing" in China*. New York: Norton.

Light, Donald W. 1969. "Strategies of Protest: Developments in Conflict Theory." Pp. 74–99 in *Black Power and Student Rebellion: Conflict on the American Campus*, edited by J. McEvoy and A. Miller. Belmont, CA: Wadsworth.

Lindholm, Charles. 1990. *Charisma*. Cambridge, MA: Basil Blackwell.

Lipset, Seymour Martin. 1963. *Political Man*. New York: Doubleday.

Lipset, Seymour Martin, Martin Trow, and James S. Coleman. 1956. *Union Democracy: The Internal Politics of the International Typographical Union*. Glencoe, IL: Free Press.

Lipsky, Michael. 1968. "Protest as a Political Resource." *American Political Science Review* 62(4, December):1144–58.

Lo, Clarence Y. 1982. "Countermovements and Conservative Movements in the Contemporary U.S." *Annual Review of Sociology* 8:107–34.

Lofland, John. [1966] 1977. *Doomsday Cult: A Study of Conversion, Proselytization, and Maintenance of Faith* (enlarged ed.). New York: Irvington. (AE)

———. 1985. *Protest: Studies of Collective Behavior and Social Movements*. New Brunswick, NJ: Transaction.

———. 1993a. *Polite Protesters: The American Peace Movement of the 1980s*. Syracuse, NY: Syracuse University Press. (AE)

———. 1993b. "Theory-Bashing and Answer-Improving in the Study of Social Movements." *American Sociologist* 24 (2, Summer):37–58.

———. 1995a. "Analytic Ethnography." *Journal of Contemporary Ethnography* 24(1, April):30–67.

———. 1995b. "Charting Movement Culture: Tasks of the Cultural Cartographer." Pp. 188–216 in *Social Movements and Culture*, edited by H. Johnston and B. Klandermans. Minneapolis, MN: University of Minnesota Press.

Lofland, John, and Joseph Fahey. 1995. "Decision-Making in Peace Groups." *Peace and War Newsletter* (Winter):4–12.

Lofland, John, and Lyn H. Lofland. 1984. *Analyzing Social Settings: A Guide to Qualitative Observation and Analysis* (2nd ed.). Belmont, CA: Wadsworth.

_____. 1995. *Analyzing Social Settings: A Guide to Qualitative Observation and Analysis* (3rd ed.). Belmont, CA: Wadsworth.

Lofland, John, and Sam Marullo. 1993. "Surge Soaring: Peace Activism, 1981–1983." Pp. 233–72 in *Polite Protesters*, by John Lofland. Syracuse, NY: Syracuse University Press.

Lofland, John, and Norman Skonovd. 1985. "Conversion Motifs." Pp. 158–71 in *Protest*, by John Lofland. New Brunswick, NJ: Transaction.

Lofland, Lyn. 1990. "Is Peace Possible? An Analysis of Sociology." *Sociological Perspectives* 33(3):313–25.

Lyman, Stanford M. (ed.). 1995. *Social Movements: Critiques, Concepts, Case-Studies*. New York: New York University Press.

Machalek, Richard, and David A. Snow. 1993. "Conversion to New Religious Movements." *Religion and the Social Order* 3B:53–74.

MacLean, Nancy. 1994. *Behind the Mask of Chivalry: The Making of the Second Ku Klux Klan*. New York: Oxford University Press.

Mannheim, Karl. [1929] 1936. *Ideology and Utopia* (translated by L. Wirth and E. Shills). New York: Harcourt, Brace.

Mao, Tse-Tung (Zedong). 1966. *Quotations from Chairman Mao Tse-tung*. Peking: Foreign Languages Press.

Marullo, Sam. 1990. "Patterns of Peacemaking in the Local Freeze Campaign." Pp. 246–64 in *Peace Action in the Eighties*, edited by S. Marullo and J. Lofland. New Brunswick, NJ: Rutgers University Press.

Marwell, Gerald, and Pamela Oliver. 1984. "Collective Action Theory and Social Movements Research." *Research in Social Movements, Conflict and Change* 7:1–27.

Marx, Gary. 1974. "Thoughts on a Neglected Category of Social Movement Participant: The Agent Provocateur and the Informant." *American Journal of Sociology* 80:402–42.

_____. 1979. "External Efforts to Damage or Facilitate Social Movements: Some Patterns, Explanations, Outcomes, and Complications." Pp. 94–125 in *The Dynamics of Social Movements: Resource Mobilization, Social Control, and Tactics*, edited by M. N. Zald and J. D. McCarthy. Cambridge, MA: Winthrop.

Marx, Gary T., and Douglas McAdam. 1994. *Collective Behavior and Social Movements: Process and Structure*. Englewood Cliffs, NJ: Prentice-Hall.

Maryanski, Alexandra, and Jonathan H. Turner. 1992. *The Human Cage: Human Nature and the Evolution of Society*. Stanford, CA: Stanford University Press.

Mauss, Armand L. 1975. *Social Problems as Social Movements*. Philadelphia: J. B. Lippincott.

McAdam, Doug. 1982. *Political Process and the Development of Black Insurgency 1930–1970*. Chicago: University of Chicago Press.

_____. 1983. "Tactical Innovation and the Pace of Insurgency." *American Sociological Review* 48(December):735–54.

_____. 1986. "Recruitment to High-Risk Activism: The Case of Freedom Summer." *American Journal of Sociology* 92:64–90.

_____. 1988a. *Freedom Summer*. New York: Oxford University Press.

_____. 1988b. "Micromobilization Contexts and Recruitment to Activism." *International Social Movement Research* 1:125–54.

————. 1989. "The Biographical Consequences of Activism." *American Sociological Review* 54(4, October):744–60.

————. 1992. "Gender as a Mediator of the Activist Experience: The Case of Freedom Summer." *American Journal of Sociology* 97(5, March):1211–40.

McAdam, Doug, John D. McCarthy, and Mayer N. Zald. 1988. "Social Movements." Pp. 695–737 in *Handbook of Sociology*, edited by N. J. Smelser. Newbury Park, CA: Sage.

McAdam, Doug, and Ronnelle Paulsen. 1993. "Specifying the Relationship between Social Ties and Activism." *American Journal of Sociology* 99(3, November):640–67.

McCarthy, John D., David W. Britt, and Mark Wolfson. 1991. "The Institutional Channeling of Social Movements by the State in the United States." *Research in Social Movements, Conflict and Change* 13:45–76.

McCarthy, John D., and Jim Castelli. 1994. *Working for Justice: The Campaign for Human Development and Poor Empowerment Groups*. Washington, DC: Life Cycle Institute, Catholic University of America.

McCarthy, John D., Clark McPhail, and John Crist. 1995. "The Emergence and Diffusion of Public Order Management Systems: Protest Cycles and Police Responses." Paper presented at the Conference on Cross-National Influences and Social Movement Research, Mont Perelin, Switzerland, June.

McCarthy, John D., Clark McPhail, and Jackie Smith. In press. "Images of Protest: Dimensions of Selection Bias in Media Coverage of Washington Demonstrations, 1982, 1991." *American Sociological Review*.

McCarthy, John D., and Mark Wolfson. 1992. "Consensus Movements, Conflict Movements, and Cooptation of Civic and State Infrastructures." Pp. 273–97 in *Frontiers in Social Movement Theory*, edited by A. D. Morris and C. M. Mueller. New Haven, CT: Yale University Press.

————. In press. "Agency, Strategy and Structure in Grass-Roots Resource Mobilization." *American Sociological Review*.

McCarthy, John D., and Mayer N. Zald. 1987a. "The Trend of Social Movements in America: Professionalization and Resource Mobilization." Pp. 337–91 in *Social Movements in an Organizational Society*, edited by M. N. Zald and J. D. McCarthy. New Brunswick, NJ: Transaction. [Article originally published by General Learning Press, 1973.]

————. 1987b. "Resource Mobilization and Social Movements: A Partial Theory." Pp. 15–42 in *Social Movements in an Organizational Society*, edited by M. N. Zald and J. D. McCarthy. New Brunswick, NJ: Transaction. [Article originally published in *American Journal of Sociology* 82(6, May 1977): 1212–42.]

McEachern, Diane. 1994. *Enough Is Enough: The Hellraiser's Guide to Community Activism*. New York: Avon.

McPhail, Clark. 1991. *The Myth of the Madding Crowd*. Hawthorne, NY: Aldine de Gruyter.

————. 1996. *Acting Together: The Social Organization of Crowds*. Hawthorne, NY: Aldine de Gruyter.

Melton, J. Gordon. 1992. *Encyclopedic Handbook of Cults in America* (revised and updated ed.). New York: Garland.

Melucci, Alberto. 1989. *Nomads of the Present: Social Movements and Individual Needs in Contemporary Society*. Philadelphia: Temple University Press.

Messinger, Sheldon. 1955. "Organizational Transformation: A Case Study of a Declining Social Movement." *American Sociological Review* 20(February): 3–10. (AE)

Meyer, David S. 1990. *A Winter of Discontent: The Nuclear Freeze and American Politics*. New York: Praeger.

Meyer, David S., and Nancy Whittier. 1994. "Social Movement Spillover." *Social Problems* 41(2, May):277–98.

Michels, Robert. [1911] 1959. *Political Parties: A Sociological Study of the Oligarchical Tendencies of Modern Democracy*. New York: Dover. [Republication of the English translation first published in 1915. First published in German].

Miles, Matthew B., and A. Michael Huberman. 1994. *Qualitative Data Analysis: An Expanded Sourcebook* (2nd ed.). Thousand Oaks, CA: Sage.

Mills, C. Wright. 1959. *The Sociological Imagination*. New York: Oxford University Press.

Mirowsky, John, and Catherine E. Ross. 1981. "Protest Group Success: The Impact of Group Characteristics, Social Control, and Context." *Sociological Focus* 14:177–92.

Molotch, Harvey. 1975. "Accidental News: The Great Oil Spill as Local Occurrence and National Event." *American Sociological Review* 39:101–12.

———. 1979. "Media and Movements." Pp. 71–93 in *The Dynamics of Social Movements: Resource Mobilization, Social Control, and Tactics*, edited by M. N. Zald and J. D. McCarthy. Cambridge, MA: Winthrop.

Molotch, Harvey, and Marilyn Lester. 1974. "News as Purposive Behavior: On the Strategic Use of Routine Events, Accidents, and Scandals." *American Sociological Review* 39:101–12.

Morris, Aldon D. 1981. "Black Southern Student Sit-In Movement: An Analysis of Internal Organization." *American Sociological Review* 46 (December): 744–67.

———. 1984. *The Origins of the Civil Rights Movement: Black Communities Organizing for Change*. New York: Free Press.

———. 1993. "Birmingham Confrontation Reconsidered: An Analysis of the Dynamics and Tactics of Mobilization." *American Sociological Review* 58 (October):621–36. (AE)

Morris, Aldon D., and Cedric Herring. 1987. "Theory and Research in Social Movements: A Critical Review." Pp. 137–98 in *Annual Review of Political Science* (Volume 2), edited by S. Long. Norwood, NJ: Ablex.

Morris, Aldon D., and Carol McClung Mueller (eds.). 1992. *Frontiers in Social Movement Theory*. New Haven, CT: Yale University Press.

Morrison, Denton. 1971. "Some Notes toward Theory on Relative Deprivation, Social Movement Participation, and Social Change." *American Behavioral Scientist* 14:675–90.

Mottl, Tahi L. 1980. "The Analysis of Countermovements." *Social Problems* 27(5, June):620–33.

Moyer, Bill. 1988. *Movement Action Plan (MAP)*. San Francisco: Movement Improvement Project.

Murray, Robert K. 1955. *Red Scare: A Study of National Hysteria, 1919–1920*. New York: McGraw-Hill.

Nagel, Joane. 1994. "Constructing Ethnicity: Creating and Recreating Ethnic Identity and Culture." *Social Problems* 41(1, February):152–76.

National Historical Publications and Records Commission. 1988. *Directory of Archives and Manuscript Repositories in the United States*. Phoenix: Oryx.

Nechayev, Sergei. 1989. *Catechism of the Revolutionist*. London: Violette Nozieres; San Francisco: A. K. Press Distribution.

Neil, Mary. 1990. "Rhetorical Styles of the Physicians for Social Responsibility." Pp. 167–79 in *Peace Action in the Eighties*, edited by S. Marullo and J. Lofland. New Brunswick, NJ: Rutgers University Press. (AE)

Neitz, Mary Jo. 1987. *Charisma and Community: A Study of Religious Commitment Within the Charismatic Renewal*. New Brunswick, NJ: Transaction.

Nelkin, Dorothy, and Jane Poulsen. 1990. "When Do Social Movements Win? Three Campaigns against Animal Experiments." Paper presented at the 85th annual meetings of the American Sociological Association, Washington, August 25.

Nolan, Kathleen Lopez. 1994. *Gale Directory of Databases*. Detroit: Gale Research.

Nye, Peter. 1994. "Surge of SLAPP Suits Chills Public Debate." *Public Citizen* (Summer):14–15, 18–19.

O'Mahony, Sean. 1987. *Frongoch: University of Revolution*. Dublin: FDR Teoranta.

O'Toole, Roger. 1977. *The Precipitous Path: Studies in Political Sects*. Toronto: Martin.

Oberschall, Anthony. 1973. *Social Conflict and Social Movements*. Englewood Cliffs, NJ: Prentice-Hall.

———. 1993. *Social Movements: Ideologies, Interests, Identities*. New Brunswick, NJ: Transaction.

Oegama, Dirk, and Bert Klandermans. 1994. "Why Social Movement Sympathizers Do Not Participate: Erosion and Nonconversion of Support." *American Sociological Review* 59:703–22.

Ofshe, Richard. 1980. "The Social Development of the Synanon Cult: The Managerial Strategy of Organizational Transformation." *Sociological Analysis* 41(2): 109-127. (AE)

Oliver, Pamela E. 1983. "The Mobilization of Paid and Volunteer Activists in the Neighborhood Movement." *Research in Social Movements, Conflicts and Change* 5:133–70.

———. 1984. " 'If You Don't Do It, Nobody Else Will': Active and Token Contributors to Local Collective Action." *American Sociological Review* 49 (October):601–10.

———. 1989. "Bringing the Crowd Back In: The Nonorganizational Elements of Social Movements." *Research on Social Movements, Conflicts and Change* 11:1–30.

Oliver, Pamela E., and Gerald Marwell. 1992. "Mobilizing Technologies of Collective Action." Pp. 251–73 in *Frontiers in Social Movement Theory*, edited by A. D. Morris and C. M. Mueller. New Haven, CT: Yale University Press.

Olson, Mancur. 1965. *The Logic of Collective Action: Public Goods and the Theory of Groups*. Cambridge, MA: Harvard University Press.

Opp, Karl-Dieter. 1988. "Grievances and Participation in Social Movements." *American Sociological Review* 53 (December):853–64.

Peterson, Roger Tory. 1990. *A Field Guide to Western Birds: A Completely New Guide to Field Marks of All Species Found in North America West of the 100th Meridian and North of Mexico* (3rd completely revised and enlarged ed.). Boston: Houghton Mifflin.

Piven, Frances Fox, and Richard Cloward. 1977. *Poor People's Movements: Why They Succeed, How They Fail.* New York: Random House.

PR Watch. 1993. "Gathering 'Intelligence' on Activists." *PR Watch* (First Quarter):3 [Publication of the Center for Media & Democracy, Inc., Madison, WI.]

Price, Edward. 1990. "Historical Generations in Freeze Member Mobilization." Pp. 207–16 in *Peace Action in the Eighties*, edited by S. Marullo and J. Lofland. New Brunswick, NJ: Rutgers University Press.

Pruitt, Dean G., Jeffrey Z. Rubin, and Sung Hee Kim. 1994. *Social Conflict: Escalation, Stalemate, and Settlement* (2nd ed.). New York: McGraw-Hill.

Prus, Robert. 1994. "Generic Social Processes and the Study of Human Lived Experiences: Achieving Transcontextality in Ethnographic Research." Pp. 436–58 in *Symbolic Interaction: An Introduction to Social Psychology*, edited by N. J. Herman and L. T. Reynolds. Dix Hills, NY: General Hall.

Public Citizen. 1991. *Masks of Deception: Corporate Front Groups in America.* Washington, DC: Author.

Rambo, Lewis R. 1993. *Understanding Religious Conversion.* New Haven, CT: Yale University Press.

Rauch, Jonathan. 1993. *Kindly Inquisitors: The New Attacks on Free Thought.* Chicago: University of Chicago Press.

Reed, Linda. 1991. *Simple Decency and Common Sense: The Southern Conference Movement, 1938–1963.* Bloomington: Indiana University Press.

Rheingold, Howard. 1994. *The Millennium Whole Earth Catalog: Access to Tools and Ideas for the Twenty-First Century.* New York: HarperCollins.

Rhodes, James M. 1980. *The Hitler Movement: A Modern Millenarian Revolution.* Stanford, CA: Hoover Institution.

Richardson, James T. (ed.). 1988. *Money and Power in the New Religions.* Lewiston, NY: E. Mellen.

———. 1992. "Public Opinion and the Tax Evasion Trial of Reverend Moon." *Behavioral Sciences and the Law* 10:53–63.

———. 1993. "A Social Psychological Critique of 'Brainwashing' Claims about Recruitment to New Religions." *Religion and the Social Order* 3B:75–97.

Richardson, James T., Mary Stewart, and Robert Simmonds. 1979. *Organized Miracles: A Study of a Contemporary, Youth, Communal, Fundamentalist Organization.* New Brunswick, NJ: Transaction.

Riley, Matilda White, Robert L. Kahn, and Anne Foner. 1995. *Age and Structural Lag: Society's Failure to Provide Meaningful Opportunities in Work, Family, and Leisure.* New York: Wiley.

Roberts, Ron E., and Robert Marsh Kloss. 1979. *Social Movements: Between the Balcony and the Barricades* (2nd ed.). St. Louis, MO: C. V. Mosby.

Roche, John P, and Stephen Sachs. 1955. "The Bureaucrat and the Enthusiast: An

Exploration of Leadership in Social Movements." *Western Political Quarterly* 8(2, June):248–61.

Rochford, E. Burke. 1982. "Recruitment Strategies, Ideology, and Organization in the Hare Krishna Movement." *Social Problems* 29(4, April):399–410.

_____. 1989. "Factionalism, Group Defection and Schism in the Hare Krishna Movement." *Journal for the Scientific Study of Religion* 28:162–79.

Rockwell, Paul. 1992. "Remembering Dr. King's Real Message." *Sacramento Bee* (January 15):B9.

Rokeach, Milton. 1968. *Beliefs, Attitudes, and Values: A Theory of Organization and Change.* San Francisco: Jossey-Bass.

Rothschild, Joyce and J. Allen Whitt. 1986. *The Cooperative Workplace: Potentials and Dilemmas of Organizational Democracy and Participation.* New York: Cambridge University Press.

Rothschild-Whitt, Joyce. 1976. "Conditions Facilitating Participatory-Democratic Organizations." *Sociological Inquiry* 46(2):75–86.

Rucht, Dieter. 1991. *Research on Social Movements: The State of the Art in Western Europe and the USA.* Boulder, CO: Westview.

Rule, James B. 1988. *Theories of Civil Violence.* Berkeley: University of California Press.

Ryan, Charlotte. 1991. *Prime Time Activism: Media Strategies for Grassroots Organizing.* Boston: South End.

Saliba, John A. 1993. "The New Religions and Mental Health." *Religion and the Social Order* 3B:99–113.

Schein, Edgar. 1961. *Coercive Persuasion.* New York: Norton.

Schiffman, Josepha. 1991. "Fight the Power: Two Groups Mobilize for Peace." Pp. 58–79 in *Ethnography Unbound: Power and Resistance in the Modern Metropolis,* edited by M. Burawoy, A. A. Ferguson, K. J. Fox, J. Gamson, N. Gartrell, L. Hurst, C. Kurzman, L. Salzinger, J. Schiffman, and S. Ui. Berkeley: University of California Press. (AE)

Schultz, Ted. 1989. *The Fringes of Reason: A Whole Earth Catalog.* New York: Crown.

Schwartz, Carol A., and Rebecca L. Turner. 1995. *Encyclopedia of Associations* (29th ed.). Detroit: Gale Research.

Schwartz, Michael, and Shuva Paul. 1992. "Resource Mobilization versus the Mobilization of People: Why Consensus Movements Cannot Be Instruments of Social Change." Pp. 205–23 in *Frontiers in Social Movement Theory,* edited by A. D. Morris and C. M. Mueller. New Haven, CT: Yale University Press.

Scott, James C. 1985. *Weapons of the Weak: Everyday Forms of Peasant Resistance.* New Haven, CT: Yale University Press.

_____. 1990. *Domination and the Arts of Resistance: Hidden Transcripts.* New Haven, CT: Yale University Press.

Selznick, Philip. [1952] 1960. *The Organizational Weapon: A Study of Bolshevik Strategy and Tactics.* Glencoe, IL: Free Press.

Sexton, Patricia Cayo. 1991. *The War on Labor and the Left: Understanding America's Unique Conservatism.* Boulder, CO: Westview.

Sharp, Gene. 1973. *The Politics of Nonviolent Action.* Boston: P. Sargent.

Sheely, E. P., with the assistance of R. G. Keckeissen. 1986. *The Guide to Reference Books* (10th ed.). Chicago: American Library Association.

Sherkat, Darren E., and T. Jean Blocker. 1992. "Protest and Alternation: Sixties Activists in Adulthood." Paper presented at the 87th Annual Meetings of the American Sociological Association, Pittsburgh, August 30.

———. 1993. "Environmental Activism in the Protest Generation." *Youth and Society* 25(1, September):140–61.

———. 1994. "The Political Development of Sixties Activists: Identifying the Influence of Class, Gender, and Socialization on Protest Participation." *Social Forces* 72(3, March):821–42.

Shibutani, Tamotsu. 1970. "On the Personification of Adversaries." Pp. 223–233 in *Human Nature and Collective Behavior: Papers in Honor of Herbert Blumer*, edited by T. Shibutani. Englewood Cliffs, NJ: Prentice-Hall.

Shils, Edward. 1968. "The Concept and Function of Ideology." Pp. 66–75 in *International Encyclopedia of the Social Sciences*, Volume 7, edited by D. Sills. New York: Macmillan.

Shlay, Anne B., and Robert R. Faulkner. 1984. "The Building of a Tenants Protest Organization: An Ethnography of a Tenants Union." *Urban Life* 4(4, January):445–65. (AE)

Shupe, Anson D., and David G. Bromley. 1980. "Walking the Tightrope: Dilemmas of Participant Observation of Groups in Conflict." *Qualitative Sociology* 2(January):3–21.

Simmel, Georg. 1959. "The Adventure." Pp. 243–58 in *Georg Simmel*, edited by K. H. Wolff. Columbus: Ohio State University Press.

Simmons, Herbert W. 1981. "The Rhetoric of Political Movements." Pp. 417–44 in *Handbook of Political Communications*, edited by D. Nimmo and K. Sanders. Beverly Hills, CA: Sage.

Simmons, Herbert W., E. W. Mechling, and H. Schreier. 1985. "Function of Communication in Mobilizing for Collective Action from the Bottom Up: The Rhetoric of Social Movements." Pp. 135–67 in *Handbook of Rhetorical and Communication Theory*, edited by C. Arnold and J. Bowers. Boston: Allyn & Bacon.

Simmons, J. L. 1964. "On Maintaining Deviant Belief Systems: A Case Study." *Social Problems* 11:250–56. (AE)

Skonovd, Norman. 1981. *Apostasy: The Process of Defection from Religious Totalism*. Ph.D. dissertation, Department of Sociology, University of California, Davis. (AE)

Smelser, Neil J. 1962. *Theory of Collective Behavior*. New York: Free Press.

———. 1995. "Endorsement of Riley, Kahn, Foner, *Age and Structural Lag*." P. 273 in *Program, 90th Annual Meeting of the American Sociological Association*, edited by A. Etzioni. Washington, DC: American Sociological Association.

Smith, Allen. 1990. "The Hidden Dynamics of Consensus." *Nonviolent Activist* (February):13–14.

Snow, David A. 1979. "A Dramaturgical Analysis of Movement Accommodation: Building Idiosyncrasy Credit as a Movement Mobilization Strategy." *Symbolic Interaction* 2(2):23–44. (AE)

Snow, David A., and Robert D. Benford. 1988. "Ideology, Frame Resonance, and Participant Mobilization." *International Social Movement Research* 1:197–217.

———. 1992. "Master Frames and Cycles of Protest." Pp. 133–55 in *Frontiers in Social Movement Theory*, edited by A. D. Morris and C. M. Mueller. New Haven, CT: Yale University Press.

Snow, David A., and Richard Machalek. 1982. "On the Presumed Fragility of Unconventional Beliefs." *Journal for the Scientific Study of Religion* 21(1, March):15–25.

———. 1983. "The Convert as a Social Type." Pp. 259–88 in *Sociological Theory 1983*, edited by R. Collins. San Francisco: Jossey-Bass.

———. 1984. "The Sociology of Conversion." *Annual Review of Sociology* 10: 167–90.

Snow, David A., and Pamela E. Oliver. 1995. "Social Movements and Collective Behavior: Social Psychological Dimensions and Considerations." Pp. 571–99 in *Sociological Perspectives on Social Psychology*, edited by K. Cook, G. A. Fine, and J. S. House. Boston: Allyn and Bacon.

Snow, David A., E. Burke Rochford, Steven Worden, and Robert Benford. 1986. "Frame Alignment Processes, Micromobilization, and Movement Participation." *American Sociological Review* 51:464–81.

Snow, David A., and Steven Worden. 1993. "Symbolic Crusades." Pp. 341–45 in *Sociology and Language*, edited by W. S. Brainbridge. New York: Pergamon.

Snow, David A., Louis Zurcher, and Sheldon Eckland-Olson. 1980. "Social Networks and Social Movements: A Microstructural Approach to Differential Recruitment." *American Sociological Review* 45(May):786–801.

Somit, Albert. 1968. "Brainwashing." Pp. 138–43 in *International Encyclopedia of the Social Sciences* (Volume 2), edited by D. Sills. New York: Macmillan.

Springer, Philip B., and Marcello Truzzi. 1973. *Revolutionaries on Revolution: Participants' Perspectives on the Strategies of Seizing Power*. Pacific Palisades, CA: Goodyear.

Staggenborg, Suzanne. 1986. "Coalition Work in the Pro-Choice Movement: Organizational and Environmental Opportunities and Obstacles." *Social Problems* 33:374–90. (AE)

———. 1988. "The Consequences of Professionalization and Formalization in the Pro-Choice Movement." *American Sociological Review* 53(August):585–606. (AE)

———. 1989a. "Stability and Innovation in the Women's Movement: A Comparison of Two Movement Organizations." *Social Problems* 36(1, February): 75–92. (AE)

———. 1989b. "Organizational and Environmental Influences on the Development of the Pro-Choice Movement." *Social Forces* 68:204–40. (AE)

Staples, Lee. 1984. *Roots to Power: A Manual for Grassroots Organizing*. Westport, CT: Praeger.

Stark, Rodney. 1987. "How New Religions Succeed: A Theoretical Model." Pp. 11–29 in *The Future of New Religious Movements*, edited by D. G. Bromley and P. E. Hammond. Macon, GA: Mercer University Press.

Stark, Rodney, and William Sims Bainbridge. 1980. "Networks of Faith: Interpersonal Bonds and Recruitment to Cults and Sects." *American Journal of Sociology* 85(6, May):1376–95.

———. 1985. *The Future of Religion: Secularization, Revival and Cult Formation.* Berkeley: University of California Press.

———. 1987. *A Theory of Religion.* New York: Peter Lang.

Stark, Rodney, and Laurence R. Iannaccone. 1993. "Rational Choice Propositions About Religious Movements." *Religion and the Social Order* 3A:241–61.

Starr, Paul. 1979. "The Phantom Community." Pp. 245–73 in *Co-ops, Communes & Collectives,* edited by J. Case and R. C. R. Taylor. New York: Pantheon.

Stearns, Peter N. 1974. *1848: The Revolutionary Tide in Europe.* New York: Norton.

Stewart, David W., and Michael A. Kamins. 1993. *Secondary Research: Information Sources and Methods* (2nd ed.). Thousand Oaks, CA: Sage.

Straus, Roger A. 1979. "Religious Conversion as a Personal and Collective Accomplishment." *Sociological Analysis* 40:158–165.

Strauss, Anselm L., and Juliet Corbin. 1990. *Basics of Qualitative Research: Grounded Theory Procedures and Techniques.* Newbury Park, CA: Sage.

Sudo, Ken. 1975. *120-Day Workshop Training Manual.* Barrytown, NY: Unification Church Barrytown International Training Center.

Swarthmore College. 1981. *Guide to the Swarthmore College Peace Collection* (2nd ed.). Swarthmore, PA: Swarthmore College Press.

Sykes, Charles J. 1992. *A Nation of Victims: The Decay of the American Character.* New York: St. Martin's.

Tarrow, Sidney. 1994. *Power in Movement: Social Movements, Collective Action and Politics.* New York: Cambridge University Press.

Taylor, David. 1978. *The Social Organization of Recruitment in the Unification Church.* M.A. thesis, Department of Sociology, University of Montana, Billings.

Taylor, Verta. 1989. "Social Movement Continuity: The Women's Movement in Abeyance." *American Sociological Review* 54(October):761–75. (AE)

Taylor, Verta, and Nicole C. Raeburn. 1995. "Identity Politics as High-Risk Activism: Career Consequences for Lesbian, Gay, and Bisexual Sociologists." *Social Problems* 42(2, May):252–73.

Taylor, Verta, and Nancy Whittier. 1992. "Collective Identity in Social Movement Communities: Lesbian Feminist Mobilization." Pp. 104–30 in *Frontiers in Social Movement Theory,* edited by A. D. Morris and C. M. Mueller. New Haven, CT: Yale University Press.

Tenabe, Jennifer P. 1992. "Exploring Our Comprehensive Philosophical System." *Unification News* (December):18.

Thorne, Barrie. 1975. "Protest and the Problem of Credibility: Uses of Knowledge and Risk-Taking in the Draft Resistance Movement of the 1960's." *Social Problems* 23(December):111–23. (AE)

Tilly, Charles. 1978. *From Mobilization to Revolution.* Reading, MA: Addison-Wesley.

———. 1981a. "Introduction." Pp. 13–25 in *Class Conflict and Collective Action,* edited by L. A. Tilly and C. Tilly. Beverly Hills, CA: Sage.

———. 1981b. "The Web of Contention in Eighteenth-Century Cities." Pp. 27–51 in *Class Conflict and Collective Action,* edited by L. A. Tilly and C. Tilly. Beverly Hills, CA: Sage.

_____. 1983. "Speaking Your Mind without Elections, Surveys, or Social Movements." *Public Opinion Quarterly* 47:461–78.

Toch, Hans. 1965. *The Social Psychology of Social Movements*. Indianapolis: Bobbs-Merrill.

Traugott, Mark. 1978. "Reconceiving Social Movements." *Social Problems* 26(October):38–49.

Troshynski-Thomas, Karn, and Deborah M. Burek. 1996. *Gale Directory of Publications and Broadcast Media*. Detroit: Gale Research.

Tuchman, Barbara W. 1984. *The March of Folly from Troy to Vietnam*. New York: Ballantine.

Tuchman, Gaye. 1994. "Historical Social Science: Methodologies, Methods, Meanings." Pp. 306–23 in *Handbook of Qualitative Research*, edited by N. Denzin and Y. S. Lincoln. Thousand Oaks, CA: Sage.

Turabian, Kate L., revised by J. Grossman and A. Bennett. 1996. *A Manual for Writers of Term Papers, Theses, and Dissertations* (6th ed.). Chicago: University of Chicago Press.

Turner, Ralph, and Lewis Killian. 1972. *Collective Behavior* (2nd ed.). Englewood Cliffs, NJ: Prentice-Hall.

Turner, Ralph, and Lewis Killian. 1987. *Collective Behavior* (3rd ed.). Englewood Cliffs, NJ: Prentice-Hall.

Ullmann, John, and Jan Colbert. 1991. *The Reporter's Handbook: An Investigator's Guide to Documents and Techniques* (2nd ed.). New York: St. Martin's.

Useem, Bert. 1980. "Solidarity Model, Breakdown Model, and the Boston Anti-Busing Movement." *American Sociological Review* 45:357–69.

Villarejo, Don. 1980. *Research for Action: A Guidebook to Public Records Investigation for Community Activists*. Davis, CA: California Institute for Rural Studies.

Volkogonov, Dmitri. 1994. *Lenin: A New Biography*. New York: Free Press.

Voss, Kim. 1993. *The Making of American Exceptionalism: The Knights of Labor and Class Formation in the Nineteenth Century*. Ithaca, NY: Cornell University Press.

Walker, Jack L. 1991. *Mobilizing Interest Groups in America: Patrons, Professions, and Social Movements*. Ann Arbor: University of Michigan Press.

Wallis, Roy. 1977. *The Road to Total Freedom: A Sociological Analysis of Scientology*. New York: Columbia University Press. (AE)

Walls, David. 1993. *The Activist's Almanac: The Concerned Citizen's Guide to the Leading Advocacy Organizations in America*. New York: Fireside, Simon & Schuster.

Walsh, Edward J. 1981. "Resource Mobilization and Citizen Protest in Communities around Three Mile Island." *Social Problems* 29(1, October):1–21.

_____. 1986. "The Role of Target Vulnerabilities in High-Technology Protest Movements: The Nuclear Establishment at Three Mile Island." *Sociological Forum* 1(2):199–218.

Walum, Laurel Richardson. 1978. "The Changing Door Ceremony: Notes on the Operation of Sex Roles in Everyday Life." Pp. 51–60 in *Interaction in Everyday Life: Social Strategies*, edited by J. Lofland. Beverly Hills, CA: Sage. (AE)

Walzer, Michael. 1974. *The Revolution of the Saints: A Study in the Origins of Radical Politics*. New York: Atheneum.

Waskow, Arthur I. 1966. *From Race Riot to Sit-In, 1919 and the 1960s: A Study of the Connection between Conflict and Violence*. Garden City, NY: Anchor.

Weber, Max. 1958. *From Max Weber: Essays in Sociology* (translated, edited, and with an introduction by H. H. Gerth and C. Wright Mills). New York: Oxford University Press.

Weir, David, and Dan Noyes. 1983. *Raising Hell: How the Center for Investigative Reporting Gets the Story*. Reading, MA: Addison-Wesley.

Weitzman, Eben A., and Matthew B. Miles. 1995. *Computer Programs for Qualitative Data Analysis: A Software Sourcebook*. Thousand Oaks, CA: Sage.

Werner, Paul. 1978. "Personality and Attitude-Activism Correspondence." *Journal of Personality and Social Psychology* 36:1375–90.

Wernette, D. R. 1990. "The Freeze Movement at the Local Level." Pp. 140–54 in *Peace Action in the Eighties*, edited by S. Marullo and J. Lofland. New Brunswick, NJ: Rutgers University Press. (AE)

Whalen, Jack, and Richard Flacks. 1989. *Beyond the Barricades: The Sixties Generation Grows Up*. Philadelphia: Temple University Press.

White, Robert W. 1989. "From Peaceful Protest to Guerilla War: Micromobilization of the Provisional Irish Republican Army." *American Journal of Sociology* 94(May):1277–1302.

Wilcox, Laird (ed.). 1994a. *Guide to the American Left: Directory and Bibliography* (16th ed.). Olathe, KS: Editorial Research Service.

———— (ed.). 1994b. *Guide to the American Right: Directory and Bibliography* (19th ed.). Olathe, KS: Editorial Research Service.

————. (ed.). 1994c. *Spectrum: Guide to the Independent Press* (23rd ed.). Olathe, KS: Editorial Research Service.

Wilson, James Q. [1974] 1995. *Political Organizations*. Princeton, NJ: Princeton University Press.

Wilson, John. 1973. *An Introduction to Social Movements*. New York: Basic.

————. 1995. "Review of *New Social Movements* by Larana, Johnston and Gusfield." *Social Forces* 73(June):1663–65.

Wolfe, Tom. 1970. *Radical Chic and Mau-Mauing the Flak Catcher*. New York: Farrar, Straus, Giroux.

Wollman, Neil, Michael Wexler, and Michael Priddy. 1994. "Psychology and Activism." *Nonviolent Activist* (November–December):12–13.

Wood, James L., and Maurice Jackson. 1982. *Social Movements: Development, Participation, Dynamics*. Belmont, CA: Wadsworth.

Wright, Stuart A., and Helen Rose Ebaugh. 1993. "Leaving New Religions." *Religion and the Social Order* 3B:117–38.

Wright, Talmadge, Felix Rodriquez, and Howard Waitzkin. 1986. "Corporate Interests, Philanthropies, and the Peace Movement." *International Journal of Health Services* 16(1):33–41.

Zablocki, Benjamin. 1980. *The Joyful Community: An Account of the Bruderhof, A Communal Movement Now in Its Third Generation*. Chicago, IL: University of Chicago Press. (AE)

————. 1991. "Review of *Charisma* by Charles Lindholm." *Contemporary Sociology* 20(6, November):963–64.

Zald, Meyer N., and Roberta Ash. 1966. "Social Movement Organizations: Growth, Decay, and Change." *Social Forces* 44:327–40.

Zald, Mayer N, and John D. McCarthy. 1987. "Social Movement Industries: Competition and Conflict Among SMOs." Pp. 161–84 in *Social Movements in an Organizational Society*, edited by M. N. Zald and J. D. McCarthy. New Brunswick, NJ: Transaction. [Article originally published in *Research in Social Movements, Conflict and Change* 3(1980):1–20.]

Zald, Mayer N., and Bert Useem. 1987. "Movement and Countermovement Interaction: Mobilization, Tactics and State Involvement." Pp. 247–72 in *Social Movements in an Organizational Society*, edited by M. N. Zald and J. D. McCarthy. New Brunswick, NJ: Transaction.

Zimmerman, Richard. 1992. *What Can I Do to Make a Difference?: A Positive Action Sourcebook*. New York: Penguin.

Zurcher, Louis A., and Russell L. Curtis. 1973. "A Comparative Analysis of Propositions Describing Social Movement Organizations." *Sociological Quarterly* 14(Spring):175–88.

Zurcher, Louis A., and David A. Snow. 1981. "Collective Behavior: Social Movements." Pp. 447–82 in *Social Psychology: Sociological Perspectives*, edited by M. Rosenberg and R. Tuner. New York: Basic.

Index